Continuations and Natural Language

OXFORD STUDIES IN THEORETICAL LINGUISTICS

Recent Titles

34 Dissolving Binding Theory
by Johan Rooryck and Guido Vanden Wyngaerd

35 The Logic of Pronominal Resumption
by Ash Asudeh

36 Modals and Conditionals
by Angelika Kratzer

37 The Theta System
Argument Structure at the Interface
edited by Martin Everaert, Marijana Marelj, and Tal Siloni

38 Sluicing
Cross-Linguistic Perspectives
edited by Jason Merchant and Andrew Simpson

39 Telicity, Change, and State
A Cross-Categorial View of Event Structure
edited by Violeta Demonte and Louise McNally

40 Ways of Structure Building
edited by Myriam Uribe-Etxebarria and Vidal Valmala

41 The Morphology and Phonology of Exponence
edited by Jochen Trommer

42 Count and Mass Across Languages
edited by Diane Massam

43 Genericity
edited by Alda Mari, Claire Beyssade, and Fabio Del Prete

44 Strategies of Quantification
edited by Kook-Hee Gil, Steve Harlow, and George Tsoulas

45 Nonverbal Predication
Copular Sentences at the Syntax-Semantics Interface
by Isabelle Roy

46 Diagnosing Syntax
edited by Lisa Lai-Shen Cheng and Norbert Corver

47 Pseudogapping and Ellipsis
by Kirsten Gengel

48 Syntax and its Limits
edited by Raffaella Folli, Christina Sevdali, and Robert Truswell

49 Phrase Structure and Argument Structure
A Case Study of the Syntax-Semantics Interface
by Terje Lohndal

50 Edges in Syntax
Scrambling and Cyclic Linearization
by Heejeong Ko

51 The Syntax of Roots and the Roots of Syntax
edited by Artemis Alexiadou, Hagit Borer, and Florian Schäfer

52 Causation in Grammatical Structures
edited by Bridget Copley and Fabienne Martin

53 Continuations and Natural Language
by Chris Barker and Chung-chieh Shan

For a complete list of titles published and in preparation for the series, see pp. 229–30.

Continuations and Natural Language

CHRIS BARKER AND CHUNG-CHIEH SHAN

OXFORD
UNIVERSITY PRESS

OXFORD
UNIVERSITY PRESS

Great Clarendon Street, Oxford, OX2 6DP,
United Kingdom

Oxford University Press is a department of the University of Oxford.
It furthers the University's objective of excellence in research, scholarship,
and education by publishing worldwide. Oxford is a registered trade mark of
Oxford University Press in the UK and in certain other countries

First published 2014

Published in the United States of America by Oxford University Press
198 Madison Avenue, New York, NY 10016, United States of America

British Library Cataloguing in Publication Data
Data available

Library of Congress Cataloging in Publication Data
Data available

ISBN 978–0–19–957501–5

Contents

General preface

The theoretical focus of this series is on the interfaces between subcomponents of the human grammatical system and the closely related area of the interfaces between the different subdisciplines of linguistics. The notion of 'interface' has become central in grammatical theory (for instance, in Chomsky's Minimalist Program) and in linguistic practice: work on the interfaces between syntax and semantics, syntax and morphology, phonology and phonetics, etc. has led to a deeper understanding of particular linguistic phenomena and of the architecture of the linguistic component of the mind/brain.

The series covers interfaces between core components of grammar, including syntax/morphology, syntax/semantics, syntax/phonology, syntax/pragmatics, morphology/phonology, phonology/phonetics, phonetics/speech processing, semantics/pragmatics, and intonation/discourse structure, as well as issues in the way that the systems of grammar involving these interface areas are acquired and deployed in use (including language acquisition, language dysfunction, and language processing). It demonstrates, we hope, that proper understandings of particular linguistic phenomena, languages, language groups, or inter-language variations all require reference to interfaces.

The series is open to work by linguists of all theoretical persuasions and schools of thought. A main requirement is that authors should write so as to be understood by colleagues in related subfields of linguistics and by scholars in cognate disciplines.

The interactions between linear order, syntactic structure, and semantic scope have been at the heart of generative grammar for decades. In this monograph, Barker and Shan delineate a new perspective on this problem that appeals to the notion that the semantic context of a quantificational expression can, in effect, function as an argument of that expression, and that the natural language phenomena that have been so puzzling over the years can be understood as deriving from the order of semantic evaluation of such contexts. This perspective allows the authors to weave together the puzzling structural and linear ordering effects that have been discovered over the years into a unified theoretical explanation, which they extend to related phenomena in natural language.

David Adger
Hagit Borer

Notational conventions

$\texttt{e} \to \texttt{t}$ Types: Instead of writing $\langle \tau, \sigma \rangle$ for the type of a function from objects of type τ into objects of type σ, we follow the convention in computer science, and write $\tau \to \sigma$. So the type of an extensional verb phrase will be $\texttt{e} \to \texttt{t}$.

saw j m Associativity for values: Values associate from left-to-right. An expression written **saw j m** is equivalent to (**saw j**) **m**.

$\texttt{e} \to \texttt{e} \to \texttt{t}$ Associativity for types: Since values associate from left-to-right, types correspondingly associate from right-to-left. This means that the type $\texttt{e} \to \texttt{e} \to \texttt{t}$ is shorthand for $\texttt{e} \to (\texttt{e} \to \texttt{t})$ (an extensional transitive verb). The type of an extensional generalized quantifier must be written with parentheses, i.e., $(\texttt{e} \to \texttt{t}) \to \texttt{t}$.

$\lambda abc.M$ Dot notation for lambda abstraction: We adopt the standard convention that $\lambda a \lambda b \lambda c M$ can be abbreviated as $\lambda abc.M$. We will assume that the scope of the lambdas before the dot extends as far to the right as possible. Therefore the expression $\lambda x.$ **yesterday** (**call** x) **m** is equivalent to $\lambda x\big(($**yesterday** (**call** x)) **m**$\big)$.

$g[\ ]$ Contexts, holes, and plugs: Throughout the book, we will consider logical expressions that have a **hole** ('[ ]') somewhere in them, e.g., $\lambda x.(x[\ ])y$. We will say that an expression that contains exactly one hole is a (certain kind of) *context*. Contexts can have their holes plugged. This means replacing the hole ('[ ]') with some expression. For instance, if $g[\ ] = \lambda x.(x[\ ])y$, then $g[w] = \lambda x.(xw)y$. Plugs can be complex expressions ($g[(ww)] = \lambda x.(x(ww))y$). We allow a context to be plugged by a context. For instance, if we plug the hole in $g[\ ]$ with itself, we get $g[g[\ ]] = \lambda x.x(\lambda x.(x[\ ])y)y$, which has exactly one hole in it, so the net result is once again a context. See sections 1.3 and 13.2, as well as Shan (2005):26 ff., and Shan (2005) chapter 3 for additional discussion.

Acknowledgments

With Barker (2001, 2002) and Shan (2001a,b) as starting points, Part I is largely based on joint work reported in Shan and Barker (2006), Barker and Shan (2006), and Barker and Shan (2008), as developed and elaborated in Shan (2004, 2005) and in Barker (2009, 2012, 2014a). Part II is based on Barker (2007) and Barker (2013). The technical results in chapter 17 have not previously appeared, and constitute new joint work. With the exception of that chapter, most of the writing and preparation of this book was (joyfully) undertaken by the first author (Barker), relying on the inspiration, advice, and commentary of the second author (Shan).

Most of the material in this book has benefited from feedback from courses, tutorials, conferences, and workshops. Special thanks to Sascha Bargmann, Raffaella Bernardi, Dylan Bumford, Lucas Champollion, Simon Charlow, John Davey, Paul Elbourne, Kate Gilks, Svetlana Godjevac, Christopher Götze, Philippe de Groote, Daniel Gutzmann, Polly Jacobson, Chris Kennedy, Oleg Kiselyov, Dan Lassiter, Tim Leffel, Salvador Mascarenhas, Michael Moortgat, Jim Pryor, Mike Solomon, Anna Szabolcsi, Michael Tabatowski, Dylan Thurston, Gert Webelhuth, ESSLLIs in 2004, 2005, and 2007, and colleagues at Goethe University who field-tested a draft of this book.

We're grateful to Anna Szabolcsi for urging us to make the system easier to understand, pressure which more or less directly resulted in creating the tower notation; and to Oleg Kiselyov, who suggested using contexts to simplify the semantic part of the tower notation.

List of abbreviations

AR	Argument Raising
CBN	call-by-name Continuation Passing style
CBV	call-by-value Continuation Passing style
CL	Combinatory Logic
CPS	Continuation Passing style
DMG	Dynamic Montague Grammar
DP	determiner phrase
DPL	Dynamic Predicate Logic (Groenendijk and Stokhof 1991)
I	identity function (λxx)
κ	variable over continuations
LF	Logical Form
LG	Lambek-Grishin logic (Bernardi and Moortgat 2010)
N	noun
NEG	negation
NL_{CL}	non-associative Lambek grammar (NL) augmented with Combinatory Logic
NL_{λ}	non-associative Lambek grammar (NL) augmented with λ-abstraction
NP	noun phrase
NPI	negative polarity item
$\mathcal{P}$	variable over pronoun meanings (category pn)
PF	Phonetic Form
pn	category of a simple pronoun $\dfrac{\text{DP} \rhd \text{S} \mid \text{S}}{\text{DP}}$
PP	prepositional phrase
PTQ	'proper treatment of quantification' (Montague 1974)
Q	DP?S (the kind of question that asks for an individual)
QP	quantificational DP
QR	Quantifier Raising
S	clause/sentence
S^{-}	a proper subset of the category S
VP	verb phrase
VPE	verb phrase ellipsis
VR	Value Raising

Introduction

This book is about continuations. It argues that continuations are an essential component of a complete understanding of natural language meaning.

(1) **The continuation hypothesis**: some natural language expressions denote functions on their continuations, i.e., functions that take their own semantic context as an argument.

The main way that we will argue in favor of this hypothesis is by providing analyses of a variety of natural language phenomena whose insights depend on explicit reference to continuations.

What is a continuation?

A **continuation** is a portion of the context surrounding an expression.

(2) John said [**Mary called** everyone **yesterday**] with relief.

In (2), the continuation of the expression *everyone*, relative to the bracketed embedded clause that contains it, is the remainder of the embedded clause after *everyone* has been removed. This material includes the lexical items *Mary*, *called*, and *yesterday*.

Based on the string presentation, this might appear to be a discontinuous object, but the contiguous nature of the continuation becomes immediately apparent when we consider the syntactic phrase structure tree:

(3)

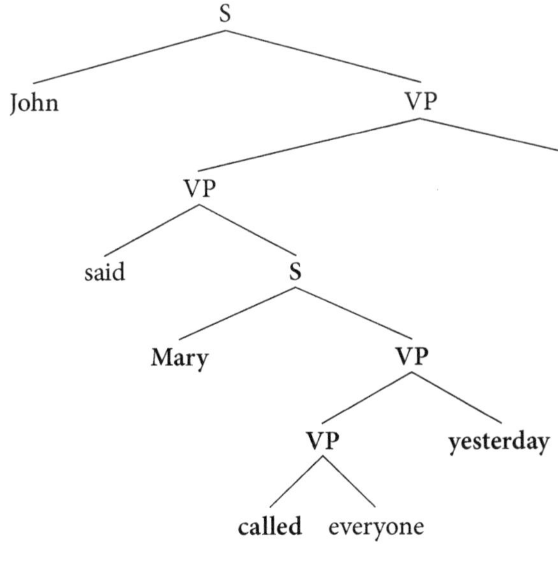

In this tree, the continuation of *everyone* relative to the embedded clause is the contiguous portion of the tree dominating *Mary*, *called*, and *yesterday*, but with *everyone* removed. More schematically, we have the following diagram:

(4)

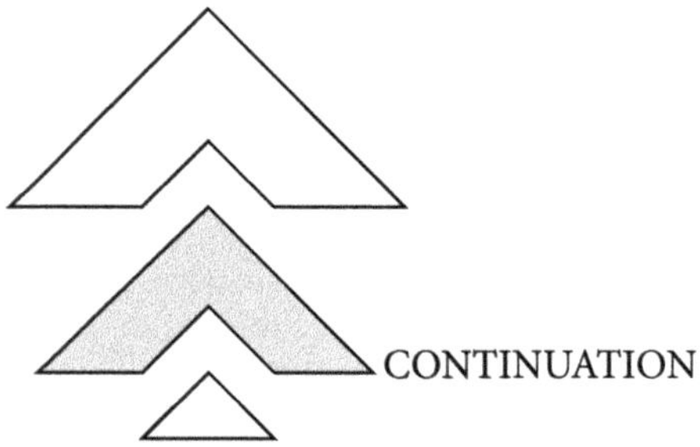

In the example at hand, the unshaded upper notched triangle corresponds to the portion of the structure in which the smaller clause is embedded, and includes *John*, *said*, and *with relief*. The middle gray notched triangle corresponds to the material over which the scope-taker *everyone* takes scope—its continuation. And the smallest unshaded unnotched triangle corresponds to the scope-taker *everyone*.

We will use schematic diagrams like this one from time to time throughout the book. We'll call them *tangram diagrams*, after the puzzle game in which a set of flat geometric shapes are rearranged into a variety of larger shapes.

Since we will be primarily concerned with meaning, we will concentrate on *semantic* context, rather than, say, phonological context or syntactic context. In the example above, then, the semantic continuation of *everyone* relative to the bracketed clause is the meaning of that clause with the contribution of *everyone* abstracted, namely, the property of being called yesterday by Mary, which can be rendered as $\lambda x.\textbf{yesterday}(\textbf{called}\, x)\ \textbf{m}$.

What makes continuations essential?

The semantic continuation identified in (2) is what the quantifier *everyone* takes for its semantic argument, its 'nuclear scope'. In general, identifying the semantic argument of a scope-taking expression is the same thing as identifying (one of its) continuations. Thus scope-taking is the most compelling application of continuations in natural language.

But it is not enough for us to show that continuations provide an elegant way to conceptualize scope-taking, given that there are other effective strategies for handling scope-taking that do not explicitly involve continuations, such as Quantifier Raising, Flexible Montague Grammar, and so on. To make a strong case that continuations are essential, we must argue that continuations provide insights that are not available in other approaches.

We find inspiration for such insights in neighboring disciplines. Continuations are an idea that has been explored in some depth in the theory of computer programming languages, where they have been used (among many applications) to characterize **order of evaluation** of expressions in a computer program, as explained in section 12.1. And in general, one of the distinctive advantages of continuations is that they provide a way to reason explicitly about the order in which a computation unfolds.

We will argue that a number of phenomena in natural language depend on order of evaluation. These include quantificational binding, crossover, reconstruction, negative polarity licensing, and donkey anaphora.

In particular, one of the central results will be a robust explanation of crossover in terms of order of evaluation.

(5) a. Everyone$_i$ loves his$_i$ mother.
    b. *His$_i$ mother loves everyone$_i$.

When the quantifier *everyone* precedes the pronoun *his*, as in (5a), the binding relationship indicated by the subscripts is available, in which case (5a) expresses a generalization about filial duty: every person loves that person's mother. But when the quantifier follows the pronoun, as in (5b), the indicated binding relationship is not possible: (5b) cannot express a general thought about family relationships, namely, that each person's mother loves that person. We will say that (5b) is a weak crossover violation.

Ever since Reinhart (1983), standard approaches to crossover (e.g., Büring 2005) have rejected the relevance of linear order in favor of purely hierarchical relationships based on c-command. However, as explained in chapter 2, following Shan and Barker (2006) and Barker (2012), we believe that c-command is not a requirement for quantificational binding. As a result, we endorse a minority tradition including Bresnan (1994, 1998), Safir (2004a,b), and Jäger (2005), who argue that in English and in many other languages, some kind of order plays a role in crossover.

Crucially, we will develop an explanation for crossover not in terms of *linear* order, but rather in terms of *evaluation* order. One reason linear order is not an adequate explanation is that there are systematic cases in which a quantifier can linearly follow a pronoun that it nevertheless can bind:

(6) a. Which of his$_i$ relatives does every man$_i$ love the most?
    b. The relative of his$_i$ that every man$_i$ loves most is his mother.

We explain in some detail how our continuation-based approach accounts for these so-called reconstruction effects. In brief, the independently-motivated semantics of wh-fronting and relative clause formation *delay* the evaluation of the pronoun until after the evaluation of the quantifier. So on our continuation-based analysis, these exceptions follow automatically from the meaning of the expressions involved. The net prediction is that it is precisely in reconstruction cases that evaluation order comes apart from linear order.

In recognition of the importance of evaluation order to building a case that continuations are indispensable, Part I of the book is devoted to an in-depth case study of crossover and related phenomena, including in-situ wh and wh-fronting, donkey anaphora, coordination, and the order-sensitivity of negative polarity licensing. The analysis is expressed in a continuation-based grammar presented in what we call tower notation, as introduced in, e.g., Barker and Shan (2008). This formalism is expressly designed to be as easy to learn as possible, and in particular, easy to work with on paper and on a blackboard.

But a principled treatment of evaluation order is not the only distinctive advantage of taking a continuation-based view. Part II of the book investigates phenomena that do not depend on evaluation order. The first of the two main case studies involves scope-taking adjectives such as *same* and *different*.

(7) Ann and Bill read the same book.

The sentence-internal reading (the reading that does not depend on identifying some salient book from context) is notoriously difficult to treat compositionally (see, e.g., Carlson 1987, Keenan 1992). Following the parasitic-scope approach of Barker (2007), we show how a continuation-based analysis follows naturally from an analysis of nominal uses of *same*.

Because parasitic scope requires higher-order continuations (categories of the form $A\backslash\!\!\backslash(B\backslash\!\!\backslash C)$), which are beyond the expressive power of the grammar from Part I, we develop the analyses in Part II in a continuation-based type-logical grammar first introduced in Barker (2007).

The second main case study in Part II is sluicing.

(8) [John made someone happy], but I don't know who __.

The interpretation of the embedded interrogative *who* __ takes its meaning from the content of an antecedent clause, in this case, the bracketed initial clause. Furthermore, the wh-phrase *who* corresponds (in a sense made precise below) to the indefinite *someone*. In fact, the elided content is exactly the antecedent clause with the wh-correlate removed, namely, *John made* [ ] *happy*. But of course, this is exactly a continuation, namely, the continuation of *someone* relative to the bracketed antecedent clause. Following Barker (2013), we suggest that sluicing is anaphora to a continuation. If so, then we need a grammar that explicitly recognizes continuations, so that it can make them available to serve as potential antecedents.

The answer to the question "What makes continuations essential?", then, is that continuations enable new and potentially insightful analyses of crossover, reconstruction, NPI licensing, and other order-sensitive phenomena in terms of evaluation order; and that continuations provide robust, potentially insightful analyses of parasitic scope and sluicing.

A continuation is the rest of an expression, e.g., a scope remnant. In some sense, then, continuations are anti-constituents: the complement of an expression relative to some enclosing expression. Analyzing natural language without explicitly using continuations is like performing arithmetic without ever using negative numbers: many useful tasks can still be accomplished, but a full understanding requires taking a broader view.

Why are continuations so hard to understand?

Continuations have been studied in computer science, in logic, and in natural language semantics. No matter which discipline, they have a reputation for being hard to understand. Apparently, continuations are intrinsically hard to understand, at least at first.

We will spend considerable effort explaining what continuations are, concentrating especially on showing in detail how analyses that make use of continuations work on a practical level.

Furthermore, since no single presentation works best for everyone, we will come at continuations from several different directions. The majority of the book will be concerned with a grammar that we develop incrementally in Part I, with step-by-step explanations and many derivations and diagrams. Then we'll develop a different continuation-based grammar in Part II. The hope is that comparing these two different formalisms will clarify the essence of (one kind of) continuation.

In our experience, grasping continuations requires working with them. Therefore, we have provided a number of exercises throughout Part I, with complete solutions at the end of the book. Offering exercises is unusual for a research monograph in linguistics. We have included them with the encouragement of our editors, as well as of many of our students and colleagues. We hope that they're useful to some of our readers. If you aren't interested in doing exercises, you can think of them as a kind of footnote.

We can't promise that we will make continuations easy to understand. We can, however, promise three things. First, we promise we'll do our best to make understanding them as easy as possible. Second, we promise that, given a modest amount of effort on the part of the reader, it will be possible to understand in detail how a continuation-based analysis works. Finally, we promise that we'll do our best to make understanding continuations worth the effort, in terms of new insights into natural language semantics.

Audience

The level of the discussion in the first half of the book is aimed at readers who understand the standard tools and techniques of natural language semantics at the level of a first-year graduate student or of an advanced undergraduate. As usual, this amounts to some familiarity with phrase structure grammars, the first-order Predicate Calculus, the (simply-typed) lambda calculus, and, ideally, the basic ideas of generalized quantifiers in the spirit of Montague, as in, for example, Heim and Kratzer (1998).

Familiarity with techniques from the theory of programming languages will help, but is not necessary. van Eijck and Unger (2010) is a particularly congenial presentation of computational techniques in the service of semantic analysis.

Once the core of the approach has been established in the first several chapters, the theoretical and empirical investigations will begin to go deeper, and the level of the discussion will approach the usual level of a research monograph in terms of speed of presentation and assumptions about familiarity with standard literature.

Like any non-trivial formal technique, a complete understanding of continuations requires working through problems. We strongly urge the reader to complete a few key exercises on paper. The tower system has been designed specifically to make this both practical and rewarding.

We'll also do our best to help readers go beyond this operational-level understanding to a deeper appreciation, with comparisons with a number of other approaches, and pointers into the literature.

Ways to read this book

The heart of the book is an attempt to use continuations to gain a deeper understanding of natural language. The core ideas are presented in this introductory chapter, and in the two following chapters, chapters 1 and 2. These chapters develop continuations and the tower system up to a simple account of scope, binding, and crossover. Chapter 3 fits these ideas into a larger theoretical landscape, showing how taking a continuations-based perspective unifies Montague's generalized quantifier theory of DP meaning with the dynamic semantics perspective on sentence meaning, by treating them as two special cases of a more general interpretive strategy. If your goal is to merely get an impression of what continuations are and how they can be used to model natural language, these first four chapters will provide that much.

The remainder of Part I extends and deepens the core ideas and techniques both empirically and theoretically. The empirical extensions include reconstruction, order effects in negative polarity licensing, and donkey anaphora. The theoretical discussions include Partee and Rooth's (1983) theory of Generalized Coordination (section 7.1), Hendriks' (1993) Flexible Montague Grammar approach to scope-taking (section 7.2), Jacobson's (1999) Variable Free Semantics (sections 11.1 and 11.2), Steedman's (2012) theory of scope as surface constituency (section 11.3), and Plotkin's (1975) Continuation Passing-Style approach to evaluation order in the lambda calculus (section 12.1).

Part II analyzes sentence-internal uses of *same*, verb phrase ellipsis, and sluicing. Part II does not depend on Part I, and should be understandable even if it is read independently of Part I. Theoretical comparisons include Morrill's et al. (2011) Discontinuous Lambek Grammar (section 15.2), de Groote's (2001) application of the $\lambda\mu$-calculus to scope (section 18.1), and Bernardi and Moortgat's (2010) Lambek-Grishin calculus (section 18.2).

Historical notes

The research reported in this book began roughly at the turn of the millennium. In the case of Barker, this included a manuscript first circulated in 2000. An early version was published as Barker (2001), and a revised version was published as Barker (2002). In the case of Shan, many of the ideas developed in this book first appeared in Shan (2001a) and Shan (2001b), some of which are developed further in Shan (2005).

Continuations have been rediscovered many times in computer science, as related by Reynolds (1993), and the same is true in the study of natural language: we are by no means the first semanticists to make use of continuations. In fact, it is the burden of chapter 3 to argue that Montague's conception of DP meanings as generalized quantifiers is a form of continuation passing. Likewise, as that chapter also argues, we consider the dynamic conception of meaning (on which a sentence is a context update function, as in, e.g., Groenendijk and Stokhof 1990) as a different version of the same core idea of continuization. And yet again, we will suggest that Partee's (1987) treatment of generalized coordination (see section 7.1), as well as Hendriks' (1993) treatment of scope-taking (chapter 7.2) also make implicit use of continuations.

Nor are we the only researchers to study natural language semantics with explicit consideration of continuations. Around the same time we began our work, de Groote (2001) applied the $\lambda\mu$-calculus to natural language scope (section 18.1). He presented this work at the 2001 Amsterdam Colloquium, the same conference where Shan presented Shan (2001b). A few years later, de Groote (2006) gave a different continuation-based treatment of donkey anaphora (discussed in section 18.3). Among the growing list of continuation-based analyses of natural language, another one in particular that we will discuss below is Bernardi and Moortgat's (2010) Lambek-Grishin calculus (see section 18.2).

In other words, this book is neither the first word nor the last word on continuations in natural language. Our goal here is to explain what continuations are, how they work, and why they are potentially interesting to someone who studies the structure of language and meaning.

Part I

Towers: Scope and Evaluation Order

This first of the two main parts of the book presents a particular continuation-based grammar. The presentation and the grammar itself are designed to be as easy to learn and use as possible. The system is a combinatory categorial grammar with a small number of type-shifters, all of which apply freely and without constraint. Categories and semantic values are presented in a grid format we call "tower notation". Using this system, we incrementally develop a fragment that addresses quantifier scope, quantificational binding, dynamic anaphora, wh-fronting, relative clauses, and more.

The main explanatory goal is to provide a reconception of scope-taking. The main advantage for adopting a continuation perspective is that continuations allow fine-grained control over the order in which expressions are evaluated. If we assume that the order of evaluation defaults to left-to-right, we have an explanation for linear scope bias, as well as for crossover. At the same time, we show that various systematic exceptions to a simple left-to-right constraint on quantificational binding, in particular, certain reconstruction effects, fall out from independently-motivated assumptions about the meaning of the expressions involved.

Because the elements of the formal grammar are presented one by one, throughout the text, here is a complete list of where to find the introduction of each piece: the combination schema, (16); the four type-shifters, namely, LIFT (18), LOWER (21), BIND (29), and FRONT (62); the principle of applying type-shifters to subparts of categories, section 4.1; and the lexical schema for syntactic gaps, $A /\!/ A$, section 5.1.

There is a compact description of a slightly refactored but equivalent grammar in section 12.2. (The modifications are motivated to make the grammar more computationally tractable.)

The first publication of an essentially equivalent formal grammar is Shan and Barker (2006); the first publication of the tower presentation is Barker and Shan (2008).

1

Scope and towers

This chapter gives a continuation-based grammar in the tower presentation, with just enough machinery to handle scope-taking. This will require defining a set of syntactic categories, and providing a way to combine expressions into complex expressions. In addition, there will be two complementary type-shifters, LIFT and LOWER. The next chapter adds binding, and the rest of Part I will build on the basic fragment, extending it when necessary, to handle a wide range of additional sentence types, concentrating on crossover and reconstruction.

The fragment is a combinatory categorial grammar similar in nature to the systems in Jacobson (1999) or Steedman (2012), in which a small number of type-shifters ("combinators") apply freely and without constraint. It is faithful in spirit and in many details to the Shan and Barker (2006) analysis, though it uses the 'tower' notation introduced in Barker and Shan (2008).

1.1 Scope

Scope-taking is one of the most fundamental, one of the most characteristic, and one of the most dramatic features of the syntax and semantics of natural languages.

A phrase **takes scope** over a larger expression that contains it when the larger expression serves as the smaller phrase's semantic argument:

(9)

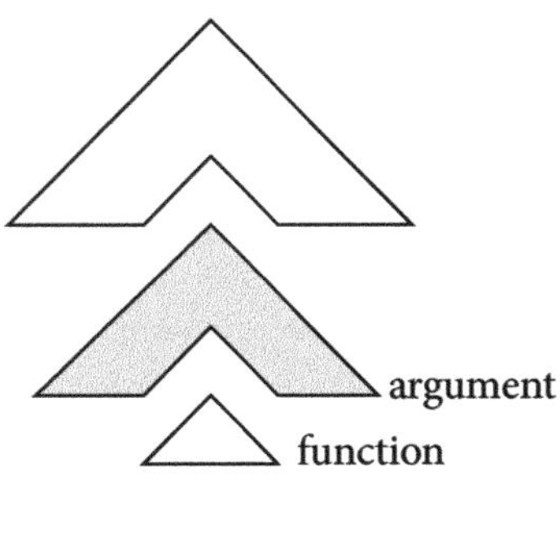

(10) John said [**Mary called** [everyone] **yesterday**] with relief.

In this schematic picture, the context *John said* [ ] *with relief* corresponds to the upper unshaded notched triangle, the embedded context *Mary called* [ ] *yesterday* corresponds to the middle gray notched triangle, and the scope-taker *everyone* corresponds to the lower unshaded triangle.

In (10), *everyone* takes scope over the rest of the embedded clause that surrounds it, namely, *Mary called* [ ] *yesterday*. Semantically, *everyone* denotes a function that takes as its argument the property $\lambda x.\textbf{yesterday}(\textbf{called}\, x)\ \textbf{m}$. We will call the expression over which the scope-taker takes scope (the gray region in the diagram) its **nuclear scope.**

The challenge for a theory of scope is to explain how it is possible for a scope-taker to reverse the direction of function/argument composition, that is, how it is possible to provide the scope-taking element with access to material that properly surrounds it.

The diagram of scope-taking is essentially identical to the diagram in (4) of the introductory chapter, the diagram that explained what a continuation is. This similarity is not accidental: the material over which a scope-taker takes scope is exactly what we are calling a continuation. This is what makes scope a particularly natural and compelling application for continuations in natural language.

Crucially, although all nuclear scopes can be viewed as continuations, the reverse is not true: the full range of continuations discussed in this book go beyond any standard analysis of scope-taking.

1.2 Syntactic categories: adjacency vs. containment

We'll need a set of syntactic category labels. This section develops a notation based on the categorial grammar tradition that we will use throughout the rest of the book.

Normally, functors combine with arguments that are syntactically adjacent to them, either on the left or on the right. In the notation of categorial grammar (e.g., Lambek 1958), a functor in category $A\backslash B$ combines with an argument of category A to its left to form a B. So if *John* has category DP, and *left* has category DP\S, *John left* has category S.

(11)
$$\left(\begin{array}{cc} \text{DP} & \text{DP}\backslash\text{S} \\ \textit{John} & \textit{left} \\ \textbf{j} & \textbf{left} \end{array}\right) = \begin{array}{c} \text{S} \\ \textit{John left} \\ \textbf{left}(\textbf{j}) \end{array}$$

Syntactically, we will call the operation that combines a functor with its argument 'merge'. Semantically, merge corresponds to function application, as usual. This means that the semantic type of an expression in category $A\backslash B$ will be $\alpha \rightarrow \beta$, where α is the type of expressions in category A, and β is the result type of the merged expression.

Schematically, for ordinary function application we have:

(12)

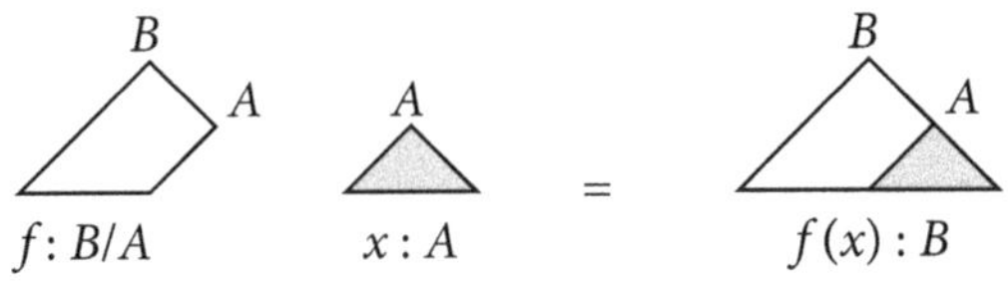

The functor category (here, B/A) is represented as a clear triangle with one corner missing: it would be a complete expression of category B if only we supply the missing corner of category A. The category of the argument (here, A) must match the category needed by the functor category, the category underneath the slash. This picture shows combination with a right-leaning slash, i.e., B/A instead of $A\backslash B$, as we had above in (11). The result after combination is a complete expression of category B.

For scope-taking, linear adjacency is not sufficient. After all, a scope-taker is not adjacent to its argument, it is contained within its argument. In (10), for instance, the scope-taker *everyone* is neither to the left or to the right of its nuclear scope—in fact, it's right in the middle. What we need, then, is a syntactic notion of 'surrounding' and 'being surrounded by'. Therefore we will augment the set of category labels with a second kind of slash: $A\mathbin{\backslash\!\!\backslash}B$ and $B /\!\!/ A$. On paper or on a blackboard, we write these symbols as double slash marks. Syntactically, we will see that these hollow slashes correspond to in-situ scope-taking.

Pursuing this idea, we will build up to a suitable category for a scope-taker such as *everyone* in two steps. First, consider again the schematic picture of scope-taking given above in (9), with some category labels added:

(13)

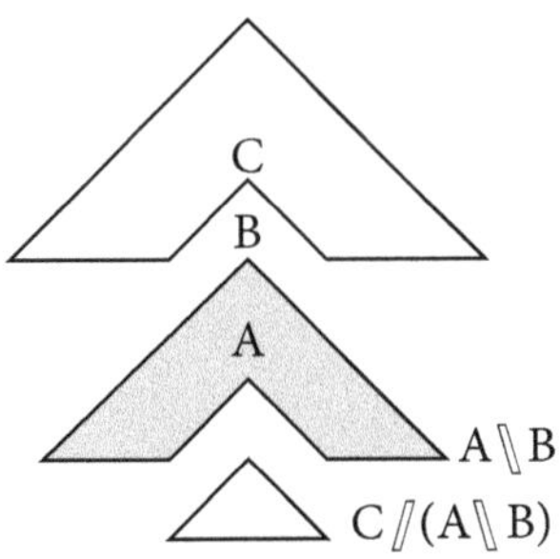

The category of the gray notched triangle in the middle—the nuclear scope—will be $A\mathbin{\backslash\!\!\backslash}B$: something that would be a complete expression of category B, except that it is missing an expression of category A somewhere (specific) inside of it. Just like $A\backslash B$, $A\mathbin{\backslash\!\!\backslash}B$ will have semantic type $\alpha \rightarrow \beta$: a function from objects of type α to objects of type β, assuming that α and β are the semantic types of expressions in categories A and B.

As may already be clear by now, an expression in a category of the form $A\mathbin{\backslash\!\!\backslash}B$ will play the role of a continuation.

The second step in arriving at a category for a scope-taker is to consider the scope-taker itself, the small lower triangle in the diagram. It takes the continuation above it as its semantic argument. But once again, it is not adjacent to its argument. Rather, it is *surrounded* by its argument. Just as we needed a notion of 'missing something somewhere inside of it', we now need a notion of 'missing something surrounding it'. If $A\backslash\!\!\backslash B$ means 'something that would be a B if we could add an A somewhere (specific) inside of it', then we'll use $C /\!\!/ D$ to mean 'would be a C if we could add a D surrounding it'. Of course these two notions complement each other; and in fact, a little thought will reveal that the surrounding D will most naturally be a continuation, since continuations are the kind of expression that require something to be inserted inside of them.

The general form of a scope-taker, then, will be $C /\!\!/ (A\backslash\!\!\backslash B)$, as indicated in the diagram: something that combines with a continuation of category $A\backslash\!\!\backslash B$ surrounding it to form a complex expression in category C.

For example, consider the sentence *John called everyone yesterday*. The nuclear scope is the sentence missing the scope-taker: *John called* [ ] *yesterday*. This is an expression that would be an S except that it is missing a DP somewhere specific inside of it. So this continuation has category DP$\backslash\!\!\backslash$S. When the quantifier *everyone* combines with this continuation, it will form a complete sentence of category S. Therefore the syntactic category of the quantifier will be S$/\!\!/$(DP$\backslash\!\!\backslash$S): the kind of expression that needs a continuation of category DP$\backslash\!\!\backslash$S surrounding it in order to form a complete S.

1.3 Tower notation

A simple example of scope-taking will serve to introduce the tower notation:

$$(14)\quad \left(\begin{array}{cc} \dfrac{\mathrm{S}|\mathrm{S}}{\mathrm{DP}} & \dfrac{\mathrm{S}|\mathrm{S}}{\mathrm{DP\backslash S}} \\ \textit{everyone} & \textit{left} \\ \dfrac{\forall y.[\;]}{y} & \dfrac{[\;]}{\textbf{left}} \end{array} \right) = \begin{array}{c} \dfrac{\mathrm{S}|\mathrm{S}}{\mathrm{S}} \\ \textit{everyone left} \\ \dfrac{\forall y.[\;]}{\textbf{left}\ y} \end{array}$$

There are several elements in this derivation that will be carefully explained in the course of the next few sections.

First, purely as a matter of notation, syntactic categories of the form $C /\!\!/ (A\backslash\!\!\backslash B)$ can optionally be written as $\dfrac{C|B}{A}$. This is what we call the 'tower' convention. The categories in this chapter have only two levels, and so don't really deserve to be called towers; however, in later chapters, categories will grow to include three or more layers.

Towers can be read counterclockwise, starting at the bottom: expressions in a category $\dfrac{C|B}{A}$ function locally (i.e., with respect to function/argument combination) as an A, take scope over an expression of category B, and return a new expression of category C. So, as explained above, the syntactic category given here for *everyone* will be $\mathrm{S} /\!\!/ (\mathrm{DP} \backslash\!\!\backslash \mathrm{S}) \equiv \frac{\mathrm{S} | \mathrm{S}}{\mathrm{DP}}$: something that functions locally as a DP, takes scope over an S, and returns as a result a new expression of category S.

Semantically, *everyone* will denote the usual generalized quantifier, namely, $\lambda\kappa.\forall y.\kappa y$, where κ is a variable of type $\mathtt{e} \to \mathtt{t}$. But, as illustrated above in (14), we can write semantic values in tower notation too:

(15)

$$\begin{array}{ccc} \mathrm{S} /\!\!/ (\mathrm{DP} \backslash\!\!\backslash \mathrm{S}) & & \frac{\mathrm{S} | \mathrm{S}}{\mathrm{DP}} \\ \textit{everyone} & \equiv & \textit{everyone} \\ \lambda\kappa.\forall y.\kappa y & & \frac{\forall y.[\,]}{y} \end{array}$$

In general, a function of the form $\lambda\kappa.g[\kappa f]$ can optionally be written as $\frac{g[\,]}{f}$.

Here, $\forall y.[\,]$ and $g[\,]$ are *contexts*, i.e., logical expressions containing a single hole. This notation is often seen in theoretical discussions of formal languages (for instance, Barendregt 1981: 29), including programming languages (e.g., Felleisen 1987), as well as in discussions of logical languages (for instance, in discussions of the cut rule in substructural logics, e.g., (Moortgat, 1997: 106) or (Restall, 2000: 112); see also chapter 13.

Contexts are not so familiar in linguistic discussions. However, because syntactic and semantic towers are completely equivalent with their flat (i.e., non-tower) counterparts, it is always possible to give a full analysis that does not rely on contexts that contain holes, if desired.

EXERCISE 1

What are the flat notational counterparts of the syntactic and semantic towers $\frac{\mathrm{S} | \mathrm{S}}{\mathrm{DP}\backslash \mathrm{S}}$ and $\frac{\forall x.[\,]}{\text{left } x}$?

1.4 The combination schema

Continuing the explanation of the derivation in (14), the combination of two multi-level towers cannot be simple functional application. Rather, it is described by the following schema:

(16) **The combination schema ('/' variant):**

$$\left(\begin{array}{cc} \dfrac{C|D}{B/A} & \dfrac{D|E}{A} \\ \text{left.exp} & \text{right.exp} \\ \dfrac{g[\;]}{f} & \dfrac{h[\;]}{x} \end{array}\right) = \begin{array}{c} \dfrac{C|E}{B} \\ \text{left.exp right.exp} \\ \dfrac{g[h[\;]]}{f(x)} \end{array}$$

On the syntactic tier, the horizontal line divides two different combination regimes. Beneath the horizontal line, B/A and A combine as usual to form a B; above the line, $C|D$ and $D|E$ combine to form $C|E$.

In parallel, on the semantic tier, below the horizontal line, combination is function application. Above the horizontal line, $g[\;]$ and $h[\;]$ combine to form $g[h[\;]]$. For instance, if $g[\;] = \forall x.[\;]$, and $h[\;] = \exists y.[\;]$, then $g[h[\;]] = \forall x[\exists y.[\;]]$.

EXERCISE 2

If $g[\;] = \lambda x.(x\,[\;])y$ and $g[h[\textbf{saw m}]] = \lambda x.(x(\textbf{thinks}(\textbf{saw m})))y$, what must $h[\;]$ be?

It is important to distinguish plugging a hole in a context from beta reduction in the lambda calculus. Unlike beta reduction, plugging a hole can result in variable capture. If $g[\;] = \lambda x.(x\,[\;])y$, then $g[x] = \lambda x.(xx)y$: plugging the hole in $g[\;]$ with x results in an expression in which the plug x is bound by the lambda.

Because the tower notation and flat notation are completely equivalent, if there is any uncertainty over the interaction of context holes with variable capture, in any concrete example it is always possible to translate the tower in question back into flat notation, and then make use of the usual rules of beta reduction.

The combination schema in (16) will be the general mode of composition that will be used throughout Part I. As we will explain in detail below, it embodies the general principle that expressions, by default, must be evaluated from left-to-right, so it is at the heart of our explanation of crossover, reconstruction, and other evaluation-order effects.

A tangram diagram will help unpack what is going on here conceptually.

(17)

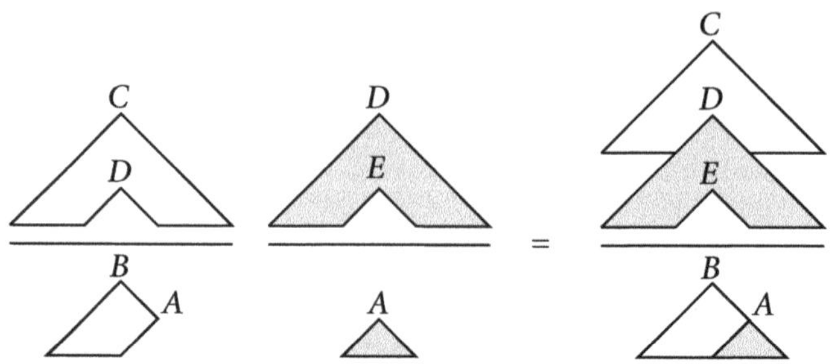

Focusing first on the layer below the horizontal lines, the unshaded trapezoidal functor element has category B/A, and the small gray triangle has category A. They combine according to the normal function/argument pattern: the A categories match and cancel, forming an expression of category B. This is just diagram (12) repeated.

In the layer above the horizontal line, the syntactic categories D match (note that the labels in the diagram match the categories in the schema given above in (16) exactly), meaning that it is coherent to use the result of the notched gray continuation as the input to the unshaded continuation. This composition is indicated graphically on the right by inserting the gray subcomputation (E to D) into the notch of the unshaded computation (D to C). The result after combination is an expression that is waiting for a continuation that would fit in the space occupied by the horizontal line, namely, a computation that can turn a B into an E (i.e., a continuation of category $B\backslash\!\!\backslash E$). If such a continuation were supplied, the net result would be a complete expression of category C.

> **EXERCISE 3**
>
> The combination schema in (16) has a right-leaning slash in the syntactic category of its leftmost expression. What should the combination schema be when the two elements have categories $\frac{C|D}{A}$ and $\frac{D|E}{A\backslash B}$? It may help to draw the tangram diagram.

1.5 Types and continuations

The semantic types of the expressions in this grammar are straightforward. Expressions in category DP have semantic type e, the type of individuals, and expressions in category S have semantic type t, the type of truth values. As mentioned, expressions in category $A\backslash B$ have semantic type $\alpha \to \beta$, where α is the type of A and β is the type of B. Likewise, expressions in category $A\backslash\!\!\backslash B$ also have semantic type $\alpha \to \beta$, as do expressions in categories B/A and $B/\!\!/A$.

Thus since the syntactic category of *everyone* is $\frac{\mathrm{S}|\mathrm{S}}{\mathrm{DP}} \equiv \mathrm{S}/\!\!/(\mathrm{DP}\backslash\!\!\backslash\mathrm{S})$, the semantic type of *everyone* is $(\mathtt{e} \to \mathtt{t}) \to \mathtt{t}$. This is exactly what we expect for an extensional generalized quantifier.

And since the semantic value of *everyone* as given above in (14) is $\frac{\forall y.[\,]}{y} \equiv \lambda\kappa.\forall y.\kappa y$, the typing correspondence forces x to be a variable of type e, and κ to be a variable of type $\mathtt{e} \to \mathtt{t}$. In other words, as discussed in more depth in chapter (3), the continuation-based approach has led us more or less directly to the standard treatment of generalized quantifiers of Montague (1974) and Barwise and Cooper (1981).

Where in the semantics are the continuations? As suggested by the choice of variable symbol, κ stands for 'continuation'. For instance, in the case of *everyone*, the key fact is that the continuation of a DP relative to the clause it takes scope over will be a function of type $\mathtt{e} \to \mathtt{t}$, exactly the type we just assigned to κ.

1.6 The LIFT type-shifter

Another element that needs comment in the derivation in (14) above is that the syntax and semantics for *left* does not match the treatment it received in (11). The reason is that non-scope-taking elements such as *left* must be adjusted in order to combine with scope-takers. Just as Montague recognized that the denotations of proper names (which according to Partee (1987) are fundamentally of type $\mathtt{e}$) must be adjusted in order to coordinate with properly quantificational DPs (type $(\mathtt{e} \to \mathtt{t}) \to \mathtt{t}$), so too must *left* be adjusted here. In both cases, the adjustment mechanism is the same: a generalization of Partee's (1987) LIFT type-shifter. In general, for all categories A and B, and for all semantic values x:

(18)
$$\begin{array}{ccc} & & \dfrac{B \mid B}{A} \\ A & \text{LIFT} & \\ \textit{phrase} & \Rightarrow & \textit{phrase} \\ x & & \dfrac{[\,]}{x} \end{array}$$

If x is the semantic value of an expression in category A, then the semantic value of the LIFTed A is $\dfrac{[\,]}{x} \equiv \lambda\kappa.\kappa x$.

The tangram version shows how LIFT turns a value into an expression that is expecting a continuation.

(19)

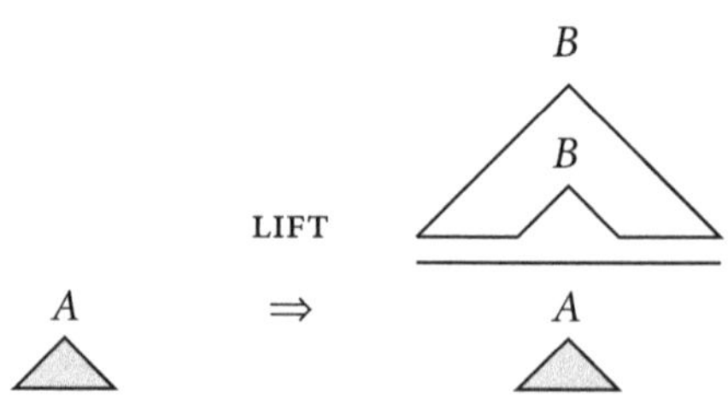

Looking at the result, the horizontal line represents the place where the continuation will fit. This expression expects a continuation that surrounds an expression of category A to build an expression of category B. The idea of the LIFT operation is that it is easy for an expression of category A to use a continuation of category $A\mathbin{\backslash\!\!\backslash}B$ to produce a result of category B: simply apply the continuation to the original expression of category A. In other words, the semantic content of the unshaded notched triangle above the horizontal line on the right is simply an identity function.

Two examples will serve to illustrate:

(20)

$$\text{(a)}\ \begin{array}{c}\text{DP}\\ \textit{John}\\ \mathbf{j}\end{array} \ \overset{\text{LIFT}}{\Rightarrow}\ \begin{array}{c}\dfrac{\text{S}|\text{S}}{\text{DP}}\\ \textit{John}\\ \dfrac{[\,]}{\mathbf{j}}\end{array} \qquad \text{(b)}\ \begin{array}{c}\text{DP}\backslash\text{S}\\ \textit{left}\\ \mathbf{left}\end{array} \ \overset{\text{LIFT}}{\Rightarrow}\ \begin{array}{c}\dfrac{\text{S}\,|\,\text{S}}{\text{DP}\backslash\text{S}}\\ \textit{left}\\ \dfrac{[\,]}{\mathbf{left}}\end{array}$$

For instance, LIFTing the proper name *John* yields the usual generalized quantifier syntax and semantics, since $\frac{[\,]}{\mathbf{j}} \equiv \lambda\kappa.\kappa(\mathbf{j})$. Likewise, when the simple version of *left* given in (11) undergoes the LIFT typeshifter, the result is the verb phrase that appears above in the derivation of *everyone left* in (14).

Semantically, just as the generalized-quantifier version of *John* has no detectable scope-taking effect (it is 'scopeless'), so too the LIFTed *left* has no detectable scope-taking effect. This is evident from the fact that the semantics of the LIFT operator supplies just an empty context '[ ]' above the horizontal line (equivalent in flat notation to the identity function).

As chapter 3 will emphasize, continuizing throughout the grammar allows us to generalize Partee's LIFT type-shifter from something that originally only applied sensibly to expressions of type e to something that can apply to expressions in any category.

1.7 The LOWER type-shifter

The final element in the derivation of *everyone left* that requires explanation is the fact that the derivation as given above ends with a multi-level syntactic category. That is, the final syntactic category is $\frac{\text{S}|\text{S}}{\text{S}}$ instead of a plain S. A derivation like this would be appropriate if the clause were embedded in a larger expression over which the quantifier takes scope; but if we imagine that this is a complete utterance, we need a way to close off the scope domain of the quantifier. We accomplish this with the following type-shifter.

For all categories A, for all contexts $f[\ ]$, and for all semantic values x:

(21)

$$\begin{array}{ccc} \dfrac{A|\mathrm{S}}{\mathrm{S}} & \text{LOWER} & A \\ \textit{phrase} & \Rightarrow & \textit{phrase} \\ \dfrac{f[\ ]}{x} & & f[x] \end{array}$$

If F is the semantic value of the original expression, then $F(\lambda\kappa.\kappa)$ is the value of the shifted expression. The idea is that the semantic tower is collapsed by plugging the hole in the context above the line with the material below the line:

(22)

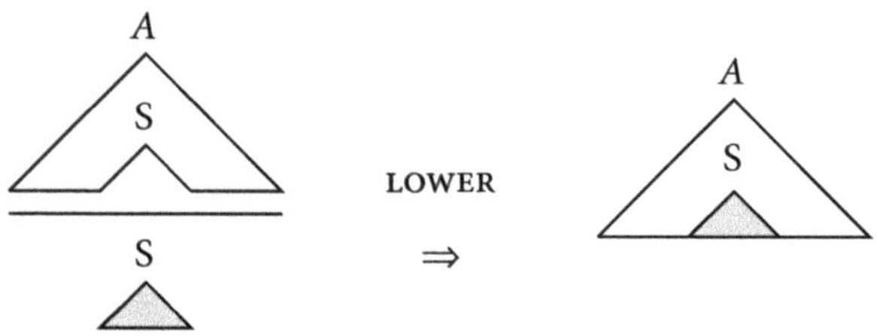

This diagram makes it clear how it is possible to remove the horizontal line and collapse two levels into one, provided that the category of the plug (the lower gray element) matches the category expected by the context (the element above the line).

Crucially, the LOWER rule as given in (21) restricts the lowering operation to situations in which the category of the plug is S. Thus this lowering rule only applies to scope-taking elements that take scope over a clause. This limitation plays an important role in the explanation for crossover, as discussed in section 4.3.

Using the LOWER type-shifter, we can complete the derivation of *everyone left*:

(23)

$$\begin{array}{ccc} \dfrac{\mathrm{S}|\mathrm{S}}{\mathrm{S}} & \text{LOWER} & \mathrm{S} \\ \textit{everyone left} & \Rightarrow & \textit{everyone left} \\ \dfrac{\forall y.[\ ]}{\mathbf{left}\ y} & & \forall y.\ \mathbf{left}\ y \end{array}$$

The combinator lowers the category of the sentence back to a plain S.

Though lowering operations are not as common in the literature as lifting, the LOWER type-shifter plays a role here that is closely similar to Groenendijk and Stokhof's (1990) '↓' operator. We will comment further on this connection in section 3.3.

1.8 A linear scope bias

As we have mentioned, the explanation for crossover will depend heavily on imposing a left-to-right evaluation regime. This bias is already embodied in the combination schema given above in (16). As one symptom of the fact that the combination schema enforces left-to-right evaluation order, note that when a sentence contains two quantifiers, the quantifier on the left takes scope over the one on the right, at least as a default:

(24)
$$\begin{array}{c}\dfrac{S\,|\,S}{DP}\\ \textit{someone}\\ \dfrac{\exists x.\,[\,]}{x}\end{array}\left(\begin{array}{c}\dfrac{S\,|\,S}{(DP\backslash S)/DP}\\ \textit{loves}\\ \dfrac{[\,]}{\textbf{loves}}\end{array}\quad\begin{array}{c}\dfrac{S\,|\,S}{DP}\\ \textit{everyone}\\ \dfrac{\forall y.\,[\,]}{y}\end{array}\right)$$
$$= \begin{array}{c}\dfrac{S\,|\,S}{S}\\ \textit{someone loves everyone}\\ \dfrac{\exists x.\,\forall y.\,[\,]}{\textbf{loves}\,y\,x}\end{array} \quad\overset{\text{LOWER}}{\Rightarrow}\quad \begin{array}{c} S\\ \textit{someone loves everyone}\\ \exists x.\,\forall y.\,\textbf{loves}\,y\,x\end{array}$$

This derivation involves two applications of the combination schema: once for the verb (the LIFTed *loves*) combining with its direct object (*everyone*), and once for the subject (*someone*) combining with the verb phrase.

> **EXERCISE 4**
>
> Give the intermediate result of combining *loves* with *everyone*.

As a result of the left-to-right bias built into the combination schema, this evaluates to $\exists x \forall y.\textbf{loves}\,y\,x$, in which the existential quantifier takes linear (i.e., surface) scope over the universal.

Of course, we will also need a way to arrive at inverse scope; that will be postponed to chapter 4.

1.9 A scope ambiguity due to LOWER

In addition to its role as a derivation finisher, LOWER also serves as a way to delimit the region that a scope-taker takes scope over. Like all of the type-shifters in this book, LOWER is allowed to freely apply or not whenever its schema is matched. Whether or not LOWER applies can determine which interpretation an ambiguous sentence receives.

(25) Mary wants everyone to leave.

For instance, if LOWER applies to the embedded clause *everyone to leave* before it combines with the matrix verb *wants*, then the scope of the quantifier will be limited to the embedded clause, and the interpretation of the sentence will be **wants**($\forall x$.**leave** x) **m**. In this interpretation, Mary has a single desire: that everyone leave.

But if LOWER does not apply until the end of the derivation, a different interpretation emerges:

(26)
$$\begin{array}{c}\dfrac{S|S}{DP}\\ \textit{Mary}\\ \dfrac{[\,]}{\mathbf{m}}\end{array} \left(\begin{array}{c}\dfrac{S\,|\,S}{(DP\backslash S)/S}\\ \textit{wants}\\ \dfrac{[\,]}{\mathbf{wants}}\end{array}\left(\begin{array}{c}\dfrac{S|S}{DP}\\ \textit{everyone}\\ \dfrac{\forall x.[\,]}{x}\end{array}\quad\begin{array}{c}\dfrac{S\,|\,S}{DP\backslash S}\\ \textit{to leave}\\ \dfrac{[\,]}{\mathbf{leave}}\end{array}\right)\right)$$

$$= \begin{array}{c}\dfrac{S|S}{S}\\ \textit{M.w.e.t.l}\\ \dfrac{\forall x.[\,]}{\mathbf{wants}(\mathbf{leave}\,x)\,\mathbf{m}}\end{array} \quad\overset{\text{LOWER}}{\Rightarrow}\quad \begin{array}{c}S\\ \textit{Mary wants everyone to leave}\\ \forall x.\mathbf{wants}(\mathbf{leave}\,x)\,\mathbf{m}\end{array}$$

In this interpretation, Mary has a multiplicity of desires: for each person x, Mary wants x to leave.

This ability of LOWER to encapsulate scope within a circumscribed domain is closely analogous to what Danvy and Filinski (1990) call a 'reset' in their theory of layered continuations. It is also similar to the mechanism for limiting scope in Barker (2002). See Charlow (2014) for discussion of reset as a mechanism for enforcing a general theory of scope islands in the context of a continuation-based grammar.

We now have a grammar that allows scope-taking elements to take scope over a portion of the material that surrounds them. At this point, we can handle sentences with multiple quantifiers, though we are for the moment limited to linear scope. We can also explain some scope ambiguities, if the scope-taking element interacts with some other element in the sentence (here, the verb *wants*).

2

Binding and crossover

When a quantifier follows a pronoun it is trying to bind, the usual result is a mild kind of ungrammaticality known as a crossover violation.

(27) a. Everyone$_i$ loves his$_i$ mother.
     b. *His$_i$ mother loves everyone$_i$.

As discussed in the introduction, a quantifier can bind a pronoun that follows it, as in (27a), but usually not when the pronoun precedes it, as in (27b). In this chapter, we will extend the grammar to account for this basic contrast, and then build a progressively more refined account of the phenomenon in later chapters.

In order to discuss crossover, we will first need to provide a way for quantifiers to bind pronouns. This will involve adding a new connective to the syntactic categories: $A \rhd B$ will be a syntactic category whenever A and B are syntactic categories. Its semantic type will be $\alpha \rightarrow \beta$, where α and β are the types of A and B. This will be the category of something that is basically an expression in category B, but that contains a pronoun of category A needing to be bound.

Just as in Jacobson (1999), the presence of an unbound pronoun will be recorded on the category of each larger expression that contains it. In particular, a clause containing an unbound pronoun will have category $\mathrm{DP} \rhd \mathrm{S}$ rather than plain S. In order to accomplish this, the essential assumption here is that a pronoun must take scope, as advocated by, e.g., Dowty (2007): it will function locally as a DP, take scope over an S, and turn that S into an open proposition:

(28)
$$\left(\begin{array}{cc} \dfrac{\mathrm{DP} \rhd \mathrm{S} \,|\, \mathrm{S}}{\mathrm{DP}} & \dfrac{\mathrm{S} \,|\, \mathrm{S}}{\mathrm{DP\backslash S}} \\ \textit{he} & \textit{left} \\ \dfrac{\lambda y.[\,]}{y} & \dfrac{[\,]}{\textbf{left}} \end{array}\right) = \begin{array}{c} \dfrac{\mathrm{DP} \rhd \mathrm{S} \,|\, \mathrm{S}}{\mathrm{S}} \\ \textit{he left} \\ \dfrac{\lambda y.[\,]}{\textbf{left}\ y} \end{array} \begin{array}{c} \textsc{lower} \\ \Rightarrow \end{array} \begin{array}{c} \mathrm{DP} \rhd \mathrm{S} \\ \textit{he left} \\ \lambda y.\,\textbf{left}\ y \end{array}$$

Note that the lexical denotation of the pronoun, $\dfrac{\lambda y.[\,]}{y} \equiv \lambda \kappa y.\kappa y$, is a (two-place) identity function.

On this view, sentences with free pronouns do not have the same category as sentences without pronouns (e.g., *John left*). This difference reflects the fact that a sentence containing a pronoun means something different from an ordinary sentence: it does not express a complete thought until the value of the pronoun has been specified, whether by binding or by the pragmatic context. However, the two sentence types still share a common core; this commonality is captured here by the fact that in the tower notation, below the line, they are both S's, and it is only above the line that their differences are marked.

Once a pronominal dependency has been created, how will it be satisfied? Certainly, it must be possible for the value of the embedded pronoun to be supplied by the pragmatic context. But it must also be possible for some other element within the utterance to control (i.e., to bind) the value of the pronoun. We accomplish this by providing a type shifter called BIND, which enables an arbitrary DP to bind a downstream pronoun. For any categories A and B:

(29)
$$\boxed{\begin{array}{ccc}
\dfrac{A \,|\, B}{\text{DP}} & \text{BIND} & \dfrac{A \,|\, \text{DP} \rhd B}{\text{DP}} \\
\textit{phrase} & \Rightarrow & \textit{phrase} \\
\dfrac{f[\;]}{x} & & \dfrac{f[[\;]x]}{x}
\end{array}}$$

Intuitively, this type-shifter feeds a copy of x to the function that will be used to plug the hole in $f[\;]$. For example:

(30)
$$\begin{array}{ccc}
\dfrac{\text{S} \,|\, \text{S}}{\text{DP}} & \text{BIND} & \dfrac{\text{S} \,|\, \text{DP} \rhd \text{S}}{\text{DP}} \\
\textit{everyone} & \Rightarrow & \textit{everyone} \\
\dfrac{\forall x.[\;]}{x} & & \dfrac{\forall x.[\;]x}{x}
\end{array}$$

The shifted expression has category S//(DP\\(DP $\rhd$ S)) and semantics $\lambda\kappa\forall x.\kappa\, x\, x$: something that knows how to turn a surrounding sentence containing a pronoun (DP $\rhd$ S) into a plain clause (S). It accomplishes this semantically by quantifying over individuals ($\forall x$), and then applying the continuation κ to two copies of each individual x ($\kappa x x$), rather than to just one.

We immediately have an account of quantificational binding:

(31)
$$\begin{array}{c}
\dfrac{\text{S} \,|\, \text{DP} \rhd \text{S}}{\text{DP}} \\
\textit{everyone} \\
\dfrac{\forall x.[\;]x}{x}
\end{array}
\left(
\begin{array}{c}
\dfrac{\text{DP} \rhd \text{S} \,|\, \text{DP} \rhd \text{S}}{(\text{DP}\backslash\text{S})/\text{DP}} \\
\textit{loves} \\
\dfrac{[\;]}{\textbf{loves}}
\end{array}
\left(
\begin{array}{cc}
\dfrac{\text{DP} \rhd \text{S} \,|\, \text{S}}{\text{DP}} & \dfrac{\text{S} \,|\, \text{S}}{\text{DP}\backslash\text{DP}} \\
\textit{his} & \textit{mother} \\
\dfrac{\lambda y.[\;]}{y} & \dfrac{[\;]}{\textbf{mom}}
\end{array}
\right)\right)$$

$$
= \begin{array}{c} \dfrac{S \mid S}{S} \\ \textit{Everyone loves his mother} \\ \dfrac{\forall x.(\lambda y.\,[\;])x}{\textbf{loves}\ (\textbf{mom}\ y)\ x} \end{array}
\quad \overset{\textsc{lower}}{\Rightarrow} \quad
\begin{array}{c} S \\ \textit{Everyone loves his mother} \\ \forall x.(\lambda y.\textbf{loves}\ (\textbf{mom}\ y)\ x)x \end{array}
$$

Note that the syntactic tower for *loves* gets its upper layer by choosing $B = \text{DP} \rhd \text{S}$ when applying LIFT. After beta reduction (i.e., lambda conversion), the semantic value is $\forall x.\ \textbf{loves}\ (\textbf{mom}\ x)\ x$. This is an interpretation on which the quantifier binds the pronoun, as desired.

EXERCISE 5

Compute the functions denoted by *his mother* and by *loves his mother*.

2.1 The irrelevance of c-command

Since c-command has no special status in our theory of binding, it is perfectly possible to have binding without c-command.

(32)
$$
\left(\begin{array}{c} \dfrac{S \mid DP \rhd S}{DP} \\ \text{everyone's} \\ \dfrac{\forall x.[\;]x}{x} \end{array}
\quad
\begin{array}{c} \dfrac{DP \rhd S \mid DP \rhd S}{DP\backslash DP} \\ \text{mother} \\ \dfrac{[\;]}{\textbf{mother}} \end{array} \right)
\left(\begin{array}{c} \dfrac{DP \rhd S \mid DP \rhd S}{(DP\backslash S)/DP} \\ \text{loves} \\ \dfrac{[\;]}{\textbf{loves}} \end{array}
\quad
\begin{array}{c} \dfrac{DP \rhd S \mid S}{DP} \\ \text{him} \\ \dfrac{\lambda y.[\;]}{y} \end{array} \right)
$$

The final interpretation is equivalent to $\forall y.\ \textbf{loves}\ y\ (\textbf{mom}\ y)$. The quantifier is able to bind the pronoun even though the quantifier is embedded in possessor position inside the subject, and so therefore does not c-command the pronoun.

One way to see what is going on here is to consider the upper level of the syntactic towers in (32): there is a chain of matching DP $\rhd$ S's connecting the possessor with the pronoun, and this chain is not disrupted by the major constituent boundary between the subject and the verb phrase. Put another way, it is often possible to ignore syntactic constituency when computing the upper levels of a tower.

Allowing a quantifier to bind a pronoun without c-commanding it is unorthodox. Since Reinhart (1983), it is almost universally assumed that quantificational binding requires c-command. Indeed, in textbooks such as Heim and Kratzer (1998:261) and Büring (2005:91), the very definition of binding requires the binder to c-command to bindee. Notable dissenters include Bresnan (1994, 1998), Safir (2004a,b), and Jäger (2005). Building on Shan and Barker (2006), Barker (2012) makes a case in some detail that there is abundant empirical motivation for rejecting this requirement.

Here is a representative sample of the data discussed in Barker (2012):

(33) a. [Everyone$_i$'s mother] thinks he$_i$'s a genius.
b. [Someone from every$_i$ city] hates it$_i$.
c. John gave [to each$_i$ participant] a framed picture of her$_i$ mother.
d. We [will sell no$_i$ wine] before it$_i$s time.
e. [After unthreading each$_i$ screw], but before removing it$_i$ ...
f. The grade [that each$_i$ student receives] is recorded in his$_i$ file.

This data shows that quantifiers can bind pronouns even when the quantifier is embedded in a possessive DP, in a nominal complement, in a prepositional phrase, in a verb phrase, in a temporal adjunct, even when embedded inside of a relative clause. In each example, the quantifier does not c-command the pronoun. Various modifications and extensions of c-command have been proposed to handle some of the data, but Barker (2012) argues that none of these redefinitions covers all of the data.

Furthermore, as the derivation in (32) demonstrates, it is perfectly feasible to build a grammar in which a quantifier binds a pronoun without c-commanding it. Nothing special needs to be said; indeed, we would need to take special pains to impose a c-command requirement. In view of the data and the discussion in Barker (2012), then, we will assume that there is no c-command requirement on quantificational binding.

There is, of course, one important class of examples where a c-command restriction on quantificational binding makes good predictions, namely, crossover configurations. Any analysis that tries to do without a c-command restriction must supply an explanation for crossover that does not depend on c-command. This is exactly what we will do, in considerable detail, starting with the next sections, and continuing in later chapters.

2.2 The standard approach to crossover

The name "crossover" comes from Postal's (1971:62) proposal for a general constraint on movement, roughly: a DP may not move across a coindexed pronoun. This prohibition is usually implemented by taking advantage of multiple stages for the derivation of a sentence. Reinhart's (1983) is an influential example, and Büring (2001, 2004) provides a more recent analysis that uses the same basic strategy. The idea is to postulate two distinct levels of representation: first, a level of surface structure at which binding is established by some syntactic relationship based on c-command, then a level of Logical Form at which quantifiers take their semantic scope. This way, even though a quantifier may raise at LF to take scope over a pronoun, it can nevertheless only bind the pronoun if it c-commands the pronoun from its surface position.

Of course, this strategy is only available if binding depends on c-command. Because we reject c-command as a requirement for quantificational binding for the reasons given in the previous section, we cannot adopt the traditional strategy.

What, then, determines crossover? A simple leftness condition (linear precedence) would cover some of the data, but, as mentioned in the introduction, there are systematic counterexamples involving reconstruction, repeated here from (6):

(34) a. Which of his$_i$ relatives does every man$_i$ love the most?
b. The relative of his$_i$ that every man$_i$ loves most is his mother.

On the standard approach, reconstruction examples require syntactically moving some material, including the pronoun, back into the gap position before checking compliance with the syntactic c-command requirement, so that crossover violations can only be assessed at a strictly intermediate stage of the derivation.

The explanation developed here is that quantificational binding depends not on c-command or on simple leftness, but rather, on evaluation order.

2.3 A first crossover example

Because continuations are well-suited for reasoning about evaluation order (see the discussion in section 12.1), they enable us to explain crossover as an effect of the order in which the various elements of the sentence are processed (evaluated).

Here is what happens in a classic weak crossover configuration, i.e., when we try to allow a quantifier to bind a pronoun when the quantifier follows the pronoun.

(35)
$$\left(\begin{array}{c} \dfrac{\mathrm{DP} \rhd \mathrm{S} \mid \mathrm{S}}{\mathrm{DP}} \\ \text{his} \end{array} \begin{array}{c} \dfrac{\mathrm{S} \mid \mathrm{S}}{\mathrm{DP\backslash DP}} \\ \text{mother} \end{array} \right) \left(\begin{array}{c} \dfrac{\mathrm{S} \mid \mathrm{S}}{\mathrm{(DP\backslash S)/DP}} \\ \text{loves} \end{array} \begin{array}{c} \dfrac{\mathrm{S} \mid \mathrm{DP} \rhd \mathrm{S}}{\mathrm{DP}} \\ \text{everyone} \end{array} \right) = \begin{array}{c} \dfrac{\mathrm{DP} \rhd \mathrm{S} \mid \mathrm{DP} \rhd \mathrm{S}}{\mathrm{S}} \\ \text{his mother loves everyone} \end{array}$$

Combination proceeds smoothly, and the complete string is recognized as a syntactic (and semantic) constituent. However, the result is not a complete derivation of a clause. In particular, it can't be lowered, since the category of the expression does not match the input to the LOWER type-shifter. The reason is that LOWER requires the subcategories in the upper right corner of the tower (here, DP ▷ S) and beneath the horizontal line (S) to match. Even more restrictively, it requires these subcategories to be S. (See section 4.3 for a discussion of the explanatory status of these syntactic restrictions.) This means that in the derivation in (35), the pronoun continues to need a binder, and the quantifier continues to need something to bind.

> **EXERCISE 6**
>
> Compute the semantic value of the expression derived in (35).

Thus even though the quantifier takes scope over the entire clause, it is unable to bind a pronoun that precedes it.

We will discuss additional examples of crossover, as well as apparent exceptions to crossover, including reconstruction, in the chapters to follow.

2.4 Strong crossover

The derivation just shown concerns weak crossover, in which the pronoun to be bound does not c-command the quantifier in question. Situations in which the pronoun does c-command the quantifier are know as strong crossover. There is a qualitative difference between strong crossover and weak crossover.

(36) a. *He$_i$ loves everyone$_i$.
b. ?His$_i$ mother loves everyone$_i$.

The standard judgment is that weak crossover examples can be interpreted with some effort, but that strong crossover examples are irredeemable. (We will speculate about what might be going on when a comprehender makes the effort to interpret a weak crossover example in the next section.)

Although the account here rules out weak crossover and strong crossover alike, nothing in the formal system as presented distinguishes strong crossover from weak crossover. Presumably, strong crossover is due to some factor over and above whatever characterizes weak crossover, perhaps something along the lines of Safir's (2004b) (chapter 3) Independence Principle. The Independence Principle entails that a pronoun must not c-command anything that binds it.

2.5 Reversing the order of evaluation

In order to explore the role that order of evaluation plays in the crossover explanation, we can temporarily replace the combination schema given above in (16) with a variant that imposes a right-to-left processing bias.

(37)
$$\left(\begin{array}{cc} \dfrac{D \mid E}{A/B} & \dfrac{C \mid D}{B} \\ \mathit{left} & \mathit{right} \\ \dfrac{g[\ ]}{f} & \dfrac{h[\ ]}{x} \end{array} \right) = \begin{array}{c} \dfrac{C \mid E}{A} \\ \mathit{left\ right} \\ \dfrac{h[g[\ ]]}{f(x)} \end{array}$$

Here, it is the *outer* corner categories of the syntactic towers that must match (the *D*'s). On the semantic tier, now it is the rightmost context ($h[\ ]$) that takes scope over the leftmost context ($g[\ ]$).

EXERCISE 7

Draw the tangram diagram similar to (17) for the right-to-left variant of the combination schema as given in (37).

We can illustrate how this variant combination schema delivers reversed evaluation order bias by showing a derivation of *Someone loves everyone*:

(38)
$$\begin{array}{c} \mathrm{S}|\mathrm{S} \\ \hline \mathrm{DP} \\ \textit{someone} \\ \exists x.[\,] \\ \hline x \end{array} \left(\begin{array}{c} \mathrm{S}\;|\;\mathrm{S} \\ \hline (\mathrm{DP}\backslash \mathrm{S})/\mathrm{DP} \\ \textit{loves} \\ [\,] \\ \hline \mathbf{loves} \end{array} \quad \begin{array}{c} \mathrm{S}|\mathrm{S} \\ \hline \mathrm{DP} \\ \textit{everyone} \\ \forall y.[\,] \\ \hline y \end{array} \right)$$

$$= \begin{array}{c} \mathrm{S}|\mathrm{S} \\ \hline \mathrm{S} \\ \textit{Someone loves everyone} \\ \forall y\, \exists x.[\,] \\ \hline \mathbf{loves}\; y\, x \end{array} \overset{\text{LOWER}}{\Rightarrow} \begin{array}{c} \mathrm{S} \\ \textit{Someone loves everyone} \\ \forall y.\, \exists x.\, \mathbf{loves}\; y\, x \end{array}$$

Using the variant combination schema in (37), the key thing to note is that the universal quantifier now takes scope over the existential, that is, the variant delivers inverse scope by default.

Crucially here, the right-to-left combination schema also enables a quantifier to bind a pronoun that precedes it:

(39)
$$\begin{array}{c} \mathrm{DP} \rhd \mathrm{S}|\mathrm{S} \\ \hline \mathrm{DP} \\ \textit{he} \\ \lambda x.[\,] \\ \hline x \end{array} \left(\begin{array}{c} \mathrm{DP} \rhd \mathrm{S}|\mathrm{DP} \rhd \mathrm{S} \\ \hline (\mathrm{DP}\backslash \mathrm{S})/\mathrm{DP} \\ \textit{loves} \\ [\,] \\ \hline \mathbf{loves} \end{array} \quad \begin{array}{c} \mathrm{S}|\mathrm{DP} \rhd \mathrm{S} \\ \hline \mathrm{DP} \\ \textit{everyone} \\ \forall y.\, ([\,]\, y) \\ \hline y \end{array} \right)$$

$$= \begin{array}{c} \mathrm{S}|\mathrm{S} \\ \hline \mathrm{S} \\ \textit{He loves everyone} \\ \forall y\, (\lambda x.\, ([\,]\, y)) \\ \hline \mathbf{loves}\; y\, x \end{array} \overset{\text{LOWER}}{\Rightarrow} \begin{array}{c} \mathrm{S} \\ \textit{He loves everyone} \\ \forall y.\, (\lambda x.\, \mathbf{loves}\; y\, x)\, y \end{array}$$

The way in which the alternative combination schema incorrectly allows the derivation of this ungrammatical crossover interpretation is by requiring the *outer* corners of the syntactic towers to match, not the inner corners, as we have been assuming so far. Because of this, the BIND type-shifter and the LOWER type-shifter do not need to be adjusted in order for this crossover derivation to go through. After lambda reduction, the final result is $\forall y.\textbf{loves}\, y\, y$.

Incidentally, if there is an independent prohibition against a pronoun c-commanding a binder, this strong crossover example will be correctly ruled out, but the right-to-left schema would still incorrectly derive weak crossover examples such as ?*His$_i$ mother loves everyone$_i$*.

EXERCISE 8

Show that with only the right-to-left version of combination available, it is no longer possible to derive *Everyone$_i$ loves his$_i$ mother*.

2.6 Default evaluation order is left-to-right

Following Shan and Barker (2006), in view of the bias for linear (surface) quantifier scope, as well as the ungrammaticality of crossover interpretations, we will adopt the following hypothesis:

(40) By default, natural language expressions are processed from left-to-right.

Here, "left-to-right" means the temporal order in which expressions are produced and perceived. We will implement this hypothesis by assuming that the only combination schema available for normal processing is the left-to-right schema given above in (16).

Now, precisely because weak crossover is weak, it is possible to overcome the default bias and find an interpretation for a crossover example. Shan and Barker (2006) suggest that one possible explanation for this might be that if pressed by pragmatic context, a comprehender can exceptionally resort to a right-to-left evaluation schema. (Strong crossover would continue to be fully ungrammatical by virtue of violating some separate requirement such as Safir's Independence Principle.)

There are other possible explanations. For instance, we will consider a second possible explanation involving a variant of the LOWER type-shifter below in section 4.3.

In any case, we have seen that replacing the combination schema with a variant creates multiple effects related to a global reversal of the default order of evaluation, including default inverse scope and crossover amelioration. At the very least, this shows how continuations provide a principled way to reason about order.

We will continue to develop our account of crossover and its exceptions step by step throughout Part I, giving special attention to cases in which evaluation order is correctly predicted to diverge from linear order. For example, in reconstruction examples such as *the relative of his$_i$ that everyone$_i$ loves the most*, a pronoun linearly precedes the quantifier that binds it.

But the key ingredients of our explanation are already in place: we have a continuation-based system that allows scope-taking expressions such as *everyone* to take scope over a portion of a larger expression, a mechanism for DPs to bind pronouns, and a default left-to-right bias in composition that, in simple examples, prevents a quantifier from binding a pronoun that precedes it.

3

From generalized quantifiers to dynamic meaning

The last two chapters presented a basic continuation-based grammar that handled a limited form of scope-taking and binding, including some simple examples of crossover. The empirical robustness of the approach will be addressed in later chapters, but in the meantime this chapter pauses to comment on what is going on conceptually.

More specifically, we'll show how taking a continuation-based perspective enables us to unify two fundamental breakthroughs in semantics that might otherwise seem independent: Montague's conception of DPs as generalized quantifiers on the one hand, and the central idea of dynamic semantics on the other hand, namely, the conception of sentences as update functions on their contexts. Here's how: we've already seen that generalized quantifiers are functions on DP continuations. We shall see that dynamic sentence meanings are functions on S continuations. Because a continuation-based grammar provides access to continuations systematically to every expression type, explicit use of continuations allows us to recognize these two major insights as special cases of a single more general strategy.

3.1 Capturing the duality of DP meaning

The puzzle is a familiar one. Proper names such as *John*, *Mary*, and *Bill* behave syntactically (almost) exactly like quantificational expressions such as *everyone, someone* and *no one*: they can all serve as subjects, direct objects, indirect objects, they can all passivize, participate in raising constructions, and so on. Yet their internal semantics is radically different: names (on some accounts) refer to entities, but the quantificational expressions do not refer at all; rather, they quantify over some class of entities. This contrast gives rise the following question:

(41) **Duality of DP meaning**: What (if anything) unifies the meanings of quantificational versus non-quantificational DPs?

The answer here will be that DPs uniformly have access to their continuations (just like any expression type). The difference between a name and a quantificational DP is that the quantificational DP makes non-trivial use of its continuation.

Once we have an answer to the duality question, we can go on to ask the following questions:

(42) **Scope displacement**: Why does the semantic scope of a quantificational DP sometimes differ from its syntactic scope?

The answer that we will give here depends on the fact that continuations deliver surrounding semantic context up to some larger enclosing constituent (typically, a clause). As a result, supposing that quantifiers denote functions on their own continuation entails that they can take scope over a larger expression.

What do other theories have to say about these two questions?

We take Quantifier Raising (QR) at a level of Logical Form (LF) to be the dominant view of natural language quantification among linguists and perhaps among philosophers, or at the very least, the most universally familiar one. The QR story is enormously persuasive and robust, both from a descriptive and from an explanatory point of view. For the sake of concreteness, we will use Heim and Kratzer (1998) (see especially their chapters 6 and 7) as our reference version for the standard QR view.

On Heim and Kratzer's standard version of the story, non-quantificational DPs denote entities (type e). Quantificational DPs (henceforth, 'QPs') denote generalized quantifiers (type $(\mathtt{e} \to \mathtt{t}) \to \mathtt{t}$), and typical transitive verbs denote relations over entities (type $\mathtt{e} \to \mathtt{e} \to \mathtt{t}$). Heim and Kratzer assume that composition is driven by types: the direction of function/argument combination is determined by whichever of the constituents has a type that is a function on objects corresponding to the type of the other constituent. Thus when a QP occurs in subject position, type-driven composition allows (indeed, requires) it to take the verb phrase (type $\mathtt{e} \to \mathtt{t}$) as an argument. However, when a QP occurs in a non-subject position, including direct object position, a type mismatch occurs: neither the verb nor the quantificational object denotes a function of the right type to take the other as an argument. Since interpretation would otherwise be impossible, QR moves the offending QP to adjoin higher in the tree, leaving behind a bound trace of type e in the original DP position, and triggering a special interpretation rule called Predicate Abstraction. These adjustments repair the type mismatch, and simultaneously explain scope displacement.

Under the QR account, the best we can say in answer to the duality question is that a generalized quantifier is what a subject DP would have to denote in order to take a verb phrase as an argument. But why are subjects special? And why repair type-mismatches via QR, rather than, say, prohibiting QPs in non-subject positions? There may be reasonable answers to these questions, perhaps along the lines of claiming that since QR resembles overt syntactic movement, we can use it 'for free'. Our point is that the fact that these questions require answers shows that duality and scope displacement are distinct phenomena according to the QR view.

Choosing the other horn of the dilemma, Montague (1974) gives a compelling answer to the duality question: non-quantificational DPs and QPs all denote generalized quantifiers. That is why they have closely similar syntactic distribution. Indeed, in the PTQ fragment, predicates accept generalized quantifiers in any NP position without any type mismatch.

But nothing in the type system forces QPs to take wide scope. As a result, Montague needs to stipulate a separate operation of Quantifying In to account for scope displacement. Once again we fail to provide a unified answer to both questions.

Therefore consider the following proposal:

(43) **The continuation hypothesis** (repeated from (1)): some natural language expressions denote functions on continuations, i.e., on their own semantic context.

In particular, assume that QPs denote functions on their continuations.

With respect to DP duality, QPs are just the continuation-aware version of non-quantificational DPs. Once the entire grammar is continuized, there is no type clash when they occur in object position, or in any other DP argument positions, since we can freely LIFT non-quantificational DPs so that they function as generalized quantifiers. To the extent that the availability of LIFT is stipulated, duality may be less than inevitable here; though see the type-logical treatment in Part II, on which LIFT is a theorem, and does not need to be stipulated.

As for scope displacement, because of the nature of continuations, merely stating the truth conditions of a QP in terms of continuations automatically guarantees that it will have semantic scope over an entire clause—in other words, scope displacement follows directly from the semantic nature of quantification. In sum, both the duality of DP meaning and scope displacement follow from the single assumption that determiner phrase meanings have access to their continuations.

3.2 Deriving context update functions

If we continuize uniformly throughout the grammar, then we will continuize both the category DP and the category S in one move. But saying that a clause denotes a function on its continuation amounts to deducing one of the core ideas of dynamic semantics.

We can show what we have in mind by giving an analysis of a simple discourse. If we make the usual assumption that a sequence of declarative sentences can be interpreted via (ordinary, non-dynamic) conjunction (category $(S\backslash S)/S$), we immediately have an analysis of the mini-discourse *Someone*$_i$ *entered. He*$_i$ *left*:

(44)

$$\left(\begin{array}{c}\dfrac{\mathrm{S}|\mathrm{DP}\rhd\mathrm{S}}{\mathrm{DP}}\\ \textit{someone}\\ \dfrac{\exists y.\,([\;]\,y)}{y}\end{array}\quad\begin{array}{c}\dfrac{\mathrm{DP}\rhd\mathrm{S}|\mathrm{DP}\rhd\mathrm{S}}{\mathrm{DP\backslash S}}\\ \textit{entered}\\ \dfrac{[\;]}{\textbf{entered}}\end{array}\right)\left(\begin{array}{c}\dfrac{\mathrm{DP}\rhd\mathrm{S}|\mathrm{DP}\rhd\mathrm{S}}{\mathrm{(S\backslash S)/S}}\\ \textit{[period]}\\ \dfrac{[\;]}{\&}\end{array}\left(\begin{array}{c}\dfrac{\mathrm{DP}\rhd\mathrm{S}|\mathrm{S}}{\mathrm{DP}}\\ \textit{he}\\ \dfrac{\lambda x.[\;]}{x}\end{array}\quad\begin{array}{c}\dfrac{\mathrm{S}\,|\,\mathrm{S}}{\mathrm{DP\backslash S}}\\ \textit{left}\\ \dfrac{[\;]}{\textbf{left}}\end{array}\right)\right)$$

$$=\begin{array}{c}\dfrac{\mathrm{S}|\mathrm{S}}{\mathrm{S}}\\ \textit{Someone entered. He left}\\ \dfrac{\exists y.\lambda x.[\;]\,y}{\&(\textbf{entered}\ y)(\textbf{left}\ x)}\end{array}\quad\overset{\textsc{lower}\text{, beta}}{\Rightarrow}\quad\begin{array}{c}\mathrm{S}\\ \textit{Someone entered. He left}\\ \exists y.\&(\textbf{entered}\ y)(\textbf{left}\ y)\end{array}$$

In this analysis, the scope of the indefinite determiner extends over the subsequent clause. On the treatment here, this is just the indefinite taking wide scope over more than one clause; see chapter 9 for a more thorough discussion.

The same mechanism that explains crossover above is operative here as well, and predicts that no matter what the scope of the indefinite, it will only be able to bind pronouns that are evaluated after it. Thus a discourse containing the same sentences in reverse order (*He left. Someone entered.*) is correctly predicted not to have an interpretation on which the pronoun covaries with the indefinite.

Note that, unlike some dynamic treatments such as Heim (1983), there is no need here to stipulate any order-sensitive details in the lexical entry of the sequencing operator that conjoins sentences in a discourse. Schlenker (2007), among others, criticizes the dynamic approach for such stipulations. Rather, here, the order asymmetry is part of the general compositional schema, independent of the lexical details of conjunction or any other operator. In fact, the conjunction plays no active role in the anaphoric link established in the derivation above, beyond merely allowing the syntactic part of the link to pass through unimpeded. This is achieved by having the basic lexical entry for conjunction (here, (S\S)/S) undergo the LIFT schema with $A = \mathrm{DP} \rhd \mathrm{S}$. (See section 7.1 for a more general treatment of coordination that accommodates coordination of a wider range of syntactic categories.)

The ability of the continuation grammar to account for dynamic binding and order asymmetries in a principled and general way depends on analyzing clause meaning as continuation-aware, that is, as a function on sentence updates. Analyzing sentences as category $\frac{\mathrm{S}|\mathrm{S}}{\mathrm{S}}$ instead of just category S allows binding information to travel along the upper layer of the diagrams. Because the combination schema introduced in chapter 1 is inherently left-to-right, it provides a unified explanation for order sensitivity in crossover and in anaphora.

3.3 Comparison with Dynamic Montague Grammar

The dynamic approach to natural language meaning includes Kamp (1981), Heim (1982), Groenendijk and Stokhof (1991), Groenendijk and Stokhof (1990), and many more; see Dekker (2012) for a recent perspective. We concentrate here on Groenendijk and Stokhof's (1990) Dynamic Montague Grammar (DMG), since it is a paradigm example of a dynamic treatment that has some striking similarities to our approach, yet with significant technical, empirical, and philosophical differences.

DMG introduces a type-shifter '↑' to turn a static clause meaning q into its dynamic counterpart $\uparrow q$.

(45) $\uparrow q = \lambda p.\, q \wedge {}^{\vee}p$

In this definition, the down operator $^{\vee}$ (a symbol borrowed from intensional logic, but given a different meaning than usual) deals in assignments ('states') rather than worlds.

The connective ';' conjoins two dynamic sentence meanings.

(46) $\phi ; \psi = \lambda p.\, \phi({}^{\wedge}\psi(p))$

For example, *John walks and John talks* translates as

(47) $(\uparrow \mathbf{walk(j)})\, ;\, (\uparrow \mathbf{talk(j)}) = \lambda p.\, \mathbf{walk(j)} \wedge \mathbf{talk(j)} \wedge {}^{\vee}p.$

An additional type-shifter '↓' extracts a static truth condition from a dynamic sentence meaning.

(48) $\downarrow \phi = \phi({}^{\wedge}\mathbf{true})$

For example, applying ↓ to (47) yields the truth condition

(49) $\mathbf{walk(j)} \wedge \mathbf{talk(j)} \wedge {}^{\vee\wedge}\mathbf{true} = \mathbf{walk(j)} \wedge \mathbf{talk(j)}.$

These elements of DMG manage the composition of a proposition p in (45), (46), and (48) much as the elements of our system manage continuations: roughly, DMG's '↑' corresponds to (a special case of) our LIFT; DMG's ';' corresponds to (a special case of) our combination schema (16) and (likewise) stipulates left-to-right evaluation; and DMG's '↓' corresponds to our LOWER. Indeed, when Groenendijk and Stokhof (1990) write that "we can look upon the propositions which form the extension of a sentence as something giving the truth conditional contents of its possible continuations", they use the word 'continuation' in an informal sense that coincides closely with what it means for us in the context of a discussion of clause meaning.

Is DMG a continuation semantics, then? Perhaps, but if so, an incomplete one. DMG only lifts clause meanings: from **walks(j)** to ↑ **walks(j)**. Analogously, for quantification, Montague's PTQ only lifts noun-phrase meanings: from the individual **j** to the continuation-consumer $\lambda\kappa.\,\kappa\mathbf{j}$. In contrast to DMG and PTQ, our grammar allows lifting any constituent, not just sentences or noun phrases. This uniformity allows our analysis to treat the mechanism by which quantifiers find their scopes as one and the same as the mechanism by which pronouns find their antecedents.

3.4 Unification of generalized quantifiers with dynamic semantics

So Montague continuizes only the category DP. Dynamic semantics continuizes only the category S. The continuation strategy advocated here continuizes uniformly throughout the grammar, including DP and S as special cases of a systematic pattern. As a result, continuations unify the generalized quantifier conception of DP meaning and the dynamic view of sentences as context update functions. They both are instances of the same shift in perspective, on which expressions can not only denote values, but also functions on their own semantic context.

4

Multi-level towers: Inverse scope

In this chapter, we generalize our system from one level of continuations to multiple levels. This generalization lets us account for inverse scope and for multiple pronouns while maintaining the empirical advantages of left-to-right evaluation order—in particular, the explanation for crossover.

The analyses in previous chapters have all involved towers with at most two levels. For instance, the category of a quantificational DP is $\frac{S \mid S}{DP}$. The bottom level (beneath the horizontal line) tracks function/argument combination, and the upper level provides a mechanism for long-distance semantic effects, such as taking scope or binding a pronoun. But with just one long-distance channel, there is little room for combining multiple effects, say, allowing two arbitrary pronouns to be bound by different quantifiers.

More subtly, with just two-level towers, there is no adequate way to represent the full pattern of quantifier scope ambiguity. The problem is not that we can't accommodate more than one quantifier in the same sentence; we've already seen a multi-quantifier derivation of *Someone loves everyone* above in (24). Rather, the problem is that this sentence is generally believed to be ambiguous, depending on the relative scope of the quantifiers. On the two-level tower system, however, the only available scoping is the default left-to-right scoping imposed by the combination schema.

Our solution to both of these issues is to allow towers with more than two layers. This will involve generalizing the combination schema and the type-shifters LIFT, BIND and LOWER. Once we have multi-level towers, keeping binding information separate is a simple matter of making use of different levels. Likewise, taking inverse scope is a matter of exploiting higher tower levels. From the point of view of accounting for crossover, the danger will be that allowing inverse scope might allow crossover. As it turns out, this is not a problem: the natural way of generalizing to multiple levels automatically gives the desired result.

4.1 Accounting for scope ambiguity

In fact, the current version of LIFT already generates towers of arbitrary height. Here is the LIFT type-shifter, repeated without modification from (18) above.

(50)

$$\boxed{\begin{array}{ccc} & & \dfrac{B|B}{A} \\ A & \textsc{lift} & \\ \textit{phrase} & \Rightarrow & \textit{phrase} \\ x & & \dfrac{[\ ]}{x} \end{array}}$$

Since the input category schema A can range over arbitrary categories, this type-shifter can apply to a tower that already has two levels:

(51)

$$\begin{array}{ccc} & & \dfrac{B|B}{\dfrac{\mathrm{S}|\mathrm{S}}{\mathrm{DP}}} \\ \dfrac{\mathrm{S}|\mathrm{S}}{\mathrm{DP}} & \textsc{lift} & \\ \textit{everyone} & \Rightarrow & \textit{everyone} \\ \dfrac{\forall y.[\ ]}{y} & & \dfrac{[\ ]}{\dfrac{\forall y.[\ ]}{y}} \end{array}$$

Here, the type-shifter applies by instantiating A as the entire input tower, i.e., $A = \dfrac{\mathrm{S}|\mathrm{S}}{\mathrm{DP}}$.

We can likewise lift all the other elements in a sentence, as long as we generalize the combination schema in the obvious way.

(52)

$$\begin{array}{ccccc} \dfrac{E|F}{\dfrac{C|D}{A}} & \dfrac{F|H}{\dfrac{D|G}{A\backslash B}} & & \dfrac{E|H}{\dfrac{C|G}{B}} \\ \textit{left} & \textit{right} & = & \textit{left right} \\ \dfrac{h[\ ]}{\dfrac{g[\ ]}{x}} & \dfrac{j[\ ]}{\dfrac{i[\ ]}{f}} & & \dfrac{h[j[\ ]]}{\dfrac{g[i[\ ]]}{f(x)}} \end{array}$$

On the syntactic tier, inner categories must match on each upper level (D with D, and F with F). On the semantic tier, contexts on the left ($g[\ ]$ and $h[\ ]$) take scope over contexts on the right ($i[\ ]$ and $j[\ ]$).

EXERCISE 9

Which of the following two ways of thinking about syntactic towers is coherent?

$$\dfrac{\dfrac{\mathrm{E}\mid\mathrm{F}}{\mathrm{C}\mid\mathrm{D}}}{\mathrm{A}} \equiv \dfrac{\left(\dfrac{\mathrm{E}\mid\mathrm{F}}{\mathrm{C}\mid\mathrm{D}}\right)}{\mathrm{A}}\ ? \qquad \dfrac{\mathrm{E}\mid\mathrm{F}}{\left(\dfrac{\mathrm{C}\mid\mathrm{D}}{\mathrm{A}}\right)}\ ?$$

Hint: figure out how to write the syntactic category in question in flat (non-tower) notation.

EXERCISE 10

Work out the flat notational equivalent for the semantic value $\dfrac{\dfrac{h[\,]}{g[\,]}}{x}$. Hint: the constituent structure of a semantic value mirrors exactly the constituent structure of the corresponding syntactic category (see previous exercise).

But the LOWER type-shifter is not able to apply to multi-story towers. Here is the LOWER type-shifter again:

(53)
$$\begin{array}{ccc} \dfrac{A\mid \mathrm{S}}{\mathrm{S}} & \text{LOWER} & A \\ \textit{phrase} & \Rightarrow & \textit{phrase} \\ \dfrac{f[\,]}{x} & & f[x] \end{array}$$

The reason is that the schema requires the category at the bottom of the tower to be S, which is a literal atomic category symbol, and not a variable over categories. Similar remarks apply to BIND, which has the literal category DP at the bottom.

The obvious move is to allow type-shifters to apply to subtowers. More precisely, we want to guarantee that for all type-shifters τ, if $\tau(x : A) = x' : A'$, then $\tau\left(\dfrac{g[\,]}{x} : \dfrac{C\mid B}{A}\right) = \dfrac{g[\,]}{x'} : \dfrac{C\mid B}{A'}$. That is, we must allow type-shifters to apply to the lower levels of a tower without disturbing the upper levels. (Incidentally, the implementation notes in section 12.2 show how to refactor the type-shifters in a way that builds in this sub-tower application principle.)

This gives us a different way to apply LIFT to *everyone*:

(54)
$$\begin{array}{c}\dfrac{\mathrm{S}\,|\,\mathrm{S}}{\mathrm{DP}}\\ \textit{everyone}\\ \dfrac{\forall x.[\,]}{x}\end{array} \quad \overset{\textsc{lift}}{\Rightarrow} \quad \begin{array}{c}\mathrm{S}\,|\,\mathrm{S}\\ \hline B\,|\,B\\ \hline \mathrm{DP}\\ \textit{everyone}\\ \forall x.[\,]\\ \hline [\,]\\ \hline x\end{array}$$

The difference is that instead of applying LIFT by matching the category variable A with the entire input tower ($A = \dfrac{\mathrm{S}\,|\,\mathrm{S}}{\mathrm{DP}}$), as we did before, we match it with just the lowest level ($A = \mathrm{DP}$).

> **EXERCISE 11**
>
> Give a lambda term that will take the semantic value of the tower on the left of (54) and return the semantic value of the tower on the right.

Note that when LIFT adds a new layer on top to the lexical entry for *everyone*, the quantification takes place on the middle level of the three-layer result, as the semantic value of (51) shows. When LIFT adds a new layer in the middle of the lexical entry, the quantification takes place on the highest level (compare (51) with (54)). This is exactly the variability we need to account for scope ambiguity.

After all, if you decide to add a new floor to a physical tower, there are two ways to go about it: either you add a new floor on the top of the old building (the original LIFT strategy), or you jack up an existing floor and build the new floor in the space in between. This second process is sometimes called 'roof lifting'.

In any case, with this alternative way to LIFT in hand, we can derive the inverse scope reading of *Someone loves everyone*:

(55)
$$\begin{array}{c}\mathrm{S}\,|\,\mathrm{S}\\ \hline \mathrm{S}\,|\,\mathrm{S}\\ \hline \mathrm{DP}\\ \textit{someone}\\ [\,]\\ \hline \exists x.[\,]\\ \hline x\end{array} \left(\begin{array}{c}\mathrm{S}\,|\,\mathrm{S}\\ \hline \mathrm{S}\,|\,\mathrm{S}\\ \hline (\mathrm{DP}\backslash\mathrm{S})/\mathrm{DP}\\ \textit{loves}\\ [\,]\\ \hline [\,]\\ \hline \mathbf{loves}\end{array} \quad \begin{array}{c}\mathrm{S}\,|\,\mathrm{S}\\ \hline \mathrm{S}\,|\,\mathrm{S}\\ \hline \mathrm{DP}\\ \textit{everyone}\\ \forall y.[\,]\\ \hline [\,]\\ \hline y\end{array} \right) = \begin{array}{c}\mathrm{S}\,|\,\mathrm{S}\\ \hline \mathrm{S}\,|\,\mathrm{S}\\ \hline \mathrm{S}\\ \textit{someone loves everyone}\\ \forall y.[\,]\\ \hline \exists x.[\,]\\ \hline \mathbf{loves}\ y\ x\end{array}$$

$$\overset{\text{Lower}}{\Rightarrow}\quad \begin{array}{c} \dfrac{\mathrm{S}|\mathrm{S}}{\mathrm{S}} \\ \textit{someone loves everyone} \\ \dfrac{\forall y.[\;]}{\exists x.\, \mathbf{loves}\; y\, x} \end{array} \quad \overset{\text{Lower}}{\Rightarrow}\quad \begin{array}{c} \mathrm{S} \\ \textit{someone loves everyone} \\ \forall y.\, \exists x.\, \mathbf{loves}\; y\, x \end{array}$$

Here are some of the details of the derivation: *someone* undergoes ordinary LIFTing, which adds a layer on top; *loves* undergoes ordinary LIFTing twice, adding two layers on top; *everyone* undergoes the variant LIFT, as described above, inserting a layer in the middle; two instances of multi-tower combination occur, producing a three-level tower in which the universal quantification occurs on the highest level, and the existential quantification occurs on the middle level; the variant application of LOWER collapses the bottom two levels, producing a two-level tower; and an ordinary application of LOWER collapses the final two levels.

From this example, it is clear that the details of LOWER guarantee that operators on higher levels always outscope operators on lower levels. Taking inverse scope, then, is a matter of applying LIFT in such a way that the quantificational effect occurs on a higher level. It should be clear how a sentence with three quantifiers will be predicted to be six ways ambiguous.

EXERCISE 12

Which scoping of *Most professors gave a grade to every student* requires four-level towers?

4.2 Binding without indices: variable-free semantics

One of the ideas explored in this book is that binding can be analyzed as a kind of scope-taking. On this approach, the pronoun or gap has one component that lives on the lowest level of the tower (playing the role of the variable), and another component that lives on a higher level (playing the role of the binding operator), and that participates in scope-taking. The pronoun will take scope just below the scope of the element that binds it.

Sentences in which multiple pronouns are bound by different quantifiers, then, are quite literally a special case of scope ambiguity.

Note that pronouns in the tower fragment do not have any indices for distinguishing one occurrence from another. Instead, the role of indices is played by the different levels of a multi-level tower. The way in which different pronoun occurrences select which quantifier will bind them is by selecting which level they will take scope at. We can see this by examining a derivation for *Someone*$_i$ *told everyone*$_j$ *he*$_i$ *saw him*$_j$.

(56)
$$
\begin{array}{c}\begin{array}{c|c} S & S \\ \hline S & DP \rhd S \\ \hline \end{array} \\ DP \\ \textit{someone} \\ \begin{array}{c} [\;] \\ \hline \exists x.\,([\;]\,x) \\ \hline x \end{array}\end{array}
\left(\left(\begin{array}{c}\begin{array}{c|c} S & S \\ \hline DP \rhd S & DP \rhd S \\ \hline \end{array} \\ ((DP\backslash S)/S)/DP \\ \textit{told} \\ \begin{array}{c} [\;] \\ \hline [\;] \\ \hline \textbf{told} \end{array}\end{array}
\;\begin{array}{c}\begin{array}{c|c} S & DP \rhd S \\ \hline DP \rhd S & DP \rhd S \\ \hline \end{array} \\ DP \\ \textit{everyone} \\ \begin{array}{c} \forall y.\,([\;]\,y) \\ \hline [\;] \\ \hline y \end{array}\end{array}\right)\right.
$$
$$
\left.\left.\left(\begin{array}{c}\begin{array}{c|c} DP \rhd S & DP \rhd S \\ \hline DP \rhd S & S \\ \hline \end{array} \\ DP \\ \textit{he} \\ \begin{array}{c} [\;] \\ \hline \lambda x.[\;] \\ \hline x \end{array}\end{array}
\left(\begin{array}{c}\begin{array}{c|c} DP \rhd S & DP \rhd S \\ \hline S & S \\ \hline \end{array} \\ (DP\backslash S)/DP \\ \textit{saw} \\ \begin{array}{c} [\;] \\ \hline [\;] \\ \hline \textbf{saw} \end{array}\end{array}
\;\begin{array}{c}\begin{array}{c|c} DP \rhd S & S \\ \hline S & S \\ \hline \end{array} \\ DP \\ \textit{him} \\ \begin{array}{c} \lambda y.[\;] \\ \hline [\;] \\ \hline y \end{array}\end{array}\right)\right)\right)\right)
$$

The subject, *someone*, takes scope at the middle level, and there is a chain of subcategories DP $\rhd$ S on the middle level connecting *someone* to the pronoun that it binds (*he*). The direct object, *everyone*, takes scope on the upper level, and there is a separate chain of DP $\rhd$ S's on that level connecting it with the pronoun that it binds (*him*). The choice of variables in the semantic towers (x for *someone* and *he*, y for *everyone* and *him*) were chosen to enhance readability, but play no role in the binding relationships.

In fact, this fragment is variable-free in the sense of Jacobson (1999) (see section 11.1 below): every constituent denotes a combinator, i.e., a lambda term with no free variables. In other words, there is no essential use of variable symbols.

EXERCISE 13

Derive a reading of *Someone*$_i$ *told everyone*$_j$ *he*$_i$ *saw his*$_i$ *mother* with binding as indicated using towers that have at most two levels (where a tower of the form $\dfrac{C \,|\, B}{A}$ counts as having two levels).

4.3 The role of LOWER in the explanation for crossover

Now that later quantifiers are able to take scope over earlier ones, we must make sure that the explanation for crossover still works. That is, we must make sure that allowing a quantifier to take inverse scope over a pronoun does not allow the quantifier to bind that pronoun.

It will turn out that preventing inverse scope from incorrectly deriving crossover hinges on syntactic details of the LOWER type-shifter, namely, on the fact that LOWER is restricted to applying to towers that have simple clauses (category S) on their lowest level. (Though see the Afterword for a translation of the basic analysis into a substructural logic that does not involve LOWER.)

In order for a later quantifier to take inverse scope over an earlier quantifier, the later quantifier must occupy a higher layer in the tower. In any attempt to incorrectly derive a crossover violation, then, the pronoun must take effect at a lower level than the quantifier that is trying to bind it. That is, if the binding effect of the pronoun inhabits level 2, the quantifier that is trying to bind it must occupy at least level 3. Here is such an attempt for the sentence *his*$_i$ *mother loves everyone*$_i$:

(57)
$$\left(\begin{array}{cc}
\begin{array}{c|c} \mathrm{S} & \mathrm{S} \\ \hline \mathrm{DP} \rhd \mathrm{S} & \mathrm{S} \\ \hline \multicolumn{2}{c}{\mathrm{DP}} \end{array} &
\begin{array}{c|c} \mathrm{S} & \mathrm{S} \\ \hline \mathrm{S} & \mathrm{S} \\ \hline \multicolumn{2}{c}{\mathrm{DP\backslash DP}} \end{array} \\
\textit{his} & \textit{mother} \\
\begin{array}{c} [\,] \\ \hline \lambda y.[\,] \\ \hline y \end{array} &
\begin{array}{c} [\,] \\ \hline [\,] \\ \hline \mathbf{mom} \end{array}
\end{array}\right)
\left(\begin{array}{cc}
\begin{array}{c|c} \mathrm{S} & \mathrm{S} \\ \hline \mathrm{S} & \mathrm{S} \\ \hline \multicolumn{2}{c}{\mathrm{(DP\backslash S)/DP}} \end{array} &
\begin{array}{c|c} \mathrm{S} & \mathrm{DP} \rhd \mathrm{S} \\ \hline \mathrm{S} & \mathrm{S} \\ \hline \multicolumn{2}{c}{\mathrm{DP}} \end{array} \\
\textit{loves} & \textit{everyone} \\
\begin{array}{c} [\,] \\ \hline [\,] \\ \hline \mathbf{loves} \end{array} &
\begin{array}{c} \forall x.[\,]x \\ \hline [\,] \\ \hline x \end{array}
\end{array}\right)$$

$$= \begin{array}{c}
\begin{array}{c|c} \mathrm{S} & \mathrm{DP} \rhd \mathrm{S} \\ \hline \mathrm{DP} \rhd \mathrm{S} & \mathrm{S} \\ \hline \multicolumn{2}{c}{\mathrm{S}} \end{array} \\
\textit{Everyone loves his mother} \\
\begin{array}{c} \forall x.[\,]\,x \\ \hline \lambda y.[\,] \\ \hline \mathbf{loves}\,(\mathbf{mom}\,y)\,x \end{array}
\end{array}
\quad \overset{\textsc{lower}}{\Rightarrow} \quad
\begin{array}{c}
\begin{array}{c|c} \mathrm{S} & \mathrm{DP} \rhd \mathrm{S} \\ \hline \multicolumn{2}{c}{\mathrm{DP} \rhd \mathrm{S}} \end{array} \\
\textit{Everyone loves his mother} \\
\begin{array}{c} \forall x.[\,]\,x \\ \hline \lambda y.\,\mathbf{loves}\,(\mathbf{mom}\,y)\,x \end{array}
\end{array}$$

At this point, the derivation cannot continue. In particular, the LOWER type-shifter cannot apply, since LOWER requires an atomic S category below the line.

Yet there is no semantic obstacle to generalizing LOWER to apply to any category in which the bottom and the top right corner match (schematically, any category of the form $\frac{B|A}{A}$). If we did generalize LOWER in this way, the semantic result would simply plug the bottom value into the hole in the context above the line. The final result would be $\forall x.(\lambda y.\,\mathbf{loves}\,(\mathbf{mom}\,y)\,x)\,x$, which reduces to $\forall x.\,\mathbf{loves}\,(\mathbf{mom}\,x)\,x$. This is exactly the crossover reading we were hoping to rule out. But as long as LOWER requires that the bottom and top right categories must not only match, they must also specifically be S, we correctly rule out crossover.

This suggests a second possible strategy for explaining the weakness of weak crossover. In section (2.5), we observed that if we suppose that comprehenders can exceptionally resort to a right-to-left processing strategy, it would be possible to arrive at an interpretation for crossover examples. In the presence of multi-level towers that allow inverse scope, another possibility would be to exceptionally generalize the LOWER type-shifter, so that it applies to cases such as the derivation immediately above.

The claim, then, is that the full explanation for crossover is partly syntactic: that quantificational binders are able to take scope (i.e., undergo LOWER) only over expressions whose category is a simple S, not over expressions whose category is DP$\triangleright$S (a clause with a functional dependency).

EXERCISE 14

This claim does not mean that a quantifier can't have a pronoun inside its scope domain that is bound outside that scope domain, as long as the pronoun takes scope on a higher tower level than the quantifier. Show this by deriving a reading for *Mary$_i$ thinks everyone saw her$_i$* on which *everyone* takes scope only over the embedded clause.

The net effect is that a quantifier can take inverse scope over material to its left, but still cannot bind pronouns to its left. In order for a pronoun to be bound by a quantifier, the quantifier and the pronoun must take effect at the same level in the tower, and the pronoun must follow the quantifier.

There is a systematic exception to this generalization about linear order, of course, namely, reconstruction. The next two chapters show how reconstruction fits into the picture.

5

Movement as delayed evaluation: Wh-fronting

In order to develop the treatment of evaluation order in more depth, it will be necessary to extend the fragment to cover additional expression types. Reconstruction in particular involves relative clauses and wh-questions. This chapter, then, introduces elements that will underwrite the derivations in later chapters. Yet this chapter does not merely develop tools needed later, but tells an essential part of the larger story: the analysis of syntactic fronting, motivated independently of any concerns about reconstruction, embodies the concept of **delayed evaluation** that will be crucial for the explanation of reconstruction effects. In addition, the same basic analysis of wh-fronting immediately explains superiority as an evaluation-order effect.

Just to be clear, there is no literal movement in this fragment. Expressions combine in the order determined by syntactic constituency, sometimes with their categories and semantic values adjusted by type-shifters. In the analysis here of a wh-question such as *Who does John like __?*, there is no level of representation corresponding to what a movement analysis would consider the structure before movement. Yet the syntax and the semantics guarantee that the sentence will be interpreted as if the fronted wh-phrase had been evaluated in the gap position.

5.1 Simple relative clauses: gaps

In order to emphasize the correspondences between relative clauses and wh-phrases, we'll concentrate on relative clauses that contain relative pronouns such as *who* and *which*. The first puzzle is to decide what should serve as the syntactic category of the constituent that a relative pronoun combines with to form a relative clause:

(58) a. the woman who [left]
b. the woman who [__ left]
c. the woman who [John likes __]

We assign the nominal *woman* to the syntactic category N, with semantic type $\mathtt{e} \to \mathtt{t}$.

In (58a), the complement of the relative pronoun appears to be a verb phrase. In (58c), however, the complement is *John likes*, a full clause missing a direct object. In view of (58c), then, we can reanalyze the VP case in (58a) as a clause missing its subject, as shown in (58b). In the general case, then, relative pronouns take a clause missing a DP somewhere inside.

This is where continuations enter the picture. A clause with a DP missing somewhere inside is exactly the kind of expression that is in the category DP$\backslash\!\!\backslash$S. For instance, in *Mary called everyone yesterday*, the quantifier *everyone* has category S$/\!\!/$(DP$\backslash\!\!\backslash$S): something that combines with an expression in the category DP$\backslash\!\!\backslash$S—that is, a clause missing a DP—to form a (quantified) S. The difference between the quantifier case and the relative clause case is that for the quantifier, the clause missing a DP surrounds the quantifier. That is, the quantifier combines with the DP$\backslash\!\!\backslash$S from the inside, as it were, from the very position of the missing DP; this is the nature of in-situ scope-taking. In order to complete the analysis of relative clauses, we need only find a way to recognize a clause missing a DP as a member of the category DP$\backslash\!\!\backslash$S from the outside.

The mechanism that will allow us to do this will be a silent pronoun-like element in the gap position, written '__'. It is an element in the category (DP$\backslash\!\!\backslash$S)$/\!\!/$(DP$\backslash\!\!\backslash$S) (more generally, it is a member of any category of the form $A/\!\!/A$), and, like a pronoun, will denote an identity function. This gives the following analysis:

(59)
$$\begin{array}{c}\dfrac{\mathrm{DP}\backslash\!\!\backslash\mathrm{S}\,|\,\mathrm{DP}\backslash\!\!\backslash\mathrm{S}}{\mathrm{DP}}\\ \textit{John}\\ \dfrac{[\;]}{\mathbf{j}}\end{array}
\left(\begin{array}{c}\dfrac{\mathrm{DP}\backslash\!\!\backslash\mathrm{S}\,|\,\mathrm{DP}\backslash\!\!\backslash\mathrm{S}}{(\mathrm{DP}\backslash\mathrm{S})/\mathrm{DP}}\\ \textit{likes}\\ \dfrac{[\;]}{\mathbf{likes}}\end{array}\quad
\begin{array}{c}\dfrac{\mathrm{DP}\backslash\!\!\backslash\mathrm{S}\,|\,\mathrm{S}}{\mathrm{DP}}\\ __\\ \dfrac{\lambda y.[\;]}{y}\end{array}\right)
= \begin{array}{c}\dfrac{\mathrm{DP}\backslash\!\!\backslash\mathrm{S}\,|\,\mathrm{S}}{\mathrm{S}}\\ \textit{John likes}\ __\\ \dfrac{\lambda y.[\;]}{\mathbf{likes}\ y\ \mathbf{j}}\end{array}$$

$$\begin{array}{cc} \text{LOWER} & \mathrm{DP}\backslash\!\!\backslash\mathrm{S}\\ \Rightarrow & \textit{John likes}\ \_\_\\ & \lambda y.\mathbf{likes}\ y\ \mathbf{j}\end{array}$$

This derivation is identical semantically to the derivation of *John likes him* given above in chapter (2). The only difference is that the final syntactic category here is DP$\backslash\!\!\backslash$S (a clause missing a DP) rather than DP $\rhd$ S (a clause containing an unbound pronoun).

Thus the gap is not only a semantic identity function, but a *syntactic* identity function. To see this, note that the syntactic category of the gap is (DP$\backslash\!\!\backslash$S)$/\!\!/$(DP$\backslash\!\!\backslash$S), which has the form $A/\!\!/A$, i.e., a syntactic identity function. It turns a continuation surrounding it into something that can be recognized as a continuation from the outside. This is why it makes sense for a gap to be silent: silence is what you add to a string in order to turn it from a phrase in a category A into a phrase in the same category A. In algebraic terms, silence is a unit for the syntactic merge operation, just as multiplying by an identity fraction of the form x/x is a unit for multiplication. That is, $3 * (x/x) = 3$ for any choice of x. The logic of gaps as identity operators is developed further in Part II, especially in sections 16.6 and 17.10.

The relative pronoun *who* will be the kind of thing that can take a relative clause and turn it into a nominal modifier. We'll give a lexical entry for this relative pronoun in the next section, after discussing the question word *who*.

> **EXERCISE 15**
>
> Nothing prevents the gap from taking scope across several clause boundaries. Check this claim by assigning a category to *thinks* that will allow you to derive *woman who Mary thinks John likes* __.

Given an analysis of gapped clauses, we can turn to building wh-questions.

5.2 From in-situ wh to ex-situ wh: FRONT

In-situ wh resembles in-situ quantification, in that in both cases a DP takes scope over surrounding material. The only difference is that while a quantified DP turns the clause that contains it into a quantified clause, an in-situ wh-phrase turns the clause that contains it into a question.

We won't say much about the meaning of questions in this book (though see Shan and ten Cate 2002, Shan 2002b, 2003b). We assume that the account here is neutral across most theories of question meaning. We will, however, track in the syntax the kind of constituent that has been questioned. Thus DP?S will be a question in which a DP has been questioned (e.g., *Who left?*), (DP/N)?S will be a question in which a determiner (category DP/N) has been questioned (e.g., *Which person left?*), and so on. In general, for any categories A and B with semantic types α and β, $A?B$ will be a complex category label whose semantic type is whatever your favorite theory of questions says should be the kind of question built from a function of type $\alpha \to \beta$.

Then *who* has syntactic category $(\text{DP?S}) /\!\!/ (\text{DP} \backslash\!\!\backslash \text{S})$: something that functions locally like a DP, takes scope over an S, and returns a question of category DP?S.

(60)
$$\begin{array}{c} \text{DP?S} \mid \text{DP?S} \\ \hline \text{DP} \\ \textit{John} \\ [\,] \\ \hline \mathbf{j} \end{array} \left(\begin{array}{c} \text{DP?S} \mid \text{DP?S} \\ \hline (\text{DP}\backslash\text{S})/\text{DP} \\ \textit{likes} \\ [\,] \\ \hline \mathbf{likes} \end{array} \quad \begin{array}{c} \text{DP?S} \mid \text{S} \\ \hline \text{DP} \\ \textit{who} \\ \mathbf{who}(\lambda y.[\,]) \\ \hline y \end{array} \right)$$

$$\overset{\textsc{lower}}{\Rightarrow} \quad \begin{array}{c} \text{DP?S} \\ \textit{John likes who?} \\ \mathbf{who}(\lambda y.\mathbf{likes}\, y\, \mathbf{j}) \end{array}$$

This analysis proceeds exactly like the derivation of the relative clause *John likes* __ given immediately above, except that instead of delivering a property, the result is the question version of a property, which can be glossed as 'who has the property of being liked by John?'.

Now, although in-situ wh-phrases are common in the world's languages (e.g., in Japanese), in English, in-situ wh-phrases for the most part must be interpreted as echo questions or metalinguistic questions, in which the questioner is asking for the identification of a word, rather than an individual. In ordinary non-echo wh-questions in English, in contrast, the wh-phrase must appear at the front of the clause.

In movement-based grammars, the wh-phrase originates in the gap position and moves to sentence-initial position. We achieve the desired effect here without movement by making use of the gap motivated above for relative clauses, and by assigning *who* to a slightly different additional syntactic category, (DP?S)/(DP$\backslash\!\!\backslash$S) instead of (DP?S)$/\!\!/$(DP$\backslash\!\!\backslash$S). The only difference between the in-situ *who* and the ex-situ version is that the fronted wh-phrase combines with the rest of the question using the ordinary categorial slash, '/', rather than with the continuation-mode slash, '$/\!\!/$'. As a result of this small change, the wh-phrase precedes the rest of the question, rather than appearing inside of the question:

(61)	(DP?S)/(DP$\backslash\!\!\backslash$S)	DP$\backslash\!\!\backslash$S		DP?S
	who	*does John like* __	=	*Who does John like* __*?*
	$\lambda\kappa.\mathbf{who}(\lambda x.\kappa x)$	$\lambda x.\mathbf{like}\ x\ \mathbf{j}$		$\mathbf{who}(\lambda x.\mathbf{like}\ x\ \mathbf{j})$

The "fronted" wh-phrase combines with the question body via ordinary function/argument combination.

Here and below, we analyze *does* for convenience as a trivial syntactic element with category S/S and identity-function semantics $\lambda p.p$. The question body (*does John like* __) is essentially the same as the relative clause derived above in (59).

Every wh-word will need an ex-situ variant that is systematically related to its in-situ lexical entry. We can codify the relationship between the versions using a new (and final) type-shifter called FRONT:

(62)

FRONT
$A_F /\!\!/ B \quad \Rightarrow \quad A/B$

The syntactic feature *F* determines when the fronting rule will apply. The reason we need to add this feature is that without some means of syntactic regulation, not only wh-phrases, but ordinary quantifiers could front as well. Although this kind of overt quantifier fronting may happen in some languages, it does not happen in English. See Kayne (1998) and Brody and Szabolcsi (2003) for relevant discussion of overt scope in English versus Hungarian.

The effect of the type-shifter is purely syntactic, and does not change the semantic value of the shifted expression in any way. Syntactically, the type-shifter replaces the hollow forward slash (‘$/\!\!/$’) with a solid slash (‘/’). The hollow slash, as we have seen, says that the nuclear scope of the wh-phrase must *surround* it (i.e., that the wh-phrase is in-situ). The solid slash says that the nuclear scope of the wh-phrase must *follow* it (i.e., that the wh-phrase has been fronted).

So we have the following lexical entries for the relative pronoun who_{rel} and the question word who_q:

(63)
$$\begin{array}{ccc} \dfrac{(\mathrm{N}\backslash\mathrm{N})_F \,|\, \mathrm{S}}{\mathrm{DP}} & \textsc{front} & (\mathrm{N}\backslash\mathrm{N})/(\mathrm{DP}\backslash\!\!\backslash\mathrm{S}) \\ who_{rel} & \Rightarrow & who_{rel} \\ \dfrac{\lambda Qx.(Qx)\wedge[\,]}{x} & & \lambda\kappa Qx.(Qx)\wedge(\kappa x) \end{array}$$

(64)
$$\begin{array}{ccc} \dfrac{(\mathrm{DP?S})_F \,|\, \mathrm{S}}{\mathrm{DP}} & \textsc{front} & (\mathrm{DP?S})/(\mathrm{DP}\backslash\!\!\backslash\mathrm{S}) \\ who_{q} & \Rightarrow & who_{q} \\ \dfrac{\mathbf{who}(\lambda x.[\,])}{x} & & \lambda\kappa.\mathbf{who}(\lambda x.\kappa x) \end{array}$$

Making use of the derivation of the gapped clause *did John see* __ given above, we now have a derivation of a complete relative clause and of a complete wh-question:

(65)
$$\begin{array}{cccc} (\mathrm{N}\backslash\mathrm{N})/(\mathrm{DP}\backslash\!\!\backslash\mathrm{S}) & \mathrm{DP}\backslash\!\!\backslash\mathrm{S} & & \mathrm{N}\backslash\mathrm{N} \\ who_{rel} & \textit{John likes}\ \_\_ & = & who_{rel}\ \textit{John likes}\ \_\_ \\ \lambda\kappa Qx.(Qx)\wedge(\kappa x) & \lambda y.\mathbf{likes}\,y\,\mathbf{j} & & \lambda Qx.(Qx)\wedge(\mathbf{likes}\,x\,\mathbf{j}) \end{array}$$

This phrase is ready to combine with the nominal *woman* to form the modified nominal *woman who John likes* __, giving it the meaning $\lambda x.(\mathbf{woman}\,x)\wedge(\mathbf{likes}\,x\,\mathbf{j})$.

(66)
$$\begin{array}{cccc} (\mathrm{DP?S})/(\mathrm{DP}\backslash\!\!\backslash\mathrm{S}) & \mathrm{DP}\backslash\!\!\backslash\mathrm{S} & & \mathrm{DP?S} \\ who_{q} & \textit{does John like}\ \_\_ & = & who_{q}\ \textit{does John like}\ \_\_ \\ \mathbf{who} & \lambda y.\mathbf{like}\,y\,\mathbf{j} & & \mathbf{who}(\lambda y.\mathbf{likes}\,y\,\mathbf{j}) \end{array}$$

This question meaning asks which individuals have the property of being liked by John.

5.3 Pied piping

Sometimes more than just a single wh-word appears in fronted position. The movement metaphor is that when the wh-word moves to the front, it brings (“pied-pipes”) some of the surrounding words with it. For example, in addition to *Who did John speak to* __, we have *To whom did John speak* __, in which the preposition has pied-piped along with the wh-word.

Pied piping is handled here by postponing the application of the FRONT type-shifter until the wh-phrase has already combined with additional material. For example, in order to derive questions in which *to whom* or *which man* has been fronted, we derive as follows:

(67)
$$\begin{array}{ccccc}
\dfrac{(\mathrm{DP?S})_F \mid (\mathrm{DP?S})_F}{\mathrm{PP/DP}} & \dfrac{(\mathrm{DP?S})_F \mid \mathrm{S}}{\mathrm{DP}} & & \dfrac{(\mathrm{DP?S})_F \mid \mathrm{S}}{\mathrm{PP}} \\
\textit{to} & \textit{whom} & = & \textit{to whom} \\
\dfrac{[\ ]}{\mathbf{to}} & \dfrac{\mathbf{who}(\lambda x[\ ])}{x} & & \dfrac{\mathbf{who}(\lambda x[\ ])}{\mathbf{to}(x)}
\end{array}$$

$$\overset{\text{FRONT}}{\Rightarrow} \quad \begin{array}{c} (\mathrm{DP?S})/(\mathrm{PP}\backslash\!\!\backslash \mathrm{S}) \\ \textit{to whom} \\ \lambda\kappa.\mathbf{who}(\lambda x.\kappa(\mathbf{to}(x))) \end{array}$$

(68)
$$\begin{array}{ccccc}
\dfrac{((\mathrm{DP/N})?\mathrm{S})_F \mid \mathrm{S}}{\mathrm{DP/N}} & \dfrac{\mathrm{S} \mid \mathrm{S}}{\mathrm{N}} & & \dfrac{((\mathrm{DP/N})?\mathrm{S})_F \mid \mathrm{S}}{\mathrm{DP}} \\
\textit{which} & \textit{man} & = & \textit{which man} \\
\dfrac{\mathbf{which}(\lambda f.[\ ])}{f} & \dfrac{[\ ]}{\mathbf{man}} & & \dfrac{\mathbf{which}(\lambda f.[\ ])}{f(\mathbf{man})}
\end{array}$$

$$\overset{\text{FRONT}}{\Rightarrow} \quad \begin{array}{c} ((\mathrm{DP/N})?\mathrm{S})/(\mathrm{DP}\backslash\!\!\backslash \mathrm{S}) \\ \textit{which man} \\ \lambda\kappa.\mathbf{which}(\lambda f.\kappa(f(\mathbf{man}))) \end{array}$$

In each case of pied piping, the lexical entry for the wh-word introduces an F feature, which remains part of the category of each successively larger constituent until the FRONT rule is applied. The net result is that a larger constituent surrounding the wh-word can appear in the fronted position. Because the FRONT typeshifter does not affect the semantic value, the interpretation of a sentence that involves pied piping will always be the same as one in which pied piping has not occurred:

(69) a. [Who] did John speak to? $\mathbf{who}(\lambda x.\mathbf{speak}\ (\mathbf{to}(x))\ \mathbf{j})$
b. [To whom] did John speak? $\mathbf{who}(\lambda x.\mathbf{speak}\ (\mathbf{to}(x))\ \mathbf{j})$

(70) a. [Which man] did John speak to? $\mathbf{which}(\lambda f.\mathbf{speak}\ (\mathbf{to}(f(\mathbf{man})))\ \mathbf{j})$
b. [To which man] did John speak? $\mathbf{which}(\lambda f.\mathbf{speak}\ (\mathbf{to}(f(\mathbf{man})))\ \mathbf{j})$

Note that the category of the gap will depend on whether the fronted phrase is a DP or a PP.

EXERCISE 16

Propose a constraint on the form of possible gap categories that will rule out Left Branch extractions, including ** Which did John see __ man.*

Pied piping is not universally available. Some languages (such as German) do not allow pied piping at all, in which case the FRONT type-shifter must be limited to the lexicon.

5.4 Preview of delayed evaluation

The derivations in this chapter so far have all involved no more than two levels, and the gap is always a simple function on individuals. In the next chapter, we will consider more elaborate examples in which the gap is a function on more complicated types. This will reveal a semantic effect that we call *delayed evaluation*. In delayed evaluation, the semantic contribution of the fronted wh-phrase will be exactly as if the wh-phrase had been evaluated in the position of the gap. Obviously, this is exactly what is required in order to handle reconstruction effects. As explained in the next chapter, Sternefeld (1997) and others call this technique 'semantic reconstruction'. For us, semantic reconstruction is an automatic consequence of the straightforward fronting analysis given in this chapter.

The key to delayed evaluation is that the FRONT type-shifter does not change any semantic property of the wh-phrase. All the type-shifter does is determine whether the wh-phrase appears syntactically embedded in-situ within its argument, or adjacent to it. The net effect is that the syntax and the semantics of the fronted wh-phrase will be exactly as if it had been interpreted in the gap position.

The next chapter will consider delayed evaluation and reconstruction in some detail.

5.5 Multiple wh-questions, and an account of superiority

There is an order-sensitive restriction on wh-fronting called superiority that is reminiscent of crossover. On the account here, superiority follows from the same evaluation-order effect that accounts for crossover.

Kuno and Robinson (1972:474) observe that moving a wh-phrase across an in-situ wh-phrase results in ungrammaticality.

(71) a. Who ate what?
 b. *What did who eat __?

The term "superiority" comes from Chomsky's (1973) proposal for a general constraint that prohibits moving a phrase if a superior (roughly, a c-commanding) phrase could have been moved instead. As a result, (71b) is ruled out because the wh-phrase in object position moved when the superior wh-phrase in subject position could have moved instead. Unlike the traditional crossover cases in chapter 2, here the quantificational element (the wh-phrase) moves overtly rather than covertly, and the crossed element is an in-situ wh-phrase rather than a bound pronoun.

Building on Chierchia's (1991, 1993) analysis of pair-list readings, Hornstein (1995), Dayal (1996), and Comorovski (1996) all argue that superiority reduces to weak crossover.

(72) a. Who$_i$ __$_i$ bought [*pro*$_i$ what]?
 b. *What$_i$ did [*pro*$_i$ who] buy __$_i$?

For instance, on Hornstein's analysis, an in-situ wh-phrase denotes a Skolem function of type $\mathsf{e} \to \mathsf{e}$ whose argument corresponds to a silent pronoun (*pro*). If we stipulate that in-situ wh-phrase pronominals must be bound by the raised wh-phrase, then superiority violations create a classic weak crossover configuration, as suggested by the movement analyses sketched in (72).

Although we agree with Hornstein, Dayal, and Comorovski that crossover and superiority share an essential explanatory element—in our case, sensitivity to order of evaluation—we do not attempt to reduce superiority to crossover per se. In fact, for us crossover violations and superiority violations arise from different binding mechanisms: crossover arises from the fact that binders must be evaluated before the pronoun that they bind. Superiority, as we will see, arises from the fact that a raised wh-word can only bind its wh-trace if the wh-trace is evaluated before any in-situ wh-word. It is the fact that both of these binding mechanisms are sensitive to order of evaluation that accounts for the resemblance between crossover and superiority.

Here is a derivation of the grammatical multiple wh-question *Who __ ate what?*. First, we derive the question body, __ *ate what*:

(73)
$$\begin{array}{c} \dfrac{\mathrm{DP}\backslash\!\!\backslash(\mathrm{DP?S}) \mid \mathrm{DP?S}}{\mathrm{DP}} \\ \text{—} \\ \dfrac{\lambda y.[\,]}{y} \end{array} \left(\begin{array}{c} \dfrac{\mathrm{DP?S} \mid \mathrm{DP?S}}{(\mathrm{DP}\backslash \mathrm{S})/\mathrm{DP}} \\ \textit{ate} \\ \dfrac{[\,]}{\mathbf{ate}} \end{array} \quad \begin{array}{c} \dfrac{\mathrm{DP?S} \mid \mathrm{S}}{\mathrm{DP}} \\ \textit{what} \\ \dfrac{\mathbf{what}(\lambda x.[\,])}{x} \end{array} \right)$$

$$= \begin{array}{c} \dfrac{\mathrm{DP}\backslash\!\!\backslash(\mathrm{DP?S}) \mid \mathrm{S}}{\mathrm{S}} \\ \text{__ } \textit{ate what} \\ \dfrac{\lambda y.\mathbf{what}(\lambda x.[\,])}{\mathbf{ate}\ x\ y} \end{array} \quad \begin{array}{c} \textsc{lower} \\ \Rightarrow \end{array} \quad \begin{array}{c} \mathrm{DP}\backslash\!\!\backslash(\mathrm{DP?S}) \\ \text{__ } \textit{ate what} \\ \lambda y.\mathbf{what}(\lambda x.\mathbf{ate}\ x\ y) \end{array}$$

Note that the gap category, $(\mathrm{DP}\backslash\!\!\backslash(\mathrm{DP?S}))/\!\!/(\mathrm{DP}\backslash\!\!\backslash(\mathrm{DP?S}))$, has the required general form of $A/\!\!/A$, and denotes an identity function.

Before we can complete the derivation, we must generalize the syntactic entry for wh-words like *who* that was given above in (64).

(74)
$$\begin{array}{c} \dfrac{(\mathrm{DP?}A)_F \mid A}{\mathrm{DP}} \\ \textit{who}_q \\ \dfrac{\mathbf{who}(\lambda x.[\;])}{x} \end{array}$$

Here, A schematizes over S, DP?S, DP?(DP?S), and so on: however many elements in the clause have already been questioned, *who* adds one more. The semantics remains the same for each of these syntactic categories. In the case in hand, we instantiate this syntactic schema by choosing $A = \mathrm{DP?S}$. After applying FRONT, the syntactic category will be $(\mathrm{DP?(DP?S)})/(\mathrm{DP}\backslash\!\!\backslash(\mathrm{DP?S}))$.

This category combines directly via ordinary function application with the question body derived above in (73) to yield the desired result: after beta reduction, we have the multiple wh-question $\mathbf{who}(\lambda y.\mathbf{what}(\lambda x.\mathbf{ate}\; x\; y)) : \mathrm{DP?(DP?S)}$. It is easy to extend the derivation above to a derivation *Who did Mary say __ ate what?*.

Now consider a superiority violation such as **What$_i$ did who eat __$_i$?*: an in-situ wh-word (*who*) intervenes between the fronted wh-word (*what*) and its gap. Because the fronted wh-word requires an argument of the form $\mathrm{DP}\backslash\!\!\backslash A$ (for some choice of A), the gap must take widest scope. Therefore the gap must take scope over the intervening wh-word. By the reasoning given in chapter 4, in order for the gap to take scope over something to its left, the gap must type-shift to operate at a higher continuation level. Here is the way a derivation of the question body *who ate __* would have to go:

(75)
$$\begin{array}{c} \dfrac{\mathrm{DP}\backslash\!\!\backslash \mathrm{S} \mid \mathrm{DP}\backslash\!\!\backslash \mathrm{S}}{\dfrac{\mathrm{DP?S} \mid \mathrm{S}}{\mathrm{DP}}} \\ \textit{who} \\ \dfrac{[\;]}{\dfrac{\mathbf{who}(\lambda x.[\;])}{x}} \end{array} \left(\begin{array}{c} \dfrac{\mathrm{DP}\backslash\!\!\backslash \mathrm{S} \mid \mathrm{DP}\backslash\!\!\backslash \mathrm{S}}{\dfrac{\mathrm{S} \mid \mathrm{S}}{(\mathrm{DP}\backslash \mathrm{S})/\mathrm{DP}}} \\ \textit{ate} \\ \dfrac{[\;]}{\dfrac{[\;]}{\mathbf{ate}}} \end{array} \quad \begin{array}{c} \dfrac{\mathrm{DP}\backslash\!\!\backslash \mathrm{S} \mid \mathrm{S}}{\dfrac{\mathrm{S} \mid \mathrm{S}}{\mathrm{DP}}} \\ \_\_ \\ \dfrac{\lambda y.[\;]}{\dfrac{[\;]}{y}} \end{array} \right)$$

$$= \begin{array}{c} \dfrac{\mathrm{DP}\backslash\!\!\backslash \mathrm{S} \mid \mathrm{S}}{\dfrac{\mathrm{DP?S} \mid \mathrm{S}}{\mathrm{S}}} \\ \textit{who ate \_\_} \\ \dfrac{\lambda y.[\;]}{\dfrac{\mathbf{who}(\lambda x.[\;])}{\mathbf{ate}\; y\; x}} \end{array} \quad \overset{\text{LOWER}}{\Rightarrow} \quad \begin{array}{c} \dfrac{\mathrm{DP}\backslash\!\!\backslash \mathrm{S} \mid \mathrm{S}}{\mathrm{DP?S}} \\ \textit{who ate \_\_} \\ \dfrac{\lambda y.[\;]}{\mathbf{who}(\lambda x.\mathbf{ate}\; y\; x)} \end{array}$$

Because LOWER only matches a plain S below the horizontal line, there is no way to continue the derivation.

The upshot is that a wh-trace must be evaluated before any in-situ wh-phrase in the same clause. Given left-to-right evaluation, this generally means that the trace must precede any in-situ wh-phrases.

EXERCISE 17

Provide a derivation that shows that the right-to-left combination schema temporarily considered above in section 2.5 generates superiority violations such as **What did who eat* __. Hint: after studying the wh-word schema in (74), consider how to choose A when you instantiate the gap schema $A /\!\!/ A$.

There are a number of issues concerning multiple wh-questions that we will not explore here. See Shan and Barker (2006) for a discussion of how to extend this analysis to D-linked wh-words such as *which*, which have been claimed to ameliorate superiority violations, and see Shan (2002a) for an explanation for how a continuation-based strategy can account for Baker's ambiguity, as described in Baker (1968).

6

Reconstruction effects

This chapter explores an approach to reconstruction that falls into the general category of 'semantic reconstruction'. In semantic reconstruction, the syntax and the semantics collaborate in order to account for a number of reconstruction effects, but without any syntactic movement. The notion of semantic reconstruction was first articulated by von Stechow in unpublished work we do not have access to, and was further developed by Cresti (1995), Rullmann (1995), and Sternefeld (1997, 2001). This chapter builds on work reported in Shan and Barker (2006), Barker (2009), and Barker (2014a).

The key idea of the analysis here is that allowing pronouns and gaps to denote higher-order functions can delay evaluation (in our terms) in a way that explains some reconstruction effects. The fragment here is just one specific implementation of this strategy. One of the points of interest here is that the higher-order functions do not have to be stipulated in order to describe reconstruction, but rather follow from the independently motivated aspects of the fragment developed in previous chapters.

In chapter 2, we proposed an analysis of crossover that depends on a left-to-right evaluation bias built into the basic composition schema. Reconstruction appears at first glance to pose a sharp challenge to any approach based on order:

(76) a. Which of his_i relatives does everyone_i love __?
b. the relative of his_i that everyone_i loves __

In the wh-question in (76a) (possible answer: *his mother*), the pronoun precedes the quantifier, yet there is a salient interpretation of this sentence on which the pronoun is bound by the quantifier. On this reading, the value of the pronoun varies with the person selected by the quantifier. Likewise, there is a bound reading for the relative clause in (76b) (possible continuation: . . . *is his mother*). We shall see that this sort of quantificational binding, as well as other types of reconstruction effects, are in fact perfectly compatible with an evaluation-order explanation for crossover.

Crucially, we will show that the possibility of backwards quantificational binding in the examples in (76) does not mean that evaluation order restrictions have been suspended. In particular, crossover effects can emerge when the wh-trace precedes the quantifier:

(77) a. *Which of her$_i$ relatives __ loves everyone$_i$?
b. *the relative of hers$_i$ who __ loves everyone$_i$

We take it that these expressions have the same status as typical weak crossover violations. The difference between the examples in (76) and the examples in (77) is that in (77), the (semantically) reconstructed position of the pronoun, marked with '__', precedes the quantifier. The rough descriptive generalization, then, is that a quantifier can bind a pronoun just in case the quantifier is evaluated before the *reconstructed* pronoun. What we will show is that, given a default evaluation order of left-to-right, the facts above follow.

On syntactic reconstruction approaches, material including the pronoun syntactically moves into the reconstruction position. Or, in some versions (e.g., Munn 1994), there is an unpronounced copy of the syntactic material within the gap site. On the approach here, the meaning of the constituent containing the pronoun will be packaged semantically in such a way that its evaluation will be delayed. The net result will be that the evaluation of the pronoun will be timed as if the pronoun had appeared in its reconstructed position.

In order to justify optimism that our approach to reconstruction is robust, we will consider a range of reconstruction effects, including binding of anaphors, idiom licensing, and especially crossover phenomena, in the context of wh-interrogatives, relative clauses, and wh-relatives.

(78) a. Which strings did John pull?
b. the strings that John pulled

(79) a. Which picture of herself does Mary like?
b. the picture of herself that Mary likes

(80) a. Which pictures of each other did they like?
b. the pictures of each other that they liked

The example in (78a) has an idiomatic interpretation on which it means that John used his political influence in order to accomplish some goal.

We will develop a detailed enough picture of reconstruction effects to argue that evaluation order remains a viable strategy for crossover, at the same time that it accounts for a substantial range of reconstruction effects.

6.1 Reconstructing quantificational binding in a question

Given the emphasis in this book on quantificational binding, our key example of a reconstruction effect will be a wh-question in which a quantifier binds a pronoun that linearly precedes it.

All of the details of the grammar developed in previous chapters, including the analyses of in-situ scope, binding, wh-fronting and pied piping, were motivated without any view towards handling reconstruction. Nevertheless, we are now in a position to derive at least some reconstruction effects without any additional assumptions.

The derivations will be somewhat more complicated than the derivations given so far. But they involve no new mechanisms or techniques: just LIFTing, LOWERing, and FRONTing, with gaps having the category $A /\!\!/ A$ for some choice of A.

The essential element in the analysis that gives rise to reconstruction effects is the FRONT type-shifter. This type-shifter captures the similarity of the semantic scope-taking behavior of in-situ wh-phrases with the syntactic scope-taking behavior of fronted wh-phrases. Because the type-shifter does not affect semantic interpretation, it guarantees that the semantic value of the fronted wh-question will be exactly the same as if it had occurred in-situ in the wh-gap position.

For instance:

(81) Which of his$_i$ relatives does everyone$_i$ love __?

In order to provide complete details of the derivation of this example, we will discuss its two main syntactic constituents in turn: the fronted wh-phrase *which of his relatives*, followed by a derivation of the question body *does everyone love* __.

Recall that the category of a simple pronoun is $\dfrac{\mathrm{DP} \rhd \mathrm{S} \mid \mathrm{S}}{\mathrm{DP}}$, which we will abbreviate in derivations as 'pn'.

(82)
$$\begin{array}{c} \dfrac{((\mathrm{DP/N})?\mathrm{S})_F \mid \mathrm{S}}{\mathrm{DP} \rhd \mathrm{S} \mid \mathrm{DP} \rhd \mathrm{S}} \\ \mathrm{DP/N} \\ \textit{which} \\ \dfrac{\dfrac{\mathbf{which}(\lambda f.[\,])}{[\,]}}{f} \end{array} \left(\begin{array}{c} \dfrac{\mathrm{S} \mid \mathrm{S}}{\mathrm{DP} \rhd \mathrm{S} \mid \mathrm{DP} \rhd \mathrm{S}} \\ \mathrm{N/DP} \\ \textit{relative-of} \\ \dfrac{\dfrac{[\,]}{[\,]}}{\mathbf{rel}} \end{array} \quad \begin{array}{c} \dfrac{\mathrm{S} \mid \mathrm{S}}{\mathrm{DP} \rhd \mathrm{S} \mid \mathrm{S}} \\ \mathrm{DP} \\ \textit{his} \\ \dfrac{\dfrac{[\,]}{\lambda z.[\,]}}{z} \end{array} \right) = \begin{array}{c} \dfrac{((\mathrm{DP/N})?\mathrm{S})_F \mid \mathrm{S}}{\mathrm{DP} \rhd \mathrm{S} \mid \mathrm{S}} \\ \mathrm{DP} \\ \textit{which rel of his} \\ \dfrac{\dfrac{\mathbf{which}(\lambda f.[\,])}{\lambda z.[\,]}}{f(\mathbf{rel}\ z)} \end{array}$$

$$\equiv \begin{array}{c} ((\mathrm{DP/N})?\mathrm{S})_F /\!\!/ (\mathrm{pn} \backslash\!\!\backslash \mathrm{S}) \\ \textit{which rel of his} \end{array} \overset{\text{FRONT}}{\Rightarrow} \begin{array}{c} ((\mathrm{DP/N})?\mathrm{S})/(\mathrm{pn} \backslash\!\!\backslash \mathrm{S}) \\ \textit{which rel of his} \end{array}$$

Note that we have LIFTed in such a way that the main semantic effect of the wh-word *which* occupies a higher layer than that of the pronoun (i.e., it outscopes the pronoun). There is another, irrelevant derivation on which the pronoun outscopes the wh-word, as when the pronoun is interpreted deictically.

The semantic value of the fronted wh-phrase as displayed in the tower is $\lambda\gamma.\mathbf{which}(\lambda f.\gamma(\lambda\kappa\lambda z.\kappa(f(\mathbf{rel}\ z))))$, where γ is a variable over two-layered (higher-typed) continuations.

We next derive the body of the question (ignoring the contribution of *does* for simplicity):

(83)

$$\begin{array}{c|c} \text{pn}\backslash\!\!\backslash\text{S} & \text{pn}\backslash\!\!\backslash\text{S} \\ \hline \text{S} & \text{DP} \rhd \text{S} \end{array} \left(\begin{array}{c|c} \text{pn}\backslash\!\!\backslash\text{S} & \text{pn}\backslash\!\!\backslash\text{S} \\ \hline \text{DP} \rhd \text{S} & \text{DP} \rhd \text{S} \end{array} \quad \begin{array}{c|c} \text{pn}\backslash\!\!\backslash\text{S} & \text{S} \\ \hline \text{DP} \rhd \text{S} & \text{S} \end{array} \right)$$

$$\begin{array}{c} \text{DP} \\ \textit{everyone} \\ [\,] \\ \hline \forall y.[\,]y \\ \hline y \end{array} \left(\begin{array}{c} (\text{DP}\backslash\text{S})/\text{DP} \\ \textit{love} \\ [\,] \\ \hline [\,] \\ \hline \textbf{love} \end{array} \quad \begin{array}{c} \text{DP} \\ \_\_ \\ \lambda\mathcal{P}.[\,] \\ \hline \mathcal{P}(\lambda w.[\,]) \\ \hline w \end{array} \right)$$

$$= \begin{array}{c} \begin{array}{c|c} \text{pn}\backslash\!\!\backslash\text{S} & \text{S} \\ \hline \text{S} & \text{S} \end{array} \\ \hline \text{S} \\ \textit{(does) everyone love}\,\_\_ \\ \lambda\mathcal{P}.[\,] \\ \hline \forall y.(\mathcal{P}(\lambda w.[\,]))\,y \\ \hline \textbf{love}\ w\ y \end{array} \quad \begin{array}{c} \text{LOWER (twice)} \\ \Rightarrow \end{array} \quad \begin{array}{c} \text{pn}\backslash\!\!\backslash\text{S} \\ \textit{(does) everyone love}\,\_\_ \\ \lambda\mathcal{P}.\forall y.(\mathcal{P}(\lambda w.\textbf{love}\ w\ y))\,y \end{array}$$

Here, $\mathcal{P}$ is a variable over pronoun meanings (category pn). The idea is that instead of having a simple gap in which an individual of category DP is missing, as in (20), we have a higher-order gap in which a pronoun is missing, with type $(\mathtt{e} \rightarrow \mathtt{t}) \rightarrow (\mathtt{e} \rightarrow \mathtt{t})$. Note that the higher-order gap is still an identity function both syntactically and semantically (see Barker 2009:20).

Putting the two halves of the example together, we have:

(84)

$$\begin{array}{cc} ((\text{DP}/\text{N})?\text{S})/(\text{pn}\backslash\!\!\backslash\text{S}) & \text{pn}\backslash\!\!\backslash\text{S} \\ \textit{which relative of his} & \textit{does everyone love}\,\_\_ \\ \lambda\gamma.\textbf{which}(\lambda f.\gamma(\lambda\kappa\lambda z.\kappa(f(\textbf{rel}\ z)))) & \lambda\mathcal{P}.\forall y.\mathcal{P}(\lambda w(\textbf{love}\ w\ y))\ y \end{array}$$

This is a simple function/argument construction. The category of the entire question, then, will be (DP/N)?S: a question asking for a function from nominals to entities (as discussed below).

In order to understand how semantic reconstruction leads to delayed evaluation of the pronoun, it is instructive to consider the series of beta reductions that leads to a simplified representation of the semantic value of the question. As the reduction proceeds, the material to be reconstructed—the semantic contribution of the constituent *relative of his*—is underlined. The reconstructed material is destined to be the value of the gap variable $\mathcal{P}$:

(85) $(\lambda\gamma.\mathbf{which}(\lambda f.\gamma\,\underline{(\lambda\kappa\lambda z.\kappa(f(\mathbf{rel}\,z)))}))(\lambda\mathcal{P}.\forall y.\mathcal{P}(\lambda w.\mathbf{love}\,w\,y)\,y)$

$\rightsquigarrow \mathbf{which}(\lambda f.(\lambda\mathcal{P}.\forall y.\mathcal{P}(\lambda w.\mathbf{love}\,w\,y)\,y)\underline{(\lambda\kappa\lambda z.\kappa(f(\mathbf{rel}\,z)))})$

$\rightsquigarrow \mathbf{which}(\lambda f.\forall y.\underline{(\lambda\kappa\lambda z.\kappa(f(\mathbf{rel}\,z)))}(\lambda w.\mathbf{love}\,w\,y)\,y)$

$\rightsquigarrow \mathbf{which}(\lambda f.\forall y.\mathbf{love}(f(\mathbf{rel}\,y))\,y)$

Gloss: 'For what choice function f does every person y love f(y's relatives)?' A possible answer for this question might be *the tallest*. In order to arrive at the traditional answer, namely, *his mother*, we need yet higher types; that derivation is somewhat more complicated, but requires no additional assumptions. Full details are provided in Barker (2009).

It is worth emphasizing that there is no syntactic movement, nor is there any sense in which the semantic beta reductions are actually moving semantic material from one place to another. That is, the lambda calculus is an equational theory: the series of reductions are a series of equivalences, not transformations. In other words, the analysis here is directly compositional in the sense of Jacobson (2002): every syntactic constituent has a well-formed semantic interpretation that does not depend on any material outside of the constituent.

6.2 Despite reconstruction, crossover effects remain in force

In the simplest examples, crossover occurs when a pronoun precedes the quantifier that binds it, as shown above in (35). In reconstruction examples, a pronoun is allowed to precede a quantifier that binds it. But this does not mean that reconstruction suspends crossover effects:

(86) ?Which of his$_i$ relatives __ loves everyone?

In the analysis of *Which of his relatives does everyone love __?*, the binding analysis requires the quantifier *everyone* to bind the virtual pronoun inside the gap site in the manner illustrated above in (83). This requires the quantifier to precede the gap site, conforming to the left-to-right restrictions on binding imposed by the combination schema. In (86), in contrast, since the gap site precedes the quantifier, there is no way for the quantifier to bind into the gap, for exactly the same reason that the simple crossover binding attempts failed in (35).

In other words, even though semantic reconstruction can allow a quantifier to bind a pronoun that precedes it, crossover restrictions remain in effect even in reconstruction situations. In each reconstruction analysis below, we will argue that crossover effects remain in force.

6.3 Principle C effects are not expected

Principle C of the binding theory prohibits names and other referring expressions from being c-commanded by a coreferent pronoun.

(87) *He$_i$ likes John$_i$'s friends.

If reconstruction involved syntactic movement, reconstruction would potentially create Principle C violations.

(88) Which of John$_i$'s friends does he$_i$ like __?

That is, if a portion of *which of John's friends* including the pronoun syntactically reconstructed into the gap position, the pronoun would c-command the name, and the coreferent interpretation indicated by the subscripts would be predicted bad. However, as (Safir, 1999:609) observes, this example is perfectly fine on the relevant interpretation.

On the approach here, reconstruction is entirely semantic, so reconstruction does not have any effect on c-command relations. This means that there should be no Principle C effects arising from the movement of a name into a reconstructed gap position.

(Safir, 1999:609) provides a wide range of examples in which a syntactic theory of reconstruction incorrectly predicts Principle C violations, including these:

(89) a. Which biography of Picasso$_i$ do you think he$_i$ wants to read?
b. Which witness's attack on Lee$_i$ did he$_i$ try to get expunged from the trial records?
c. Whose criticism of Lee$_i$ did he$_i$ choose to ignore?

On our account, the sentences in (88) and (89) are correctly expected to be fine.

An approach involving overt syntactic reconstruction, on the other hand, must consider Principle C violations to be the default, and then explain how some examples like these escape ungrammaticality through some separate mechanism. For instance, Safir suggests that reconstructed referring expressions sometimes function as if they were pronouns for the purposes of the binding constraints; he suggests that this is a species of 'vehicle change'.

The empirical status of Principle C violations in reconstruction contexts is subtle and intricate. In addition to Safir (1999, 2004a) and Safir (2004b), see Heycock (1995), Büring (2005), Sportiche (2006), and many others for discussions. In any case, the grammaticality of these examples is exactly what is predicted under the semantic reconstruction account developed here.

6.4 Reconstruction into relative clauses

As noted above in (76), it has long been observed that wh-questions bear a striking resemblance to some kinds of relative clauses:

(90) a. [Which relative of his] does everyone love __?
b. [the relative of his] that everyone loves __

Just as there can be a quantificational binding relationship between *everyone* and *his* in (90a), there can be a similar binding relationship in (90b). On the account here, this suggests that the definite determiner *the* may have a lexical entry that closely resembles the pied piping lexical entry for the wh-determiner *which*. Here is a candidate for such a lexical entry for *the*:

(91)
$$\frac{((\mathrm{DP}/\mathrm{N})?\mathrm{S})_F \,|\, \mathrm{S}}{\mathrm{DP}/\mathrm{N}} \qquad\qquad \frac{\mathrm{DP}_F \,|\, \mathrm{S}}{\mathrm{DP}/\mathrm{N}}$$
which *the*
$$\frac{\mathbf{which}(\lambda f.[\ ])}{f} \qquad\qquad \frac{\mathbf{the}(\lambda f.[\ ])}{f}$$

Positing a lexical ambiguity specific to *the* is too flat-footed, since examples parallel to (90b) exist for *a*, *some*, *many*, etc., so there is some systematic type-shifting going on here. But in any case, no matter how we arrive at the variant lexical entry for *the*, we get the following analyses in parallel with the reconstruction derivation given above in section 6.1 for wh-questions:

(92) a. Which relative of his does everyone love __?
b. $\mathbf{which}(\lambda f.\forall y.\mathbf{love}(f(\mathbf{rel}\ y))\ y)$

(93) a. the relative of his that everyone loves __
b. $\mathbf{the}(\lambda f.\forall y.\mathbf{love}(f(\mathbf{rel}\ y))\ y)$

One possible answer to the wh-question is *the tallest*; the corresponding completion to the relative clause is . . . *is always the tallest*. In other words, this is an analysis on which the reconstruction version of the definite description receives (at least by default) a functional interpretation rather than a strictly referential one. See Barker (2014a) for details of a functional semantics for the reconstructing determiner.

On the topic of functional (intensional) descriptions, Grosu and Krifka (2007) note that reconstruction is relevant for understanding what they call equational intensional reconstruction relatives:

(94) a. the gifted mathematician that John claims to be
b. $\mathbf{the}(\lambda f.\mathbf{claim}(\mathbf{be}(f(\mathbf{gifted\text{-}mathematician}))\ \mathbf{j}))$

As they note, one of the hallmarks of this construction is that the referent of the description is not entailed to be a gifted mathematician. This is exactly what we would expect by using the version of *the* from (91), since the semantic material contributed by *gifted mathematician* will be (semantically) reconstructed into the gap position, which is in the scope of *claim*. There are many special properties of this construction that we cannot explore here; nevertheless, the general approach to reconstruction here may provide some insight into how the interaction of reconstruction and intensionality in this construction can be implemented in a framework that does not make use of syntactic movement.

We do not assume that (91) is the only lexical entry for *the*. There will be an ordinary, non-reconstruction version of *the* as well. The judgments of reconstruction examples involving relative clauses are notoriously variable; but as, e.g., Bargmann et al. (2013) observe, the fact that there are any grammatical examples requires the availability of a reconstruction analysis such as that provided by (91).

6.5 Relative pronouns with pied piping

Of course, one place where wh-phrases and relative clause formation overlap is in relative pronouns:

(95)

$$\text{Relative pronouns:} \quad \frac{(A\backslash\!\!\backslash S)_F \,|\, S}{A} \quad \textit{who(se)/which} \quad \frac{\lambda x.[\,]}{x}$$

Given that the feature *F* triggers the pied-piping mechanism, we correctly predict that that relative pronouns can participate in pied piping:

(96) a. the man [who] John saw
b. the man [whose mother] John saw
c. the man [the mother of whom] John saw

In addition, we also expect that when a relative pronoun pied-pipes another pronoun along with it, the reconstructed ordinary pronoun can be bound by a quantifier that follows it:

(97) John is a man [[whose opinion of her$_i$] every woman$_i$ respects __]

Likewise, we predict that if the relative pronoun pied-pipes a quantificational binder, if the reconstruction site follows a pronoun, an attempt at binding should give rise to crossover effects:

(98) a theory [[every proponent$_i$ of which] {?he$_i$/?his$_i$ advisor} cites __]

Native speakers report that this sentence is somewhat hard to process. Our theory predicts in addition to any other processing difficulties, it should have the status of a weak crossover violation.

6.6 Idioms

Idiom chunks—DPs that serve as parts of idioms, such as *care* in *take good care of someone*, or *lip service*, as in *pay lip service to*—generally must occur as an argument of a limited, specific set of verbs in order to receive their idiomatic interpretation. Yet they can sometimes be separated from the relevant verb in wh-interrogatives and in relative clauses:

(99) a. How much care did Mary say that John took of Bill?
b. the lip service that Mary said that John paid to civil liberties

In order for the idiomatic interpretations to be licensed, there must be some mechanism for transmitting information about the identity of the idiom chunk from its displaced position to the rest of the idiomatic expression. This has traditionally served as an argument for syntactic reconstruction (see, e.g., Sportiche 2006), since one way to make the needed connection is to syntactically reconstruct the idiom chunk, at which point it will be reunited with the rest of its idiom.

Although the approach here is primarily semantic, nevertheless a limited amount of syntactic information does flow between the gap site and the fronted constituent, as we have seen above in pied piping examples. To handle idiom licensing, we need only provide some fine-grained syntactic features that will enable suitable syntactic bookkeeping to take place. For example, if the relevant idiomatic sense of *strings* as in *to pull strings* subcategorizes for a DP_{str} ('*str*' for strings), then the noun *strings* will itself have category N_{str}. We will need a generalization of the lexical entry given above in (91) for interrogative *which* that copies the relevant features from its nominal complement to the category of the kind of gap it expects to find in its gapped-clause complement. Finally, we need to instantiate the gap schema ($A /\!\!/ A$) by choosing $A = \mathrm{DP}_{str}\backslash\!\!\backslash \mathrm{S}$. Then we have the following derivation for *Which strings did John pull?* (the auxiliary *did* has once again been omitted for clarity):

(100)
$$\left(\begin{array}{c} \dfrac{((\mathrm{DP}/\mathrm{N})?\mathrm{S})_F \mid \mathrm{S}}{\mathrm{DP}_\gamma/\mathrm{N}_\gamma} \\ \textit{which} \\ \dfrac{\mathbf{which}(\lambda f.[\ ])}{f} \end{array} \quad \begin{array}{c} \dfrac{\mathrm{S} \mid \mathrm{S}}{\mathrm{N}_{str}} \\ \textit{strings} \\ \dfrac{[\ ]}{\mathbf{connections}} \end{array} \right)$$

$$\left(\begin{array}{c} \dfrac{\mathrm{DP}_{str}\backslash\!\!\backslash \mathrm{S} \mid \mathrm{DP}_{str}\backslash\!\!\backslash \mathrm{S}}{\mathrm{DP}} \\ \textit{John} \\ \dfrac{[\ ]}{\mathbf{j}} \end{array} \left(\begin{array}{c} \dfrac{\mathrm{DP}_{str}\backslash\!\!\backslash \mathrm{S} \mid \mathrm{DP}_{str}\backslash\!\!\backslash \mathrm{S}}{(\mathrm{DP}\backslash \mathrm{S})/\mathrm{DP}_{str}} \\ \textit{pull} \\ \dfrac{[\ ]}{\mathbf{use}} \end{array} \quad \begin{array}{c} \dfrac{\mathrm{DP}_{str}\backslash\!\!\backslash \mathrm{S} \mid \mathrm{S}}{\mathrm{DP}_{str}} \\ \text{—} \\ \dfrac{\lambda x.[\ ]}{x} \end{array} \right) \right)$$

The remainder of the derivation goes exactly as in (61) except that the category of the question body is $DP_{str}\backslash\!\!\backslash S$ instead of $DP\backslash\!\!\backslash S$, and likewise for the category that the fronted wh-phrase is seeking to combine with. If *strings* were replaced with an ordinary nominal, or if this special sense of *pull* were replaced with an ordinary transitive verb, the two halves of the derivation would not match appropriately. Because the gap faithfully carries with it the detailed syntactic category expected at the gap site, further embedding of the idiomatic verb (e.g., *Which strings did Mary get so upset that John pulled?*) will not disrupt the licensing connection.

6.7 Reflexives and *each other* anaphors

One classic reconstruction effect involves reflexives. Normally, reflexives must be bound by some less oblique coargument in the same clause:

(101) a. John liked a picture of himself.
b. *Mary liked a picture of himself.
c. *John claimed Mary liked a picture of himself.
d. *A picture of himself was liked by John.

But in reconstruction situations, the reflexive can be separated from its binder:

(102) a. Which picture of himself does John like __?
b. the picture of herself that Mary likes __

Assuming that the anaphors in (102) are grammatically bound, our account requires (semantic) reconstruction.

The approach here follows the suggestion of Dowty (2007:97) that reflexives are scope-taking expressions, building on the suggestion of Szabolcsi (1992) that reflexives express the duplicator combinator $\mathbf{W} = \lambda\kappa x.\kappa x x$:

(103)
$$\begin{array}{c}\dfrac{\mathrm{DP\backslash S} \,|\, \mathrm{DP\backslash S}}{\mathrm{(DP\backslash S)/DP}}\\ \textit{saw}\\ \dfrac{[\ ]}{\textbf{saw}}\end{array}\quad \begin{array}{c}\dfrac{\mathrm{DP\backslash S} \,|\, \mathrm{DP\backslash S}}{\mathrm{DP}}\\ \textit{himself}\\ \dfrac{\lambda x.[\ ]x}{x}\end{array}\quad = \quad \begin{array}{c}\dfrac{\mathrm{DP\backslash S} \,|\, \mathrm{DP\backslash S}}{\mathrm{DP\backslash S}}\\ \textit{saw himself}\\ \dfrac{\lambda x.[\ ]x}{\textbf{saw}\ x}\end{array}$$

$$\begin{array}{cc} \textsc{lower} & \mathrm{DP\backslash S}\\ \Rightarrow & \textit{saw himself}\\ & \lambda x.\textbf{saw}\ x\ x\end{array}$$

On this view, reflexives are an in-situ VP modifier: they take scope over a VP, and return a new VP whose next argument (the subject) gets copied into the anaphor position. See chapter 15 below for a more general version of this anaphoric strategy.

Once we have a treatment of ordinary uses of reflexive pronouns, we can combine it with our reconstruction analysis.

(104) Which picture of himself did John see?

(105)
$$\begin{array}{c}\dfrac{((\mathrm{DP/N})?\mathrm{S})_F \;\big|\; \mathrm{S}}{\mathrm{DP\backslash S} \;\big|\; \mathrm{DP\backslash S}}\\ \mathrm{DP/N}\\ \textit{which}\\ \dfrac{\dfrac{\mathbf{which}(\lambda f.[\;])}{[\;]}}{f}\end{array} \qquad \begin{array}{c}\dfrac{\mathrm{S} \;\big|\; \mathrm{S}}{\mathrm{DP\backslash S} \;\big|\; \mathrm{DP\backslash S}}\\ \mathrm{N}\\ \textit{picture of himself}\\ \dfrac{\dfrac{[\;]}{\lambda x.[\;]x}}{\mathbf{pic}\ x}\end{array}$$

$$\overset{\text{FRONT}}{\Rightarrow} \quad \begin{array}{c}((\mathrm{DP/N})?\mathrm{S})/(\dfrac{\mathrm{DP\backslash S} \;\big|\; \mathrm{DP\backslash S}}{\mathrm{DP}} \mathbin{\backslash\!\!\backslash} \mathrm{S})\\ \textit{which picture of himself}\\ \lambda \gamma.\mathbf{which}(\lambda f.\gamma(\dfrac{\lambda x.[\;]x}{f(\mathbf{pic}\ x)}))\end{array}$$

The only difference between this analysis and the one for quantificational binding of an ordinary pronoun is that the the gap within the pied-piped material is a reflexive-pronoun type gap rather than a standard pronoun.

Once again, the category of the fronted wh-phrase reflects the fact that it contains a particular kind of anaphor. Instead of containing an ordinary bindable pronoun, as in (76), here it is a reflexive pronoun, with corresponding changes in the details of the category.

One additional wrinkle: as (106a) shows, a reconstructed reflexive can even take an antecedent that is not in the same minimal clause as the reconstruction site.

(106) a. Which picture of himself does John claim Mary liked __?
b. *John claimed Mary liked a picture of himself.

Our analysis generates both of these examples. To the extent that the indicated contrast between the reconstruction example in (106a) and the non-reconstruction example in (106b) is systematic, it suggests that reconstruction somehow enables a reflexive to take advantage of a wider range of possible binders than it would have been able to if it had been generated in the reconstruction position. One possible strategy in the approach taken here would be to impose restrictions on the categories of the towers that clause-embedding predicates can take as complements; but we leave this for future research.

Reconstruction of anaphors such as *each other* can be handled analogously:

(107) a. Which of each other's papers did they read __?
b. the descriptions of each other that they offered __

Like reflexives, *each other* must generally be c-commanded by the element that binds it. We can therefore give *each other* a scope-taking analysis on which it takes scope just equal to the scope of its binder, e.g., category $\frac{\mathrm{DP\backslash S} \mid \mathrm{DP\backslash S}}{\mathrm{DP}}$. The semantics will require that the binder be the kind of object that the quantificational part of *each other* can distribute over, but otherwise the derivation will proceed exactly as shown above for *himself*.

The analyses in this section (and only in this section) require adjusting the details of the LOWER type-shifter. Examination of the derivation in (103) will show that we have applied the LOWER type-shifter to a tower in which the matching corners have the category DP\S rather than just S. There are several possible adjustments, depending on what you think the right explanation is: if what the example shows is that it is possible to evaluate verb phrases in addition to clauses, then the LOWER rule needs to be generalized to accept either S or DP\S as a lowering target; if what the example shows is that lowering can happen in many different places, then the statement of the LOWER rule needs to be stated in a way that it applies to any tower with matching corner categories, as long as those matching categories are not of the form DP $\triangleright$ *A*.

6.8 Conclusions concerning reconstruction

We've proposed that crossover in general follows from two assumptions: that pronouns find their binders by taking scope, and so participate in the same scope-taking system as their binders; and that the evaluation order that governs scope relations defaults to left-to-right.

This chapter, building on Shan and Barker (2006), Barker (2009), and Barker (2014a) explores a number of reconstruction effects, including quantificational binding, wh-questions, relative clauses, and wh-relatives, idioms, and reflexives. In each case, the analysis hinges on the application of the FRONT type-shifter, repeated here:

(108)

FRONT
$A_F /\!\!/ B \quad \Rightarrow \quad A/B$

This type shifter turns what would otherwise be an in-situ scope-taker (such as a wh-phrase) into an expression that has been syntactically displaced to the left. Because it adjusts the syntactic category of an expression without adjusting its semantic value, the semantic value of the resulting expression is guaranteed to be exactly as if the displaced constituent were evaluated in the position of the gap. We call this *delayed evaluation.* This is what accounts for the semantic reconstruction effects, including bindability as well as ability to bind.

Crucially, the effects due to the FRONT type-shifter are perfectly compatible with default left-to-right evaluation, so the reconstruction effects discussed do not constitute counterexamples to the continuation-based approach to crossover. Indeed, quite the contrary: we have presented empirical data from a range of constructions that crossover is not suspended in reconstruction situations. For instance, if a reconstructed quantifier follows a pronoun, it cannot bind the pronoun, so crossover remains in effect even in the presence of reconstruction, as predicted by our account.

Furthermore, since the FRONT type-shifter does not involve syntactic movement, there is no syntactic reconstruction. This is why reconstruction typically does not trigger Principle C violations, since there is no syntactic structure inside the reconstruction gap site.

We would like to emphasize that the FRONT type-shifter is motivated entirely by a desire to give the simplest possible analysis to wh-question formation, without considering reconstruction examples. Nevertheless, it provides analyses not only of syntactic pied piping, but also a variety of reconstruction effects, in a way that remains fully compatible with a principled explanation for crossover.

7

Generalized coordination, Flexible Montague Grammar

This chapter considers two semantic analyses that are related to each other both historically and conceptually: Partee and Rooth's (1983) generalized coordination, and Hendriks' (1993) Flexible Montague Grammar. We argue that these analyses both make implicit use of continuations. More specifically, we argue that generalized coordination depends on a limited form of continuation-capturing, and that the relevance of continuation-passing to Flexible Montague Grammar is even more clearly evident.

Generalized coordination provides an application in natural language of a technique that is common in programming with continuations, namely, repeated execution of a single continuation.

We argue that although Flexible Montague Grammar provides a robust continuation-based account of scope-taking, it is not well suited to reasoning about evaluation order, and therefore does not provide an account of crossover, reconstruction, or other order-sensitive effects.

7.1 Generalized coordination as re-executing a continuation

Partee and Rooth's (1983) generalized coordination can be viewed as a form of context capturing. The net effect is that a coordinated phrase such as *A and B* denotes a function that takes its continuation, copies it, applies one copy to *A* and the other to *B*, and then logically conjoins the results.

Partee and Rooth's starting point is the observation that natural-language conjunction (likewise, disjunction) can coordinate expressions in a wide range of categories:

(109) a. John left and John slept. **and(left j)(slept j)**
b. John left and slept. **and(left j)(slept j)**
c. John saw and liked Mary. **and(saw m j)(liked m j)**
d. John and Mary left. **and(left j)(left m)**

These examples illustrate coordination of S's, VPs, transitive verbs, and DPs. As the translations indicate, the truth conditions of (the relevant reading) of each of these sentences can be accurately expressed by unpacking the coordination into conjoined clauses. Of course, there are are a variety of other uses of *and* that cannot be paraphrased by means of conjoined clauses (*John and Mary are a happy couple*; *the flag is red and white*) that we will not discuss see the more complete disclaimer in Partee and Rooth (1983:361). We will call the sense of *and* whose meaning is equivalent to conjoined sentences GENERALIZED *and*.

Partee and Rooth (1983), building on work of Gazdar (1980), von Stechow, and Keenan and Faltz (1985), give an analysis of generalized coordination that has three parts. First, they stipulate that a CONJOINABLE TYPE is any type "ending in t". Examples include sentences (type t), verb phrases and common nouns (type $e \rightarrow t$), and quantificational NPs (type $(e \rightarrow t) \rightarrow t$), but not the basic (i.e., lexical) type of proper names (type e).

Second, they rely on a syntactic schema to generalize over the conjoinable syntactic categories.

	SYNTAX	SEMANTICS
(110)	$X \rightarrow X_l$ and X_r	$\mathbf{and}_{\langle\alpha,\beta\rangle}\ ([\![X_l]\!])([\![X_r]\!])$

Third, they provide a recursive rule characterizing how the meaning of generalized *and* for complex semantic types relates to the meaning of *and* for simpler types. More specifically, let L and R be meanings of type $\alpha \rightarrow \beta$. Partee and Rooth (1983) have:

(111) $\mathbf{and}_{\langle\alpha,\beta\rangle}(L)(R) = \lambda a.\mathbf{and}_{\beta}(L(a))(R(a))$

where a is a variable over objects of type α. The base case says that $\mathbf{and}_{t}$ is the standard binary boolean operator over truth values.

On this analysis generalized *and* has a single meaning, but that meaning is type-polymorphic (i.e., able to take arguments of different semantic types). For instance, if we instantiate the syntactic schema for coordinating VPs, then the denotation of *and* takes properties of type $e \rightarrow t$ as arguments; but if we instantiate the syntactic schema for coordinating transitive verbs, then the denotation of *and* takes relations as arguments, type $e \rightarrow e \rightarrow t$.

Equivalently, it is possible to think of (111) as a type-shifting rule, in which case *and* is polysemous, where each distinct homophonous version of *and* takes arguments of a single semantic type. Then there is one basic lexical meaning for *and* (namely, the operator over truth values), and the various other senses of *and* are related to each other and ultimately to the basic lexical meaning by means of a type-shifting rule resembling (111). See Heim and Kratzer (1998:182) for a discussion of this approach.

On either construal (type-polymorphic versus type-shifting), the claim is that *and* has a meaning that is capable of relating properties, or relations, or any other semantic object having a conjoinable type, in addition to truth values.

Now consider one way of achieving a similar analysis of generalized coordination in a continuized grammar. There is no need for a recursive semantic rule; all that is needed is a single lexical schema for *and*:

(112) $$\left(\frac{\mathrm{S}|B}{A} \Big\backslash \frac{\mathrm{S}|B}{A}\right) \Big/ \frac{\mathrm{S}|B}{A}$$
and
$$\lambda r l \kappa.(l\kappa) \wedge (r\kappa)$$

This entry for generalized coordination takes two expressions with matching categories and builds a coordinated expression of the same category. The only requirement placed on the coordinated category is that the final result after taking scope must be an S (this is the 'ends in `t`' part). The coordinated expression takes for its semantic argument the continuation of an A relative to some enclosing B. The generalized *and* takes that continuation (κ) and uses it twice: once by feeding it to the value of the left hand conjunct (l), and again by feeding it to the value of the right hand conjunct (r), and conjoining the result.

EXERCISE 18

Derive *John left and slept.*

EXERCISE 19

Derive *John and everyone left.*

If we think of a continuation as the default future of a computation, i.e., what is about to happen to a value, we can gloss this lexical entry as saying "Whatever you are planning to do with the value of the coordinate structure, do that to the left conjunct, also do it to the right conjunct, and conjoin the resulting truth values".

Thus the compositional pattern expressed by Partee and Rooth's recursive type-shifting rule is built in to our continuation-based grammar. Or, to put it a bit differently, the recursive denotation required for generalized coordination gives a glimpse of the more general compositional structure provided by a continuation-based grammar.

In section 3.2, we provided a simple lexical entry for *and* that coordinated sentences, and noted that it made good predictions about the interaction of linear order with dynamic anaphora, without stipulating any order asymmetry in the lexical entry for *and*. The analysis in this section generalizes that simple lexical entry to handle coordination of multiple expression types, but there is still no need to stipulate the order of update. The left-to-right evaluation default imposed by the combination schema generalizes smoothly as well, so that we not only correctly predict a contrast between *John*$_i$ *entered and he*$_i$ *spoke* versus *He*$_i$ *entered and John*$_{?i}$ *spoke*, in which full sentences are conjoined, we also correctly predict an analogous contrast between *John met Mary*$_i$ *and spoke to her*$_i$ versus *John met her*$_i$ *and spoke to Mary*$_{?i}$, in which verb phrases are conjoined. This interaction between order and dynamic anaphora is not predicted by standard dynamic treatments, e.g., Groenendijk and Stokhof (1991), which continuizes only at the sentence level rather than uniformly throughout the grammar.

7.2 Flexible Montague Grammar: implicit continuations

Building on ideas of Partee and Rooth (1983) and Keenan (1987), Hendriks (1988, 1990, 1993) proposes a type-shifting system for scope-taking called Flexible Montague Grammar.

Because Flexible Montague Grammar involves type-shifters that (we will argue) constitute a form of continuation-passing, it makes an especially useful comparison with the explicitly continuation-based system developed here.

We will see that although Flexible Montague Grammar provides a robust account of scope, it does not also provide an account of evaluation order in general, or crossover in particular.

Hendriks (1993:75) provides three type-shifting rules. One concerns intensionality, and we will not discuss it here. The two essential rules for scope-taking are Argument Raising and Value Raising, which we will discuss in turn.

7.3 Argument Raising

In order to allow a generalized quantifier to appear in a position where an individual-denoting expression is expected, a type-shifting rule called Argument Raising does two things simultaneously: it shifts the type of that argument position to generalized quantifier type, and gives that argument scope over the other arguments of the predicate.

Argument Raising (AR): if an expression ϕ has type

$$a_1 \rightarrow a_2 \rightarrow \ldots \rightarrow a_i \rightarrow \ldots \rightarrow a_n \rightarrow r$$

and translation f, then ϕ also has type

$$a_1 \rightarrow a_2 \rightarrow \ldots \rightarrow ((a_i \rightarrow r) \rightarrow r') \rightarrow \ldots \rightarrow a_n \rightarrow r',$$

with translation $\lambda x_1 x_2 \ldots x_i \ldots x_n . x_i(\lambda x . f x_1 x_2 \ldots x \ldots x_n)$.

For instance, in order to combine an ordinary verb phrase of type $\texttt{e} \to \texttt{t}$ such as *left* with a generalized quantifier subject of type $(\texttt{e} \to \texttt{t}) \to \texttt{t}$ such as *everyone*, the verb phrase must first undergo Argument Raising:

(113)
$$\begin{array}{ccc} \texttt{e} \to \texttt{t} & \text{Arg Raise} & \dfrac{\texttt{t} \mid \texttt{t}}{\texttt{e}} \to \texttt{t} \\ \textit{left} & \Rightarrow & \textit{left} \\ \textbf{left} & & \lambda \mathcal{P}.\mathcal{P}\ \textbf{left} \end{array}$$

For ease of comparison, we are displaying the semantic types of Flexible Montague Grammar as if they were syntactic categories in our tower system. For instance, the type $(\texttt{e} \to \texttt{t}) \to \texttt{t}$ is displayed above as if it had been category $\texttt{t} /\!\!/ (\texttt{e} \backslash\!\!\backslash \texttt{t})$.

In this example, the Argument Raising type shifter replaces an argument of type e with an argument of type $\dfrac{\texttt{t} \mid \texttt{t}}{\texttt{e}}$. This means that the predicate *left* shifts from taking an individual-denoting argument to taking a generalized quantifier argument, at which point it is able to combine with a generalized quantifier subject.

The formulation of Argument Raising given here is slightly generalized compared to Hendriks' original formulation. To get Hendriks' exact rule, choose $r' = r$. This generalization allows a scope-taking operator to deliver a final result type (r') that is different from the original result type r. As we have discussed in chapter 5, in general scope-taking operators can have result types that are different from the category of the expression they take scope over. For example, in our analysis, the wh-word *who* takes scope over a sentence, which has category S, but returns a question, with category DP?S.

Unlike the tower system, Flexible Montague Grammar places no restrictions on evaluation order. The order in which the Argument Raising schema applies to a functor reflects the order in which the arguments of that functor will be evaluated, and there are no restrictions on the order in which different instantiations of Argument Raising apply. For instance, if our goal is to model the two scopings of *Someone saw everyone*, we need to apply Argument Raising to the verb *saw* twice.

(114)
$$\begin{array}{ccc} \texttt{e} \to \texttt{e} \to \texttt{t} & \text{AR} & \dfrac{\texttt{t} \mid \texttt{t}}{\texttt{e}} \to \texttt{e} \to \texttt{t} \\ \textit{saw} & \Rightarrow & \textit{saw} \\ \lambda xy.\textbf{saw}\ x\ y & & \lambda \mathcal{X} y.\mathcal{X}(\lambda x.\textbf{saw}\ x\ y) \end{array}$$

$$\begin{array}{cc} \text{AR} & \dfrac{\texttt{t} \mid \texttt{t}}{\texttt{e}} \to \dfrac{\texttt{t} \mid \texttt{t}}{\texttt{e}} \to \texttt{t} \\ \Rightarrow & \textit{saw} \\ & \lambda \mathcal{X}\mathcal{Y}.\mathcal{Y}(\lambda y.\mathcal{X}(\lambda x.\textbf{saw}\ x\ y)) \end{array}$$

When this doubly-type-shifted denotation for *saw* combines with *everyone* and with *someone*, the second argument (syntactically, the subject) takes scope over the first argument (the direct object), giving linear scope. If we had applied Argument Raising in the opposite order, we would have the same final type, but a denotation with the other evaluation order, namely $\lambda\mathcal{X}\mathcal{Y}.\mathcal{X}(\lambda x.\mathcal{Y}(\lambda y.\mathsf{saw}\ x\ y))$, giving inverse scope.

Argument Raising gives one argument of a predicate access to one of its continuations. More specifically, it allows that argument to take scope exactly over the domain of its local functor, as well as over the remaining arguments of that functor.

In the terms of the discussion in chapter 3, the single rule of Argument Raising simultaneously accounts for the duality of DP meaning, as well as at least some portion of scope displacement and scope ambiguity.

Unfortunately, the rule of Argument Raising alone does not provide a complete analysis of scope displacement and scope ambiguity. At least one additional type-shifting schema (Value Raising) is needed in order for a scope-taking expression to take scope over more than its local co-arguments.

7.4 Value Raising

The second main type shifting rule, Value Raising, allows expressions to take scope wider than their most local constituent. The role of continuations is even clearer for Value Raising:

Value Raising (VR): if an expression ϕ has type

$$a_1 \to a_2 \to \ldots \to a_n \to r$$

and translation f, then ϕ also has type

$$a_1 \to a_2 \to \ldots \to a_n \to (r \to r') \to r',$$

with translation $\lambda x_1 x_2 \ldots x_n \kappa.\kappa(f x_1 x_2 \ldots x_n)$.

By lifting the result type of a predicate from r to $\dfrac{r' \mid r'}{r}$, Value Raising explicitly makes the result type a function on its continuation (here, κ).

Argument Raising and Value Raising interact in such a way that the continuation variable κ of type $r \to r'$ introduced by Value Raising will come to have for its value the continuation of the phrase in question, delimited by some enclosing constituent whose result type is r'.

For example, Value Raising allows quantifiers such as *everyone* to be embedded in possessives such as *everyone's mother left*. Assume that the basic type of the relational noun *mother* is a function of type $\mathsf{e} \to \mathsf{e}$ mapping people to their mothers. Then in addition to its basic type, *mother* will have a number of shifted types, including:

(115)
$$\begin{array}{ccccc} \texttt{e} \to \texttt{e} & \text{Val Raising} & \texttt{e} \to \dfrac{\texttt{t}|\texttt{t}}{\texttt{e}} & & \\ \textit{mother} & \Rightarrow & \textit{mother} & & \\ \textbf{mom} & & \lambda x\kappa.\kappa(\textbf{mom}\ x) & & \\ & & & \text{AR} & \dfrac{\texttt{t}|\texttt{t}}{\texttt{e}} \to \dfrac{\texttt{t}|\texttt{t}}{\texttt{e}} \\ & & & \Rightarrow & \textit{mother} \\ & & & & \lambda\mathcal{P}\kappa.\mathcal{P}(\lambda x.\kappa(\textbf{mom}\ x)) \end{array}$$

This doubly-shifted version of the *mother* function is suitable for transmitting scope-taking ability from a generalized quantifier in possessor position to the possessed DP as a whole:

(116) $[\![\textit{mother}]\!]([\![\textit{everyone}]\!]) = [\lambda\mathcal{P}\kappa.\mathcal{P}(\lambda x.\kappa(\textbf{mom}\ x))](\textbf{everyone})$
$= \lambda\kappa.\textbf{everyone}(\lambda x.\kappa(\textbf{mom}\ x))$

On this analysis, the doubly-shifted *mother* functions as a modifier of generalized quantifiers. Clearly, using shifted relational nouns, we can stack possessee phrases as high as we like: *everyone's mother's mother left* (i.e., everyone's grandmother left) comes out as $\textbf{everyone}(\lambda x.\textbf{left}(\textbf{mom}(\textbf{mom}\ x)))$, and so on.

This derivation for *everyone's mother* can be combined with the shifted *left* from above in (113).

(117) $[\![\textit{(everyone's mother) left}]\!] = [\lambda\mathcal{P}.\mathcal{P}\textbf{left}](\lambda\kappa.\textbf{everyone}(\lambda x.\kappa(\textbf{mom}\ x)))$
$= \textbf{everyone}(\lambda x.\textbf{left}(\textbf{mom}\ x))$

We can gain perspective on how this derivation works by examining the shifted types:

(118)
$$\left(\begin{array}{cc} \dfrac{\texttt{t}|\texttt{t}}{\texttt{e}} & \dfrac{\texttt{t}|\texttt{t}}{\texttt{e}} \to \dfrac{\texttt{t}|\texttt{t}}{\texttt{e}} \\ \textit{everyone's} & \text{AR}(\text{VR}(\textit{mother})) \end{array}\right) \begin{array}{c} \dfrac{\texttt{t}|\texttt{t}}{\texttt{e}} \to \texttt{t} \\ \text{AR}(\textit{left}) \end{array}$$

Chaining Argument Raising and Value Raising can allow a scope-taker to take scope over an arbitrarily large context.

> **EXERCISE 20**
>
> The type-shifting parts of Argument Raising and Value Raising are highly parallel: both involve replacing one element in the type (either x_i in the case of Argument Raising, or r in the case of Value Raising) with some lifted type. What prevents writing a single more general type-shifter that handles both Argument Raising and Value Raising in a single schema?

7.5 So how flexible is Flexible Montague Grammar?

Clearly Flexible Montague Grammar provides systematic access to continuations. But how many of the continuation-based analyses developed here can be reproduced within Flexible Montague Grammar? The answer we will give is: many, but by no means all.

Emphasizing first the parallels between Flexible Montague Grammar and the tower system, Flexible Montague Grammar has two levels of well-formedness checking: a syntactic level of function/argument composition, and a semantic filter making sure that the type of (possibly shifted) arguments match that of their (possibly shifted) functors. We can think of the official syntactic categories as the public syntax, the rules which characterize which strings can combine with which other strings. The semantic types, then, are private syntactic categories, a record of the internal adjustments that an expression makes in order to prepare for combination with their possibly shifted siblings. This is parallel to the formal system in Part I, with the role of public syntax played by the syntactic categories below the horizontal line in the tower system, with the categories in the layers above the horizontal line tracking type-shifting.

More substantively, like the tower system, Flexible Montague Grammar provides a general lifting mechanism: for any type τ with translation f, choose $n = 0$ and apply Value Raising to derive $(\tau \to \tau_2) \to \tau_2$ with translation $\lambda\kappa.\kappa f$.

In contrast with our system, Flexible Montague Grammar does not provide a general LOWERing mechanism. Instead, Argument Raising combines the effects of lifting, scoping, and lowering into a single shifting operation. We will suggest below that the absence of a separate, generally available LOWER operation prevents Flexible Montague Grammar from allowing full control over order of evaluation.

Nevertheless, Flexible Montague Grammar is able to deliver a wide range of scoping analyses. One source of this flexibility is that each application of Value Raising introduces a new scope-taking layer, where each layer corresponds to one level in a type tower. Using layers, it is possible to interleave the scopes of scope-taking operators embedded in different predicates.

(119) Someone called two aides from every borough.

For instance, Flexible Montague Grammar can provide an analysis of this sentence on which *every* outscopes *someone*, which in turn outscopes *two*. We will present a derivation of this reading in some detail, despite the somewhat intricate details involved, since it illustrates the sense in which Flexible Montague Grammar in effect constructs continuation layers on the fly.

Before presenting the derivation, we should note that many authors claim that the interleaved interpretation is not among the meanings that can be expressed by the sentence in question (see Heim and Kratzer 1998:233 for discussion). Certainly the interleaved interpretation is more difficult for most native speakers than the other relative scopings. This issues makes it all the more revealing of an example of the expressive power of Flexible Montague Grammar.

We can do all our type shifting for lexical items in advance:

(120)

VR(AR(two))	$\frac{\mathtt{t} \mid \mathtt{t}}{\mathtt{e} \to \mathtt{t}} \to \begin{array}{c}\mathtt{t} \mid \mathtt{t} \\ \hline \mathtt{t} \mid \mathtt{t} \\ \hline \mathtt{e}\end{array}$	$\lambda P'\kappa.P'(\lambda P.\kappa(\mathbf{two}\ P))$
aides	$(\mathtt{e} \to \mathtt{t})$	**aides**
AR(VR(from))	$\frac{\mathtt{t} \mid \mathtt{t}}{\mathtt{e}} \to (\mathtt{e} \to \mathtt{t}) \to \frac{\mathtt{t} \mid \mathtt{t}}{\mathtt{e} \to \mathtt{t}}$	$\lambda\mathcal{P}P\kappa.\mathcal{P}(\lambda x.\kappa(\mathbf{from}\ x\ P))$
every	$(\mathtt{e} \to \mathtt{t}) \to \frac{\mathtt{t} \mid \mathtt{t}}{\mathtt{e}}$	**every**
borough	$(\mathtt{e} \to \mathtt{t})$	**borough**

In order to allow a quantifier to take scope in between the cardinal and the universal, it is necessary for the universal to occupy a distinct layer from the cardinal. The relevant layer is created by an application of VR to *from* (since *from* is the first local predicate taking *every borough* as an argument). There is a corresponding application of VR in the next predicate up (i.e., the cardinal *two*).

(121)

$$\underbrace{\frac{\mathtt{t} \mid \mathtt{t}}{\mathtt{e} \to \mathtt{t}} \to \begin{array}{c}\mathtt{t} \mid \mathtt{t} \\ \hline \mathtt{t} \mid \mathtt{t} \\ \hline \mathtt{e}\end{array}}_{\textit{two}} \left(\underset{\textit{aides}}{(\mathtt{e} \to \mathtt{t})} \left(\underset{\textit{from}}{\frac{\mathtt{t} \mid \mathtt{t}}{\mathtt{e}} \to (\mathtt{e} \to \mathtt{t}) \to \frac{\mathtt{t} \mid \mathtt{t}}{\mathtt{e} \to \mathtt{t}}} \left(\underset{\textit{every}}{(\mathtt{e} \to \mathtt{t}) \to \frac{\mathtt{t} \mid \mathtt{t}}{\mathtt{e}}} \ \underset{\textit{borough}}{(\mathtt{e} \to \mathtt{t})} \right)\right)\right)$$

(122)

$$\begin{array}{c}\mathtt{t} \mid \mathtt{t} \\ \hline \mathtt{t} \mid \mathtt{t} \\ \hline \mathtt{e}\end{array} : \lambda\kappa.(\mathbf{every\ borough})(\lambda x.\kappa(\mathbf{two}(\mathbf{from}\ x\ \mathbf{aides})))$$

The quantifier introduced by *every* occupies the highest layer, and the quantifier introduced by *two* occupies the middle layer. Thus the continuation variable κ provides access to a scope position intermediate between *every* and *two*.

When combination reaches the matrix predicate *called*, we interleave the scope of the quantifiers by interleaving applications of Argument Raising: AR first targets the direct object argument (giving narrowest scope to the lower layer of *two aides from every borough*), then the subject (giving intervening scope to the *someone*), and finally, targeting the direct object again, giving widest scope to the higher layer of the direct object.

(123)

$$\begin{array}{rll}
\text{called} & \mathtt{e} \to \mathtt{e} \to \mathtt{t} & \mathbf{call} \\[1ex]
\text{AR} \Rightarrow \text{called} & \dfrac{\mathtt{t} \mid \mathtt{t}}{\mathtt{e}} \to \mathtt{e} \to \mathtt{t} & \lambda \mathcal{P} y.\mathcal{P}(\lambda x.\mathbf{call}\; y\; x) \\[2ex]
\text{AR} \Rightarrow \text{called} & \dfrac{\mathtt{t} \mid \mathtt{t}}{\mathtt{e}} \to \dfrac{\mathtt{t} \mid \mathtt{t}}{\mathtt{e}} \to \mathtt{t} & \lambda \mathcal{P}\mathcal{Q}.\mathcal{Q}(\lambda y.\mathcal{P}(\lambda x.\mathbf{call}\; x\; y)) \\[3ex]
\text{AR} \Rightarrow \text{called} & \dfrac{\mathtt{t} \mid \mathtt{t}}{\dfrac{\mathtt{t} \mid \mathtt{t}}{\mathtt{e}}} \to \dfrac{\mathtt{t} \mid \mathtt{t}}{\mathtt{e}} \to \mathtt{t} & \lambda \mathcal{P}'\mathcal{Q}.\mathcal{P}'(\lambda \mathcal{P}.\mathcal{Q}(\lambda y.\mathcal{P}(\lambda x.\mathbf{call}\; x\; y)))
\end{array}$$

Applying the (multiply shifted) interpretation of *called* to the derived interpretation of *two aides from every borough* shows how the the scope-taking layers contributed by the direct object make a sandwich, with the subject denotation in the middle.

(124)
$$\begin{array}{l}
([\lambda \mathcal{P}'\mathcal{Q}.\mathcal{P}'(\lambda \mathcal{P}.\mathcal{Q}(\lambda y.\mathcal{P}(\lambda x.\mathbf{call}\; x\; y)))] \\
\quad (\lambda \kappa.(\mathbf{every\ borough})(\lambda x.\kappa(\mathbf{two}(\mathbf{from}\; x\; \mathbf{aides}))))) \\
= \lambda \mathcal{Q}.(\mathbf{e.b.})(\lambda x.\mathcal{Q}(\lambda y.[\mathbf{two}(\mathbf{from}\; x\; \mathbf{aides})](\lambda x.\mathbf{call}\; x\; y)))
\end{array}$$

Once we apply this verb phrase meaning to the generalized quantifier denoted by the subject *someone*, we have *every* taking scope over *someone*, which takes scope over *two*, which was our goal.

Although Flexible Montague Grammar generates a wide range of scope ambiguities, as we have just seen, it is not a fully general scope-taking mechanism. In particular, there is no way for effects introduced by a functor to take wide scope over its arguments. For instance, in Barker and Shan (2008:30), quantificational determiners can take wide scope over their nominal arguments. In order to see why this is not possible in Flexible Montague Grammar, imagine that the type of the quantificational determiner is $(\mathtt{e} \to \mathtt{t}) \to (\mathtt{e} \to \mathtt{t}) \to \mathtt{t}$ (as usual). If the first argument (the nominal) contains a quantifier (or other effect), it can shift via Argument Raising, but any application of Argument Raising will necessarily give the nominal's effect wide scope over the quantification introduced by the quantifier.

For a second example, it is not clear how to extend Flexible Montague Grammar to handle the sort of parasitic scope advocated by Barker (2007) and discussed in detail in Part II of this book.

Whatever the merits of these analyses, our point here is that there are proposals for scope-taking in the literature that go beyond the expressive power of Flexible Montague Grammar.

7.6 Adding binding to Flexible Montague Grammar

Because Flexible Montague Grammar separates scope-taking into layers, we can consider adding a Bind type-shifter that serves the same purpose as the one given in our main system.

Binding for Flexible Montague Grammar: if an expression ϕ has type

$$a_1 \to a_2 \to \ldots \to ((\mathsf{e} \to r) \to r') \to \ldots \to a_n \to r$$

and translation f, then ϕ also has type

$$a_1 \to a_2 \to \ldots \to ((\mathsf{e} \to (\mathsf{e} \to r)) \to r') \to \ldots \to a_n \to r,$$

with translation $\lambda x_1 x_2 \ldots x_i \ldots x_n . f x_1 x_2 \ldots (\lambda x . x_i x x) \ldots x_n$.

If we give pronouns the category DP and the type $\frac{\mathsf{e} \to \mathsf{t} \,|\, \mathsf{t}}{\mathsf{e}}$, then we would have a suitable derivation for the bound reading of, say, *Everyone$_i$ loves his$_i$ mother*. (This strategy relies on the slight generalization of Argument Raising discussed above, since it depends on the ability of a scope-taking element to manipulate result types.)

However, because there are no restrictions on the order in which Argument Raising applies to the arguments of a predicate, it would be equally easy to incorrectly derive the weak crossover example **His$_i$ mother loves everyone$_i$*. We could imagine adding constraints based on linear order, but only if we abandon Hendriks' strategy of basing his type-shifters purely on the semantic types of the expressions involved. This is feasible, of course, although there will have to be a considerable number of versions of both Argument Raising and of Value Raising (basically, a different version for each possible linear configuration of arguments). We could then forbid Argument Raising from targeting any argument to the left of an argument targeted by a previous application of Argument Raising.

If we did so, then we would be faced with the problem of restoring the ability to take inverse scope. We could do this by adding a variant of Value Raising that allowed a rightmost argument to take its quantificational effect at a higher layer. But because there is no way to eliminate layers in unembedded expressions, we would then need to add a general Lower typeshifter independent of Argument Raising.

Of course, once we add a binding type-shifter, make the system sensitive to linear order, restore inverse scope with an internal Lift type-shifter, and add a Lower type-shifter, we will have in effect recreated our main system.

Conclusion: Flexible Montague Grammar is a continuation-based system that is adequate for generating a wide range of scope relationships, but it is not well suited for exploring the role of evaluation order on interpretation.

8

Order effects in negative polarity licensing

We've argued that continuations are a natural fit for scope-taking, and that one of the main advantages of using continuations for scope is that it makes possible a principled account of order sensitivity for crossover and for reconstruction. What other effects of evaluation order might there be? We suspect that the importance of order has been under-appreciated, in part because the lack of formal tools for accounting for order effects has prevented people from looking for them, or from pursuing them when they find them.

In subsequent chapters, chapters 9 and 10, we will explore evaluation order effects in donkey anaphora.

This chapter shows how evaluation order can shed light on what has long been a puzzling sensitivity to linear order in negative polarity licensing.

(125) a. No one saw anyone.
 b. *Anyone saw no one.

In general, negative polarity items (NPIs) such as *anyone* require the presence of a licensor, illustrated here with the downward-entailing quantifier *no one*. We can assume that the licensor quantifier takes scope over the entire sentence in both examples. But it is not enough for the licensor to take scope over the NPI—it must also precede the NPI.

(126) a. I gave nothing to anybody.
 b. *I gave anything to nobody.
 c. I gave nobody anything.
 d. *I gave anybody nothing.

Ladusaw (1979) notes this mystery in his Inherent Scope Condition: "If the NPI is clausemate with the trigger, the trigger must precede" (section 4.4). He goes on (section 9.2) to speculate that this left-right requirement is related to quantifier scope and sentence processing, just as we are claiming:

I do not at this point see how to make this part of the Inherent Scope Condition follow from any other semantic principle. This may be because the left-right restriction, like the left-right rule for unmarked scope relations, should be made to follow from the syntactic and semantic processing of sentences ....

This is exactly the kind of explanation our formal system aims to provide. More precisely, we will suggest that a trigger for licensing a negative polarity item must not only take scope over the NPI, it must be evaluated before the NPI.

8.1 Negative polarity, order, and scope

The field of negative polarity licensing is vast and intricate, and we cannot attempt a full-scale analysis here. Our more modest goal is to show how evaluation order can interact with a rudimentary analysis in a way that improves the accuracy of that analysis. Our hope is that an evaluation-order bias can be factored into a more sophisticated account of NPI licensing.

Which polarity items are licensed or prohibited in a given linguistic environment depends, to a high but limited degree, on semantic properties of that environment, as argued by Ladusaw (1979), Krifka (1995), Giannakidou (2011) and Chierchia (2013), inter alia. For example, some NPIs can be licensed in certain downward-entailing contexts, such as under the scope of a monotonically decreasing quantifier. A quantifier q, of type $(\mathtt{e} \to \mathtt{t}) \to \mathtt{t}$, is monotonically decreasing just in case

(127) $\forall s_1.\, \forall s_2.\, \big(\forall x.\, s_2(x) \to s_1(x)\big) \to (q(s_1) \to q(s_2)).$

Thus (128a) is acceptable because the scope of *no one* is downward-entailing, while (128b) and (128c) are unacceptable.

(128) a. No one saw anyone.
b. *Everyone saw anyone.
c. *Alice saw anyone.

Note that it is a requirement that the negative polarity item be in the scope of the licensor. To see this, observe that (128a) is unambiguous, and means only $\neg\exists x \exists y.\mathbf{saw}\, y\, x$. If *anyone* could take wide scope, we would incorrectly predict that (128a) could mean $\exists y \neg\exists x.\mathbf{saw}\, y\, x$.

Yet merely being in the scope of a downward-entailing quantifier is not a sufficient condition.

(129) *No one thought everyone saw anyone.

In this example, based on Linebarger (1980), even though *anyone* is in the nuclear scope of *no one*, the intervening presence of the upward-entailing *everyone* disrupts the licensing relation. Like many researchers, we take such facts to show that although negative polarity licensing is primarily semantic, it has an irreducible syntactic component, and requires careful attention to the syntax/semantics interface.

Going one level deeper, whether an operator disrupts NPI licensing in a particular sentence is not purely a function of syntactic configuration, but also depends on scope relations. If the potential disruptor does not take scope over the NPI in question, there is no disruption:

(130) a. No one gave anyone everything.
b. $\neg\exists z\exists y\forall x.\mathbf{gave}\ x\ y\ z$
c. $*\neg\exists z\forall x\exists y.\mathbf{gave}\ x\ y\ z$

If the indefinite NPI *anyone* outscopes the universal *everything*, as in the paraphrase in (130b), the subject quantifier *no one* licenses the NPI, so that (130a) is grammatical on the given interpretation. These truth conditions require only that no single person received everything.

If the universal does take scope over the NPI, as in the paraphrase in (130c), the truth conditions require in addition that no one gives away everything, not even by distributing the gifts across several recipients. In this case there is an intervention effect, and the sentence is ungrammatical on this construal. Kroch (1974), Linebarger (1980), and Szabolcsi (2004) discuss such intervention cases.

In other words, we need a system that does the following things: it must track both syntactic and semantic features, it must impose a linear order bias, and it must automatically take into account the interaction of scope with a syntactically-mediated dependency. This describes in general terms exactly the system we have developed above for explaining the interaction of scope with binding.

In this analogy, the connection between an NPI and its licensor corresponds to the connection between a pronoun and its binder. In order to emphasize the parallel with quantificational binding, here are some examples in which the ability of the quantifier *no one* to bind a pronoun behaves similarly to its ability to license the negative polarity item *anyone*:

(131) a. No one$_i$ called his$_i$ mother.
b. No one called anyone's mother.

A quantifier in subject position can bind a pronoun inside the direct object, just as an NPI licensor can license an NPI in a similar configuration.

(132) a. [No one$_i$'s mother] called him$_i$.
b. [No one's mother] called anyone.

Just as in quantificational binding, it is not necessary for the quantifier to c-command the NPI in order to license it.

(133) a. *His$_i$ mother called no one$_i$.
b. *Anyone's mother called no one.

In the same configuration in which we see a crossover violation, the NPI licensing does not go through. Apparently, in some configurations, it is not enough for the licensor to take scope over the dependent element, it must also precede the NPI.

Because Fry (1997, 1999), Bernardi (2002), and Bernardi and Moot (2001) focus on quantification and scope, they easily characterize how *no* must scope over *any* in order to license it, but they leave it a mystery why *no* must precede *any* in order to license it. In particular, they wrongly accept all of (125)–(126).

Developing the analogy with crossover further, we now turn to cases in which the licensor and the NPI both follow the verb.

(134) a. John sent no one$_i$ his$_i$ grade.
b. John sent no one$_i$ anyone's grade.

(135) a. John sent no one$_i$ to his$_i$ home town.
b. John sent no one$_i$ to anyone's home town.

Whether in the double-object construction, as in (134), or with a preposition-marked indirect object, as in (135), binding and NPI licensing are fine when the quantifier in question precedes the pronoun or NPI.

Note also that if we replace *no one* with *no one's mother* in each of these examples, grammaticality is unaffected, showing once again that surface c-command is not required for NPI licensing. Just to drive home this point:

(136) John gave [the phone number of no one's mother] to anyone.

This example provides an example in which the licensor is deeply embedded within the direct object, yet can still license a following negative polarity item.

But if the order of the quantifier and the dependent element is reversed, both binding and NPI licensing are disrupted.

(137) a. *John sent his$_i$ mother no one$_i$.
b. *John sent anyone's mother no one$_i$.

(138) a. ?John sent his$_i$ grade to no one$_i$'s mother.
b. *John sent anyone's grade to no one's mother.

The examples in which the pronoun precedes the quantifier give rise to crossover violations, and likewise the examples in which the NPI precedes the quantifier are ungrammatical.

8.2 An evaluation-order account

The analysis here is based on discussion in Shan (2004), Shan (2003a), and Barker and Shan (2006).

Our hypothesis is that continuations provide precisely the missing link between linear order and quantifier scope.

Just as in our account of binding, there will be a chain of matching syntactic categories that links the dependent element to the thing that it depends on. Because this kind of linking can only be established within a single continuation layer, it is subject to the left-to-right evaluation default.

In order to track licensing environments syntactically, we will make use of clause subtyping, in the spirit of the approaches to negative polarity licensing in Dowty (1994), and Bernardi (2002), Bernardi and Moot (2001), Bernardi and Szabolcsi (2008), Fry (1997, 1999), and others. Then let 'S^-' be a special kind of clause, a proper subset of the the category 'S'. We can now assign the following categories to different quantifiers in the lexicon:

(139) everyone: $\dfrac{S \mid S}{DP}$, no one: $\dfrac{S \mid S^-}{DP}$, anyone: $\dfrac{S^- \mid S^-}{DP}$.

The type of *everyone* is unchanged: it takes scope over a normal clause to form a normal clause. The types of *no one* and *anyone* involve the newly introduced S^-: they both take scope over a negative clause, but *no one* forms a neutral clause, whereas *anyone* forms a negative clause. As long as only neutral clauses count as complete utterances, the only way for an NPI to be licensed is for there to be some trigger upstream that knows how to turn a S^- into an S.

(140)
$$\left(\begin{matrix}\dfrac{S \mid S^-}{DP} & \dfrac{S^- \mid S^-}{DP\backslash DP} \\ \textit{no one's} & \textit{mother} \\ \dfrac{\neg\exists x.[\;]}{x} & \dfrac{[\;]}{\textbf{mother}}\end{matrix}\right)\left(\begin{matrix}\dfrac{S^- \mid S^-}{(DP\backslash S)/DP} & \dfrac{S^- \mid S}{DP} \\ \textit{loves} & \textit{anyone} \\ \dfrac{[\;]}{\textbf{loves}} & \dfrac{\exists y.[\;]}{y}\end{matrix}\right)$$

In this grammatical example, the category after combination and LOWERing is a plain S, as desired. Note that just as with quantificational binding, c-command is irrelevant in this approach for negative polarity licensing.

Clearly, if the order of the quantifier and the NPI are reversed, the derivation will not constitute a complete utterance: the final category will be $\dfrac{S^- \mid S^-}{S}$, which does not match the input schema of the LOWER type-shifter.

Accounting for the way that upward-monotone quantifiers disrupt licensing depending on their scope interpretation, as discussed above for (130), is also straightforward:

$$(141)\quad \begin{array}{c} S\,|\,S^- \\ \hline DP \\ \textit{no one} \\ \neg\exists x.[\,] \\ \hline x \end{array} \left(\left(\begin{array}{c} S^- \,|\, S^- \\ \hline ((DP\backslash S)/DP)/DP \\ \textit{gave} \\ [\,] \\ \hline \textbf{gave} \end{array} \quad \begin{array}{c} S^-\,|\,S \\ \hline DP \\ \textit{anyone} \\ \exists y.[\,] \\ \hline y \end{array} \right) \begin{array}{c} S\,|\,S \\ \hline DP \\ \textit{everything} \\ \forall z.[\,] \\ \hline z \end{array} \right)$$

In this derivation, both *no one* and the NPI *anyone* take linear scope over *everyone.* The licensing relation goes through, deriving the attested interpretation described in (130b).

If we try to allow the universal to take intermediate scope, the licensing relation is disrupted. In order for the universal to take inverse scope over the NPI, the universal must LIFT, since that is the only way to achieve inverse scope. But since we're aiming for an interpretation on which the subject quantifier takes widest scope, it must also LIFT. But this is incompatible with *no one* satisfying the need created by *anyone* to have its S^- category replaced by a normal S.

$$(142)\quad \begin{array}{c} S\,|\,S^- \\ \hline S^-\,|\,S^- \\ \hline DP \\ \textit{no one} \\ \forall x.[\,]x \\ \hline [\,] \\ \hline x \end{array} \left(\left(\begin{array}{c} S^-\,|\,S^- \\ \hline S^-\,|\,S^- \\ \hline ((DP\backslash S)/DP)/DP \\ \textit{gave} \\ [\,] \\ \hline [\,] \\ \hline \textbf{gave} \end{array} \quad \begin{array}{c} S^-\,|\,S^- \\ \hline S^-\,|\,S \\ \hline DP \\ \textit{anyone} \\ [\,] \\ \hline \exists y.[\,] \\ \hline y \end{array} \right) \begin{array}{c} S^-\,|\,S^- \\ \hline S\,|\,S \\ \hline DP \\ \textit{everything} \\ \forall z.[\,] \\ \hline [\,] \\ \hline z \end{array} \right)$$

The S^-'s on the top layer are forced by the lexical entry for *no one.* The S^-'s on the middle layer are forced by the lexical entry for *anyone.* After combination, we are stuck with the category $\begin{array}{c} S\,|\,S^- \\ \hline S^-\,|\,S \\ \hline S \end{array}$. We can LOWER once at the bottom level, but S^- categories remain uneliminated, and the derivation is not complete.

Once again, in a way that is highly parallel to the situation with weak crossover, inverse scope has disrupted a syntactically-mediated connection.

Of course, there are many other NPI licensors besides downward-entailing quantifiers. To give just one example, we can give auxiliary-verb sentence negation *not* the category $\frac{S\,|\,S^-}{\text{Aux}}$ (where 'Aux' is the syntactic category of a verb phrase modifier). Then we correctly predict that the NPI in *Alice did not see anyone* is licensed, but not **Anyone did not see Alice.*

EXERCISE 21

What problem occurs when an NPI licensor like *no one* or *not* occurs in a sentence in which there is no negative polarity item? Propose two solutions, one in the form of a type-shifting rule, and one that involves multiple lexical items.

EXERCISE 22

Why not assign *anyone* the simpler category $\frac{S^- | S}{DP}$? Derive *No one gave anyone anything*.

EXERCISE 23

Show that doubly-licensed NPIs are correctly predicted to be grammatical, e.g., *No one doubted anyone left*. Assume *doubted* licenses NPIs, as in *John doubts anyone left*.

8.3 Other theories of order in NPI licensing

Recent works on negative polarity, even thorough and wide-ranging surveys such as Giannakidou (2011), do not address order effects. We are currently aware of only two theories of NPI licensing that consider contrasts corresponding to a difference in order: de Swart (1998), and Collins and Postal (2014).

de Swart (1998) argues that a trigger must c-command an NPI in order to license it, unless the sentence entails or implicates a fact that is 'positive' in some informational sense.

(143) a. Examples with any relevance didn't come up in the discussion.
b. Examples with no relevance did come up in the discussion.

According to this hypothesis, the reason the NPI in (143a) can precede its licensor (the sentence negation) is because the sentence implicates the positive fact in (143b). But even granting that examples like (143a) are systematically grammatical, and that informational structure is crucial in exactly the way suggested by de Swart, there would still be a linear order mystery that remained to be explained. The reason is that, given the many counterexamples presented throughout the chapter, we have to conclude that c-command is not a requirement for licensing an NPI. Nor can we detect any difference in the kind of entailments or implicatures between the members of minimal pairs such as that in (125). This means that an explanation for the full pattern of sensitivity to linear order requires more than sensitivity to informational structure. Our suggestion, of course, is that the required extra element is a general requirement that a quantificational trigger must be evaluated before any NPI it licenses.

Collins and Postal (2014) (chapter 6) do not explicitly address linear order, but they do discuss the following contrast:

(144) a. No man loves any woman.
b. *Any man loves no woman.

On their account, the subject and the direct object form a discontinuous 'polyadic' quantifier, quantifying over man-woman pairs. This situation arises when there is a single abstract determiner [NEG SOME] that forms a part of two different DPs, implemented perhaps by allowing a single expression token to participate in two distinct merge operations. (A later rule inserts distinct copies into each position.) So initially, the subject DP [[NEG SOME] man] and the object DP [[NEG SOME] woman] are completely parallel with respect to their determiner position, and it is up for grabs which one will surface as "no N" and which one as "any N".

The symmetry is broken by a rule (see chapters 6 and 8 of Collins and Postal 2014) that deletes the NEG part of any component of a discontinuous determiner that is c-commanded at LF by some other component. Then a morphological rule spells out [NEG SOME] as *no*, and [SOME] as *any*. Therefore it is only when we add the assumption that [[NEG SOME] man] c-commands [[NEG SOME] woman] at LF that we get (144a) correctly predicted good, and (144b) correctly predicted ungrammatical. The order effects hinge, then, on making sure that the leftmost element of the polyadic quantifier c-commands the other elements at LF.

The question, then, is what guarantees this? Collins and Postal assume that DPs may be moved into LF position by Quantifier Raising. But, as they note in their chapter 8, Quantifier Raising certainly does not guarantee that scope relations at LF mirror linear order: to allow for inverse scope with ordinary (non-NPI) quantifiers, it must be possible for, say, a direct object quantifier to c-command a subject quantifier at LF.

Furthermore, it would be problematic to assume that c-command relations at LF mirror c-command relations at the surface, even restricting attention specifically to polyadic quantifiers. In fact, as expected on our account and as illustrated in (140), a quantifier can license an NPI even if the quantifier does not c-command the NPI on the surface.

(145) a. John gave [the address of no one's mother] to anyone.
b. *John gave [the address of anyone's mother] to no one.

To the extent that there is a contrast between these examples, the challenge to the syntactic approach of Collins and Postal (2014) is that it appears that it is order, and not c-command relations, that determines which element can surface as an NPI.

On our account, the contrast in (145) follows directly from the left-to-right evaluation order built into the combination schema.

9

Donkey anaphora and donkey crossover

In chapter 3, we suggested that the dynamic view of meaning arises naturally from taking a continuation-aware perspective on composition. The reason is that on the continuations view, a sentence denotes a function on its own continuation, just like every expression type does. That is the same thing as denoting a function on the remainder of the discourse in which it is embedded, which is the essence of the dynamic view.

One of the main applications of dynamic semantics has been anaphora in general, as discussed briefly in chapter 3, concentrating on donkey anaphora in particular (e.g., Groenendijk and Stokhof 1991, 1990). We should consider, then, what the tower fragment has to say about donkey anaphora.

In this chapter, we will consider donkey anaphora in conditional clauses, and we will stick fairly closely to the proposal in Barker and Shan (2008). In the next chapter, we will consider several strategies for dealing with donkey anaphora when the donkey indefinite is embedded within a DP.

Our account has a number of unusual features. Most notably, on our analysis, an indefinite will only bind a pronoun if the indefinite takes scope over the pronoun. As we will discuss, this is an assumption which runs very much against the grain of other analyses, which perhaps universally assume that a donkey pronoun is not in the scope of the indefinite that controls its value.

We should say what we mean by being in the scope of an indefinite. On the traditional dynamic view, there are supposed to be several kinds of scope-taking. Since quantifier scope ambiguity is handled by the usual Quantifier Raising technique, an indefinite's *logical* scope will be the material that it c-commands at LF. But since binding is handled by treating clauses as updates on sets of assignment functions, an indefinite's *binding* scope will be the region over which it is able to affect the value of a variable. Most dynamic theories are designed to enable the binding scope of an indefinite to be larger than its logical scope.

In contrast, on the account here, there is only one kind of scope, namely, the scope that corresponds to the continuation of the quantifier. A pronoun or other expression will be in the scope of a quantifier just in case it is part of the material that contributes to the continuation that serves as the semantic argument of the quantifier. One way of stating the hypothesis developed in this chapter, then, is that an indefinite's binding scope is contained within its logical scope.

This aspect of our analysis is not forced by taking a continuation-based approach. Rather, as we will explain, it arises in large part from a desire to keep the formal complexity of the system as simple as possible. If we wanted to allow a pronoun to covary with an indefinite that did not take scope over it, we would need to add extra compositional mechanisms such as assignment functions, or model-theoretic situations, or some other discourse-referent tracking mechanism, all of which we have so far done without in this book. There would be no difficulty adding such mechanisms if desired; Charlow (2014) explains one way of integrating additional machinery into a continuation-based core grammar.

But even if a separate mechanism for indefinites is ultimately necessary, it will still be instructive and worthwhile to see how far we can get using only LIFT, LOWER, BIND, FRONT, and the combination schema. We'll argue that we can get quite far even with our minimalist architecture.

After developing the basic account, we will return to the larger theme of Part I, namely, evaluation order. We will show that the proposed analysis makes good predictions about the effect of evaluation order on the availability of donkey anaphora, including examples of so-called 'donkey crossover'. Despite the fact that traditional dynamic accounts are explicitly concerned with order effects with respect to at least anaphora and coordination, those accounts at best fail to make predictions about donkey crossover. (This is a point emphasized by Charlow 2014.)

9.1 Donkey anaphora as in-scope binding

'Donkey anaphora' is the name for situations in which an indefinite and a pronoun covary exactly as if the indefinite were binding the pronoun, yet there is some reason to suspect that the indefinite should not be able to bind the pronoun.

(146) a. If a farmer owns a donkey, he beats it.
b. Every farmer who owns a donkey beats it.

In both of these examples, for each relevant case of a farmer and a donkey, the value of the pronoun *it* tracks the choice of the donkey. The issue, then, is whether the indefinite takes scope over and binds the pronoun, or whether the covariance is achieved through indirect means.

In order to fit this discussion into the larger landscape explored in this book, we already know that scope and binding can come apart in one way: crossover examples are exactly cases in which a quantifier can take scope over a syntactic position that it cannot bind. For instance, in *Someone likes everyone*, the quantifier *everyone* can take scope over the subject *someone*, since on the inverse-scope reading, there is a potentially different choice of liker for each choice of likee, but in *His mother likes everyone*, it is not possible for the quantifier to bind the pronoun in subject position. So there is strong evidence that the scope domain for a quantifier can include regions that are excluded from the binding domain for that quantifier. Our explanation for this fact is that binding depends both on scope and on evaluation order. Since the requirements for binding are more stringent than the requirements for taking scope, the scope domain of a quantifier can be strictly larger than its binding domain.

Donkey anaphora is supposed to be a case in which scope and binding come apart in the other direction, where the binding domain of an indefinite is strictly larger than its scope domain. The evidence for this claim, we will argue, is not so strong. In fact, we will make a case in favor of the view that donkey anaphora is ordinary quantificational binding, in which the donkey indefinite both takes scope over and binds the donkey pronoun.

One reason people discount the possibility that the indefinite binds the pronoun in the ordinary way in examples like those in (146) is a tradition going back at least to Evans (1977) and chapter 3 of May (1977) that says that the scope of all quantifiers is clause bounded.

(147) a. *[Everyone$_i$ arrived] and [she$_i$ spoke].
b. A woman$_i$ arrived and she$_i$ spoke.

If *everyone* can only take scope over the first clausal conjunct in (147a), that explains why it cannot bind the pronoun in the second. But it has been known at least since Farkas (2003) (first published in 1981; see Barker 2014b or Szabolcsi 2010 for a fuller picture of the data) that the scope options for indefinites are strikingly different from those of *every* and certain other quantifiers. And in fact when *everyone* in (147a) is replaced with an indefinite, as in (147b), covariation becomes possible, as indicated by coindexing. We will continue to assume, as we have throughout the previous chapters, that this fact has a simple explanation: indefinites are able to take wide scope—in many cases, wider than the minimal clause that contains them.

A second common reason to reject postulating a binding relationship in (146) is the widespread belief that quantificational binding requires c-command. But for reasons discussed in section 2.1, we assume that c-command simply isn't required for quantificational binding. In any case, as we have emphasized repeatedly, our formal system certainly allows a quantifier to bind a pronoun that it doesn't c-command (e.g., as in the derivation in (32)). So in particular, a failure to c-command is no impediment here to having indefinites take scope over their respective donkey pronouns and bind them.

Thus we will suppose that the reason donkey indefinites appear to bind donkey pronouns is because they do bind them, with exactly the same sort of binding that holds between the quantifier and the pronoun in *Everyone$_i$ thinks he$_i$ left*.

However, we must still confront the fact that on our view, in order for the indefinite to bind the pronoun, it must take scope over the pronoun. Clearly, giving the indefinite scope over the entire sentence does not lead to the desired set of truth conditions:

(148) a. If a donkey eats, it sleeps.
b. $\exists d.\ (\mathbf{donkey}\ d) \wedge (\mathbf{eats}\ d \rightarrow \mathbf{sleeps}\ d)$

If the indefinite takes scope over the entire sentence, we get the truth conditions for (148a) given in (148b). Given a sufficiently rich context, the sentence probably has a reading along these lines (setting aside for now the oversimplification of using material implication to model the semantics of the conditional). But as Evans (1980:342) points out, the most natural reading of (148a) is not that there is some special donkey that sleeps when it eats, but rather that when *any* donkey eats, that donkey sleeps. Evans concludes that the indefinite must take scope inside the antecedent clause, leaving the pronoun unbound.

This conclusion is too strong. A more conservative conclusion is that the indefinite must scope underneath whatever operator delivers the universal force of the generalization. Since this universalizing operator clearly takes scope over the entire sentence, it remains possible for the indefinite to take scope under that operator, and yet still take scope over the entire clause, including over the consequent.

More concretely, if we associate the universalist force of the conditions with the lexical item *if*, we have the following situation: as long as the donkey indefinite takes scope under the *if*, we get reasonable truth conditions for the indefinite. And as long as the *if* takes scope over the entire sentence, as it must in order to arrive at the appropriate truth conditions, the indefinite will be free to scope over the donkey pronoun, and to bind it.

The way in which we will make *if* a scope-taking operator is by giving it the following lexical entry:

(149)
$$\begin{array}{c} \mathrm{S}\,|\,\mathrm{S} \\ \hline (\mathrm{S}/\mathrm{S})/\mathrm{S} \\ \textit{if} \\ \neg[\ ] \\ \hline \lambda pq.p \wedge \neg q \end{array}$$

Crucially, in the semantic tower, the outer negation is above the horizontal line, where it can take scope over the entire conditional. The conjunction and the inner negation are below the line, in order to combine first with the antecedent, and then with the consequent.

(150)

$$\begin{array}{c} \dfrac{\mathrm{S} \mid \mathrm{S}}{(\mathrm{S/S})/\mathrm{S}} \\ \textit{if} \\ \dfrac{\neg[\,]}{\lambda pq.p \wedge \neg q} \end{array} \left(\begin{array}{c} \dfrac{\mathrm{S} \mid \mathrm{DP} \rhd \mathrm{S}}{\mathrm{DP}} \\ \textit{someone} \\ \dfrac{\exists y.[\,]y}{y} \end{array} \quad \begin{array}{c} \dfrac{\mathrm{DP} \rhd \mathrm{S} \mid \mathrm{DP} \rhd \mathrm{S}}{\mathrm{DP\backslash S}} \\ \textit{knocked} \\ \dfrac{[\,]}{\mathbf{knocked}} \end{array} \right) \left(\begin{array}{c} \dfrac{\mathrm{DP} \rhd \mathrm{S} \mid \mathrm{S}}{\mathrm{DP}} \\ \textit{she} \\ \dfrac{\lambda x.[\,]}{x} \end{array} \quad \begin{array}{c} \dfrac{\mathrm{S} \mid \mathrm{S}}{\mathrm{DP\backslash S}} \\ \textit{left} \\ \dfrac{[\,]}{\mathbf{left}} \end{array} \right)$$

The indefinite takes scope over the consequent and binds the pronoun, which accounts for covariance. The outer negation contributed by the *if* takes even wider scope. It is the interaction of the negation with the existential that delivers the universal force of the conditional. After combination, we have

(151)

$$\begin{array}{c} \dfrac{\mathrm{S} \mid \mathrm{S}}{\mathrm{S}} \\ \dfrac{\neg\exists y.((\lambda x.[\,])\,y)}{\mathbf{knocked}\,y \wedge \neg(\mathbf{left}\,x)} \end{array} \quad \overset{\text{Lower}}{\Rightarrow} \quad \begin{array}{c} \mathrm{S} \\ \neg\exists y.\,\mathbf{knocked}\,y \wedge \neg(\mathbf{left}\,y) \end{array}$$

These truth conditions say that no one knocked without leaving, which is a reasonable approximation of the truth conditions of a donkey conditional.

We know of one other proposal that a lexical item could introduce a negation that takes scope separate from other semantic elements introduced by that lexical item: Jacobs (1980) advocates decomposing German *kein* 'no' into negation plus existential quantification so that other quantificational elements can take scope between the negation and the existential. The proposal remains controversial (Jacobs 1980, Geurts 1996, de Swart 2000, Penka and Zeijlstra 2005, Penka 2012, among others). In particular, Geurts (1996) criticizes lexical decomposition as implemented by Jacobs as an unwelcome extension of the expressive power of the formal system. However, that criticism does not apply here, since our analysis for *if* does not rely on any formal resources beyond those already required for basic quantification.

The next few sections will work through some of the basics that any account of donkey anaphora has to deal with, including: the ability of universal quantifiers to disrupt donkey anaphora; how the system distinguishes among multiple indefinites, leading to a particularly satisfying solution to the problem of indistinguishable participants; and the interaction of donkey anaphora with disjoined antecedents. We do not, however, explore extending the analysis to an intensional account of the conditional; see Barker and Shan (2008) section 3.3 for one way to do this.

In section 9.7, we discusses the interaction of our donkey anaphora analysis with crossover phenomena. We argue there that our general evaluation-order constraint on combination makes good predictions about order asymmetries in donkey anaphora.

9.2 Why does *every* disrupt donkey anaphora?

If a universal occurs in the antecedent, donkey anaphora is no longer possible:

(152) If everyone owns a donkey, it brays.

More precisely, there is no interpretation on which the indefinite takes narrow scope with respect to the universal and still binds the pronoun.

As discussed above in section 3.3, previous dynamic accounts such as Dynamic Predicate Logic and Dynamic Montague Grammar define *everyone* in terms of static negation, which is stipulated to block anaphora between an indefinite taking scope inside the negation and a pronoun outside the scope of negation.

Our account needs no such stipulation: the binding relationships follow immediately from getting the scope of the quantifiers right. Recall from (147) that, unlike indefinites, the scope of *everyone* is generally limited to its minimal clause. In this case, the minimal clause is the antecedent. That means that the only possible analysis of the antecedent in (152) must close off the scope of *everyone* by applying LOWER before the antecedent combines with *if*:

(153)
$$\frac{\mathrm{S}\,|\,\mathrm{S}}{\mathrm{S}} \quad \xRightarrow{\text{LOWER}} \quad \mathrm{S}$$
$$\textit{Everyone owns a donkey} \quad \Rightarrow \quad \textit{Everyone owns a donkey}$$
$$\frac{\forall x.\, \exists y.\, \textbf{donkey}\, y \wedge [\;]}{\textbf{owns}\, y\, x} \qquad \forall x.\, \exists y.\, \textbf{donkey}\, y \wedge \textbf{owns}\, y\, x$$

Because eliminating the quantificational level at which *everyone* takes scope also eliminates any other quantifier on the same level and lower levels, whenever the indefinite takes narrow scope with respect to the universal, the scope of the indefinite must also be limited to the antecedent clause.

There is no obvious semantic reason why universals can't take wide scope beyond their minimal clause, so their scope limitations are presumably purely syntactic. Like most leading accounts of donkey anaphora (including Groenendijk and Stokhof 1991, 1990, Elbourne 2006), we provide no formal mechanism here that bounds the scope-taking of universals, though see Barker and Shan (2006) section 6 for one strategy, and see Charlow (2014) for discussion.

9.3 Multiple indefinites: tracking bishops

The standard example of donkey anaphora contains more than one indefinite (namely, *a farmer* and *a donkey*). In most treatments of binding, multiple binders are distinguished by means of different subscript indices, e.g., x_i versus x_j. As explained in chapter 4, in the tower system, since each binder can occupy a different scope-taking level, there is no need for subscripts.

In addition, we shall see that providing distinct layers for each binding relationship solves the celebrated bishop problem discussed by Heim (1990), Elbourne (2006), and others.

We begin with the antecedent clause. We first apply the indefinite determiner *a* to each of the two common nouns *farmer* and *donkey*, illustrated below for *farmer*.

(154)
$$\begin{array}{ccccc}
\left(\dfrac{S|S}{DP}\right)\Big/N & & N & & \dfrac{S|S}{DP} \\
a & & \textit{farmer} & = & \textit{a farmer} \\
\lambda P.\ \dfrac{\exists x.\,Px \wedge [\,]}{x} & & \textbf{farmer} & & \dfrac{\exists x.\,(\textbf{farmer}\ x) \wedge [\,]}{x}
\end{array}$$

The following chapter, chapter 10, discusses other possible lexical entries for the determiner *a*, in addition to the one displayed here.

We then apply BIND and LIFT to each of the two indefinite DPs *a farmer* and *a donkey*, so that they occupy different binding levels from each other.

(155)
$$\begin{array}{ccccc}
 & \dfrac{S|DP \rhd S}{DP} & & \dfrac{\dfrac{S|DP \rhd S}{S|S}}{DP} \\
\overset{\text{BIND}}{\Rightarrow} & \textit{a farmer} & \overset{\text{LIFT}}{\Rightarrow} & \textit{a farmer} \\
 & \dfrac{\exists x.\,(\textbf{farmer}\ x) \wedge ([\,]x)}{x} & & \dfrac{\exists x.\,(\textbf{farmer}\ x) \wedge ([\,]x)}{\dfrac{[\,]}{x}}
\end{array}$$

We build the antecedent clause from three three-level meanings.

(156)
$$\begin{array}{ccc}
\dfrac{\dfrac{S|DP \rhd S}{S|S}}{DP} & \dfrac{\dfrac{DP \rhd S|DP \rhd S}{S|S}}{(DP\backslash S)/DP} & \dfrac{\dfrac{DP \rhd S|DP \rhd S}{S|DP \rhd S}}{DP} \\
\textit{a farmer} & \textit{owns} & \textit{a donkey} \\
\dfrac{\exists x.\,(\textbf{farmer}\ x) \wedge ([\,]x)}{\dfrac{[\,]}{x}} & \dfrac{[\,]}{\dfrac{[\,]}{\textbf{owns}}} & \dfrac{[\,]}{\dfrac{\exists y.\,(\textbf{donkey}\ y) \wedge ([\,]y)}{y}}
\end{array}$$

And we have a complete antecedent clause. Note that we cannot apply LOWER, since each continuation layer still has unresolved side effects (the DP $\rhd$ S's). We will eventually lower after the consequent has been combined with the antecedent, at which point both pronominal dependencies will have been resolved.

Next, we build the consequent by LIFTing two pronouns, waiting to be bound at two different levels.

(157)
$$
\begin{array}{c|c}
\mathrm{DP} \rhd \mathrm{S} & \mathrm{S} \\ \hline
\mathrm{DP} \rhd \mathrm{S} & \mathrm{DP} \rhd \mathrm{S} \\ \hline
\multicolumn{2}{c}{\mathrm{DP}} \\
\multicolumn{2}{c}{\textit{he}} \\
\multicolumn{2}{c}{\dfrac{\lambda z.\,[\;]}{\dfrac{[\;]}{z}}}
\end{array}
\qquad
\begin{array}{c|c}
\mathrm{S} & \mathrm{S} \\ \hline
\mathrm{DP} \rhd \mathrm{S} & \mathrm{DP} \rhd \mathrm{S} \\ \hline
\multicolumn{2}{c}{(\mathrm{DP}\backslash \mathrm{S})/\mathrm{DP}} \\
\multicolumn{2}{c}{\textit{beats}} \\
\multicolumn{2}{c}{\dfrac{[\;]}{\dfrac{[\;]}{\mathbf{beats}}}}
\end{array}
\qquad
\begin{array}{c|c}
\mathrm{S} & \mathrm{S} \\ \hline
\mathrm{DP} \rhd \mathrm{S} & \mathrm{S} \\ \hline
\multicolumn{2}{c}{\mathrm{DP}} \\
\multicolumn{2}{c}{\textit{it}} \\
\multicolumn{2}{c}{\dfrac{[\;]}{\dfrac{\lambda w.\,[\;]}{w}}}
\end{array}
$$

We finish the derivation using the lexical entry for *if* given in (149) above (adjusted by an application of LIFT).

(158)
$$
\begin{array}{c|c}
\mathrm{S} & \mathrm{S} \\ \hline
\mathrm{S} & \mathrm{S} \\ \hline
\multicolumn{2}{c}{(\mathrm{S}/\mathrm{S})/\mathrm{S}} \\
\multicolumn{2}{c}{\textit{if}} \\
\multicolumn{2}{c}{\dfrac{\neg[\;]}{\dfrac{[\;]}{\lambda p \lambda q.\, p \wedge \neg q}}}
\end{array}
\qquad
\begin{array}{c|c}
\mathrm{S} & \mathrm{DP} \rhd \mathrm{S} \\ \hline
\mathrm{S} & \mathrm{DP} \rhd \mathrm{S} \\ \hline
\multicolumn{2}{c}{\mathrm{S}} \\
\multicolumn{2}{c}{\textit{a farmer owns a donkey}} \\
\multicolumn{2}{c}{\dfrac{\exists x.\,(\mathbf{farmer}\,x) \wedge ([\;]x)}{\dfrac{\exists y.\,(\mathbf{donkey}\,y) \wedge ([\;]y)}{\mathbf{owns}\,y\,x}}}
\end{array}
\qquad
\begin{array}{c|c}
\mathrm{DP} \rhd \mathrm{S} & \mathrm{S} \\ \hline
\mathrm{DP} \rhd \mathrm{S} & \mathrm{S} \\ \hline
\multicolumn{2}{c}{\mathrm{S}} \\
\multicolumn{2}{c}{\textit{he beats it}} \\
\multicolumn{2}{c}{\dfrac{\lambda z.\,[\;]}{\dfrac{\lambda w.\,[\;]}{\mathbf{beats}\,w\,z}}}
\end{array}
$$

$$
= \begin{array}{c|c}
\mathrm{S} & \mathrm{S} \\ \hline
\mathrm{S} & \mathrm{S} \\ \hline
\multicolumn{2}{c}{\mathrm{S}} \\
\multicolumn{2}{c}{\textit{If a farmer owns a donkey he beats it}} \\
\multicolumn{2}{c}{\dfrac{\neg\exists x.\,(\mathbf{farmer}\,x) \wedge ((\lambda z.\,[\;])x)}{\dfrac{\exists y.\,(\mathbf{donkey}\,y) \wedge ((\lambda w.\,[\;])y)}{(\mathbf{owns}\,y\,x) \wedge \neg(\mathbf{beats}\,w\,z)}}}
\end{array}
$$

With two applications of LOWER and some routine lambda conversion, we have the following analysis of the standard donkey sentence:

(159) If a farmer owns a donkey, he beats it.
$\neg\exists x.\,(\mathbf{farmer}\,x) \wedge \exists y.\,(\mathbf{donkey}\,y) \wedge (\mathbf{owns}\,y\,x) \wedge \neg(\mathbf{beats}\,y\,x)$

These truth conditions require that every farmer beats every donkey that he owns, which is one of the accepted interpretations of the donkey anaphora interpretation of the sentence.

The D-type situation-based account (using Elbourne's name for the approach; some people prefer 'E-type') first proposed by Heim (1990) (adapting ideas in Berman 1987, and further developed by Elbourne 2006) provides truth conditions for the standard donkey sentence that say, roughly, that every minimal situation of a farmer owning a donkey can be extended to a situation in which the (unique) farmer in that situation beats the (unique) donkey in that situation. These truth conditions are compatible with situations in which a farmer owns more than one donkey, since given a theory of situations such as that in Kratzer (1989), we can choose each minimal situation so small that it contains only one farmer and only one donkey, provided we also stipulate suitable persistence behavior, as discussed by Zweig (2008).

However, as pointed out by Kamp (according to Heim 1990), sometimes even the minimal situation must contain more than one entity that matches the descriptive content of a D-type pronoun.

(160) If a bishop meets a bishop, he blesses him.

The problem with (160) is that any situation in which a bishop meets a bishop, no matter how minimal, presumably contains two bishops. If we take the pronoun *he* as a D-type pronoun expressing the content *the bishop* or even *the bishop who meets a bishop*, the uniqueness implication due to the definiteness of the description fails, since there is no unique bishop in any of the relevant minimal situations.

Elbourne (2006:147) explains how to reconcile intuitions about bishops with a situation-based account. The solution depends on supposing that the implicit descriptive content of the D-type pronouns can be pragmatically enriched with a certain kind of property that distinguishes between the two bishops. (See Barker and Shan 2008 and Elbourne 2009 for more detailed discussion of Elbourne's account.)

On the present proposal, bishop sentences are perfectly straightforward and require no special assumptions. The derivation is identical to the one given above for the farmer/donkey sentence (after substituting the appropriate words), giving the following truth conditions (compare with (159) above):

(161) If a bishop meets a bishop, he blesses him.
$\neg\exists x.\,(\mathbf{bishop}\,x) \wedge \exists y.\,(\mathbf{bishop}\,y) \wedge (\mathbf{meets}\,y\,x) \wedge \neg(\mathbf{blesses}\,y\,x)$

Thus bishop sentences pose no special difficulties on our account.

9.4 Conjoined antecedents

Elbourne (2006, 2009) argues that it is a virtue of the D-type analysis that it fails to predict donkey anaphora for certain configurations of conjoined DPs.

(162) If a bishop and a bishop meet, he blesses him.

In contrast with the standard bishop sentence,

(163) If a bishop$_i$ meets a bishop$_j$, he$_i$ blesses him$_j$

—in which *meet* is used transitively—it is hard to interpret the pronouns in (162) as taking the indefinites as antecedents. On the D-type account, in the conjoined case, the situation-building algorithm treats the two indefinites perfectly symmetrically. This prevents the covert definite descriptions contributed by the pronouns from being pragmatically enriched in a way that allows distinguishing the two bishops, and the example is rendered infelicitous by the failed uniqueness presupposition of the definite descriptions.

Certainly, our account predicts that the conjuncts can serve as (separate) antecedents for the two pronouns. But in the general case, this is necessary:

(164) If a woman and a man meet, she asks him for his number.

The D-type account can also explain the availability of anaphora in this case, since each conjunct's distinctive lexical content provides plenty of semantic leverage for the covert descriptions denoted by the pronouns on the D-type account to be able to distinguish between the participants in the antecedent situation.

However, it is possible to find cases in which the conjuncts are semantically distinct, yet the overall situation is symmetric enough that donkey anaphora becomes infelicitous:

(165) a. #If John and Bill meet, he falls asleep.
b. #If a butcher and a baker meet, he pays him.
c. #If a man with a dog and a woman with a dog meet, it barks at it.

The D-type and continuations accounts both predict that these sentences have various readings involving donkey anaphora, yet anaphoric interpretations are difficult in a way that we feel is just like the difficulty of (162). The problem with the sentences in (165), then, is that they provide no traction for deciding which of the possible anaphoric relations is the intended one.

As Elbourne (2009) points out, from a purely semantic point of view, the classic bishop sentence is equally symmetric. Why then don't we feel any hesitation in selecting a binding configuration? Elbourne (2009) considers the possibility that the feeling of uncertainty disappears when the choice of a binding pattern is immaterial to the truth conditions. And indeed, if we modify the conjoined variant of the bishop sentence so the choice of anaphora resolution makes a difference to the overall truth conditions, a curious effect emerges:

(166) If a bishop meets a bishop, he is older.

Both our account and the D-type account predict that this sentence ought to have at least two grammatically distinct (but truth-conditionally equivalent) readings, depending on whether the pronoun is resolved to the first bishop or the second bishop. We judge that (166) gives rise to the same kind of uncertainty about how to resolve the pronoun as in (162) and (165).

In any case, on our account, unlike the D-type account, we assume that any infelicity of (162) must be pragmatic, and not a matter of grammar.

9.5 Disjoined antecedents

Disjoined antecedents give rise to a different set of issues. As noted by Stone (1992), disjunction constitutes a challenge for at least some dynamic theories of anaphora, including Groenendijk and Stokhof (1991) (DPL).

(167) If a farmer owns a donkey or a goat, he beats it.

The problem for DPL is that the indefinites *a donkey* and *a goat* introduce two distinct discourse referents, neither of which is a suitable antecedent for *it*. This challenge is hardly insurmountable, but does seem to require assumptions that go beyond the basic theory of DPL. For instance, one possibility is to follow Partee and Rooth (1983) and allow a phrase like *John or Bill* to introduce a new variable, independent from the discourse referent introduced by either disjunct.

The D-type analysis has no trouble with disjunction: every situation that verifies the antecedent will either have a donkey in it or a goat, so there will always be a suitable object for the pronoun *it* to describe. The descriptive content of the pronoun will be something neutral between the two descriptions, something like *the animal*, or perhaps *the donkey or goat*. (Though Leu 2005 argues that in the general case, the content of the D-type pronoun will have to be so bleached that it is essentially contentless, roughly equivalent to *the entity*.) Elbourne (2006:19) concludes that disjunction provides an argument in favor of the D-type approach over DPL.

Given the treatment of generalized coordination developed above in (112) in chapter 7, no extra assumptions are needed.

(168)
$$\left(\begin{array}{c} \mathrm{S}|\mathrm{S} \\ \hline \mathrm{DP} \\ \textit{John} \end{array}\right) \left(\left(\underset{\textit{or}}{\left(\begin{array}{c} \mathrm{S}|\mathrm{S} \\ \hline \mathrm{DP} \end{array} \Big\backslash \begin{array}{c} \mathrm{S}|\mathrm{S} \\ \hline \mathrm{DP} \end{array} \right) \Big/ \begin{array}{c} \mathrm{S}|\mathrm{S} \\ \hline \mathrm{DP} \end{array}} \; \begin{array}{c} \mathrm{S}|\mathrm{S} \\ \hline \mathrm{DP} \\ \textit{Bill} \end{array} \right) \right) \left(\begin{array}{c} \mathrm{DP} \rhd \mathrm{S}|\mathrm{S} \\ \hline \mathrm{DP}\backslash \mathrm{S} \\ \textit{called his mother} \end{array} \right)$$

$$\overset{\text{Bind}}{\Rightarrow} \left(\begin{array}{c} \mathrm{S}|\mathrm{DP} \rhd \mathrm{S} \\ \hline \mathrm{DP} \\ \textit{John or Bill} \end{array} \right) \left(\begin{array}{c} \mathrm{DP} \rhd \mathrm{S}|\mathrm{S} \\ \hline \mathrm{DP}\backslash \mathrm{S} \\ \textit{called his mother} \end{array} \right)$$

This derivation gives the truth condition

(169) $\textbf{called (mother j) j} \vee \textbf{called (mother b) b}$.

In other words, the disjunction of *John* and *Bill* is perfectly able to serve as the antecedent of a singular pronoun.

A similar derivation goes through for donkey anaphora, i.e., when the disjunction is in the antecedent and the pronoun is in the consequent:

(170) If John or Bill left, he called.
$(\textbf{left j} \rightarrow \textbf{called j}) \vee (\textbf{left b} \rightarrow \textbf{called b})$

In order to bind the pronoun, the disjunction must scope over the consequent, in which case the truth conditions come out as requiring whoever left to call.

If the disjuncts are indefinites rather than names, we get appropriate truth conditions for sentences such as

(171) If a farmer owns a donkey or a goat, he beats it.

EXERCISE 24

Provide details for the derivation of *If a donkey or a goat entered, it left.*

Stone and Elbourne claim that similar anaphora can occur with disjoined sentences (as opposed to disjoined DPs):

(172) If Mary hasn't seen John lately, or Ann misses Bill, she calls him.

On the D-type analysis, all that is required is that each minimal situation involved in the antecedent of (172) contains a man. On our system, we simply choose $A = \frac{\mathrm{S} \mid \mathrm{DP} \rhd \mathrm{S}}{\mathrm{S}}$ for the syntactic coordination schema given in (112), which allows each disjoined clause to provide its own binder independently of the other disjunct.

Thus, although disjunction poses difficulties for some specific dynamic theories of meaning (such as Groenendijk and Stokhof 1990, 1991, as discussed by Elbourne 2006), it by no means poses difficulties for all dynamic theories. In particular, it works out fine in the analysis proposed here.

9.6 Indefinites with universal force in the consequent

The semantics of the conditional allow indefinites in the antecedent to take what appears to be universal force: for *every* farmer and *every* donkey, that farmer beats that donkey. On our split-scope analysis, this is because the indefinite takes scope under a negation supplied by the lexical entry of *if* (and it is a matter of logic that an indefinite under negation has the force of a universal).

Charlow (2010) observes that our analysis predicts that indefinites in the consequent can also receive a universal-like interpretation.

(173)
$$\left(\begin{array}{cc} \dfrac{S \mid S}{(S/S)/S} & \dfrac{S|S}{S} \\ \textit{if} & \textit{it rains} \\ \dfrac{\neg[\,]}{\lambda pq.p \wedge \neg q} & \dfrac{[\,]}{\textbf{rains}} \end{array}\right)\left(\begin{array}{cc} \dfrac{S|S}{DP} & \dfrac{S \mid S}{DP\backslash S} \\ \textit{a woman} & \textit{leaves} \\ \dfrac{\exists x.\textbf{woman}\, x \wedge [\,]}{x} & \dfrac{[\,]}{\textbf{leaves}} \end{array}\right)$$

$$\overset{\text{LOWER}}{\Rightarrow} \quad \begin{array}{c} S \\ \textit{If it rains, a woman leaves} \\ \neg\,(\exists x.\textbf{woman}\, x \wedge (\textbf{rains} \wedge \neg(\textbf{left}\, x))) \end{array}$$

If the outer negation introduced by *if* outscopes the indefinite, and the indefinite takes scope over the rest of the sentence, the predicted truth conditions require that whenever it rains, every woman leaves.

For some reason, this universalist interpretation, though present, is remote in (173). However, the availability of the universal interpretation is enhanced if the subordinate *if* clause follows the consequent:

(174) A woman leaves if it rains.

In addition to an unproblematic reading on which it asserts that there is some specific woman who leaves if it rains, this sentence also has a quasi-generic interpretation that characterizes what women in general do when it rains. (See the next section for discussion of the order of the antecedent and the consequent.) The universal reading can be further enhanced by substituting *whenever* for *if*.

A universal interpretation is also enhanced in the presence of modification, even when the antecedent precedes the main clause:

(175) If it rains, a wise woman leaves.

This variant does have an interpretation that requires every wise woman to leave whenever it rains.

This phenomenon is reminiscent of subtrigging, in which indefinites receive free-choice (i.e., universal) interpretations only in the presence of modification (see, e.g., Dayal 1995, 1998 and Mascarenhas 2011 for theories and discussion of subtrigging). However, subtrigging usually requires modification by a postnominal phrase such as a relative clause, rather than by just a prenominal adjective.

Our tentative conclusion is that although the factors that promote or suppress the universalist readings are not well understood, such readings are available, as predicted by our theory.

9.7 Donkey weak crossover

Our in-scope binding analysis of donkey anaphora predicts that donkey anaphora will display the same order sensitivity as ordinary anaphora does. It is well known (e.g., Büring 2004) that donkey anaphora out of a DP can give rise to robust crossover effects.

(176) a. Most women who have a son$_i$ love his$_i$ father.
b. *His$_i$ father loves most women who have a son$_i$.

As the contrast in (176) shows, donkey anaphora requires the indefinite (*a son*) to precede the covarying pronoun (*his*), even though the quantifier *most* takes scope over the entire sentence in both (176a) and (176b).

Büring derives the contrast in (176) from his assumption that a DP that contains a donkey antecedent must c-command the donkey pronoun. Without invoking c-command, we explain donkey weak crossover just as we explain weak crossover, as a consequence of left-to-right evaluation order.

The examples in (176) involve indefinites embedded inside of DPs. We have postponed a discussion of our analysis of donkey anaphora out of DP, and how our theory of evaluation order explains the contrast in (176), until the next chapter. However, we will consider the analogous issue for donkey anaphora in conditionals.

In Barker and Shan (2008), we suggested that donkey anaphora out of conditionals also gives rise to crossover effects.

(177) a. If a farmer owns a donkey, he beats it. (= 146a)
b. *?If he owns it, a farmer beats a donkey.

The anaphora from the antecedent into the consequent in 177a is good, but the anaphora from the consequent into the antecedent in 177b is more difficult.

However, other similar examples of donkey cataphora seem to be much better, as in this example from Chierchia (1995:129):

(178) If it is overcooked, a hamburger usually doesn't taste good.

In Barker and Shan (2008), we questioned how systematic this kind of cataphora is. Elbourne (2009) criticizes us on this point, agreeing with Chierchia (1995), and citing a number of additional examples of similar cataphora. We remain skeptical of the full grammaticality of donkey cataphora, but we will offer some speculations about what might be going on in examples like (178).

Elbourne (2009) argues that the canonical syntactic position of an *if* clause is subordinate to the main clause, and we find this plausible. If so, it suggests a more complicated syntactic analysis than we have been assuming on which the initial *if* clause has been fronted. If we give *if* the syntactic category $\dfrac{S_F \mid S}{(S\backslash S)/S}$, then the FRONT typeshifter predicts that the constituent formed by the *if* along with the antecedent clause ought to be able to appear displaced at the front of the sentence, using the same analysis we gave for wh-questions in chapter 5.

> **EXERCISE 25**
>
> What is the category of the gap that would be required to complete a derivation with a fronted antecedent clause?

Support for this possibility comes from the fact that *when/whenever* conditionals are overtly wh-phrases (e.g., *Whenever it rains, it pours* means roughly the same thing as *If it rains, it pours*). We saw in chapter 5 that several varieties of wh-words trigger FRONTing, including wh-question words and relative pronouns. If antecedent clauses arrive at the beginning of a sentence through fronting, then any pronouns they contain would reconstruct in the way explained in chapter 6, providing a derivation for (178) and similar examples.

The examples discussed above do not provide strong evidence in favor of our crossover explanation. Fortunately, there remains one class of examples that we find robustly and unproblematically confirm the predictions of our theory of evaluation order. If we allow *if* clauses to appear in their canonical subordinate position after the main clause (i.e., in-situ, in the fronting analysis), donkey cataphora is quite difficult:

(179) a. *She$_i$ left if someone$_i$ knocked.
b. ?Her$_i$ mother left if someone$_i$'s father knocked.
c. ?John beats it$_i$ if he owns a donkey$_i$

Elbourne (2009) tentatively suggests that donkey cataphora is possible if the cataphoric pronoun is within the verb phrase of the main clause, but native speakers find that donkey anaphora in (179c) is difficult enough that we are comfortable predicting that it is a crossover violation.

In any case, our analysis predicts that for *if* clauses in sentence-final position, it is a systematic pattern that an attempt to have a donkey pronoun in the main clause that covaries with an indefinite in the subordinate *if* clause will have the status of a crossover violation, as illustrated in (179).

9.8 Conclusions

The picture that we have drawn is very simple: a quantifier can only bind a pronoun that it takes scope over. But since indefinites can take scope over more than their minimal clause, they can bind pronouns in subsequent clauses. In particular, they can take scope over and bind donkey pronouns. The fact that they fail to c-command those pronouns is irrelevant, because c-command is not a requirement for binding. However, since evaluation order is a requirement for binding, donkey indefinites must be evaluated before the pronouns that they bind, which means that the pronoun must follow the quantifier, or semantically reconstruct to a position to the right of the quantifier. Otherwise, donkey weak crossover results.

10

Strategies for determiners

Throughout the book so far, we have always used syntactically simple quantifiers such as *everyone* and *someone*. The only exception was the discussion of donkey anaphora in the previous chapter, in which we used indefinites like *a farmer*; however, that was primarily for the sake of the naturalness of the examples, since nothing there depended on the indefinites being syntactically complex. In this chapter, we extend the fragment to quantificational determiners.

We will consider several strategies for managing the interaction of quantificational determiners with side effects such as scope-taking and binding. The main empirical arguments distinguishing among the strategies involve donkey anaphora. Although questions about determiners will remain, we will suggest that no matter how those issues are resolved, predictions about evaluation order and crossover are borne out.

10.1 Donkey anaphora from relative clauses

There are two classic cases of donkey anaphora. The first case involves conditionals (*If a farmer owns a donkey, he beats it*), and was discussed in the previous chapter. We argued that the indefinite takes scope over and binds the donkey pronoun, contrary to the standard wisdom. This chapter extends the argument to the second case, which involves donkey indefinites inside the nominal argument of a quantificational determiner, as illustrated here using examples from Evans (1977:117):

(180) a. Most men who own a car wash it on Sundays.
b. Every man who owns a donkey beats it.

Evans provides the following assessment of these examples:

> If the sentence is to express the intended restrictions upon the major quantifier—that of being a car- or donkey-owner—it would appear that the second quantifier must be given a scope which does not extend beyond the relative clause, and this rules out a bound variable interpretation of the later pronouns.

Once again, the conclusion is too strong. The conclusion is warranted only if the only way for the indefinite to take scope wider than the relative clause is to also take scope over the quantificational determiner. Just as in the conditional case, we will show that it is perfectly possible for the indefinite to take scope wider than the relative clause yet still narrower than the quantificational determiner.

In fact, we will consider a range of strategies for analyzing quantificational determiners. This chapter owes much to discussions with Simon Charlow, and in particular to Charlow (2010) and to Charlow (2014). Developing ideas in Shan (2001a) and other work, Charlow advocates combining a continuation-based grammar with additional compositional machinery, including relativizing expressions to a sequence of individuals, and modeling indefinites via Hamblin-style alternatives. Although there is much to recommend a multi-mechanism approach, we will pursue a more parsimonious approach here, in order to see how much of the empirical landscape can be covered using only towers in their simplest form.

The larger goal of the chapter will be to argue that nothing about donkey anaphora out of DP challenges the main empirical claim of the book, which is that evaluation order can explain crossover.

To begin the discussion, consider the lexical entry given above in (154) for the indefinite determiner *a*, repeated here along with the analogous entry for *every*:

(181)

$$\frac{\mathrm{S}|\mathrm{S}}{\mathrm{DP}} \Big/ \mathrm{N} \qquad\qquad \frac{\mathrm{S}|\mathrm{S}}{\mathrm{DP}} \Big/ \mathrm{N}$$

$$\text{a} \qquad\qquad\qquad\qquad \text{every}$$

$$\lambda P. \frac{\exists x.\, Px \wedge [\,]}{x} \qquad\qquad \lambda P. \frac{\forall x.\, Px \rightarrow [\,]}{x}$$

On this analysis, these determiners combine with an argument of category N having semantic type $\mathtt{e} \rightarrow \mathtt{t}$, and return a scope-taking DP of generalized quantifier type, $(\mathtt{e} \rightarrow \mathtt{t}) \rightarrow \mathtt{t}$. This is a direct translation of the standard (extensional) treatment of quantificational determiners as in, e.g., Barwise and Cooper (1981). As far as we know, nothing goes wrong if these lexical entries are present, and we will continue to assume that they are available.

However, they are not sufficient, since they do not allow for side effects initiated within the restriction. In particular, they do not lead to an account of donkey anaphora. The reason is that in order to get the desired truth conditions for (180b), the indefinite must scope under the universal, since there must be a potentially different donkey for each farmer. But, given the lexical entry in (181), the only way for the indefinite to scope under the universal would be for the indefinite to take scope only within the relative clause, in which case the indefinite will be unable to bind a pronoun in the nuclear scope of the universal. Both of these derivations lead to grammatical interpretations, so nothing goes wrong; but neither leads to a donkey anaphora interpretation.

For the sake of explicitness, in the next two sections we will provide detailed examples illustrating these two types of derivations: one on which the indefinite scopes too low for donkey anaphora, and one on which the indefinite scopes too high. The element in the derivations to track is the extent of the scope of the indefinite.

10.2 A derivation on which the indefinite scopes too low

To see why the simple lexical entries in (181) do not lead to an account of donkey anaphora out of DP, we must first provide an analysis of the nominal *farmer who owns a donkey*, starting with the relative clause:

(182)
$$\begin{array}{c}\dfrac{\mathrm{DP}\backslash\!\!\backslash \mathrm{S}\,|\,\mathrm{S}}{\mathrm{DP}}\\ \_\_\\ \dfrac{\lambda y.[\,]}{y}\end{array}\left(\begin{array}{c}\dfrac{\mathrm{S}\,|\,\mathrm{S}}{(\mathrm{DP}\backslash \mathrm{S})/\mathrm{DP}}\\ \textit{owns}\\ \dfrac{[\,]}{\textbf{owns}}\end{array}\left(\begin{array}{c}\dfrac{\mathrm{S}\,|\,\mathrm{S}}{\mathrm{DP}}\Big/\mathrm{N}\\ a\\ \lambda P.\dfrac{\exists x.\, Px\wedge[\,]}{x}\end{array}\quad\begin{array}{c}\mathrm{N}\\ \textit{donkey}\\ \textbf{donkey}\end{array}\right)\right)$$

$$\begin{array}{c}\dfrac{\mathrm{DP}\backslash\!\!\backslash \mathrm{S}\,|\,\mathrm{S}}{\mathrm{S}}\\ \_\_\ \textit{owns a donkey}\\ \dfrac{\lambda y\exists x.\,(\textbf{donkey}\,x)\wedge[\,]}{\textbf{owns}\,x\,y}\end{array}\quad\begin{array}{c}\text{Lower}\\ \Rightarrow\\ \end{array}\quad\begin{array}{c}\mathrm{DP}\backslash\!\!\backslash \mathrm{S}\\ \_\_\ \textit{owns a donkey}\\ \lambda y.\,\exists x.\,(\textbf{donkey}\,x)\wedge(\textbf{owns}\,x\,y)\end{array}$$

Because the relative clause undergoes LOWERing, the scope of the indefinite extends only over the relative clause, and no farther. Combining this gapped clause with a relative pronoun and a nominal, we have:

(183)
$$\begin{array}{c}\mathrm{N}\\ \textit{farmer}\\ \textbf{farmer}\end{array}\left(\begin{array}{c}(\mathrm{N}\backslash\mathrm{N})/(\mathrm{DP}\backslash\!\!\backslash\mathrm{S})\\ \textit{who}_{rel}\\ \lambda\kappa Qy.(Qy)\wedge(\kappa y)\end{array}\ \begin{array}{c}\mathrm{DP}\backslash\!\!\backslash\mathrm{S}\\ \_\_\ \textit{owns a donkey}\\ \lambda y.\,\exists x.\,(\textbf{donkey}\,x)\wedge(\textbf{owns}\,x\,y)\end{array}\right)$$

$$=\quad\begin{array}{c}\mathrm{N}\\ \textit{farmer who owns a donkey}\\ \lambda y.\,(\textbf{farmer}\,y)\wedge\exists x.\,(\textbf{donkey}\,x)\wedge(\textbf{owns}\,x\,y)\end{array}$$

This derivation combines immediately with the lexical value for *every* currently under consideration, as given above in 181.

(184)
$$\begin{array}{c}\dfrac{\mathrm{S}\,|\,\mathrm{S}}{\mathrm{DP}}\\ \textit{every farmer who owns a donkey}\\ \dfrac{\forall y.\big((\textbf{farmer}\,y)\wedge\exists x.\,(\textbf{donkey}\,x)\wedge(\textbf{owns}\,x\,y)\big)\rightarrow[\,]}{y}\end{array}$$

Given the treatment of binding developed in previous chapters, the only element available to serve as a binder is the farmer participant. This derivation does not lead to any obvious bad predictions. However, there is no way to apply the BIND type-shifter that would allow the donkey DP to bind a pronoun outside of the nominal, which means that this derivation will not lead to an account of donkey anaphora.

10.3 A derivation on which the indefinite scopes too high

There is a different derivation on which the indefinite takes wider scope—but the scope is so wide it outscopes the universal, which, though grammatical, is not the donkey anaphoric reading. This derivation is similar to the derivation of the nominal given in the preceding section, except that the indefinite *a donkey* has undergone shifting by the BIND typeshifter before combining with the rest of the relative clause:

(185)

$$\frac{\mathrm{S}\,|\,\mathrm{DP} \rhd \mathrm{S}}{\mathrm{N}} \qquad \textit{farmer who owns a donkey} \qquad \frac{\exists y.\,(\mathbf{donkey}\,y) \wedge ([\,]\,y)}{\lambda z.\,(\mathbf{farmer}\,z) \wedge (\mathbf{owns}\,y\,z)}$$

> **EXERCISE 26**
>
> Give details for this derivation.

If we combine this analysis of the nominal with (a LIFTed version of) the value for *every* given in (181), we get the following.

(186)

$$\begin{array}{cc} \dfrac{\mathrm{S}\,|\,\mathrm{S}}{\dfrac{\mathrm{S}\,|\,\mathrm{S}}{\mathrm{DP}} / \mathrm{N}} & \dfrac{\mathrm{S}\,|\,\mathrm{DP} \rhd \mathrm{S}}{\mathrm{N}} \\ \textit{every} & \textit{farmer who owns a donkey} \\ \dfrac{[\,]}{\lambda P.\,\dfrac{\forall x.\,Px \rightarrow [\,]}{x}} & \dfrac{\exists y.\,(\mathbf{donkey}\,y) \wedge ([\,]\,y)}{\lambda z.\,(\mathbf{farmer}\,z) \wedge (\mathbf{owns}\,y\,z)} \end{array}$$

$$= \quad \dfrac{\mathrm{S}\,|\,\mathrm{DP} \rhd \mathrm{S}}{\dfrac{\mathrm{S}\,|\,\mathrm{S}}{\mathrm{DP}}} \qquad \textit{every farmer who owns a donkey} \qquad \dfrac{\exists y.\,(\mathbf{donkey}\,y) \wedge ([\,]\,y)}{\dfrac{\forall x.((\mathbf{farmer}\,x) \wedge (\mathbf{owns}\,y\,x)) \rightarrow [\,]}{x}}$$

On this analysis, the indefinite does take wide enough scope to bind a pronoun outside of the relative clause, but only by taking scope wider than the universal. Then *Every farmer who owns a donkey$_i$ beats it$_i$* would require the existence of some special donkey (call it Pedro), such that every farmer who owns Pedro beats Pedro. The sentence has such a reading, but this is not the classic donkey-anaphora reading we seek to explain.

10.4 Explicitly managing side effects

We need to create enough flexibility in the denotation of *every* to allow an indefinite to take scope beyond the relative clause, yet still below the universal. We will explore how to do this by explicitly managing the transmission of side-effects from the restriction to the nuclear scope of the universal.

(187)
$$\dfrac{\mathrm{S}\,|\,\mathrm{DP} \rhd \mathrm{S}}{\mathrm{DP}} \Big/ \dfrac{\mathrm{S}\,|\,\mathrm{DP} \rhd \mathrm{S}}{\mathrm{N}}$$
$$\textit{every}$$
$$\dfrac{\neg\exists x.g[\lambda y.Px \wedge \neg([\ ]y)]}{x} \Big/ \dfrac{g[\ ]}{P}$$

In order to make the intention of the semantic analysis clear (since the semantics somewhat abuses the official tower notation), the value in flat notation is $\lambda\mathcal{P}\kappa.\neg\exists x.\mathcal{P}(\lambda Py.Px \wedge \neg(\kappa xy))$.

The idea of this lexical entry is to propagate a binding side effect from the restriction to the nuclear scope "by hand", that is, by explicitly mentioning them in the lexical entry.

Here's how this lexical entry accounts for a basic donkey anaphora example.

(188)
$$\left(\begin{array}{cc} \dfrac{\mathrm{S}\,|\,\mathrm{DP} \rhd \mathrm{S}}{\mathrm{DP}} \Big/ \dfrac{\mathrm{S}\,|\,\mathrm{DP} \rhd \mathrm{S}}{\mathrm{N}} & \dfrac{\mathrm{S}\,|\,\mathrm{DP} \rhd \mathrm{S}}{\mathrm{N}} \\ \textit{every} & \textit{farmer who owns a donkey} \\ \dfrac{\neg\exists x.g[\lambda y.Px \wedge \neg([\ ]y)]}{x} \Big/ \dfrac{g[\ ]}{P} & \dfrac{\exists y.\,(\mathbf{donkey}\ y) \wedge ([\ ]\,y)}{\lambda z.\,(\mathbf{farmer}\ z) \wedge (\mathbf{owns}\ y\ z)} \end{array}\right) \begin{array}{c} \dfrac{\mathrm{DP} \rhd \mathrm{S}\,|\,\mathrm{S}}{\mathrm{DP}\backslash\mathrm{S}} \\ \textit{beats it} \\ \dfrac{\lambda z.[\ ]}{\mathbf{beats}\ z} \end{array}$$

$$= \begin{array}{c} \dfrac{\mathrm{S}\,|\,\mathrm{DP} \rhd \mathrm{S}}{\mathrm{DP}} \\ \textit{every farmer who owns a donkey} \\ \dfrac{\neg\exists x.\exists y\,(\mathbf{donkey}\ y) \wedge (\mathbf{farmer}\ x) \wedge (\mathbf{owns}\ y\ x) \wedge \neg([\ ]\,y)}{x} \end{array} \begin{array}{c} \dfrac{\mathrm{DP} \rhd \mathrm{S}\,|\,\mathrm{S}}{\mathrm{DP}\backslash\mathrm{S}} \\ \textit{beats it} \\ \dfrac{\lambda z.[\ ]}{\mathbf{beats}\ z} \end{array}$$

$$= \begin{array}{c} \dfrac{\mathrm{S}\,|\,\mathrm{S}}{\mathrm{S}} \\ \textit{every farmer who owns a donkey beats it} \\ \dfrac{\neg\exists x.\exists y\,(\mathbf{donkey}\ y) \wedge (\mathbf{farmer}\ x) \wedge (\mathbf{owns}\ y\ x) \wedge \neg((\lambda z.[\ ])\ y)}{\mathbf{beats}\ z\ x} \end{array}$$

The net result is that there is no way of choosing a farmer and a donkey such that if the farmer owns that donkey, then the farmer fails to beat that donkey. This is a reasonable approximation of the truth conditions of the donkey anaphora reading of the sentence.

Despite being embedded in a relative clause, the indefinite takes scope over the entire sentence, including the verb phrase, at the same time that it takes narrower scope than the universal introduced by *every*.

> **EXERCISE 27**
>
> Devise a lexical entry for *every* that handles more than one binding relationship originating inside the restriction and terminating inside the nuclear scope, e.g., *Every farmer who owns a donkey*$_i$ *and a mule*$_j$ *keeps pictures of him*$_i$ *and her*$_j$ *in his wallet.*

10.5 Crossover for relative clause donkey anaphora

Now that we have a provisional analysis of donkey anaphora out of DP, we can return to the main theme of Part I of this book: evaluation order and its effect on binding. (We will return to a discussion of the analysis of determiners in the next section.) Just as for donkey anaphora from conditionals, donkey anaphora from inside DPs confirm the by now familiar pattern.

(189) a. Every farmer$_i$ who owns a donkey beats it$_i$.
b. *It$_i$ loves every farmer who owns a donkey$_i$.
c. *Its$_i$ veterinarian loves every farmer who owns a donkey$_i$.
d. John photographed every farmer who owns a donkey$_i$ with it$_i$.
e. *John photographed it$_i$ with every farmer who owns a donkey$_i$.
f. Which of its$_i$ habits does no farmer who owns a donkey$_i$ hate?
g. ?Which of its$_i$ habits enrages no farmer who owns a donkey$_i$?

These examples are marked as predicted by our theory of binding and reconstruction developed in previous chapters, and the predictions match native-speaker judgments, as well as, e.g., Büring (2004). Certainly, when the donkey pronoun follows the donkey antecedent in an ordinary transitive sentence, donkey anaphora goes through. When the pronoun precedes the donkey antecedent, crossover effects emerge. Just as with ordinary quantificational binding, donkey binding is rescued by wh-fronting as in (189f), unless the wh-trace is evaluated before the donkey antecedent as in (189g).

10.6 A scope-roofing constraint

The fragment in Barker and Shan (2008) considers a different strategy for allowing side effects in the restriction to influence the interpretation of the nuclear scope. That paper gives the following lexical entry for *every*, which we'll call *every*′:

(190)
$$\begin{array}{c} \dfrac{\mathrm{S} \mid \mathrm{S}}{\left(\dfrac{\mathrm{S}\mid\mathrm{S}}{\mathrm{DP}}\right)/\mathrm{N}} \\ \textit{every}' \\ \dfrac{\neg\exists x.[\;]}{\lambda P.\dfrac{Px \wedge \neg[\;]}{x}} \end{array}$$

This lexical entry has the advantage of allowing any number of side effects from the restriction to extend into the nuclear scope. However, Charlow (2014) identifies a number of overgeneration problems created by the variant lexical entry.

First, it allows violations of a roofing constraint proposed by Brasoveanu and Farkas (2011). Roofing concerns the interaction of scope-taking with binding. Descriptively, the roofing constraint says that if a quantifier binds a pronoun contained in some DP, the quantifier must take scope over the entire DP.

(191) a. Some girl_i gave her_i picture to [every boy].
b. Some girl_i gave [every boy] her_i picture.
c. Some girl_i gave a picture to [every boy who met her_i].

In the first two examples, either one of the indefinite or the universal can take wide scope relative to the other, whether or not the indefinite binds the pronoun as indicated by the subscripts. But in (191c), the roofing constraint correctly predicts that if the indefinite *some girl* binds the pronoun *her*, the indefinite must take scope over the entire bracketed DP.

EXERCISE 28

Using (181), derive the grammatical interpretation of *Someone called every boy who met her.*

Roofing falls out fairly naturally on a QR account: in order for the universal to take scope over the indefinite, the universal must undergo QR to a position that c-commands the indefinite. Because the entire DP undergoes QR, the pronoun goes along with it. After QR, the pronoun is no longer c-commanded by the indefinite, and there is no way to give that LF an interpretation on which the pronoun is bound by the lower quantifier.

As Charlow (2010) shows, the variant lexical entry *every′* allows the roofing constraint to be violated.

(192)

$$\begin{array}{c}\begin{array}{c|c} S & S \\ \hline S & DP \rhd S \\ \hline S & S \end{array} \\ \hline DP \\ \textit{a girl} \\ [\,] \\ \hline \exists y.(\textbf{girl}\, y) \wedge ([\,]\, y) \\ \hline [\,] \\ \hline y \end{array} \left(\begin{array}{c}\begin{array}{c|c} S & S \\ \hline DP \rhd S & DP \rhd S \\ \hline S & S \end{array} \\ \hline (DP\backslash S)/DP \\ \textit{called} \\ [\,] \\ \hline [\,] \\ \hline [\,] \\ \hline \textbf{called} \end{array} \right.$$

$$\left. \left(\begin{array}{c}\begin{array}{c|c} S & S \\ \hline DP \rhd S & DP \rhd S \end{array} \\ \hline \dfrac{S|S}{DP} \Big/ N \\ \textit{every}' \\ \neg\exists x.[\,] \\ \hline [\,] \\ \hline \lambda P.\dfrac{Px \wedge \neg[\,]}{x} \end{array} \quad \begin{array}{c}\begin{array}{c|c} S & S \\ \hline DP \rhd S & S \end{array} \\ \hline N \\ \textit{boy who met her} \\ [\,] \\ \hline \lambda z.[\,] \\ \hline \lambda x.\textbf{boy}\, x \wedge (\textbf{met}\, z\, x) \end{array} \right) \right)$$

The truth conditions after LOWERing and beta reduction are $\neg\exists x.\exists y.\textbf{girl}\, y \wedge (\textbf{boy}x) \wedge (\textbf{met}\, x\, y) \wedge \neg(\textbf{called}\, x\, y)$. In words: there is no way of choosing a boy and a girl such that the boy met the girl unless the girl called the boy. If such a reading is available, it is remote.

Assuming for the sake of argument that the roofing constraint should be a matter of grammar, let us consider what options are available in the tower system. Note that in the derivation of the undesired interpretation, the universal lifts to take inverse scope over the indefinite, and the indefinite then binds the pronoun inside the DP headed by *every*′. One perspective on what is going wrong here involves the timing of restricted quantification. We can rephrase the roofing constraint in evaluation-order terms as follows: no part of the nuclear scope can be evaluated after the determiner but before any part of the restriction. The derivation just given violates this constraint, since the pronoun inside of the restriction depends (via binding) on the indefinite for its value, and the indefinite depends (via narrower scope) on the universal. Thus the indefinite (part of the nuclear scope) must be evaluated after the determiner, but before the pronoun. One diagnosis of the problem, then, is that the evaluation order timing of the quantificational elements is out of sync.

The official (non-variant) lexical entry for *every* given in (187) enforces roofing. It does this by placing the quantification introduced by *every* behind a solid slash that leans over the entire restriction. The slash blocks effects from earlier in the sentence from sneaking underneath the layer at which the universal takes effect.

The general pattern, fully respected by the official (non-variant) strategy given here, is that no element outside of the DP can take scope over any part of the DP without taking scope over the entire DP.

Barker and Shan (2008) give a schematic lexical entry similar to *every′* making use of what they call 'frege pairs', which generalizes to arbitrary (conservative) quantificational determiners. Since we are not going down the path suggested by *every′* here, we will not discuss frege pairs here.

10.7 A mystery concerning scope islands for universals

Charlow (2010) points out that the analysis in Barker and Shan (2008) overgenerates in certain cases involving a universal inside a nominal restriction. The official analysis given here overgenerates in the same way:

(193)
$$\left(\begin{array}{c} \dfrac{S|DP \rhd S}{DP} \Big/ \dfrac{S|DP \rhd S}{N} \\ a \\ \dfrac{\exists x.g[\lambda y.Px \wedge ([\ ]y)]}{x} \Big/ \dfrac{g[\ ]}{P} \end{array} \quad \begin{array}{c} \dfrac{S|DP \rhd S}{N} \\ \textit{f'mer who owns every d'ey} \\ \dfrac{\forall y.\,(\textbf{donkey}\ y) \rightarrow ([\ ]\,y)}{\lambda z.\,(\textbf{farmer}\ z) \wedge (\textbf{owns}\ y\ z)} \end{array}\right) \quad \begin{array}{c} \dfrac{DP \rhd S|S}{DP\backslash S} \\ \textit{beats it} \\ \dfrac{\lambda z.[\ ]}{\textbf{beats}\ z} \end{array}$$

This derivation is exactly parallel to the derivation of the donkey anaphora given in (188), but with the roles of the indefinite and the universal reversed. The truth conditions require that there be a farmer who owns every donkey, and that this farmer beats each of his or her donkeys. As Charlow points out, the sentence cannot express those truth conditions, so the grammar as given overgenerates.

Now, of course, we assume that distributive quantifiers such as *every*, *each* and *no* cannot take scope outside of their minimal tensed clause. That means that the scope of the universal in (193) must be trapped inside of the relative clause, and the derivation just sketched does not respect this constraint. Once the independently-motivated restriction on the scope of distributive quantifiers has been implemented, the problematic derivation sketched in (193) will also be correctly ruled out.

Interestingly, as Charlow notes, that can't be the entire story, since the same problem arises when the universal is in a prepositional complement rather than within a relative clause:

(194) A member of every committee$_i$ hates it$_i$.

We can't assume that prepositional phrases are scope islands for *every* in general, because there is a perfectly legitimate inverse-linking reading of (194) on which *every* takes wide scope over *a*. Thus it appears to be possible for *every* in this kind of construction to take scope over the entire sentence. If so, then an analysis along the lines of (193) will incorrectly predict truth conditions on which a single person who is on every committee hates each individual committee.

Nevertheless, we suggest that this problem still has to do purely with scope constraints, and does not teach us anything specifically about binding or crossover. The reason we believe this is that the same restriction governs the scope interaction of *every* with quantifiers in the verb phrase:

(195) A member of every committee missed a meeting.

Once again, an inverse-linking interpretation is perfectly fine: a different member of each committee missed a potentially different meeting in each case. But if the first indefinite takes scope over the universal (a non-inverse linking interpretation), that is, if the interpretation entails that there is a single person who is on every committee, it guarantees only that there was (at least) one meeting that was missed. There is no reading on which the meeting involved (potentially) varies with the choice of committee. This suggests that when the *member* indefinite takes scope over the universal, the scope of the universal gets trapped somehow inside its containing DP.

In any case, if a quantifier can't take scope over a pronoun, it certainly can't bind it. So if we had a way of guaranteeing the scope restriction just observed, the fact that donkey anaphora is likewise unavailable would follow for free.

One common assumption since May (1977) is that DP is a scope island. Then the universal in (194) is always trapped inside its containing DP. This explains why an embedded universal can't take scope over or bind elements outside the container. However, it then becomes necessary to adopt extra semantic mechanisms, such as situations and E-type meanings, in order to explain how the inverse-linking reading arises. See especially Elbourne (2006) and Büring (2004) for proposals, and Heim and Kratzer (1998), Sauerland (2005), Charlow (2009), Barker (2005), Barker and Shan (2008), and Elbourne (2009) for critical discussion.

To be sure, as mentioned in the previous chapter, there remain puzzles concerning how to implement constraints on the possible scope domains for distributive quantifiers; but assuming these constraints can be managed correctly, the binding facts follow. Here is our promise: if the scope constraints on quantifiers are respected, the binding possibilities fall out from evaluation order.

11

Other combinatory categorial frameworks

This chapter discusses two other combinatory categorial approaches to natural language semantics: Jacobson's Variable Free Semantics, and Steedman's scope as surface constituency.

The tower system is highly compatible with the assumptions and many of the details of Jacobson (1999, 2002), though the two systems are not equivalent, particularly with respect to their approaches to scope, crossover, and reconstruction.

Steedman (2000) and the elaborations in Steedman (2012) gives type-shifters for scope and binding. Like this book, Steedman (2012) is a complete reconceptualization of scope, with a detailed and explicit formal implementation. Although we enthusiastically endorse the project undertaken in Steedman (2012), and although many of the claims about scope in Steedman (2000) and later work have influenced our thinking, we disagree on the core data that we believe needs to be accounted for by an adequate theory of scope, as explained below.

11.1 Jacobson's Variable-Free program

As noted (e.g., in chapter 2), there are many points of similarity between our framework and the variable-free program of Jacobson (1999, 2002). One of the most salient elements in common is that our gaps and pronouns, as in Jacobson, are various syntactic flavors of the identity function.

More in general, our approach embodies several of the guiding principles of Jacobson's research program:

Direct compositionality: every syntactic constituent must have a well-formed and self-contained semantic interpretation.

Compositional transparency: the presence of unresolved semantic dependencies (e.g., unbound pronouns, gaps) must be reflected in the category of the larger constituents that contain the dependency.

Variable-free: meanings are constructed entirely from combinators, without any essential use of variables.

These three ideas are related, but not equivalent.

The deepest and most important principle is direct compositionality (see Jacobson 1999, 2002, Barker and Jacobson 2007). This principle says that any well-formed syntactic constituent is a well-formed semantic constituent. For an example of a system that is not directly compositional, consider Quantifier Raising as in the standard presentation in Heim and Kratzer (1998): in a quantified sentence such as *John called everyone*, the verb phrase *called everyone* does not have a denotation that reflects the full semantic contribution of its parts. Before Quantifier Raising takes place, there is type clash between the individual-expecting transitive verb and the generalized quantifier direct object; that means there is no well-formed semantic value. After Quantifier Raising, the quantifier has been raised to a position adjoining to the entire sentence, well outside the verb phrase. The verb phrase at this point contains a variable in the place of the quantifier. The verb phrase has a well-formed semantic interpretation, but not one that reflects the full semantic contribution of its parts, since the contribution of the quantifier is no longer present.

In the tower system, direct compositionality is guaranteed by the fact that every syntactic constituent (represented here as giant parentheses grouping syntactic elements into a tree) always has a single category and a single semantic value. Furthermore, that value represents exactly the full semantic contribution of all and only those semantic elements it was built up from.

Closely related to direct compositionality, compositional transparency is a commitment to track the presence of semantic elements that have long-distance effects, such as quantifiers or pronouns. For instance, in Jacobson's system, as in ours, if a sentence contains an unbound pronoun, then the syntactic category of that sentence will be DP $\triangleright$ S rather than plain S, since it denotes a function from individuals to sentence meanings rather than a plain sentence meaning.

It is important to emphasize that the fact that we, like Jacobson, routinely use lambdas in our semantic representations does not mean that the system isn't fully variable-free in the relevant technical sense. To see this, note that for every syntactic constituent in any of the analyses in Part I, the semantic denotation is a combinator, that is, a term containing no unbound variables.

In addition to being variable-free, the tower system in Part I is also compositionally transparent and directly compositional.

11.2 Jacobson's lgz fragment

To give a more detailed comparison with Jacobson's concrete implementation of her approach, Jacobson relies on three families of combinators. The first, l ('lift') corresponds closely to our LIFT. The only difference comes from the fact that Jacobson's grammar does not distinguish between the part of a syntactic category that determines function/argument combination versus higher levels that manage scope-taking and binding. On the type-logical approach developed in Part II, lifting is a theorem in both the merge mode and the continuation mode. It does no harm to add Jacobson's merge-mode lift to the tower system if desired.

The second crucial combinator family is the Geach combinator **g**. In a typical situation, this rule transmits a pronominal dependence from an argument to the phrase that contains it. So if f : DP\S is a verb phrase expecting a subject, $(\lambda gx.f(gx))$: (DP ▷ DP)\(DP ▷ S) is the geached verb phrase (expressed in our category notation). Assuming that the pronoun *he* is the identity function $(\lambda x.x)$: DP ▷ DP, the geached analysis predicts the sentence *He left* will be analyzed as $(\lambda x.\textbf{left}\ x)$: DP ▷ S: variable-free and directly compositional, with full compositional transparency. In the tower system, the geach rule is built into the semantic composition schema. Examination of the derivation of *He left* in (28) in chapter 2 will show how the tower system achieves an equivalent result.

Finally, the third family of combinators, the binding combinator **z**, shifts a predicate in a way that allows one of its arguments to bind into one of its other arguments. Unlike in the tower system, the **z** type-shifter shifts the predicate, not the argument that will serve as the binder.

The **lgz** fragment does not address scope displacement. Barker (2005) shows how to add Hendriks' Flexible Montague Grammar to the **lgz** fragment, discussing various strategies for accounting for binding from a non-c-commanding position, as well as some simple crossover examples. Barker (2009) compares reconstruction in the **lgz** fragment versus the tower system.

EXERCISE 29

• Explain why the geach rule is derivable in the tower system. • Given a type-shifter that allows function composition (e.g., $f\ :\ A/B \Rightarrow (\lambda gx.f(gx))\ :\ ((A/C)/(B/C))$), sketch how to use the tower system to derive the dual-binding interpretation of *Everyone loves, but no one marries, his mother*, on which it is equivalent to 'Everyone$_i$ loves his$_i$ mother, but no one$_j$ marries his$_j$ mother'. (This interpretation is a challenge for Quantifier Raising approaches.) • Derive a suitable meaning for a paycheck sentence such as the bracketed part of *John put his paycheck in the bank, but [Mary spent it]*. The desired interpretation is one on which there must be some salient function f from people to paychecks such that *Mary spent it* means that Mary spent the paycheck identified by f(Mary).

Stepping back, Jacobson's Variable-Free program and our tower strategy are closely similar in outlook, methodological philosophy, and many specific and highly detailed analyses. The distinctive aspect of our approach that we would like to emphasize is that making the role of continuations explicit enables us to reason formally at a high theoretical level about the role of evaluation order in phenomena such as scope-taking, dynamic anaphora, the linear scope bias, negative polarity licensing, crossover, and reconstruction.

11.3 Steedman's scope as surface constituency

Steedman (2000) and especially (Steedman, 2012:110) offers a combinator-based grammar that addresses scope displacement and binding.

In order to sketch how the system works, we will explain how to derive the two scopings of *Everyone loves no one*. Among the lexical entries generated by Steedman's system for *everyone* and for *no one* are the following:

(196) a. everyone$_a$ $\lambda\kappa.\forall x.\kappa x : \mathrm{S}/(\mathrm{DP}\backslash\mathrm{S})$
b. everyone$_b$ $\lambda\kappa y.\forall x.\kappa x y : ((\mathrm{DP}\backslash\mathrm{S})/\mathrm{DP})\backslash(\mathrm{DP}\backslash\mathrm{S})$
c. no one$_c$ $\lambda\kappa.\neg\exists x.\kappa x : (\mathrm{S}/\mathrm{DP})\backslash\mathrm{S}$
d. no one$_d$ $\lambda\kappa y.\neg\exists x.\kappa x y : ((\mathrm{DP}\backslash\mathrm{S})/\mathrm{DP})\backslash(\mathrm{DP}\backslash\mathrm{S})$

We have recast Steedman's notation to conform to the Lambek/type-logical tradition, in order to match the convention used throughout this book. In particular, the argument category always appears under the slash, no matter which way the slash is facing, thus: ARG\FN and FN/ARG.

Given a verb *loves* of category (DP\S)/DP, and referring to the lexical entries given in (196), we first choose version (a) of *everyone* and version (d) of *no one*. This gives linear scope:

(197)
$$\cfrac{\text{everyone}_a{:}\mathrm{S}/(\mathrm{DP}\backslash\mathrm{S}) \qquad \cfrac{\text{loves}{:}(\mathrm{DP}\backslash\mathrm{S})/\mathrm{DP} \quad \text{no one}_d{:}((\mathrm{DP}\backslash\mathrm{S})/\mathrm{DP})\backslash(\mathrm{DP}\backslash\mathrm{S})}{\text{loves no one}_d{:}\mathrm{DP}\backslash\mathrm{S}}<}{\text{everyone}_a\ (\text{loves no one}_d){:}\mathrm{S}}>$$

The $<$ and $>$ inferences are function application, with the arrow pointing in the direction of the argument. So the semantic value delivered by this derivation will be

(198) $\textbf{everyone}_a(\textbf{no one}_d\ \textbf{loves}) = \forall x \neg\exists y.\textbf{loves}\ y\ x$

In order to arrive at inverse scope, Steedman provides a type-shifter for forward function composition, **B** (Smullyan's 'Bluebird'), which allows composing the subject with the verb before combining with the direct object:

(199)
$$\cfrac{\cfrac{\text{everyone}_a{:}\mathrm{S}/(\mathrm{DP}\backslash\mathrm{S}) \qquad \text{loves}{:}(\mathrm{DP}\backslash\mathrm{S})/\mathrm{DP}}{\text{everyone}_a\ \text{loves}{:}\mathrm{S}/\mathrm{DP}}>\mathbf{B} \qquad \text{no one}_c{:}(\mathrm{S}/\mathrm{DP})\backslash\mathrm{S}}{\text{everyone}_a\ \text{loves no one}_c{:}\mathrm{S}}<$$

This derivation uses the same entry for *everyone* (namely, the (a) version), but a different lexical entry for *no one* (the (c) version instead of the (d) version). Semantically, the **B** inference corresponds to function composition:

(200) **no one**$_c$(λ*x*(**everyone**$_a$(**loves** *x*))) $= \neg\exists y \forall x.$**loves** *y x*

Function composition is independently motivated by so-called non-constituent coordination, as in Right Node Raising examples such as *Ann described and Betty built the motorboat*: function composition allows treating the strings *Ann described* and *Betty built* as predicates with category S/DP. Although we believe that limited access to function composition is necessary in order to account for non-constituent coordination, unlike most combinatory categorial grammars, and unlike many type-logical grammars, our tower system does not rely on function composition. Function composition plays no role in any of the derivations in this book outside of the current chapter.

Crucially, the order of syntactic combination differs across the two derivations: (*everyone* (*loves no one*)) for linear scope versus ((*everyone loves*) *no one*) for inverse scope. The main hypothesis of Steedman (2000) and Steedman (2012) is that inverse scope is only possible if function composition has rearranged the normal syntactic constituency, along with corresponding changes in intonation and information structure. This requires making a distinction between deep, function/argument constituency versus the constituent structure delivered by function composition, which Steedman calls surface constituency. His main claim, then, is that the nuclear scope of any scope-taker must form a surface constituent that is adjacent to the scope-taker.

Steedman (2012) develops the implications of this hypothesis in depth. One key additional assumption is an independent mechanism for the scoping of indefinites involving Skolem functions. Apart from some discussion in chapter 10, we have not addressed the differences between indefinites and other classes of scope-takers in this book; see, e.g., Szabolcsi (2010), Barker (2014b) for general discussion of the special status of indefinites, and Charlow (2014) for a discussion of indefinites in the context of a continuation-based approach.

Crucially, on the surface-constituency view, the only way for a universal to take scope is to be linearly adjacent to its nuclear scope.

(201) [[The man who builds] each clock] also repairs it.

That means, for instance, that the only way (201) can receive an inverse-linking interpretation is if the inner bracketed string *the man who builds* can be derived as a constituent. Given the typeshifter **B**, this is just function composition. One nice prediction of this account is an explanation for how the universal is able to bind a pronoun in the nuclear scope on the inverse linking reading, since the universal is in a syntactic position high enough to (almost) c-command the pronoun. This solves the problem that some QR approaches have binding from inverse linking cases as discussed by, e.g., Heim and Kratzer (1998:234–5).

In other words, Steedman denies that there is ever what we would consider genuine in-situ scope-taking, that is, scope-taking in which the scope-taking element is neither at the left edge nor the right edge of the continuation it is taking scope over.

We believe (along with many others) that scope-takers do not need to be at the edge of their nuclear scope. In addition to the many analyses of in-situ scope argued for above, we will offer here some examples of inverse linking that pose a challenge for the surface-constituency approach.

(202) a. [Some student from each department who had failed] complained.
b. [The man who puts each clock into its velvet case] also repairs it.
c. See if the nursing home is willing to give you the names of [some of each doctor's other patients in the facility]

Native speakers report that these sentences can all receive an inverse-linking interpretation. Steedman (2012:131) argues that in (202a) the relative clause *who had failed* is appositive. This is unlikely to be a viable analysis for (202b): since the locative *into its velvet case* is an obligatory argument of *put*, it must be part of the relative clause.

Likewise, in the naturally-occurring example in (202c), the only way to get the right set of names is to quantify over doctors, find their other patients, and choose some as a subset. This requires the quantifier *each doctor* to take scope over material that surrounds it both on the left and on the right. There is no way to build the required nuclear scope into a surface unit using function composition.

In addition, anticipating Part II, we can see no way for any compositional account of the truth conditions of sentence-internal *same* to manage without proper in-situ scope-taking of the quantificational licensors of *same*, including at least the accounts in Barker (2007) and Brasoveanu (2011).

We conclude that at least some of the time, it is possible for a universal quantifier to take in-situ scope from a properly non-edge position. If so, a grammar that allows scope-taking only over surface constituents, even in the presence of function composition, does not give a full account of scope-taking.

12

Computational connections

In this chapter we address two of the more overtly computational aspects of our project. First, we will consider order of evaluation from the point of view of the pure lambda calculus, one of the original inspirations for our approach.

Second, we will provide some notes on a computational implementation of the tower system, including a refactoring of the type-shifters into a group of operators that provide an effective way to search for analyses.

12.1 Order of evaluation in the lambda calculus

In computer programming languages, order matters.

(203) a.
```
x := x + 1
x := 1
print x
```

b.
```
x := 1
x := x + 1
print x
```

These two blocks of pseudocode differ only in the order of the first two statements. Nevertheless, the behavior of the two blocks will differ: the first will print the number 1, and the second will print the number 2.

What we need in order to understand this difference is some way of representing the meaning of these blocks that encodes the difference in evaluation order. The danger is that the language that we use to encode the difference will itself be order-sensitive, in which case our analysis is in danger of being circular: how can we make sure that the encoding language will be evaluated in the right way?

In order to make this problem concrete, consider representing code in the pure lambda calculus. The lambda calculus is confluent, which means that no matter which application you decided to reduce first, you can always eventually arrive at the same result. Could the lambda calculus, then, serve as an order-neutral representation of sequential computations?

The problem is that the pure lambda calculus is not completely order-neutral. If a lambda form contains subterms that do not have a normal form, the order in which we choose to reduce applications matters very much, as we will see shortly.

First, we need to be more explicit about when we will consider a lambda term to have been fully evaluated. Following Plotkin (1975), we will classify the constructions of the lambda calculus into values and programs:

(204)
x	Variable: value
(λxM)	Abstract: value
(MN)	Application: program

Here, x schematizes over variables, and M and N schematize over arbitrary lambda terms. We will consider our job of evaluating an expression to be complete if the reduced term is a value, that is, either a variable or a lambda abstract. But if the term is an application, we must reduce it if possible, continuing until we have a value.

Some terms cannot be reduced to a value:

(205) $\Omega = ((\lambda x(xx))(\lambda x(xx)))$

Because this term is an application (i.e., is of the form (MN) where $M = N = \lambda x.xx$), it is a program, and not fully reduced. If we attempt to beta-reduce this form, we get a "reduced" form that is identical to the original form (up to alphabetic variance). The result is itself an application, and therefore not fully reduced. This is the simplest "infinite loop" in the pure lambda calculus.

Now we can construct a lambda term where order of reduction makes a big difference. Let **I** be the identity function (λxx). Then

(206) $(\lambda x\mathbf{I})\Omega = (\lambda x(\lambda xx))\ ((\lambda x(xx))\ (\lambda x(xx)))$

This is an application, so we need to reduce. However, we have a term with the form $(M(NN))$, and so have two choices for what to reduce: we can reduce the leftmost (also, outermost) application first, resulting in (λxx), a value. Success! Or we could start by reducing the rightmost (innermost) application, in which case we might begin an endless series of profitless reductions, never getting closer to a value.

Obviously, in this case, we want to start on the left. As long as we agree to always reduce the leftmost application first, we can be sure that we will always arrive at a value (that is, for any expression that reduces to a value).

But, just as in our discussion of crossover in natural language, we'd like to make this policy of always working from left-to-right explicit and precise. Perhaps we'd like to make it precise by encoding it in the form of a program. And since the pure lambda calculus is Turing complete, we might naturally choose to encode the reduction algorithm in the pure lambda calculus. But if we do this, then the reduction algorithm will be expressed in a language whose semantic behavior, as we have just seen, depends on evaluation order, and we're right back where we started.

What we are wishing for is an evaluation strategy for which the order of evaluation of the analyzed expression is independent of the evaluation order of the language in which the analysis is conducted. This is where continuations come in. We adopt the following strategy of Plotkin (1975): for any given term in the language to be analyzed, we map it to a different term via some explicit mapping strategy, then we reduce the expanded term. The maps that Plotkin studied are known as Continuation Passing Style (CPS) transforms, and they make explicit use of continuations.

It turns out that a carefully-crafted CPS transform can faithfully simulate the same series of reductions that the original term would undergo given a leftmost reduction scheme (or rightmost reduction, or some more complicated regime). Yet the transformed term itself will be completely insensitive to the reduction strategy under which it is evaluated. The way the transform accomplishes this is by creating a term in which there is always exactly one redex, i.e., exactly one choice for which application to reduce next. It doesn't matter whether we reduce the leftmost redex, or the rightmost, since there is only one option. How this works will become clear as we develop the discussion in more detail.

Here is the call-by-name (CBN) Continuation Passing Style (CPS) transform from Plotkin (1975:153). If ϕ is some term in the pure lambda calculus, we'll write $[\phi]$ for the call-by-name CPS transform of ϕ.

(207)
$$\begin{aligned} [x] &= x \\ [\lambda x M] &= \lambda\kappa.\kappa(\lambda x[M]) \\ [MN] &= \lambda\kappa.[M](\lambda m.m[N]\kappa) \end{aligned}$$

Thus $[\cdot]$ maps lambda terms into (more complex) lambda terms. For instance, the mapping rules apply to our problematic term as follows:

(208)
$$\begin{aligned} [(\lambda x\mathrm{I})\Omega] &= \lambda\kappa.[\lambda x\mathrm{I}](\lambda m.m[\Omega]\kappa) \\ &= \lambda\kappa.(\lambda\kappa.\kappa(\lambda x[\mathrm{I}]))(\lambda m.m[\Omega]\kappa) \end{aligned}$$

Crucially, this transformed term encodes the computation expressed by the original term in such a way that the the desired order of evaluation is explicitly encoded. Since the transform is an abstract (it begins with "$\lambda\kappa$"), it's already a value, so we can't evaluate the transformed expression directly. In order to see the encoding unfold, we must apply this term to the trivial continuation, I, which triggers the reduction process. As reduction proceeds, unlike in the original term, at each stage there is exactly one possible reduction, so we can't possibly make the wrong choice:

(209)
$$\begin{aligned} ([(\lambda x\mathrm{I})\Omega]\mathrm{I}) &= (\underline{(\lambda\kappa.(\lambda\kappa.\kappa(\lambda x[\mathrm{I}]))(\lambda m.m[\Omega]\kappa))}\mathrm{I}) \\ &= (\underline{(\lambda\kappa.\kappa(\lambda x[\mathrm{I}]))}(\lambda m.m[\Omega]\mathrm{I})) \\ &= (\underline{(\lambda m.m[\Omega]\mathrm{I})}(\lambda x[\mathrm{I}])) \\ &= (((\lambda x[\mathrm{I}])[\Omega])\mathrm{I}) \\ &= (((\lambda x[\lambda xx])[\Omega])\mathrm{I}) \\ &= (((\lambda x(\lambda\kappa.\kappa(\lambda x[x])))[\Omega])\mathrm{I}) \end{aligned}$$

$$
\begin{aligned}
&= (((\underline{(\lambda x(\lambda\kappa.\kappa(\lambda xx)))}[\Omega])\mathrm{I})\\
&= (\underline{(\lambda\kappa.\kappa(\lambda xx))\mathrm{I}})\\
&= (\underline{\mathrm{I}}(\lambda xx))\\
&= (\lambda xx)
\end{aligned}
$$

Some of these steps are beta reductions, and some are further unfolding of the CPS transform '[·]'. For each reduction, we have underlined the only functor that is ready to be applied to an argument. Note that the underlined lambda term is always the leftmost functor. As the zipper of evaluation descends, there is at most one application that is not hidden underneath an abstract (recall that since abstracts are already values, we don't perform reductions inside of an abstract). As a result, at each step there is only one possible move. The CBN CPS transform forces us to always reduce the leftmost application first, ignoring the inner structure of the argument Ω.

Incidentally, the reason it makes sense to call this transform "call-by-name" is that the argument (in this case, the argument is Ω) is passed to the functor unevaluated. In linguistic terms, it corresponds to a de dicto interpretation: if Lars wants to marry a Norwegian, then the description "a Norwegian" is incorporated into the description of his desire unevaluated, rather than first picking out a specific de re individual (i.e., by evaluating the direct object, call-by-value) and then supplying the individual to build the desired representation. (This analogy to the de dicto/de re ambiguity is meant to spur intuition, and should not be taken too seriously in its simplest form.)

EXERCISE 30

Here is Plotkin's call-by-value transform:

$$
\begin{aligned}
[x] &= \lambda\kappa.\kappa x\\
[\lambda xM] &= \lambda\kappa.\kappa(\lambda x[M])\\
[MN] &= \lambda\kappa.[M](\lambda m.[N](\lambda n.mn\kappa))
\end{aligned}
$$

Show that this CPS transform forces evaluation of the argument first, guaranteeing the evaluation of (206) will result in an infinite loop.

In order to see the family resemblance between Plotkin's transforms and the continuation-based system here, consider the semantic part of the combination schema from (16):

(210) $\dfrac{g[\;]}{f} \cdot \dfrac{h[\;]}{x} \rightarrow \dfrac{g[h[\;]]}{f(x)}$

Translated into flat notation, this is

(211) $\lambda\kappa.g[\kappa f] \cdot \lambda\kappa.h[\kappa x] \Rightarrow \lambda\kappa.g[h[\kappa(fx)]]$

The combinator that will produce this result given the left hand value and the right hand value is $C = \lambda MN\kappa.M(\lambda m.N(\lambda n.\kappa(mn)))$. To see this, compare the following to (210).

(212) $$CMN = (\lambda MN\kappa.M(\lambda m.N(\lambda n.\kappa(mn))))(\lambda\kappa.g[\kappa f])(\lambda\kappa.h[\kappa x])$$
$$= \lambda\kappa.g[h[\kappa(fx)]]$$

The final result is exactly the linear presentation of the semantics of the result expression of the combination schema.

The details of C are not exactly the same as either Plotkin's call-by-name transform or his call-by-value transform. For one thing, Plotkin's transform makes the continuation variable κ an argument ('$mn\kappa$' in both transforms), but κ is in functor position for us ('$\kappa(mn)$'). Subtle differences in CPS transforms make for significant differences in behavior; nevertheless, the resemblance should be clear.

The main point here is that, just as a CPS transform allows explicit control over order of evaluation in the lambda calculus, so too does articulating an ordinary categorial grammar into continuation layers allow control over order of evaluation in our natural language fragment. And, just as Plotkin was able to reason about evaluation order by transforming an order-sensitive term into an order-insensitive version, so too are we able to reason about the processing order of composition by transforming the natural language expression in question into an expression in a semantic representation that is itself order-neutral.

The result is a theory in which a certain aspect of processing is represented in terms of a competence grammar. In this sense, then, we treat crossover and other order effects simultaneously as processing defaults and as part of the competence grammar that composes well-formed expressions. On this view, there is no contradiction between being a matter of processing, and simultaneously being a matter of linguistic competence, i.e., a matter of grammaticality.

12.2 Notes on a computational implementation

The tower system was designed to make it easy to construct derivations by hand. Nevertheless, it is still useful to have a machine supply most of the details of a derivation automatically. This enables quick checking of the soundness of an analysis, and also helps find all alternative parses and interpretations for an ambiguous string.

We will show how the pressures of building a practical implementation can lead to an equivalent but different set of type-shifters. The differences will help reveal how the combinators (lifting, lowering, combination, etc.) interact with one another.

The main engineering pressure comes from the fact that the search space for derivations is not bounded. For instance, since the input pattern for the LIFT type-shifter is always met, there is no limit to the number of times LIFT can be applied, so there is no limit to the number of distinct derivations for any sentence generated by a tower grammar. The challenge, then, is to figure out how to LIFT when needed, without LIFTing ad infinitum.

Our strategy here is to compile the LIFTing operation into the combination schema. The idea is that rather than LIFTing spontaneously, we will only LIFT when motivated by the need to combine with a neighboring tower.

Given that there are multiple options for LIFTing, the possible ways of combining any two expressions is a relation, not a function. Then let '$\Rightarrow$' be a three place relation between an expression in category A, an adjacent expression in category B, and the combined expression C (written '$A \cdot B \Rightarrow C$', pronounced 'an A merged with a B forms a C'). Then we can replace the type-shifters given above with the following combination rules:

(213) $A/B \cdot B \Rightarrow A$ (Slash)

(214) $B \cdot B\backslash A \Rightarrow A$ (Backslash)

(215) If $A \cdot B \Rightarrow C$, then $A \cdot \dfrac{D|E}{B} \Rightarrow \dfrac{D|E}{C}$ (LiftLeft)

(216) If $A \cdot B \Rightarrow C$, then $\dfrac{D|E}{A} \cdot B \Rightarrow \dfrac{D|E}{C}$ (LiftRight)

(217) If $A \cdot B \Rightarrow C$, then $\dfrac{D|E}{A} \cdot \dfrac{E|F}{B} \Rightarrow \dfrac{D|F}{C}$ (Combination)

(218) If $A \cdot B \Rightarrow \dfrac{\mathrm{C}|\mathrm{S}}{\mathrm{S}}$, then $A \cdot B \Rightarrow C$ (Lower)

(219) $A_F /\!\!/ B \cdot B \Rightarrow A$ (Front)

> **EXERCISE 31**
>
> Argue that an arbitrary pair of expressions will generate a finite set of combined expressions. Special reasoning is required for the case of Lower.

In this presentation, because the combination schema governs just the top layer of a pair of expressions, there is no need for more than one variant of the combination schema (compare with section 1.3). There is also no need to distinguish between simple lifting and internal lift (see the discussion in section 4.1).

The semantics of each of the schemata that don't have side conditions (namely, Slash, Backslash, and Front) will be a combinator which will first be applied to the meaning of the left constituent, then to the meaning of the right. The semantics of the Slash rule and the Front rule is simply the identity function, $\lambda x.x$. The semantics of the Backslash rule is the T combinator, $\lambda xy.yx$, so that **j**:DP · **left**:DP\S ⇒ **T j left**:S, where **T j left** reduces to **left j**.

The semantics for the other rules depend also on the semantics associated with their side condition. So their semantics will be a combinator that applies first to the semantics of the expression mentioned in the side condition, then to the semantics of the two expressions. The combinator for LiftLeft will be $\lambda zxy\kappa.x(\lambda x.\kappa(zxy))$, for LiftRight will be $\lambda zxy\kappa.y(\lambda y.\kappa(zxy))$, and for the main Combination schema, $\lambda zxy\kappa.x(\lambda x.y(\lambda y.\kappa(zxy)))$.

This derivation relation can be combined with standard chart parsing techniques to build a practical parser. Starting with the lexical entries of each word, for any two adjacent expressions L and R, add a new expression for each way of combining L and R according to the relation defined above. A derivation is complete if there is an expression whose category is S spanning the entire input string.

A derivation of the linear scope reading of *Someone saw everyone* will illustrate:

```
someone saw everyone S Lower Combination Backslash
   someone (S//(DP\\S))
   saw everyone (S//((DP\S)\\S)) LiftLeft Slash
     saw ((DP\S)/DP)
     everyone (S//(DP\\S))
```

Reading from the bottom up, the two-level direct object combines with the one-level verb by means of the LiftLeft schema on the higher level and the Slash schema on the lower level. The two-level verb phrase combines with the two-level subject by means of the Combination schema on the higher level with the Backslash schema on the lower level, followed by Lowering the result. To get inverse scope, the last step will follow the recipe `Lower LiftLeft Lower LiftRight Backlash`, which says that the two-level *someone* takes narrow scope with respect to the tower on the right (LiftLeft); that two-level tower combines with the lower level of *saw everyone* by means of the LiftRight schema on the higher level and Backslash on the lower level; and two applications of Lower complete the derivation.

One of the remaining challenges for a parser is to manage gaps, which are allowed to range over any category of the form $A /\!\!/ A$. In practice, a gap will only be useful if it matches the needs of some other independently parsed constituent. For instance, in the case of a fronted wh-phrase, the gap will mirror whatever the fronted phrase requires. This means that we can deduce the structure of the gap category we will need by looking at the wh-phrase. One practical technique for building a system that infers appropriate categories for gaps and pronouns is to allow variables as elements in categories, and then combine categories via a unification algorithm. See section 17.10 for an effective and reasonably efficient strategy for handling gaps in a continuation-based type-logical grammar.

Likewise, the BIND type-shifter can be applied an unbounded number of times. However, it will only be useful to apply BIND if there is a corresponding occurrence of the ▷ category connective elsewhere in the derivation to cancel the ▷ introduced by BIND.

EXERCISE 32

If the Combination rule in (217) were eliminated, binding and NPI licensing would no longer work. (Why?) However, scope-taking and scope ambiguity *would* work. Convince yourself of this by sketching derivations of at least some of the six readings of *Someone gave everyone nothing*. If in addition the Lower rule is generalized to apply to any matching categories, rather than to just matching S's, then binding is once again possible, but crossover violations are generated. (Demonstrate.) What would it take to restore an explanation for crossover to the modified grammar?

Part II

Logic: *Same* and Sluicing

The continuation-based tower framework explored in Part I is by no means the only way to use continuations to gain insight into natural language. Continuations are a perspective, a way of looking at composition. They can be incorporated into a concrete system in many different ways. In fact, we suspect that considering multiple different implementations of continuations is essential in triangulating on the underlying concept. In accord with this belief, in this part of the book we will develop a different continuation-based grammar, which we will call NL_λ. The emphasis will not be on order effects, as it was in Part I, but rather, on phenomena and explanations beyond the reach of the simple tower system.

Part I implemented continuations in a combinatory categorial grammar. The approach in Part II is set in a different branch of the categorial tradition, namely, type-logical grammar. Type-logical grammar stems from the work of Lambek (1958), as developed in particular by Michael Moortgat and associates (see Moortgat 1997 for an overview). The main idea is to use a formal logic—a set of formulas combined with inference rules—to reason about composition. Usually, logics are used to reason about truth: from knowing that "There's smoke" and that "Where there is smoke, there's fire", it is valid to conclude that "There's fire". Type-logical grammar reasons instead about composition: from knowing that "*John* is a DP" and that "a DP followed by a verb phrase makes a sentence", it is valid to conclude that "*John* followed by a verb phrase makes a sentence".

The most basic kind of categorial grammar (see Bar-Hillel 1953) studies function/argument combination, corresponding in the semantics to function application. Lambek (1958) adds hypothetical reasoning, corresponding in the semantics to lambda abstraction. In order to handle in-situ scope-taking, pursuing ideas of Oehrle (1994), Muskens (2001), and de Groote (2002), we will enrich the SYNTACTIC side of categorial grammar with a kind of lambda abstraction. Although this requires adding an unusual structural inference rule, we show how to factor it into more ordinary structural rules. (See chapter 17 for some of the formal properties of the system.)

The resulting continuation-aware system differs from the tower system in the first part of the book in ways both superficial and deep. One of the more striking differences is that the type-shifters LIFT and LOWER are theorems in this system, so there is no need to manage multiple levels of continuations. This makes the type-logical system simpler in a certain respect. Of course, it was exactly the rigid separation into layers that allowed control over evaluation order in Part I. Part II does not focus on issues of order, though we will suggest in the Afterword a way that control over order of evaluation could be introduced into the type-logical approach.

A second, related, difference is that the grammar here provides expressions with access not only to their own continuation, but to a portion of their context which is itself a continuation. That is, if an expression in category $A \backslash\!\!\backslash B$ is a B missing an expression of category A, then an expression in category $A \backslash\!\!\backslash (B \backslash\!\!\backslash C)$ is an expression missing two pieces, an A and a B. In the terms of Morrill, Fadda and Valentín's Discontinuous

Lambek Grammar, this is the difference between expressions containing a single point of discontinuity and expressions containing multiple points of discontinuity. We will consider the relationship between our system and Discontinuous Lambek Grammar in section 15.2.

So if Part I is about linear order, Part II is about *higher* order (types).

The main empirical application discussed here that makes essential use of higher-order continuations will be the 'parasitic scope' analysis of sentence-internal *same* developed by Barker (2007). Parasitic scope is discussed here in chapter 14.

Building on analyses of Morrill et al. (2011), we will extend the parasitic scope technique to pronominal anaphora and verb phrase ellipsis in chapter 15.

The final major empirical case study concerns sluicing. Sluicing is the kind of ellipsis involved in the sentence *Someone left, but I don't know who* __. In chapter (16), building on work of Jäger (2001, 2005), we develop an account of sluicing. Following Barker (2013), we propose that sluicing is anaphora to a continuation. If so, this supports our hypothesis that explicitly recognizing continuations is an essential part of a complete picture of natural language.

The analysis of sluicing does not require higher-order continuations. We could have provided an analysis of sluicing in the tower-based grammar of Part I, given the addition of an ad-hoc type shifter allowing continuations to serve as the value passed by a binding operator. We discuss sluicing in this part of the book instead for several reasons. For one thing, sluicing does not hinge on evaluation order in any essential way, so it does not contribute to the order-based theme of the first part of the book. Second, as a form of ellipsis, it is useful to compare the analysis of sluicing with the parasitic-scope treatment of verb phrase ellipsis using higher-order continuations given in chapter 15. Third, the type-logical setting allows us to emphasize the logic of silent modifiers, a crucial component of the explanation for sprouting (a certain class of sluicing examples such as *John left, but I don't know when*). Fourth, the type-logical setting also makes possible an analysis of implicit-argument sluices (e.g., *John ate, but I don't know what* __) in terms of multiplicative conjunction (the tensor connective '⊗').

A note on exercises: although type-logical grammars are conceptually elegant, they are not particularly well-suited to working out derivations on paper or on a blackboard. Because of this, we will not continue the tutorial aspect of the first part of the book, so there won't be any more suggested exercises.

Although we will mention connections with discussions in Part I from time to time, it should be possible to read Part II independently from Part I.

The complete formal system is presented in the next chapter, chapter 13. An equivalent grammar is given in chapter 17. These formal systems were first presented in Barker (2007).

13

NL$_\lambda$

We present NL$_\lambda$: the non-associative Lambek grammar NL, augmented with λ-abstraction in the syntax. Of course, plain Lambek grammars have λ-abstraction already, in their Curry-Howard labeling (i.e., in the semantic part of the grammar); what is innovative here is that we will have lambda abstraction in the syntactic, proof-theoretic part of the grammar. In effect, our syntactic lambda embodies the idea that an expression in category $A\backslash\!\!\backslash B$ is a B missing an A somewhere (specific) inside of it—that is, it is a B with an A *syntactically* abstracted from it.

This chapter introduces the formal system, and shows how it provides an analysis of simple in-situ scope-taking. The presentation will be relatively informal, by the standards of type-logical grammar; chapter 17 contains additional formal details. For a more complete discussion of type-logical grammar, see Moortgat (1997) or Jäger (2005).

The following chapters will use the formal system to develop a parasitic-scope analysis of *same*, a treatment of pronominal anaphora and verb phrase ellipsis, and an analysis of sluicing.

Some of the formal properties of the system are discussed in chapter 17, including a completeness result, conservativity over NL (the non-associative Lambek grammar), and decidability (effective proof search for finding derivations). These results will justify our claim that despite the introduction of syntactic lambda abstraction, the logics studied in Part II are perfectly ordinary and well-behaved substructural logics, and can be used with full confidence and without the slightest reservation.

13.1 Categories

In a type-logical grammar, the role of syntactic categories are played by logical formulas. In fact, the categories (formulas) of NL$_\lambda$ are identical to the syntactic categories developed in Part I in section 1.2, and their interpretation and behavior are conceptually parallel.

More specifically, the set of syntactic categories used in Part II will contain the same basic (atomic) categories as in Part I, namely, DP, S, and N. As in Part I, if A and B are any categories, then $A\backslash B$, A/B, $A\backslash\!\!\backslash B$, $A/\!\!/B$, and $A?B$ are also (complex) categories.

It will be convenient to use Q as an abbreviation for DP?S, where DP?S is the kind of question that asks for an individual.

Category examples:		
Determiner phrase	DP	John
Verb phrase	$DP\backslash S$	left
Clause	S	John left
Generalized quantifier	$S/\!\!/(DP\backslash\!\!\backslash S)$	everyone
Interrogative-embedding verb	$(DP\backslash S)/Q$	know
Fronted wh-phrase	$Q/(DP\backslash\!\!\backslash S)$	who

These categories match the categories used for these expression types in Part I exactly.

13.2 Structures

In type-logical grammar, *structures* play the role of syntactic trees, as well as the role of logical forms. The simplest structure is a syntactic category (a formula). That is, the set of structures includes the set of syntactic categories. In addition, if Γ and Δ are structures, then $\Gamma \cdot \Delta$ ('Γ syntactically merged with Δ') and $\Gamma \circ \Delta$ ('Γ taking scope over Δ') are also structures.

Structures:		
Determiner phrase	DP	John
Clause	$DP \cdot DP\backslash S$	John left
Clause	$DP \cdot ((DP\backslash S)/DP \cdot DP)$	John saw Mary
Verb phrase	$(DP\backslash S)/Q \cdot Q$	know who left

We will need to enlarge the set of structures below before we can provide concrete examples of useful structures involving '$\circ$', the structural punctuation for scope-taking.

13.3 Logical rules

These rules are identical to the rules given in Moortgat (1997:129). They constitute the logical core of a two-mode type-logical grammar:

(220)

$$\frac{}{A \vdash A}\text{Axiom}$$

$$\frac{\Gamma \vdash A \quad \Sigma[B] \vdash C}{\Sigma[\Gamma \cdot A\backslash B] \vdash C}\backslash L \qquad \frac{A \cdot \Gamma \vdash B}{\Gamma \vdash A\backslash B}\backslash R \qquad \frac{\Gamma \vdash A \quad \Sigma[B] \vdash C}{\Sigma[B/A \cdot \Gamma] \vdash C}/L \qquad \frac{\Gamma \cdot A \vdash B}{\Gamma \vdash B/A}/R$$

$$\frac{\Gamma \vdash A \quad \Sigma[B] \vdash C}{\Sigma[\Gamma \circ A\backslash\!\!\backslash B] \vdash C}\backslash\!\!\backslash L \qquad \frac{A \circ \Gamma \vdash B}{\Gamma \vdash A\backslash\!\!\backslash B}\backslash\!\!\backslash R \qquad \frac{\Gamma \vdash A \quad \Sigma[B] \vdash C}{\Sigma[B/\!\!/A \circ \Gamma] \vdash C}/\!\!/L \qquad \frac{\Gamma \circ A \vdash B}{\Gamma \vdash B/\!\!/A}/\!\!/R$$

Since these logical rules are completely standard, the logic NL_λ explored here will differ from other more standard two-mode type-logical grammars only in the choice of structural postulates.

In the terminology of type-logical grammar, solid slashes characterize one *mode* of syntactic combination, which we will call the MERGE mode (as in the syntactic merge operation), and the hollow slashes characterize a second mode, which we will call the CONTINUATION mode. The solid slashes '\' and '/' are the familiar slashes of categorial grammar, and have the same meaning they do there. The hollow slashes '⑊' and '⫽' are for reasoning about scope-taking, and, as mentioned, they are essentially equivalent to the hollow slashes introduced in Part I.

Just as we used contexts of the form *g*[ ] in the logical expressions used in the semantics of Part I, here we will have syntactic (structural) contexts. In the rules above, '$\Sigma[\Delta]$' is a structure Σ containing a particular occurrence of the structure Δ. Then $\Sigma[\Gamma]$ is a structure just like Σ except that the occurrence of Δ has been replaced by the structure Γ. For instance, if $\Sigma = \text{John}\cdot\text{left}$, and Δ is the occurrence of the structure *left* inside of Σ, then $\Sigma[\text{saw}\cdot\text{Mary}] = \text{John}\cdot(\text{saw}\cdot\text{Mary})$. Thus the bracket notation is a way to refer to structures and their subparts, and in particular to replace one substructure with another. This kind of substitution into a context is the same plugging operation used in Part I as part of the semantics for the tower notation, except that in Part I, holes and plugs were part of the semantic representation language, and here they are part of the syntactic representation language.

As the labels attached to the logical rules indicate, there are two types of inference patterns: *R* inferences and *L* inferences. Here is an example of an *R* inference:

$$\frac{\text{DP} \cdot \text{VP} \vdash \text{S}}{\text{VP} \vdash \text{DP}\backslash\text{S}}\ \backslash R$$

In words, reading from top to bottom: if merging a DP with a VP is one way of forming an S, then it follows that any expression in the category VP must also be in the category DP\S. This rule captures the sense in which an expression in category DP\S is the kind of expression that can be merged with a DP to its left to form an S.

And here is an example of a *L* inference:

$$\frac{\text{John} \vdash \text{DP} \qquad \text{S} \vdash \text{S}}{\text{John} \cdot \text{DP}\backslash\text{S} \vdash \text{S}}\ \backslash L$$

This rule has two premises. The first premise says that *John* is in category DP. The second premise is trivial in this instance, and merely says that everything in the category S is in the category S (as surely it must be). If both these premises hold, the conclusion on the bottom line says that *John* must be the kind of thing that can be syntactically merged with an expression in the category DP\S in order to form a complete S.

As for the other six logical rules, they differ only in whether the targeted expression appears on the left or the right of some other element, and whether we are reasoning about merging (solid slashes) or scope-taking (hollow slashes).

13.4 Proofs as derivations

By chaining inferences together, we can analyze complex sentences:

(221)
$$\dfrac{\dfrac{\text{Mary} \vdash \text{DP} \qquad \dfrac{\text{John} \vdash \text{DP} \qquad \dfrac{}{\text{S} \vdash \text{S}}\,\text{Axiom}}{\text{John} \cdot \text{DP}\backslash\text{S} \vdash \text{S}}\,\backslash L}{\text{John} \cdot ((\text{DP}\backslash\text{S})/\text{DP} \cdot \text{Mary}) \vdash \text{S}}\,/L}{\text{John} \cdot (\text{saw} \cdot \text{Mary}) \vdash \text{S}}\,\text{LEX}$$

The $\backslash L$ inference at the top was just discussed. The bottom inference, labeled LEX, simply substitutes the lexical item *saw* in the place of its syntactic category, $(\text{DP}\backslash\text{S})/\text{DP}$.

A derivation is complete if the premises at the top of the proof consist entirely of axioms (such as '$\text{S} \vdash \text{S}$') or lexical assumptions (such as '$\text{Mary} \vdash \text{DP}$').

A structure followed by '$\vdash$' and a category constitutes a **sequent**. Sequents can be interpreted here as category judgments. For instance, the sequent '$\text{John} \cdot (\text{saw} \cdot \text{Mary}) \vdash \text{S}$' asserts that the syntactic structure '$\text{John} \cdot (\text{saw} \cdot \text{Mary})$' is a member of the category S.

Since the derivation in (221) is complete, the final sequent is a theorem of the logic. Once the inference rules of a logic are chosen, linguistic analysis consists in assigning categories to lexical expressions. The goal is for every well-formed expression in the fragment of the language under study to be a theorem of the logic (and vice-versa).

13.5 Structures with holes (contexts)

The inferences and the derivations (proofs) discussed so far involve only the merge mode. In order to use the categories and logical rules governing the continuation mode, we need to add a structural rule. In order to state this structural rule, we will need to enlarge the set of structures (as promised above) to include **gapped structures**: if $\Sigma[\Delta]$ is a structure, then so is $\lambda\alpha\ \Sigma[\alpha]$, where α is a variable taken from the set $x, y, z, x_1, x_2, \ldots$. For instance, $\lambda x\ x$, $\lambda y\ y$, $\lambda x\ (x \cdot \text{left})$, $\lambda x\ (\text{John} \cdot (\text{saw} \cdot x))$, and $\lambda x\, \lambda y\ (y \cdot (\text{saw} \cdot x))$ are gapped structures.

Then we have the following structural inference rule:

(222) $\Sigma[\Delta] \equiv \Delta \circ \lambda\alpha\ \Sigma[\alpha]$

In words: if a structure Σ contains within it a structure Δ, then Δ can take scope over the rest of Σ, where 'the rest of Σ' is represented as the gapped structure $\lambda\alpha\ \Sigma[\alpha]$.

In a tangram diagram:

(223)

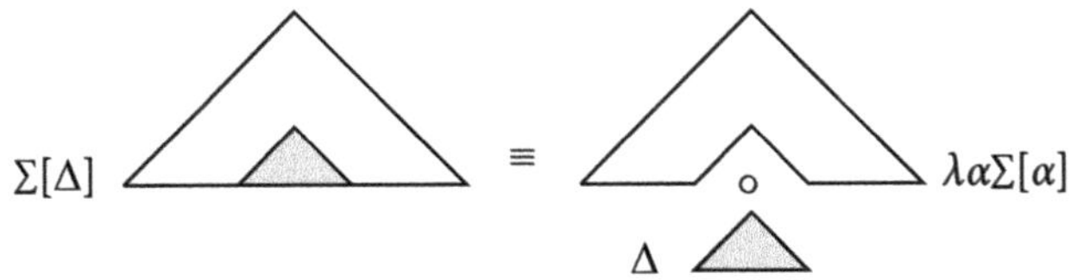

The postulate says that if Δ (the small gray triangle) is some structure embedded within a larger structure Σ (the complete larger triangle), we can present these components completely equivalently by articulating them into foreground and background, plug and context, an expression and its continuation. Then Δ will be the foregrounded expression, and its context (the clear notched triangle) will be the continuation $\lambda\alpha\,\Sigma[\alpha]$.

A technical point: the inference expressed by the structural postulate is only valid in cases in which the variable instantiating α is distinct from all other variables in Σ. This restriction is not essential; there is a variable-free implementation of the fragment in Barker (2007), which is also presented below in chapter 17.

This structural rule handles scope-taking of in-situ quantifiers, and, as we will see in subsequent chapters, a number of other semantic phenomena, including parasitic scope and sluicing.

An example will show how the rule handles simple in-situ scope-taking. If we assume that *everyone* has the syntactic category $S/\!\!/(DP\backslash\!\!\backslash S)$ (just as in Part I), then we can give the following derivation to the sentence *John saw everyone*:

(224)

$$\dfrac{\dfrac{\dfrac{\dfrac{\dfrac{\dfrac{\vdots}{\text{john}\cdot(\text{saw}\cdot \text{DP})\vdash \text{S}}}{\text{DP}\circ\lambda x\,(\text{john}\cdot(\text{saw}\cdot x))\vdash \text{S}}\equiv}{\lambda x\,(\text{john}\cdot(\text{saw}\cdot x))\vdash \text{DP}\backslash\!\!\backslash \text{S}}\backslash\!\!\backslash R \quad \text{S}\vdash\text{S}}{\text{S}/\!\!/(\text{DP}\backslash\!\!\backslash\text{S})\circ\lambda x\,(\text{john}\cdot(\text{saw}\cdot x))\vdash \text{S}}/\!\!/L}{\text{everyone}\circ\lambda x\,(\text{john}\cdot(\text{saw}\cdot x))\vdash \text{S}}\text{LEX}}{\text{john}\cdot(\text{saw}\cdot\text{everyone})\vdash \text{S}}\equiv$$

Reading from the bottom to the top, the first step is to suppose that *everyone* might take scope over the rest of the clause (second line from the bottom). This involves applying the structural postulate in a way that selects *everyone* as the focussed substructure. That is, we choose $\Sigma[\Delta] = \text{john}\cdot(\text{saw}\cdot[\text{everyone}])$. The structural equivalence delivers the second line from the bottom, since $\Delta\circ\lambda\alpha\,\Sigma[\alpha] = \text{everyone}\circ\lambda x(\text{john}\cdot(\text{saw}\cdot x))$.

In order to complete the derivation, it is necessary to prove that "the rest of the clause", corresponding here to the gapped structure $\lambda x\,(\text{john}\cdot(\text{saw}\cdot x))$, has category $DP\backslash\!\!\backslash S$. The derivation here omits some details, since the initial premise is neither a lexical correspondence nor a tautology, but the remaining steps are similar to the derivation of *John saw Mary* given above in (221).

In later derivations we will see that the structure Σ can itself be embedded within an even larger context.

What does the structural rule say? On the one hand, it plays a role in the grammar analogous to the role of Quantifier Raising. It is tempting to view the inference at the bottom of the derivation in (224) as a movement operation simulating Quantifier Raising. In fact, that is a legitimate way to understand an aspect of what the postulate is doing, and intuitions about Quantifier Raising will often be directly transferable to intuitions about applying the structural postulate, and vice-versa.

However, it is not a complete understanding. Another important way to interpret the postulate is that it says the two structures are logically equivalent. Unlike Quantifier Raising, then, the structural postulate has no effect on semantic interpretation; more technically, in terms of the model theory of the logic (the model of the logic, not the model theory of the linguistic analysis; see chapter 17), the two structures denote the same object. On this view, the structural postulate merely makes explicit a shift in perspective, a shift in what the prover is considering to be foreground and what background. This notion of a shifted perspective is developed further below in section 15.1.

13.6 Curry-Howard labeling (semantic interpretation)

One pleasant property of type-logical grammar is that the compositional semantics is completely determined by the structure of the logical rules. That is, the composition of the elements of a linguistic structure follows automatically from the logical operations that build them, according to a mapping known as the Curry-Howard correspondence. In brief (once again, see or Moortgat 1997 or Jäger 2005 for full details), Left inference rules (the ones marked '*L*') have the semantics of function application, Right rules (the ones marked '*R*') have the semantics of functional abstraction, and structural rules have no effect on the semantic labeling.

The Curry-Howard labeling of the inference rules is completely standard, exactly as given by Moortgat (1997), section 3. We illustrate by giving examples of labeled versions of the axiom rule, one *L* rule, and one *R* rule. Here, $x : A$ means that x is the semantic label for the syntactic category (formula) A.

$$\frac{}{x : A \vdash x : A}\ \text{Axiom}$$

$$\frac{\Gamma \vdash x{:}A \qquad \Sigma[N{:}B] \vdash M{:}C}{\Sigma[\Gamma \cdot f{:}(A\backslash B)] \vdash M\{N \mapsto f(x)\}{:}C}\ \backslash L \qquad \frac{x{:}A \cdot \Gamma \vdash N{:}B}{\Gamma \vdash (\lambda x N){:}(A\backslash B)}\ \backslash R$$

Here, '$M\{N \mapsto f(x)\}$' means 'the formula just like M, but with each occurrence of N replaced by $f(x)$'. In the labeling for the Right rule, note that because A is used to derive B, the label x of A will normally occur as part of the label N of B, so that when λx is prefixed to N, the lambda will bind an occurrence of x.

The labelings of the other L and R rules are parallel; see Moortgat (1997) section 3 for full details.

To see how these labeling rules interact to give a full semantic analysis, here is the same proof given immediately above, but with semantic labels prefixed to each syntactic category:

$$
\begin{array}{cl}
\mathbf{j}\text{:john} \cdot (\mathbf{saw}\text{:saw} \cdot y\text{:DP}) \vdash (\mathbf{saw}\, y\, \mathbf{j})\text{:S} & \\ \hline
y\text{:DP} \circ \lambda x(\mathbf{j}\text{:john} \cdot (\mathbf{saw}\text{:saw} \cdot x)) \vdash (\mathbf{saw}\, y\, \mathbf{j})\text{:S} & \equiv \\ \hline
\lambda x(\mathbf{j}\text{:john} \cdot (\mathbf{saw}\text{:saw} \cdot x)) \vdash (\lambda y.\mathbf{saw}\, y\, \mathbf{j})\text{:DP}\backslash\!\!\backslash\text{S} \qquad p\text{:S} \vdash p\text{:S} & \backslash\!\!\backslash R \\ \hline
Q\text{:S}/\!\!/(\text{DP}\backslash\!\!\backslash\text{S}) \circ \lambda x(\mathbf{j}\text{:john} \cdot (\mathbf{saw}\text{:saw} \cdot x)) \vdash Q(\lambda y.\mathbf{saw}\, y\, \mathbf{j})\text{:S} & /\!\!/ L \\ \hline
\mathbf{everyone}\text{:everyone} \circ \lambda x(\mathbf{j}\text{:john} \cdot (\mathbf{saw}\text{:saw} \cdot x)) \vdash \mathbf{everyone}(\lambda y.\mathbf{saw}\, y\, \mathbf{j})\text{:S} & \text{LEX} \\ \hline
\mathbf{j}\text{:john} \cdot (\mathbf{saw}\text{:saw} \cdot \mathbf{everyone}\text{:everyone}) \vdash \mathbf{everyone}(\lambda y.\mathbf{saw}\, y\, \mathbf{j})\text{:S} & \equiv
\end{array}
$$

Thus the semantic labeling automatically derives the compositional meaning from the inferences. In particular, the conclusion (the bottom line) states that if the semantic values of *John*, *saw*, and *everyone* are **j**, **saw**, and **everyone**, then the semantic value of the sentence is $\mathbf{everyone}(\lambda y.\mathbf{saw}\, y\, \mathbf{j})$.

Although Curry-Howard labeling is simple and straightforward conceptually, it is somewhat cumbersome visually, and the derivations below will include only the syntactic categories.

One crucial aspect of NL_λ is that the structural rule does not affect semantic labeling at all. To see this in the derivation above, compare the bottom line with the line immediately above it: there is no change in any of the semantic labels. This means that the structural operation that corresponds to Quantifier Raising in some sense moves (raises) a substructure to a scope-taking position, but without any effect on meaning. This seems paradoxical, but goes to the heart of the continuation strategy: semantically, a scope-taker combines with its nuclear scope simply and directly, without mediation. It is only the syntax that is unfamiliar, allowing the scope-taker (the functor) to syntactically appear within the surrounding nuclear scope (its argument). The structural rule captures scope-taking as a syntactic operation without disturbing the straightforward semantic composition.

13.7 Quantifier scope ambiguity

NL_λ automatically accounts for the two different semantic interpretations of an ambiguous sentence like *Someone loves everyone*. There are two classes of derivations such that the members of one class have the same linear scoping as their semantic labeling, and the members of the other class have the inverse scoping. Here are representative examples of each of the two classes of derivations:

$$\dfrac{\dfrac{\dfrac{\dfrac{\dfrac{\dfrac{\dfrac{\dfrac{\dfrac{\dfrac{\text{DP}\cdot(\text{loves}\cdot\text{DP})\vdash\text{S}}{\text{DP}\circ\lambda x(\text{DP}\cdot(\text{loves}\cdot x))\vdash\text{S}}\equiv}{\lambda x(\text{DP}\cdot(\text{loves}\cdot x))\vdash\text{DP}\backslash\!\!\backslash\text{S}}\backslash\!\!\backslash R\quad\text{S}\vdash\text{S}}{\text{S}/\!\!/(\text{DP}\backslash\!\!\backslash\text{S})\circ\lambda x(\text{DP}\cdot(\text{loves}\cdot x))\vdash\text{S}}/\!\!/L}{\text{everyone}\circ\lambda x(\text{DP}\cdot(\text{loves}\cdot x))\vdash\text{S}}\text{LEX}}{\text{DP}\cdot(\text{loves}\cdot\text{everyone})\vdash\text{S}}\equiv}{\text{DP}\circ\lambda x(x\cdot(\text{loves}\cdot\text{everyone}))\vdash\text{S}}\equiv}{\lambda x(x\cdot(\text{loves}\cdot\text{everyone}))\vdash\text{DP}\backslash\!\!\backslash\text{S}}\backslash\!\!\backslash R\quad\text{S}\vdash\text{S}}{\text{S}/\!\!/(\text{DP}\backslash\!\!\backslash\text{S})\circ\lambda x(x\cdot(\text{loves}\cdot\text{everyone}))\vdash\text{S}}/\!\!/L}{\text{someone}\circ\lambda x(x\cdot(\text{loves}\cdot\text{everyone}))\vdash\text{S}}\text{LEX}}{\text{someone}\cdot(\text{loves}\cdot\text{everyone})\vdash\text{S}}\equiv$$

The semantic labeling for this derivation is $\exists x\forall y.\textbf{loves}\,y\,x$. In general, the scope-taker that is focussed (i.e., targeted by the structural postulate) lower in the proof takes wider scope.

$$\dfrac{\dfrac{\dfrac{\dfrac{\dfrac{\dfrac{\dfrac{\dfrac{\dfrac{\dfrac{\text{DP}\cdot(\text{loves}\cdot\text{DP})\vdash\text{S}}{\text{DP}\circ\lambda x(x\cdot(\text{loves}\cdot\text{DP}))\vdash\text{S}}\equiv}{\lambda x(x\cdot(\text{loves}\cdot\text{DP}))\vdash\text{DP}\backslash\!\!\backslash\text{S}}\backslash\!\!\backslash R\quad\text{S}\vdash\text{S}}{\text{S}/\!\!/(\text{DP}\backslash\!\!\backslash\text{S})\circ\lambda x(x\cdot(\text{loves}\cdot\text{DP}))\vdash\text{S}}/\!\!/L}{\text{someone}\circ\lambda x(x\cdot(\text{loves}\cdot\text{DP}))\vdash\text{S}}\text{LEX}}{\text{someone}\cdot(\text{loves}\cdot\text{DP})\vdash\text{S}}\equiv}{\text{DP}\circ\lambda x(\text{someone}\cdot(\text{loves}\cdot x))\vdash\text{S}}\equiv}{\lambda x(\text{someone}\cdot(\text{loves}\cdot x))\vdash\text{DP}\backslash\!\!\backslash\text{S}}\backslash\!\!\backslash R\quad\text{S}\vdash\text{S}}{\text{S}/\!\!/(\text{DP}\backslash\!\!\backslash\text{S})\circ\lambda x(\text{someone}\cdot(\text{loves}\cdot x))\vdash\text{S}}/\!\!/L}{\text{everyone}\circ\lambda x(\text{someone}\cdot(\text{loves}\cdot x))\vdash\text{S}}\text{LEX}}{\text{someone}\cdot(\text{loves}\cdot\text{everyone})\vdash\text{S}}\equiv$$

In this case, the semantic labeling gives the universal wide scope: $\forall y\exists x.\textbf{loves}\,y\,x$.

At this point, it should be clear that NL_λ provides an account of in-situ scope taking that automatically accounts for scope ambiguity.

14

Parasitic scope for *same*

Adjectives such as *same*, *different*, *incompatible*, etc., pose a challenge for compositional semantics.

(225) Everyone read the same books.

This sentence has at least two readings. On the sentence-external (deictic) reading, there is some salient set of books such that everyone read those books. On the reading of main interest here, the sentence-internal reading, it means something roughly like 'There is a unique maximal set of books such that everyone read exactly that set'.

The problem is that on the sentence-internal reading, there is no adequate generalized quantifier meaning for the DP *the same books*, as discussed in Keenan (1992) and Barker (2007). We can try interpreting *the same books* as if it meant *exactly one set of books*. But then this quantifier would have to take scope relative to *everyone*, and neither linear nor inverse scope gives the right result: if we give *everyone* wide scope over the choice of a set of books, there will be a potentially different set of books for each person. That does not match intuitions about what (225) means at all, since there would be no requirement that anyone read books in common.

On the other hand, if we give *everyone* narrow scope with respect to the choice of a set of books, we come much closer: the requirement is that everyone read at least those books, but may have read other books in addition. But this strategy does not generalize to other quantifiers, such as *no*, nor to presumably closely-related adjectives, such as *different*:

(226) a. No one read the same books.
b. Everyone read different books.

We certainly do not want to interpret (226a) as saying that there is exactly one set of books that no one read, since those truth conditions are far too easy to satisfy. Likewise, choosing a single set of books before quantifying over readers does not lead to even remotely adequate truth conditions for (226b).

In addition, the partitive examples discussed below in section 14.4 cause additional problems for a generalized-quantifier analysis.

Thus a generalized-quantifier analysis of *the same books* will not work. Instead, we will argue, following Barker (2007) that *same* is a scope-taking adjective.

14.1 Motivating a scope-taking analysis for *same*

Internal readings for *same* arise in a wide range of contexts. We can motivate a quantificational scope-taking analysis of *same* by considering a context in which *same* is embedded inside of a nominal:

(227) John met two [women with the same name].

On the irrelevant external deictic reading, the speaker may have a specific name in mind. In contrast, on the internal reading of interest here, (227) will be true just in case there is any name such that two women in the room have that name.

To emphasize the quantificational nature of these truth conditions, note that a speaker might assert (227) on the basis of a mistaken belief that John met two women named 'Heddy'. But if, unbeknownst to the speaker, John met two women named 'Mary', the sentence is nevertheless true, albeit accidentally from the point of view of the speaker.

Given that *same* involves existential quantification, it will need to take scope. As a starting point for a scope-taking analysis, note that *same* occupies the syntactic position of an adjective. This means it will have a local syntactic category suitable for a nominal modifier, N/N, which we will abbreviate as A. Semantically, it will contribute locally a function f of type $(\texttt{e} \to \texttt{t}) \to \texttt{e} \to \texttt{t}$ that maps nominal properties to subproperties. Given that f chooses among the set of names in the example at hand, we need to quantify over possible f's in order to find a function that selects a multi-woman name.

The next step is to decide what the quantifier takes scope over. It certainly does not take scope over an entire clause, as shown by embedding the nominal in question under a downward entailing operator.

(228) a. John didn't meet two women with the same name.
b. $\exists f$.John didn't meet two women with the f(name).

If we quantify over nominal modifiers at the level of the clause, we predict that (228a) should have an interpretation on which it is true just in case there is some way f of choosing a name such that John didn't meet two women who have the f(name). But those truth conditions are extremely easy to satisfy: the sentence will incorrectly be predicted true as long as there is any name, no matter how rare, such that John didn't meet any women who have that name.

Instead, Barker (2007) suggests that *same* has category $N /\!\!/ (A \backslash\!\!\backslash N)$: something that functions locally as an adjective (i.e., as a nominal modifier, where 'A' abbreviates N/N), takes scope over a nominal, and returns a (quantified) nominal as a result. This lexical assignment gives the following analysis:

(229)

$$
\begin{array}{c}
\text{men} \cdot (\text{with} \cdot (\text{the} \cdot (\text{A} \cdot \text{name}))) \vdash \text{N} \\
\hline
\text{A} \circ \lambda x(\text{men} \cdot (\text{with} \cdot (\text{the} \cdot (x \cdot \text{name})))) \vdash \text{N} \quad \equiv \\
\hline
\lambda x(\text{men} \cdot (\text{with} \cdot (\text{the} \cdot (x \cdot \text{name})))) \vdash \text{A}\mathbin{\backslash\!\!\backslash}\text{N} \quad \mathbin{\backslash\!\!\backslash} R \qquad \text{N} \vdash \text{N} \\
\hline
\text{N}\mathbin{/\!\!/}(\text{A}\mathbin{\backslash\!\!\backslash}\text{N}) \circ \lambda x(\text{men} \cdot (\text{with} \cdot (\text{the} \cdot (x \cdot \text{name})))) \vdash \text{N} \quad \mathbin{/\!\!/} L \\
\hline
\text{same} \circ \lambda x(\text{men} \cdot (\text{with} \cdot (\text{the} \cdot (x \cdot \text{name})))) \vdash \text{N} \quad \text{LEX} \\
\hline
\text{men} \cdot (\text{with} \cdot (\text{the} \cdot (\text{same} \cdot \text{name}))) \vdash \text{N} \quad \equiv
\end{array}
$$

This is in-situ scope-taking of exactly the sort motivated in chapter 13 above; compare this derivation with, e.g., (224). The crucial step is the first step (reading from the bottom upwards), in which *same* takes scope over the enclosing nominal.

This analysis suggests the following denotation for *same*, where N abbreviates the type of a nominal, $\mathtt{e} \to \mathtt{t}$:

(230) a. type(*same*) = $((N \to N) \to N) \to N$
b. $[\![\mathit{same}]\!] = \lambda F_{(N\to N)\to N} \lambda X_{\mathtt{e}}.\exists f_{N\to N} \forall x < X : Ffx$

Inserting the denotation in (230b) into the Curry-Howard labeling of the derivation just given, we have:

(231) a. $[\![$*two men with the same name*$]\!]$ =
b. $\mathbf{two}(\lambda X.\exists f \forall x < X : [\mathbf{with}(\mathbf{the}(f(\mathbf{name})))\ (\mathbf{men})]\ (x))$
c. Objects X with cardinality 2 such that there is a modifier function f such that each proper subpart of X has f(name).

Here, X is a variable of type $\mathtt{e}$ that ranges over sets of women. The result of *same* taking scope over the nominal *women with the __ name* is a property of sets of women where each member of that set share a name. The cardinal *two* restricts these sets of equi-named women to those containing two women. When inserted in the analysis for (227), the result is a requirement that there is a pair of women such that there exists a name such that both members of the pair has that name.

The analysis of the scope-taking properties of this nominal use of *same* is completely ordinary, except that instead of taking scope over a clause of category S the way that typical quantifiers do, it takes scope over a nominal of category N.

The proposed lexical entry would work unmodified in the tower grammar developed in Part I. But *same* has other uses in which it requires more expressive power than the tower grammar is able to provide, as explored in the next section.

14.2 Parasitic scope

With a quantificational and scope-taking analysis of one use of internal *same* in place, we can consider generalizing the approach to other cases.

One important clue to the special nature of *same* is that the internal reading depends on the presence of other scope-taking elements elsewhere in the sentence.

(232) a. John read the same book.
b. Everyone read the same book.

The second sentence, in (232b), has a sentence-internal interpretation that (232a) lacks. It seems clear that the availability of the additional reading has something to do with the presence of the quantifier *everyone*. We will provide an analysis on which the scope of *same* depends on the scope of *everyone* in a certain way that Barker (2007) calls *parasitic scope*.

The syntactic category given for nominal *same* will not work without modification, since there is no suitable N node in view for *same* to take scope over. However, if we look instead for an expression with the same semantic type, namely, $\texttt{e} \rightarrow \texttt{t}$, a scope target emerges as the derivation unfolds:

(233)

$$\dfrac{\dfrac{\dfrac{\lambda x(x \cdot (\text{read} \cdot (\text{the} \cdot (\text{same} \cdot \text{book})))) \vdash \mathrm{DP}\backslash\!\!\backslash \mathrm{S} \qquad \mathrm{S} \vdash \mathrm{S}}{\mathrm{S}/\!\!/(\mathrm{DP}\backslash\!\!\backslash \mathrm{S}) \circ \lambda x(x \cdot (\text{read} \cdot (\text{the} \cdot (\text{same} \cdot \text{book})))) \vdash \mathrm{S}}\,/\!\!/L}{\mathrm{S}/\!\!/(\mathrm{DP}\backslash\!\!\backslash \mathrm{S}) \cdot (\text{read} \cdot (\text{the} \cdot (\text{same} \cdot \text{book}))) \vdash \mathrm{S}}\,\lambda}{\text{everyone} \cdot (\text{read} \cdot (\text{the} \cdot (\text{same} \cdot \text{book}))) \vdash \mathrm{S}}\,\text{LEX}$$

Reading the proof from the bottom up, *everyone* takes scope over the sentence, creating a scope remnant ($\lambda x(x \cdot (\text{read} \cdot (\text{the} \cdot (\text{same} \cdot \text{book}))))$) with category $\mathrm{DP}\backslash\!\!\backslash \mathrm{S}$. This structure is the nuclear scope of *everyone*, and has the desired semantic type, $\texttt{e} \rightarrow \texttt{t}$.

If we assume that in addition to the category $\mathrm{N}/\!\!/(\mathrm{A}\backslash\!\!\backslash \mathrm{N})$ assigned to *same* above, it is also in category $(\mathrm{DP}\backslash\!\!\backslash \mathrm{S})/\!\!/(\mathrm{A}\backslash\!\!\backslash(\mathrm{DP}\backslash\!\!\backslash \mathrm{S}))$, we can continue the derivation as follows, with no adjustment needed in the semantic value for *same* proposed in the previous section:

(234)

$$\dfrac{\dfrac{\dfrac{\dfrac{\dfrac{\dfrac{\dfrac{\mathrm{DP} \cdot (\text{read} \cdot (\text{the} \cdot (\mathrm{A} \cdot \text{book}))) \vdash \mathrm{S}}{\mathrm{DP} \circ \lambda x(x \cdot (\text{read} \cdot (\text{the} \cdot (\mathrm{A} \cdot \text{book})))) \vdash \mathrm{S}}\,\lambda}{\lambda x(x \cdot (\text{read} \cdot (\text{the} \cdot (\mathrm{A} \cdot \text{book})))) \vdash \mathrm{DP}\backslash\!\!\backslash \mathrm{S}}\,\backslash\!\!\backslash R}{\mathrm{A} \circ \lambda y \lambda x(x \cdot (\text{read} \cdot (\text{the} \cdot (y \cdot \text{book})))) \vdash \mathrm{DP}\backslash\!\!\backslash \mathrm{S}}\,\lambda}{\lambda y \lambda x(x \cdot (\text{read} \cdot (\text{the} \cdot (y \cdot \text{book})))) \vdash \mathrm{A}\backslash\!\!\backslash(\mathrm{DP}\backslash\!\!\backslash \mathrm{S})}\,\backslash\!\!\backslash R \qquad \mathrm{DP}\backslash\!\!\backslash \mathrm{S} \vdash \mathrm{DP}\backslash\!\!\backslash \mathrm{S}}{(\mathrm{DP}\backslash\!\!\backslash \mathrm{S})/\!\!/(\mathrm{A}\backslash\!\!\backslash(\mathrm{DP}\backslash\!\!\backslash \mathrm{S})) \circ \lambda y \lambda x(x \cdot (\text{read} \cdot (\text{the} \cdot (y \cdot \text{book})))) \vdash \mathrm{DP}\backslash\!\!\backslash \mathrm{S}}\,/\!\!/L}{\lambda x(x \cdot (\text{read} \cdot (\text{the} \cdot ((\mathrm{DP}\backslash\!\!\backslash \mathrm{S})/\!\!/(\mathrm{A}\backslash\!\!\backslash(\mathrm{DP}\backslash\!\!\backslash \mathrm{S})) \cdot \text{book})))) \vdash \mathrm{DP}\backslash\!\!\backslash \mathrm{S}}\,\lambda}{\lambda x(x \cdot (\text{read} \cdot (\text{the} \cdot (\text{same} \cdot \text{book})))) \vdash \mathrm{DP}\backslash\!\!\backslash \mathrm{S}}\,\text{LEX}$$

Here, as above, 'A' is the category of an adjectival nominal modifier, and abbreviates N/N.

The Curry-Howard labeling is completely standard, and we have:

(235) **everyone(same(**$\lambda f \lambda y$**.read(the(**f**(book)))** y**))**

The reason it makes sense to call this strategy parasitic scope is because *same* takes scope in between the scope-taking element *everyone* and its nuclear scope. The scope target for *same* isn't even present until some other element (in this case, *everyone*) has taken its scope. In that sense, then, the scope-taking of *same* is parasitic on the scope-taking of some other element in the sentence.

Parasitic scope goes beyond the expressive power available to the tower system. The reason is that the tower system assumes that each continuation has exactly one missing piece; as discussed below in section 15.1, parasitic scope requires continuations that are missing two pieces.

14.3 Pervasive scope-taking

One consequence of adopting the parasitic scope strategy is that everything that is able to serve as the trigger for the internal reading of *same* must be able to take scope, since that is the only way to create the scope host required for parasitic *same*. For overtly scope-taking triggers such as *everyone*, that is unproblematic. But there are other DP types that are not obviously scope-taking that nevertheless trigger internal readings for *same*, including coordinated DPs and definite plural DPs.

(236) a. Ann and Bill read the same book.
b. The men read the same book.

In order for a parasitic scope analysis to go through, it is necessary to assume that *Ann and Bill* and *the men* are able to take scope.

In the context of a combinatory categorial grammar, this would mean assuming the availability of a freely available LIFT operation, as in the tower grammar of Part I. Of course, LIFT was required independently, for instance, in order for a non-quantificational DP to coordinate with a generalized quantifier (e.g., *Ann and every student*). Furthermore, it is harmless to allow a plain DP to shift to a scope-taking generalized quantifier, since the semantics of the type shift guarantees that the truth conditions remain unchanged in the shifted derivation.

But in any case, on the type logical grammar here, $\mathrm{DP} \vdash \mathrm{S} /\!\!/ (\mathrm{DP} \backslash\!\!\backslash \mathrm{S})$ is a theorem, so there is no need to stipulate the availability of a LIFT type-shifter. This means that lifting is always available as a matter of logic, though in the usual case, it is a useless digression, since it makes no difference semantically. However, in the presence of a scope-taker like *same*, the shift can serve as a catalyst to facilitate parasitic scope-taking.

In fact, the required scope-taking is even more pervasive, since DPs are by no means the only expressions that can trigger an internal reading for *same*, as emphasized by Carlson (1987):

(237) a. John [read and reviewed] the same book.
b. John read the same book [quickly and thoroughly].
c. John read the same book [every day].
d. John [usually] read the same book.

Here, an internal reading is possible with conjoined verbs, conjoined adverbs, a quantificational adverbial containing a DP quantifier, and a quantificational adverb. It appears that *same* is unusually promiscuous syntactically, and cares only about whether it has the right kind of object to distribute over. Because continuations are available uniformly across all syntactic categories, the parasitic approach generalizes smoothly to these cases, under certain assumptions about the mereology of events and other types of objects; see Barker (2007) for details.

In general, the scope-taking mechanism allows *same* to target any element in the clause, subject to the semantic constraint that that element provides a denotation suitable for distributing over. This means that in contrast to the usual assumption that scope-taking is restricted to a limited class of quantificational DPs, if every expression has access to its continuation, then quite literally every expression can potentially take scope. In other words, on the view here, natural language is seething with scope-taking.

14.4 *Same* in the presence of partitives: recursive scope

Solomon (2011) argues that the simple parasitic scope analysis just given does not get uniqueness/maximality implications right. The point is especially compelling when *same* occurs in the presence of partitivity:

(238) Anna and Bill know [some of the same people].

On the analysis of *same* described above, the predicted truth conditions require that there is some set of people X such that Ann and Bill each know a subset of X. But nothing prevents the two subsets from being disjoint, so that there might be no one that Ann and Bill both know, contrary to intuitions about the meaning of the sentence. According to native speakers, in order for (238) to be true, Ann and Bill must have some acquaintances in common.

Solomon gives *same* the category $((DP\mathbin{\backslash\!\!\backslash}S)/\!\!/(DP\mathbin{\backslash\!\!\backslash}(DP\mathbin{\backslash\!\!\backslash}S)))/\!\!/(A\mathbin{\backslash\!\!\backslash}DP)$. It's easier to see what's going on here if we present the category in the tower notation developed in Part I:

(239) Recursive-scope *same*: $$\frac{\begin{array}{c|c} \dfrac{\mathrm{DP}\backslash\!\!\backslash \mathrm{S} \mid \mathrm{DP}\backslash\!\!\backslash \mathrm{S}}{\mathrm{DP}} & \mathrm{DP} \end{array}}{\mathrm{A}}$$

Note that result category (top left corner of the tower) is itself a tower. On this analysis, *same* sits in adjective position (A), taking scope over the DP *some of the* __ *people*; it then turns this host DP into a parasitic scope-taker that distributes over the set containing Ann and Bill.

Solomon gives the following denotation for the recursive-scope *same*, leading to an analysis for (238):

(240) a. $\lambda FRX.\exists Z \forall x < X.F(\lambda gY.RYx \wedge gy)(\lambda W.W = Z)$

b. $(\mathbf{a} \oplus \mathbf{b})(\mathbf{same}(\lambda f.\mathbf{some\text{-}of}(\mathbf{the}(f(\mathbf{people}))))(\lambda yx.\mathbf{know}\, y\, x))$

c. $\exists Z \forall x < (\mathbf{a} \oplus \mathbf{b}).\mathbf{some\text{-}of}(\mathbf{the}(\lambda Y.\mathbf{know}\, Y\, x \wedge \mathbf{people}\, Y))(\lambda W.W = Z)$

Here, $\mathbf{a} \oplus \mathbf{b}$ is the mereological sum of Anna and Bill. The net truth conditions require that there is a group Z such that for each x out of the set consisting of Anna and Bill, Z constitutes some of the people that x knows, as desired.

On the recursive-scope analysis proposed by Solomon, then, *same* is an operator that turns its nuclear scope into a new, larger scope-taking expression. Note that Solomon's analysis still relies crucially on parasitic scope.

We find Solomon's arguments compelling, and will assume that on the most general analysis of *same*, it takes recursive, parasitic scope.

Section 16.9 on Andrews Amalgams gives a second example of a recursive-scope analysis of a natural language expression type.

14.5 Other accounts of *same*

There are a number of insightful formal analyses of *same*. Some are not strictly compositional (Stump 1982, Moltmann 1992), in that they allow non-adjacent quantifiers to interact before combining with intervening material, in the style of polyadic quantifiers. Others are radically pragmatic (Dowty 1985, Beck 2000) in a way that Barker (2007) argues does not capture the crisp robust intuitions about the truth conditions of *same*.

Brasoveanu (2007, 2011) gives a fully compositional account on which the connection between *same* and *different* is mediated by a process he calls association with distributivity. See Bumford and Barker (2013) for a proposed refinement of the association with distributivity analysis, including a brief comparison with the parasitic approach presented here. Unlike the parasitic scope analysis, in the association with distributivity analysis, all of the heavy lifting is done by the distributive quantifier, which allows adjectives like *same* to express their semantic restriction in the form of a simple, non-quantificational requirement on their anaphoric referents.

On the one hand, association with distributivity makes a clean distinction between the behavior of singular *different* versus *same* and plural *different*:

(241) a. The men read a different book.
b. The men read the same book.
c. The men read different books.

Unlike the examples with *same* and plural *different* in (241b) and (241c), singular *different* in (241a) does not allow a sentence-internal reading. That is, in (241a), each man must have read a book that is different from some salient book provided by context.

On the other hand, the association-with-distributivity approach would require considerable development in order to handle nominal cases like those discussed above in section 14.1, as well as the coordinated verb examples such as (237a), discussed in detail in Barker (2007), not to mention the partitive examples given in the section above (though see optimistic remarks in Brasoveanu (2011)).

In addition to association-with-distributivity, there are promising compositional analyses due to Solomon (2011) and Bumford (2013) based on constructing what they call functional witnesses (Skolem functions). In addition to handling many cases of *same* and *different*, functional witnesses are capable of describing a wide range of challenging constructions:

(242) Everyone read a book. Then everyone read a different book.

This discourse has an interpretation on which each person is required to read two different books, although there is no requirement that different people read different books from each other. We don't extend our treatment to such examples here.

Having motivated the technique of parasitic scope, the following chapter considers a number of additional applications to natural language.

15

Scope versus discontinuity: Anaphora, VPE

Parasitic scope provides a compositional way for two elements that are not contiguous to interact semantically. In the previous chapter, those two elements were a quantificational adjective (e.g., *same*) and an independent trigger for the adjective to distribute over, usually, a quantificational or plural DP. Despite the fact that these elements were not adjacent to each other, and in fact did not even need to stand in a c-command relation syntactically, the analysis was fully compositional.

NL_λ was motivated by a desire to provide an account of in-situ scope taking that is expressive enough to handle parasitic scope analyses of *same*. But the parasitic scope technique can be applied to a wide range of problems. This chapter briefly considers parasitic scope analyses of pronoun binding and of verb phrase ellipsis. We mention some other applications of parasitic scope in section 15.5.

The Discontinuous Lambek Grammar (Morrill et al. 2011, Valentín 2012) is also a type-logical grammar, and also handles interaction of non-adjacent elements. It takes a dramatically different perspective, treating expressions that we analyze as higher-order continuations as discontinuous. It counts as a compositional grammar only if you are willing to consider expressions with an unbounded number of points of discontinuity as a syntactic constituent. We consider how the two approaches—NL_λ and Discontinuous Lambek Grammar—illuminate each other in section 15.2.

15.1 The tangram picture of parasitic scope

Here is a schematic diagram of parasitic scope:

(243)

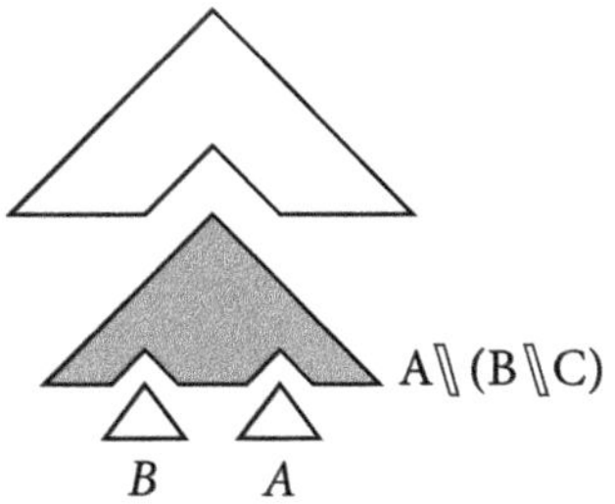

The doubly-notched gray triangle is what we have been calling a higher-order continuation. It is something that would have been a C, except that it is missing not one substructure, but two. If one of the notches were filled, the resulting complex structure would still have a notch in it; that is, the result of the first combination operation will be an ordinary continuation. That means that we can schematically represent the category of the doubly-notched structure as $A \backslash\!\!\backslash (B \backslash\!\!\backslash C)$: an expression in this category is ready to combine with a filler of category A. Once we fill the A notch, the singly-notched result will be ready to combine with a filler of category B, to form a complete C.

For instance, in the analysis of *same* given in the previous chapter, $A = \mathrm{N/N}$ (the category of an adjectival nominal modifer), and $B = \mathrm{DP}$. The scope-taking adjective *same* has category $\dfrac{\mathrm{DP}\backslash\!\!\backslash\mathrm{S} \mid \mathrm{DP}\backslash\!\!\backslash\mathrm{S}}{\mathrm{N/N}}$. (We're keeping things simple by not implementing the recursive-scope refinement discussed in section 14.4.) Once *same* has combined with its (doubly-notched) continuation—in the diagram above, imagine pushing the triangle above the A into the notch directly above it—the result is a singly-notched continuation of category $\mathrm{DP}\backslash\!\!\backslash\mathrm{S}$: just the right kind of thing for a quantifier such as *every* to take scope over.

15.2 Discontinuous Lambek Grammar

Morrill et al. (2011) and Valentín (2012) present a type-logical grammar **D** called Discontinuous Lambek Grammar. Though different from NL_λ in its historical development (see Morrill et al. 2011:11) and in form, the expressive power and the specific analyses it provides are closely parallel to those of NL_λ. We view the similarity as a case of two independent research efforts converging on a similar solution. At the same time, the two formalisms are interestingly different in their assumptions and their methods.

For instance, consider the gray doubly-notched triangle in the diagram in the previous section. The continuation-based grammar NL_λ views this portion of a linguistic tree as a unit: it is a constituent with two pieces excluded. All of its parts are connected, so it is a contiguous, unitary constituent.

The perspective of Discontinuous Lambek Grammar is quite different. Since type-logical grammars model languages, and since languages can be viewed as sets of strings, Morrill et al. focus their attention on the words that occupy the leaves of the tree. Instead of considering the doubly-notched contiguous region of the larger tree, they consider instead the words along the bottom edge. And because there are two notches interrupting the bottom edge, the words in question form a discontinuous string. For instance, in the sentence *Mary claimed John wanted everyone to read the same book*, the discontinuous string corresponding to the nuclear scope of *same* is *John wanted . . . to read the . . . book*. On the continuation-based view, this is a single constituent with two pieces excluded; on the Discontinuous Lambek Grammar view, it is a configuration consisting of three separate parts.

The correspondence with NL_λ is easiest to see at the level of categories. Morrill et al. define a type connective '$\uparrow$' such that $B \uparrow A$ means (roughly) "a discontinuous expression that would be of category B if one of its gaps were filled with an expression of category A". This is functionally equivalent to our $A\backslash\!\!\backslash B$ (note the reversal of the order of the subcategories). Likewise, they define a complementary connective '$\downarrow$' such that $D \downarrow C$ means "an expression that would be of category C, if only it were first substituted into a discontinuous expression of category D", which is functionally equivalent to our $C/\!\!/D$. (Note again the reversal of the categories.) So their category for a generalized quantifier is $((S_1 \uparrow DP) \downarrow S_2)$, which is equivalent to our $S_2/\!\!/(DP\backslash\!\!\backslash S_1)$.

Discontinuous Lambek Grammar builds associativity directly into the logical rules (see, e.g., Valentín 2012 section 3.3 for an explanation of how the structural rules for associativity have been absorbed into the logical rules). As a result, in order to regulate the combination of expressions which might differ in their number of points of discontinuity, it is necessary to sort the expressions into a hierarchy of classes, where each class corresponds to a different number of discontinuities.

Morrill et al. are committed to the assumption that natural language is fully associative: that the syntactic structure $p \cdot (q \cdot r)$ will be well-formed if and only if $(p \cdot q) \cdot r$ is well-formed. Associativity is well-established as an assumption in some varieties of categorial grammar. For instance, it is an essential part of the program of Steedman's scope as surface constituency, discussed above in section 11.3.

However, it is by no means clear that natural language is uniformly associative. Instead of building associativity into the basic definitions of the grammar, as Morrill et al. do, a more conservative strategy would be to build a non-associative grammar, and add associativity in a carefully regulated way, only where needed, as explained in detail in Moortgat (1997).

Although Morrill et al. present associativity as an essential part of their enterprise, Moortgat (2012) comments that there does not appear to be any reason why Discontinuous Lambek Grammar could not be rebuilt without associativity, so that it combined full tree structures instead of discontinuous strings. The details of how this might be accomplished are not clear to us, however.

In the other direction, associativity can easily be added to NL_λ by adopting a suitable structural postulate, if desired; see the discussion of (290) below in chapter 17.

15.3 Pronominal binding as parasitic scope

Adapting the analysis of Morrill et al. (2011:52), we can use parasitic scope for pronoun binding. Instead of adding a special type-shifter and a special meaning for pronouns, as in Part I, the parasitic scope analysis allows pronouns to find a binder purely by taking (parasitic) scope. This binding strategy will play a role in the sketch of verb phrase ellipsis in the next section (section 15.4), as well as in the analysis of sluicing below in chapter 16.

The idea is that a pronoun is a scope-taker (as in Part I), such that its scope is parasitic on the scope of its binder. Assuming the pronoun *he* has category $(\mathrm{DP}\backslash\!\!\backslash \mathrm{S})/\!\!/(\mathrm{DP}\backslash\!\!\backslash(\mathrm{DP}\backslash\!\!\backslash \mathrm{S}))$, we have:

(244) Everyone$_i$ said he$_i$ left.

$$
\dfrac{\dfrac{\dfrac{\dfrac{\dfrac{\dfrac{\dfrac{\dfrac{\mathrm{DP}\cdot(\mathrm{said}\cdot(\mathrm{DP}\cdot\mathrm{left}))\vdash \mathrm{S}}{\mathrm{DP}\circ\lambda x(x\cdot(\mathrm{said}\cdot(\mathrm{DP}\cdot\mathrm{left})))\vdash \mathrm{S}}\equiv}{\lambda x(x\cdot(\mathrm{said}\cdot(\mathrm{DP}\cdot\mathrm{left})))\vdash \mathrm{DP}\backslash\!\!\backslash \mathrm{S}}\backslash\!\!\backslash R}{\mathrm{DP}\circ\lambda y\lambda x(x\cdot(\mathrm{said}\cdot(y\cdot\mathrm{left})))\vdash \mathrm{DP}\backslash\!\!\backslash \mathrm{S}}\equiv}{\lambda y\lambda x(x\cdot(\mathrm{said}\cdot(y\cdot\mathrm{left})))\vdash \mathrm{DP}\backslash\!\!\backslash(\mathrm{DP}\backslash\!\!\backslash \mathrm{S})}\backslash\!\!\backslash R
\quad
\dfrac{\dfrac{\mathrm{DP}\backslash\!\!\backslash \mathrm{S}\vdash \mathrm{DP}\backslash\!\!\backslash \mathrm{S}\qquad \mathrm{S}\vdash \mathrm{S}}{\mathrm{S}/\!\!/(\mathrm{DP}\backslash\!\!\backslash \mathrm{S})\circ \mathrm{DP}\backslash\!\!\backslash \mathrm{S}\vdash \mathrm{S}}/\!\!/L}{\mathrm{everyone}\circ \mathrm{DP}\backslash\!\!\backslash \mathrm{S}\vdash \mathrm{S}}\textsc{lex}}{\mathrm{everyone}\circ((\mathrm{DP}\backslash\!\!\backslash \mathrm{S})/\!\!/(\mathrm{DP}\backslash\!\!\backslash(\mathrm{DP}\backslash\!\!\backslash \mathrm{S}))\circ\lambda y\lambda x(x\cdot(\mathrm{said}\cdot(y\cdot\mathrm{left}))))\vdash \mathrm{S}}/\!\!/L}{\mathrm{everyone}\circ(\mathrm{he}\circ\lambda y\lambda x(x\cdot(\mathrm{said}\cdot(y\cdot\mathrm{left}))))\vdash \mathrm{S}}\textsc{lex}}{\mathrm{everyone}\circ\lambda x(x\cdot(\mathrm{said}\cdot(\mathrm{he}\cdot\mathrm{left})))\vdash \mathrm{S}}\equiv}{\mathrm{everyone}\cdot(\mathrm{said}\cdot(\mathrm{he}\cdot\mathrm{left}))\vdash \mathrm{S}}\equiv
$$

From the bottom upward, first the host scope-taker *everyone* takes scope. Then the pronoun *he* takes parasitic scope just under *everyone*.

Giving *he* the semantics of the duplicator combinator $\mathbf{W} = \lambda\kappa\lambda x.\kappa xx$, and assuming that the generalized quantifier $\mathbf{everyone} = \lambda P\forall x.Px$, the semantics for the derivation is as follows:

(245)
$$
\begin{aligned}
&\mathbf{everyone}((\lambda\kappa\lambda x.\kappa xx)(\lambda y\lambda x.\mathbf{said}(\mathbf{left}\,x)\,y))\\
&= \mathbf{everyone}(\lambda x.\mathbf{said}(\mathbf{left}\,x)\,x) = (\lambda P\forall x.Px)(\lambda x.\mathbf{said}(\mathbf{left}\,x)\,x)\\
&= \forall x.\mathbf{said}(\mathbf{left}\,x)\,x
\end{aligned}
$$

This derivation gives the bound reading, on which the pronoun varies with the choice of the universal quantifier.

It will be convenient to adopt a convention in the remainder of this chapter and in the next chapter for abbreviating the syntactic category that delivers bound anaphora:

(246) $A^B \equiv (B\backslash\!\!\backslash \mathrm{S})/\!\!/(A\backslash\!\!\backslash(B\backslash\!\!\backslash \mathrm{S}))$

This is the category of an anaphor of category A taking an antecedent of category B. Usually (though not always; see Barker 2013, section 6.2), A and B will match exactly (e.g., in the derivation above, $A = B = \mathrm{DP}$).

Jäger (2005) points out that anaphora is a challenge for some of the cherished assumptions of type-logical grammar. For instance, one of the central properties of Lambek grammars in general, like all so-called substructural logics (see Restall 2000), is that they are *resource-sensitive*: unlike logics that are used to reason about truth, assumptions in a resource-sensitive logic cannot be duplicated or omitted at will. Yet anaphora appears to require duplicating its antecedent. The Morrill et al.

analysis adopted here resolves this tension: in the logic, pronoun binding makes use of each grammatical expression exactly once, so that there is no compromise of the resource-sensitive discipline. The only duplication occurs in the lexical semantics of the pronoun. In particular, there is no special logical rule for anaphora, as in Jäger (2005). Instead, the duplication is accomplished entirely within the lexical syntax and semantics of the pronoun, a strategy long advocated by Szabolcsi (1989, 1992), Dowty (2007), and others.

15.4 Verb phrase ellipsis as parasitic scope

In anticipation of the next chapter on sluicing (a form of ellipsis), we will explore another application of parasitic scope proposed by Morrill et al. involving verb phrase ellipsis. We will not develop or defend this analysis of verb phrase ellipsis in detail, but offer it for comparison with sluicing.

In verb phrase ellipsis (VPE), a verb phrase takes a nearby verb phrase as antecedent. We can model this by providing a silent proform VPEGAP with category $\mathrm{VP}^{\mathrm{VP}}$ (where 'VP' abbreviates DP\S):

(247) John left or Bill did.

$$\cfrac{\cfrac{\text{left} \circ (\textsc{vpegap} \circ \lambda y\lambda x((\text{John} \cdot x) \cdot (\text{or} \cdot (\text{Bill} \cdot y)))) \vdash \mathrm{S}}{\text{left} \circ \lambda x((\text{John} \cdot x) \cdot (\text{or} \cdot (\text{Bill} \cdot \textsc{vpegap}))) \vdash \mathrm{S}}\equiv}{(\text{John} \cdot \text{left}) \cdot (\text{or} \cdot (\text{Bill} \cdot \textsc{vpegap})) \vdash \mathrm{S}}\equiv$$

The VP proform takes the verb phrase *left* as its antecedent. The semantic value of the VP gap is once again the duplicator combinator, the same as for pronoun binding (though with different semantic types for the arguments). The net interpretation is that John left or Bill left.

The VPE analysis and the analysis of bound pronouns given above interact to provide analyses of the traditional strict versus sloppy ambiguity. To illustrate a sloppy interpretation, simply replace the verb phrase *left* in the derivation above with the following derivation of *said he left* in which the pronoun takes scope over the rest of the verb phrase (i.e., covaries with the subject of the verb phrase):

(248) John said he left or Bill did.

$$\cfrac{\cfrac{\cfrac{\mathrm{DP} \circ (\text{he} \circ \lambda y\lambda x(x \cdot (\text{said} \cdot (y \cdot \text{left})))) \vdash \mathrm{S}}{\mathrm{DP} \circ \lambda x(x \cdot (\text{said} \cdot (\text{he} \cdot \text{left}))) \vdash \mathrm{S}}\equiv}{\mathrm{DP} \cdot (\text{said} \cdot (\text{he} \cdot \text{left})) \vdash \mathrm{S}}\equiv}{\text{said} \cdot (\text{he} \cdot \text{left}) \vdash \mathrm{DP}\backslash\mathrm{S}}\backslash R$$

The interpretation in this case is that John said John left or Bill said Bill left.

In order to arrive at the strict interpretation, it is necessary for the strict antecedent (in this case, *John*) to take scope over the entire sentence, and in particular, to take wider scope than the the verb phrase ellipsis:

(249) John said he left or Bill did.

$$\dfrac{\dfrac{\dfrac{(\text{DP}\cdot(\text{said}\cdot(\text{DP}\cdot\text{left})))\cdot(\text{or}\cdot(\text{Bill}\cdot\textsc{vpegap}))\vdash \text{S}}{\text{DP}\circ(\text{DP}\circ\lambda y\lambda x((x\cdot(\text{said}\cdot(y\cdot\text{left})))\cdot(\text{or}\cdot(\text{Bill}\cdot\textsc{vpegap}))))\vdash\text{S}}\equiv,\equiv}{\lambda y\lambda x((x\cdot(\text{said}\cdot(y\cdot\text{left})))\cdot(\text{or}\cdot(\text{Bill}\cdot\textsc{vpegap})))\vdash\text{DP}\backslash\!\!\backslash(\text{DP}\backslash\!\!\backslash\text{S})}\backslash\!\!\backslash R,\backslash\!\!\backslash R \quad \text{John}\circ\text{DP}\backslash\!\!\backslash\text{S}\vdash\text{S}}{\dfrac{\text{John}\circ(\text{he}\circ\lambda y\lambda x((x\cdot(\text{said}\cdot(y\cdot\text{left})))\cdot(\text{or}\cdot(\text{Bill}\cdot\textsc{vpegap}))))\vdash\text{S}}{\dfrac{\text{John}\circ\lambda x((x\cdot(\text{said}\cdot(\text{he}\cdot\text{left})))\cdot(\text{or}\cdot(\text{Bill}\cdot\textsc{vpegap})))\vdash\text{S}}{(\text{John}\cdot(\text{said}\cdot(\text{he}\cdot\text{left})))\cdot(\text{or}\cdot(\text{Bill}\cdot\textsc{vpegap}))\vdash\text{S}}\equiv}\equiv}/\!\!/L$$

The left branch of the derivation continues by using the VP corresponding to *said* · (DP · *left*) to bind VPEGAP. The interpretation is that John said John left or Bill said John left.

Of course these examples are only the simplest, most basic type of verb phrase ellipsis. We will not evaluate here how robust the Morrill et al. parasitic scope strategy is for verb phrase ellipsis in general, though we're currently not aware of any fatal shortcomings.

15.5 Other parasitic scope analyses

Parasitic scope has been used to characterize a number of different phenomena. Kennedy and Stanley (2009) propose a parasitic scope analysis for sentences like *The average American has 2.3 kids*, solving the puzzle posed by the fact that no individual person can have a fractional number of kids.

(250) The average American has 2.3 kids.

$$\dfrac{\dfrac{2.3\circ(\text{average}\circ\lambda y\lambda x(\text{the}\cdot(y\cdot\text{American}))(\text{has}\cdot(x\cdot\text{kids})))\vdash\text{S}}{2.3\circ\lambda x(\text{the}\cdot(\text{average}\cdot\text{American}))(\text{has}\cdot(x\cdot\text{kids}))\vdash\text{S}}\equiv}{(\text{the}\cdot(\text{average}\cdot\text{American}))(\text{has}\cdot(2.3\cdot\text{kids}))\vdash\text{S}}\equiv$$

Starting from the bottom, the cardinal 2.3 takes scope, creating the right circumstance for *average* to take parasitic scope. Kennedy and Stanley provide details of the denotation for the *average* operator that gives suitable truth conditions for this analysis.

Parasitic scope analyses have also been proposed for various types of coordination in English and in Japanese (Kubota and Levine 2012, Kubota 2013).

16

Sluicing as anaphora to a continuation

Sluicing is a form of ellipsis in which the complement of a wh-phrase is missing, with its interpretation depending on material elsewhere in the discourse:

(251) Someone left, but I don't know [who __].

In this sluicing example, the (bracketed) sluiced interrogative embedded under *know* can be interpreted as if the expression *left* had been pronounced in the place of the gap ('__'). That is, (251) can mean the same thing as *Someone left, but I don't know who left.*

The antecedent clause (here, *someone left*) typically contains within it an indefinite (*someone*) whose role in the antecedent clause is parallel to the role of the wh-phrase in the sluiced interrogative. Following Chung et al. (1995), we will call the wh-phrase correlate the INNER ANTECEDENT.

Then the interpretation of the sluiced clause is given by the following recipe:

(252) sluice = wh-phrase + (antecedent-clause − inner-antecedent)

In this informal arithmetic, the sluiced clause [*who* __] in (251) can be interpreted as *who* + ([*someone left*] − *someone*) = *who* + [__ *left*]. Of course, the notion of a clause with a piece subtracted is precisely what we have been calling a continuation. Following Barker (2013), then, we will argue that sluicing is precisely anaphora to a continuation.

16.1 Other approaches

There are currently three main approaches to sluicing. The first is due to Chung et al. (1995), who suggest that the sluiced clause is constructed by copying logical form material from the antecedent. The second is due to Romero (1998) and Merchant (2001), who suggest that the complement of a wh-phrase can be silent (deleted at PF) just in case the interrogative and the antecedent clause entail each other, after factoring out the wh-phrase and the wh-phrase correlate. The third approach is the one that is closest to ours in many respects, and is a type-logical treatment due to (Jäger, 2001,

2005). Jäger suggests that sluicing is anaphora to a particular kind of clause, a clause that contains an indefinite somewhere inside of it.

There are three empirical challenges that distinguish among the approaches. One challenge is that the case of the wh-phrase must match the case of the inner antecedent (discussed below in section 16.4). Case-matching shows that there must be some amount of syntactic information that is passed between the inner antecedent and the sluice. A second challenge is that sluicing, by and large, is insensitive to syntactic islands; we will not discuss syntactic islands here, though see Barker (2013) for details. The third challenge is that sluices often do not have an overt inner antecedent:

(253) John left, but I don't know when __.

There is no temporal modifier in the antecedent clause that correlates with the wh-phrase; as discussed below, Chung et al. (1995) call this 'sprouting'.

All three approaches are empirically robust, and all three address each of the main empirical challenges, with one exception: it is not clear how to directly extend the indefinite-based type-logical anaphoric approach to sprouting. We will explain how our continuation-based type-logical approach does extend to sprouting in some detail below, so in some sense, the analysis here can be viewed as a revision of the anaphoric approach that handles sprouting. (See Barker 2013 for a more detailed discussion and comparison of competing accounts of sluicing.)

On the conceptual level, both the LF copying strategy and the PF deletion strategy rely heavily on postulating syntactic structure inside the gap site. The type-logical approaches reject this assumption, maintaining instead that there is no structure in the silence.

Our main point is this: what all of these accounts are aiming at is a way of interpreting the sluice gap as equivalent to the antecedent clause with the inner antecedent removed. The LF copying strategy does this by replacing the inner antecedent with a bound variable; the PF deletion strategy does this by abstracting over the inner antecedent as part of the algorithm for computing the appropriate sort of semantic equivalence; the indefinite-based type-logical account does this by providing a special interpretation for clauses containing an indefinite on which the indefinite is (in effect) abstracted.

We are proposing to state this generalization directly: for us, sluicing is anaphora to a clause missing a DP, that is, anaphora to an expression in category DP⫽S—anaphora to a continuation.

16.2 Basic sluicing

Before we can give an analysis for basic sluicing, we need to briefly consider the syntax of interrogatives. In order to avoid dealing with subject auxiliary inversion, we'll limit consideration to embedded interrogatives, such as *who left* in *I know who left*.

(254) a. I know [who (__ left)].
b. I know [who (John ((saw __) yesterday))].

The bracketed phrases are what we are calling embedded interrogatives.

In general, wh-phrases take as their complement a clause missing a DP somewhere inside of it. Then if Q is the category of embedded interrogatives, *who* will have the syntactic category $Q/(DP\mathbin{\backslash\!\!\backslash}S)$: something that must merge with a gapped clause to its right in order to form an interrogative. All of this is just as in Part I.

Finally, we reason that if what is missing in a sluice is the complement of a wh-phrase, and the complement of a wh-phrase has category $DP\mathbin{\backslash\!\!\backslash}S$, then the silent proform SLUICEGAP must have the anaphoric category $(DP\mathbin{\backslash\!\!\backslash}S)^{(DP\mathbin{\backslash\!\!\backslash}S)}$: anaphora to a continuation. On these assumptions, parasitic scope immediately gives a syntactic and semantic analysis of simple sluicing examples:

(255) Someone left, but I don't know who SLUICEGAP.

$$\dfrac{\dfrac{\dfrac{\dfrac{\dfrac{\dfrac{\dfrac{\dfrac{\dfrac{(\mathrm{sm1}\circ DP\mathbin{\backslash\!\!\backslash}S)\cdot(\mathrm{bidk}\cdot(\mathrm{who}\cdot DP\mathbin{\backslash\!\!\backslash}S))\vdash S}{DP\mathbin{\backslash\!\!\backslash}S\circ\lambda y((\mathrm{sm1}\circ y)\cdot(\mathrm{bidk}\cdot(\mathrm{who}\cdot DP\mathbin{\backslash\!\!\backslash}S)))\vdash S}\equiv}{\lambda y((\mathrm{sm1}\circ y)\cdot(\mathrm{bidk}\cdot(\mathrm{who}\cdot DP\mathbin{\backslash\!\!\backslash}S)))\vdash(DP\mathbin{\backslash\!\!\backslash}S)\mathbin{\backslash\!\!\backslash}S}\mathbin{\backslash\!\!\backslash}R}{DP\mathbin{\backslash\!\!\backslash}S\circ\lambda z\lambda y((\mathrm{sm1}\circ y)\cdot(\mathrm{bidk}\cdot(\mathrm{who}\cdot z)))\vdash(DP\mathbin{\backslash\!\!\backslash}S)\mathbin{\backslash\!\!\backslash}S}\equiv}{\lambda z\lambda y((\mathrm{sm1}\circ y)\cdot(\mathrm{bidk}\cdot(\mathrm{who}\cdot z)))\vdash(DP\mathbin{\backslash\!\!\backslash}S)\mathbin{\backslash\!\!\backslash}((DP\mathbin{\backslash\!\!\backslash}S)\mathbin{\backslash\!\!\backslash}S)}\mathbin{\backslash\!\!\backslash}R\qquad\dfrac{\dfrac{\dfrac{DP\cdot DP\backslash S\vdash S}{DP\circ\lambda x(x\cdot\mathrm{left})\vdash S}\equiv,\textsc{lex}}{\lambda x(x\cdot\mathrm{left})\vdash DP\mathbin{\backslash\!\!\backslash}S}\mathbin{\backslash\!\!\backslash}R\qquad S\vdash S}{\lambda x(x\cdot\mathrm{left})\circ(DP\mathbin{\backslash\!\!\backslash}S)\mathbin{\backslash\!\!\backslash}S\vdash S}\mathbin{\backslash\!\!\backslash}L}{\lambda x(x\cdot\mathrm{left})\circ(((DP\mathbin{\backslash\!\!\backslash}S)\mathbin{\backslash\!\!\backslash}S)\mathbin{/\!\!/}((DP\mathbin{\backslash\!\!\backslash}S)\mathbin{\backslash\!\!\backslash}((DP\mathbin{\backslash\!\!\backslash}S)\mathbin{\backslash\!\!\backslash}S))\circ\lambda z\lambda y((\mathrm{sm1}\circ y)\cdot(\mathrm{bidk}\cdot(\mathrm{who}\cdot z))))\vdash S}\mathbin{/\!\!/}L}{\lambda x(x\cdot\mathrm{left})\circ(\textsc{sg}\circ\lambda z\lambda y((\mathrm{sm1}\circ y)\cdot(\mathrm{bidk}\cdot(\mathrm{who}\cdot z))))\vdash S}\textsc{lex}}{\lambda x(x\cdot\mathrm{left})\circ\lambda y((\mathrm{sm1}\circ y)\cdot(\mathrm{bidk}\cdot(\mathrm{who}\cdot\textsc{sg})))\vdash S}\equiv}{(\mathrm{sm1}\circ\lambda x(x\cdot\mathrm{left}))\cdot(\mathrm{bidk}\cdot(\mathrm{who}\cdot\textsc{sg}))\vdash S}\equiv}{(\mathrm{sm1}\cdot\mathrm{left})\cdot(\mathrm{bidk}\cdot(\mathrm{who}\cdot\textsc{sg}))\vdash S}\equiv$$

Recall that $(DP\mathbin{\backslash\!\!\backslash}S)^{(DP\mathbin{\backslash\!\!\backslash}S)}$ abbreviates $((DP\mathbin{\backslash\!\!\backslash}S)\mathbin{\backslash\!\!\backslash}S)\mathbin{/\!\!/}((DP\mathbin{\backslash\!\!\backslash}S)\mathbin{\backslash\!\!\backslash}((DP\mathbin{\backslash\!\!\backslash}S)\mathbin{\backslash\!\!\backslash}S))$; here, *bidk* is an abbreviation of but-I-don't-know, and behaves as if it had syntactic category $(S\backslash S)/Q$.

The first step in the derivation (starting at the bottom) is to allow *someone* to take scope over the antecedent clause (in the second line from the bottom). Next (third line from the bottom), the scope remnant $\lambda x(x\cdot\mathrm{left})$ takes scope over the entire utterance. At this point (fourth line), the silent proform takes parasitic scope in order for the scope remnant to provide the content of the sluice gap.

16.3 Immediate good prediction: scope of inner antecedent

As Chung et al. (1995:255) note, sluicing is only possible when the inner antecedent takes scope over the rest of the antecedent clause.

(256) Everyone selected a book, but I don't know which book.

In order for a sluice to be possible, not only must the sluiced clause be interpreted giving the wh-phrase scope over the universal, in which case there must be a single book that everyone selected, the antecedent clause must also receive a parallel interpretation on which the indefinite takes wide scope over the universal. This follows from the basic analysis given here:

(257) Someone saw everyone, but I don't know who.

$$\cfrac{\cfrac{\cfrac{\lambda x(x \cdot (\text{saw} \cdot \text{everyone})) \circ (\textsc{sluicegap} \circ \lambda z \lambda y((\text{someone} \circ y) \cdot (\text{bidk} \cdot (\text{who} \cdot z)))) \vdash \text{S}}{\lambda x(x \cdot (\text{saw} \cdot \text{everyone})) \circ \lambda y((\text{someone} \circ y) \cdot (\text{bidk} \cdot (\text{who} \cdot \textsc{sluicegap}))) \vdash \text{S}} \equiv}{(\text{someone} \circ \lambda x(x \cdot (\text{saw} \cdot \text{everyone}))) \cdot (\text{bidk} \cdot (\text{who} \cdot \textsc{sluicegap})) \vdash \text{S}} \equiv}{(\text{someone} \cdot (\text{saw} \cdot \text{everyone})) \cdot (\text{bidk} \cdot (\text{who} \cdot \textsc{sluicegap})) \vdash \text{S}} \equiv$$

In order for the remnant $\lambda x(x \cdot (saw \cdot everyone))$ to become available to serve as an antecedent for the sluicegap, the inner antecedent *someone* must first take scope over the rest of the antecedent clause (second line from bottom), forcing an interpretation on which the indefinite takes wide scope with respect to the universal.

16.4 Case matching

Merchant (2001), following Ross (1969), argues that the morphological case of the wh-phrase must match the case of the inner antecedent. Examples from English will serve to illustrate this robustly cross-linguistic pattern:

(258) a. Someone spoke to John, but I don't know who/*whom.
b. John spoke to someone, but I don't know whom/%who.

In (258a), the inner antecedent is in subject position, and the wh-phrase must have nominative case. In (258b), the inner antecedent is in object position, and the wh-phrase must have accusative case. The '%' marking in (258b) reflects the fact that in most dialects of colloquial English, *who* can occur in many environments that require accusative case.

On the analysis here, just as in Jäger (2001, 2005), case matching is a matter of syntactic bookkeeping. The bookkeeping mechanism in question is independently needed in order to enforce agreement in ϕ features for bound pronouns. For instance, in English, pronouns must match their antecedents in number:

(259) a. Every boy$_i$ said he$_i$/*they$_i$ left.
b. Most boys$_i$ said they$_i$/*he$_i$ left.

If we refine the syntactic category DP into the subcategories DP.SG and DP.PL, then as long as the bound pronoun has category $\text{DP.SG}^{\text{DP.SG}}$ or $\text{DP.PL}^{\text{DP.PL}}$, the analysis of bound pronouns in the previous chapter will enforce number agreement.

In the sluicing case, naturally, we will have wh-phrases that are distinguished according to their case properties:

(260) a. who: $Q/(DP.\textsc{nom}\backslash\!\!\backslash S)$
b. whom: $Q/(DP.\textsc{acc}\backslash\!\!\backslash S)$

Then as long as sluicegaps require that the syntactic category of its antecedent (the exponent) is identical to the syntactic category of its syntactic role (the base), case matching will be enforced.

(261) a. SLUICEGAP.NOM : $(DP.\textsc{nom}\backslash\!\!\backslash S)^{(DP.\textsc{nom}\backslash\!\!\backslash S)}$
b. SLUICEGAP.ACC : $(DP.\textsc{acc}\backslash\!\!\backslash S)^{(DP.\textsc{acc}\backslash\!\!\backslash S)}$

As Jäger (2001, 2005) observes, a type-logical analysis with suitably fine-grained syntactic categories is capable of accurately describing the observed patterns of case matching.

16.5 Simple sprouting

The indefinite-based type-logical account in Jäger (2001, 2005) requires the presence of an indefinite DP somewhere inside the antecedent clause. However, sluicing can still be possible without any overt indefinite in sight:

(262) John left, but I don't know when __. (= 253)

We will show how the continuation-based account here generalizes to sprouting examples.

If some wh-phrases can be S modifiers, the analysis handles certain cases of sprouting immediately. For instance, *why* may be able to take a clausal complement:

(263) I want to know why Mary decided John left.

The sentence in (263) can only be used to raise the issue of Mary's motivations, not John's. This suggests that the syntactic category of *why* can be Q/S: something that combines with a complete clause. If so, then the reason (263) is unambiguous is that *why* is only able to combine with an adjacent, complete clause, in this case, *Mary decided John left*. Then if we have a silent proform WHYSLUICEGAP with category S^S, we have the following simple derivation of *John left, but I don't know why*:

(264)
$$\cfrac{\cfrac{(\text{John}\cdot\text{left})\circ(\textsc{whysluicegap}\circ\lambda y\lambda x(x\cdot(\text{bidk}\cdot(\text{why}\cdot y))))\vdash S}{(\text{John}\cdot\text{left})\circ\lambda x(x\cdot(\text{bidk}\cdot(\text{why}\cdot\textsc{whysluicegap})))\vdash S}\equiv}{(\text{John}\cdot\text{left})\cdot(\text{bidk}\cdot(\text{why}\cdot\textsc{whysluicegap}))\vdash S}\equiv$$

On this analysis, the antecedent for the sluicegap is the complete clause *John left*.

16.6 Embedded sprouting: motivating silent modifiers

If all sprouting could always be analyzed as anaphora to a full clause, it would be easy to generalize the indefinites-based type-logical analysis to cover sprouting. However, the anaphora to a clause strategy will not generalize to the full range of sprouting examples.

(265) I want to know when John wanted to leave.

Unlike (263), (265) is ambiguous: it can be used to ask when John felt a particular desire, or else to ask about John's preferred departure time. We can suppose that *when* has category $\mathrm{S}/(\textsc{adv}\backslash\!\!\backslash \mathrm{S})$, where $\textsc{adv} = (\mathrm{DP}\backslash\mathrm{S})\backslash(\mathrm{DP}\backslash\mathrm{S})$. Then the corresponding proform WHENSLGAP will have category $(\textsc{adv}\backslash\!\!\backslash \mathrm{S})^{(\textsc{adv}\backslash\!\!\backslash \mathrm{S})}$.

(266) John wanted to leave, but he didn't say when __.

In order to arrive at the most natural interpretation of (266), *when* must be interpreted as modifying the embedded verb phrase *leave*, rather than modifying the entire antecedent clause. Therefore anaphora to a clause will not work here.

On the indefinite-based type-logical account, building a suitable meaning requires constructing a function from temporal modifier meanings to sentence meanings. But in the formal treatment of Jäger (2001, 2005), the rule that constructs such meanings requires the presence of an overt indefinite in the position of the inner antecedent.

The formal technique that we will use here to explain embedded sprouting depends on inferences with empty antecedents. This technique has motivation independent of sluicing. For instance, following Barker and Shan (2006), we can make use of empty antecedents in a continuation-based grammar in order to derive silent categories that can be used as gaps in derivations involving syntactic movement.

In order to see how gaps motivate empty antecedents in the logic, we begin by assuming that the empty structure is an identity element for both the merge mode and for the continuation mode, i.e., $\Gamma \cdot ()^{\cdot} \equiv \Gamma \equiv ()^{\cdot} \cdot \Gamma$, and $\Gamma \circ ()^{\circ} \equiv \Gamma \equiv ()^{\circ} \circ \Gamma$. The justification for these structural equivalences is that adding a silent empty structure does not change the resulting syntactic structure. (It is necessary to distinguish the empty merge structure ('$()^{\cdot}$') from the empty continuation structure ('$()^{\circ}$') in order to prevent overgeneration: if the empty merge structure can be mistaken for the empty continuation structure, the grammar becomes commutative.)

If we allow the empty structure as a syntactic identity element, we can prove that the silent empty structure is a member of the following category:

(267)
$$\cfrac{\cfrac{\mathrm{DP}\backslash\!\!\backslash \mathrm{S} \vdash \mathrm{DP}\backslash\!\!\backslash \mathrm{S}}{()^{\circ} \circ \mathrm{DP}\backslash\!\!\backslash \mathrm{S} \vdash \mathrm{DP}\backslash\!\!\backslash \mathrm{S}}\equiv}{()^{\circ} \vdash (\mathrm{DP}\backslash\!\!\backslash \mathrm{S})/\!\!/(\mathrm{DP}\backslash\!\!\backslash \mathrm{S})}\,/\!\!/R$$

In general, silence will be a member of any category of the form $X|X$, where '|' is any of the four category-forming connectives ('$\backslash$', '$/$', '$\backslash\!\!\backslash$', '$/\!\!/$').

If we have empty antecedents, we can derive interrogatives with fronted wh-phrases such as *Who does John like?* as follows, where GAP abbreviates the identity category derived immediately above, namely, $(\mathrm{DP}\backslash\!\!\backslash \mathrm{S})/\!\!/(\mathrm{DP}\backslash\!\!\backslash \mathrm{S})$:

(268)

$$\dfrac{\dfrac{\dfrac{\dfrac{\dfrac{\text{does}\cdot(\text{John}\cdot(\text{like}\cdot\mathrm{DP}))\vdash \mathrm{S}}{\mathrm{DP}\circ\lambda x(\text{does}\cdot(\text{John}\cdot(\text{like}\cdot x)))\vdash \mathrm{S}}\equiv}{\lambda x(\text{does}\cdot(\text{John}\cdot(\text{like}\cdot x)))\vdash \mathrm{DP}\backslash\!\!\backslash \mathrm{S}}\backslash\!\!\backslash R \quad \mathrm{DP}\backslash\!\!\backslash \mathrm{S}\vdash \mathrm{DP}\backslash\!\!\backslash \mathrm{S}}{(\mathrm{DP}\backslash\!\!\backslash \mathrm{S})/\!\!/(\mathrm{DP}\backslash\!\!\backslash \mathrm{S})\circ\lambda x(\text{does}\cdot(\text{John}\cdot(\text{like}\cdot x)))\vdash \mathrm{DP}\backslash\!\!\backslash \mathrm{S}}/\!\!/L}{\textsc{gap}\circ\lambda x(\text{does}\cdot(\text{John}\cdot(\text{like}\cdot x)))\vdash \mathrm{DP}\backslash\!\!\backslash \mathrm{S}}\textsc{lex}}{\text{does}\cdot(\text{John}\cdot(\text{like}\cdot\textsc{gap}))\vdash \mathrm{DP}\backslash\!\!\backslash \mathrm{S}}\equiv$$

Clearly, this works exactly like the gaps that were stipulated to be of the form $A/\!\!/A$ in Part I. And, on the semantic side, just as in Part I, the Curry-Howard labeling of empty categories is always the identity function. In the syntax, they have a null effect, taking an X as complement and returning an identical X as the resulting syntactic category; and likewise in the semantics, they have a null effect, taking x as an argument and returning that same x as the resulting value. To take an arithmetic analogy, deriving an empty category is like multiplying by 2/2, or by (3/2)/(3/2), etc. But this is just multiplying by 1, which amounts to recognizing that the empty category is an identity element. In slogan form: adding nothing to a structure does not change that structure.

Empty antecedents are usually disallowed in type logical grammar. One reason to suppose they may be problematic, at least for natural-language applications, is that they can lead to trouble with adjunct modifiers. If we assume that adjectives have category N/N, and that adjective modifiers such as *very* have category (N/N)/(N/N), then we can derive a silent identity-function denoting adjective with category N/N. The prediction is that in addition to *(very · tall) · man*, we should be able to say **(very · ()) · man*. This prediction is incorrect, of course. Thus using empty antecedents requires finding a different analysis for adjectival modifiers. For instance, we might suppose that *very* can only modify gradable adjectives (**That's a very prime number*). Once we refine the category of adjectives and of *very* to track gradability, silent adjectives will presumably not count as gradable.

There is a technical reason for dispreferring empty antecedents, which is that they create issues for decidability: if it is always possible to add a new empty category, we may never be sure we have found all of the legitimate derivations. For a solution to the decidability issue, see section 17.9.

16.7 Sprouting in silence

If we have empty antecedents, we can derive embedded sprouting cases. Sprouting, then, will involve postulating an empty structure within the antecedent clause.

For instance, let ordinary adverbs have category $\textsc{adv} = (\mathrm{DP}\backslash\mathrm{S})\backslash(\mathrm{DP}\backslash\mathrm{S})$. Assume that *when* has category $\mathrm{Q}/(\textsc{adv}\backslash\!\!\backslash\mathrm{S})$, and $\textsc{whenslgap}$ has category $(\textsc{adv}\backslash\!\!\backslash\mathrm{S})^{(\textsc{adv}\backslash\!\!\backslash\mathrm{S})}$. Then we have the following derivation of the sprouting example *John left, but I don't know when*:

(269)

$$\dfrac{\mathrm{DP}\backslash\mathrm{S} \vdash \mathrm{DP}\backslash\mathrm{S}}{\mathrm{DP}\backslash\mathrm{S}\cdot()^{\cdot} \vdash \mathrm{DP}\backslash\mathrm{S}}\equiv \qquad \dfrac{\mathrm{DP}\backslash\mathrm{S}\cdot()^{\cdot} \vdash \mathrm{DP}\backslash\mathrm{S}}{()^{\cdot} \vdash (\mathrm{DP}\backslash\mathrm{S})\backslash(\mathrm{DP}\backslash\mathrm{S})}\backslash R \qquad \dfrac{()^{\cdot} \vdash (\mathrm{DP}\backslash\mathrm{S})\backslash(\mathrm{DP}\backslash\mathrm{S})}{()^{\cdot} \vdash \textsc{adv}}\,\textsc{def}$$

$$\dfrac{()^{\cdot} \vdash \textsc{adv} \qquad \mathrm{S}\cdot(\mathrm{bidk}\cdot(\mathrm{when}\cdot\textsc{adv}\backslash\!\!\backslash\mathrm{S})) \vdash \mathrm{S}}{(()^{\cdot}\circ\textsc{adv}\backslash\!\!\backslash\mathrm{S})\cdot(\mathrm{bidk}\cdot(\mathrm{when}\cdot\textsc{adv}\backslash\!\!\backslash\mathrm{S})) \vdash \mathrm{S}}\backslash\!\!\backslash L$$

$$\dfrac{(()^{\cdot}\circ\textsc{adv}\backslash\!\!\backslash\mathrm{S})\cdot(\mathrm{bidk}\cdot(\mathrm{when}\cdot\textsc{adv}\backslash\!\!\backslash\mathrm{S})) \vdash \mathrm{S}}{\textsc{adv}\backslash\!\!\backslash\mathrm{S}\circ\lambda y((()^{\cdot}\circ y)\cdot(\mathrm{bidk}\cdot(\mathrm{when}\cdot\textsc{adv}\backslash\!\!\backslash\mathrm{S}))) \vdash \mathrm{S}}\equiv$$

$$\dfrac{\textsc{adv}\backslash\!\!\backslash\mathrm{S}\circ\lambda y((()^{\cdot}\circ y)\cdot(\mathrm{bidk}\cdot(\mathrm{when}\cdot\textsc{adv}\backslash\!\!\backslash\mathrm{S}))) \vdash \mathrm{S}}{\lambda y((()^{\cdot}\circ y)\cdot(\mathrm{bidk}\cdot(\mathrm{when}\cdot\textsc{adv}\backslash\!\!\backslash\mathrm{S}))) \vdash (\textsc{adv}\backslash\!\!\backslash\mathrm{S})\backslash\!\!\backslash\mathrm{S}}\backslash\!\!\backslash R$$

$$\dfrac{\lambda y((()^{\cdot}\circ y)\cdot(\mathrm{bidk}\cdot(\mathrm{when}\cdot\textsc{adv}\backslash\!\!\backslash\mathrm{S}))) \vdash (\textsc{adv}\backslash\!\!\backslash\mathrm{S})\backslash\!\!\backslash\mathrm{S}}{\textsc{adv}\backslash\!\!\backslash\mathrm{S}\circ\lambda z\lambda y((()^{\cdot}\circ y)\cdot(\mathrm{bidk}\cdot(\mathrm{when}\cdot z))) \vdash (\textsc{adv}\backslash\!\!\backslash\mathrm{S})\backslash\!\!\backslash\mathrm{S}}\equiv$$

$$\dfrac{\textsc{adv}\backslash\!\!\backslash\mathrm{S}\circ\lambda z\lambda y((()^{\cdot}\circ y)\cdot(\mathrm{bidk}\cdot(\mathrm{when}\cdot z))) \vdash (\textsc{adv}\backslash\!\!\backslash\mathrm{S})\backslash\!\!\backslash\mathrm{S}}{\lambda z\lambda y((()^{\cdot}\circ y)\cdot(\mathrm{bidk}\cdot(\mathrm{when}\cdot z))) \vdash (\textsc{adv}\backslash\!\!\backslash\mathrm{S})\backslash\!\!\backslash((\textsc{adv}\backslash\!\!\backslash\mathrm{S})\backslash\!\!\backslash\mathrm{S})}\backslash\!\!\backslash R$$

$$\dfrac{\mathrm{John}\cdot(\mathrm{left}\cdot\textsc{adv}) \vdash \mathrm{S}}{\textsc{adv}\circ\lambda x(\mathrm{John}\cdot(\mathrm{left}\cdot x)) \vdash \mathrm{S}}\equiv \qquad \dfrac{\textsc{adv}\circ\lambda x(\mathrm{John}\cdot(\mathrm{left}\cdot x)) \vdash \mathrm{S}}{\lambda x(\mathrm{John}\cdot(\mathrm{left}\cdot x)) \vdash \textsc{adv}\backslash\!\!\backslash\mathrm{S}}\backslash\!\!\backslash R$$

$$\dfrac{\lambda x(\mathrm{John}\cdot(\mathrm{left}\cdot x)) \vdash \textsc{adv}\backslash\!\!\backslash\mathrm{S} \qquad \mathrm{S}\vdash\mathrm{S}}{\lambda x(\mathrm{John}\cdot(\mathrm{left}\cdot x))\circ(\textsc{adv}\backslash\!\!\backslash\mathrm{S})\backslash\!\!\backslash\mathrm{S} \vdash \mathrm{S}}\backslash\!\!\backslash L$$

$$\dfrac{\lambda z\lambda y((()^{\cdot}\circ y)\cdot(\mathrm{bidk}\cdot(\mathrm{when}\cdot z))) \vdash (\textsc{adv}\backslash\!\!\backslash\mathrm{S})\backslash\!\!\backslash((\textsc{adv}\backslash\!\!\backslash\mathrm{S})\backslash\!\!\backslash\mathrm{S}) \qquad \lambda x(\mathrm{John}\cdot(\mathrm{left}\cdot x))\circ(\textsc{adv}\backslash\!\!\backslash\mathrm{S})\backslash\!\!\backslash\mathrm{S} \vdash \mathrm{S}}{\lambda x(\mathrm{John}\cdot(\mathrm{left}\cdot x))\circ(\textsc{whenslgap}\circ\lambda z\lambda y((()\circ y)\cdot(\mathrm{bidk}\cdot(\mathrm{when}\cdot z)))) \vdash \mathrm{S}}/\!\!/L$$

$$\dfrac{\lambda x(\mathrm{John}\cdot(\mathrm{left}\cdot x))\circ(\textsc{whenslgap}\circ\lambda z\lambda y((()\circ y)\cdot(\mathrm{bidk}\cdot(\mathrm{when}\cdot z)))) \vdash \mathrm{S}}{\lambda x(\mathrm{John}\cdot(\mathrm{left}\cdot x))\circ\lambda y((()\circ y)\cdot(\mathrm{bidk}\cdot(\mathrm{when}\cdot\textsc{whenslgap}))) \vdash \mathrm{S}}\equiv$$

$$\dfrac{\lambda x(\mathrm{John}\cdot(\mathrm{left}\cdot x))\circ\lambda y((()\circ y)\cdot(\mathrm{bidk}\cdot(\mathrm{when}\cdot\textsc{whenslgap}))) \vdash \mathrm{S}}{(()^{\cdot}\circ\lambda x(\mathrm{John}\cdot(\mathrm{left}\cdot x)))\cdot(\mathrm{bidk}\cdot(\mathrm{when}\cdot\textsc{whenslgap})) \vdash \mathrm{S}}\equiv$$

$$\dfrac{(()^{\cdot}\circ\lambda x(\mathrm{John}\cdot(\mathrm{left}\cdot x)))\cdot(\mathrm{bidk}\cdot(\mathrm{when}\cdot\textsc{whenslgap})) \vdash \mathrm{S}}{(\mathrm{John}\cdot(\mathrm{left}\cdot()^{\cdot}))\cdot(\mathrm{bidk}\cdot(\mathrm{when}\cdot\textsc{whenslgap})) \vdash \mathrm{S}}\equiv$$

$$\dfrac{(\mathrm{John}\cdot(\mathrm{left}\cdot()^{\cdot}))\cdot(\mathrm{bidk}\cdot(\mathrm{when}\cdot\textsc{whenslgap})) \vdash \mathrm{S}}{(\mathrm{John}\cdot\mathrm{left})\cdot(\mathrm{bidk}\cdot(\mathrm{when}\cdot\textsc{whenslgap})) \vdash \mathrm{S}}\equiv$$

The first step in the proof (reading from the top downwards) is to recognize that because the empty structure is an identity element, DP\S is structurally equivalent to $(\mathrm{DP}\backslash\mathrm{S}\cdot()^{\cdot})$. The proof proceeds as usual, until the final step, when we remove the empty structure. Although the silent adverbial is syntactically and semantically inert, it serves to mark the position with respect to which the remainder (continuation) of the antecedent clause is defined. This is enough to complete the sluicing derivation in the normal way.

Thus, given independently-motivated empty antecedents, we can sprout silent identity-function denoting modifiers that are syntactically and semantically harmless, and we can sprout them whenever we need them in order to nucleate a sluicing analysis.

Note that this technique only sprouts adjuncts, such as VP modifiers, and not arguments or specifiers. This is a good thing:

(270) a. Someone's dogs barked, but I don't know who.

b. *Dogs barked, but I don't know who.

As discussed in Chung (2013), a possessor can be sluiced as long as there is an appropriate overt inner antecedent, as in (270a), but a possessor can't be sprouted, as shown in (270b). (The fact that *whose* is a grammatical sluice is irrelevant, since it takes the entire DP as the inner antecedent, with the nominal *dog* deleted via an independent ellipsis process common to possessives.) On the analysis here, the reason we can't sprout possessors is that they have category DP/N, which is not an identity category.

Section 17.10 below considers a way of compiling various structural rules into the logical rules for computational reasons. As shown there, on that variation of the logic, embedded sprouting turns out to be simple parasitic scope.

16.8 Implicit argument sluices

There is a class of examples in which the missing inner antecedent is an argument rather than an adjunct. This is generally possible only when the argument in question is optional:

(271) John ate/*dined, but I don't know what.

Whether an argument is optional is specified in the lexicon on a per-item basis.

Implicit-argument sluices are often considered as a subtype of sprouting, following the terminology of Chung et al. (1995), but on our account, implicit argument sluices require a different analysis from sprouting.

Because implicit-argument sluicing is lexically governed, type logical grammar makes available an analysis involving product categories: if A and B are syntactic categories, then so is $A \times B$, the product of A and B. Products have the logic of multiplicative conjunction:

(272) $$\frac{\Sigma[A \cdot B] \vdash C}{\Sigma[A \times B] \vdash C}\times L \qquad \frac{\Gamma \vdash A \qquad \Delta \vdash B}{\Gamma \cdot \Delta \vdash A \times B}\times R$$

Product categories are related in an intimate way to the slash categories by the residuation law: $A \vdash C/B$ iff $A \times B \vdash C$ iff $B \vdash A\backslash C$.

The logical rules for the product say that when you have something of category $A \times B$, it will behave exactly as if you had something of category A followed by something of category B. This enables a single lexeme (say, *eat*) to behave as if it contributed two independent elements into the derivation. Thus we can suppose that the intransitive *eat* has the category ((DP\S)/DP) × (S⫽(DP⑊S)): it functions as if it were a transitive verb followed by a (silent) quantifier. This gives rise to the following derivation for the sluiced sentence *John ate, but I don't know what*:

(273) $$\cfrac{\cfrac{(\text{John}\cdot(((\text{DP}\backslash\text{S})/\text{DP})\cdot \text{S}/\!\!/(\text{DP}\backslash\!\!\backslash\text{S})))\cdot(\text{bidk}\cdot(\text{what}\cdot\textsc{sluicegap}))\vdash \text{S}}{(\text{John}\cdot(((\text{DP}\backslash\text{S})/\text{DP})\times \text{S}/\!\!/(\text{DP}\backslash\!\!\backslash\text{S})))\cdot(\text{bidk}\cdot(\text{what}\cdot\textsc{sluicegap}))\vdash \text{S}}\times L}{(\text{John}\cdot\text{ate}_{\text{INTR}})\cdot(\text{bidk}\cdot(\text{what}\cdot\textsc{sluicegap}))\vdash \text{S}}\textsc{lex}$$

The remainder of the proof proceeds exactly as if there had been an overt direct object.

Naturally, just as for conjunction in, say, intuitionistic logic, the semantics for a product category is an ordered pair. In this case, the denotation for the intransitive *eat* will be an ordered pair consisting of the meaning of the transitive *eat* along with the meaning of *something* (roughly, $\lambda P \exists x.Px$).

On the analysis here, once the implicit argument has entered the derivation, there is nothing to prevent it from taking scope just like any overt existential quantifier. This makes good predictions with respect to sluicing, since the scopability analysis here requires the implicit argument to take scope over the rest of the antecedent clause in order to serve as an inner antecedent for sluicing.

(274) a. Everyone ate, but I don't know what.
b. Everyone in the room was reading, but I don't know what.

To the extent that these sentences imply that there was some particular thing that everyone ate or read, they are consistent with the claims about scoping and sluicing here.

(275) *No one ate, but I don't know what.

Likewise, the ungrammaticality of (275) can be explained by the fact that downward-entailing quantifiers such as *no one* make it difficult or impossible for an indefinite in the verb phrase to take scope over the rest of the antecedent clause.

Note that implicit arguments can be prepositional phrases that require specific prepositions:

(276) a. John was flirting, but I don't know *(with) who.
b. Ralph was astonished, but I don't know *(at) what.
c. Marian was interested, but I don't know *(in) what.

As long as the categories of the intransitive versions of these predicates are (DP\S) × PP.*with*, (DP\S) × PP.*to*, and (DP\S) × PP.*in*, where, for instance, PP.*with* is the syntactic category of a prepositional phrase headed by *with*, we correctly predict not only that the wh-phrase in the sluice must be a prepositional phrase, but which preposition is the right one.

The scope behavior of implicit arguments required for sluicing is somewhat at odds with the typical behavior of implicit arguments. Apart from sluicing, implicit arguments generally take narrowest scope: *Everyone ate* can mean that for each person, there is something that they ate, but usually isn't taken to assert that there is some particular thing that everyone ate. However, it is well known (e.g., Tancredi 1992) that focusing a phrase can enable it to take unusually wide scope. It is hard to imagine focusing an implicit argument in most situations, since it is silent. However, as suggested by Sandra Chung (personal communication), if we were to assume that sluicing guarantees that the inner antecedent must be in focus, sluicing provides a way to deduce that the implicit argument must be in focus, and therefore can take wide scope.

See Barker (2013) for additional argument structure constraints on implicit argument sluicing.

16.9 A recursive scope analysis of Andrews Amalgams

In the analysis of sluicing offered here, the elided complement of a wh-phrase gets its content from a continuation, that is, from the scope remnant of a DP. The relationship between the sluice gap and its content-providing scope remnant is treated as anaphora. But there are other ways of gaining access to a DP continuation beside anaphora. Indeed, the prototypical way to gain access to a continuation is the method that generalized quantifiers such as *everyone* or *most girls* use, that is, by taking scope over it. Could there be a sluice-like ellipsis construction that acquired its gap content directly through scope-taking?

There is a construction in English that might qualify, what Lakoff (1974) calls an Andrews Amalgam:

(277) a. Sally will eat something today, but I don't know what __.
b. Sally will eat [I don't know what __] today.

In (277a), we have an ordinary sluice, where the inner antecedent is *someone*. The (grammatical) sentence in (277b) has roughly the same meaning, but in the place of *someone* sits an entire clause containing what appears to be a sluiced interrogative. Just as in the normal sluice, (277b) entails that the speaker does not know the answer to the question of what Sally will eat today.

Providing an analysis for these amalgams is challenging under standard assumptions, not least of all because it appears to be a case of ellipsis for which there is no obvious antecedent. Strategies for extending the standard framework include positing a special merge operation that combines two complete clauses, e.g., as in Kluck (2011), or else allowing trees in which nodes have more than one mother, e.g., as in Johnson (2012).

The formalism developed here accounts for Andrews Amalgams without any extension or modification. Let $\text{G} \equiv \text{S}/\!\!/(\text{DP}\backslash\!\!\backslash\text{S})$ abbreviate the category of a scope-taking generalized quantifier, the same category as ordinary quantifiers such as *everyone* or *most girls*. Then we need only allow ourselves a silent proform, written AMALGAM, having syntactic category $\text{G}/\!\!/((\text{DP}\backslash\!\!\backslash\text{S})\backslash\!\!\backslash\text{S})$ and semantic value $\lambda F \lambda P \exists x.Px \wedge (FP)$.

Because the result category $\text{G} \equiv \dfrac{\text{S}|\text{S}}{\text{DP}}$ is itself a scope-taking category, this is a case of recursive scope. (Recall that Solomon 2011 proposes a recursive-scope analysis of *same* as discussed above in section 14.4.)

In order to see how this analysis works, it is important to understand how the AMALGAM proform turns the clause in which it is embedded into a generalized quantifier:

(278)
$$\dfrac{\dfrac{\dfrac{\dfrac{\dfrac{\text{idk}\cdot(\text{what}\cdot \text{DP}\backslash\!\!\backslash\text{S})\vdash\text{S}}{\text{DP}\backslash\!\!\backslash\text{S}\circ\lambda x(\text{idk}\cdot(\text{what}\cdot x))\vdash\text{S}}\equiv}{\lambda x(\text{idk}\cdot(\text{what}\cdot x))\vdash(\text{DP}\backslash\!\!\backslash\text{S})\backslash\!\!\backslash\text{S}}\backslash\!\!\backslash R \qquad \textsc{g}\vdash\textsc{g}}{\textsc{g}/\!\!/((\text{DP}\backslash\!\!\backslash\text{S})\backslash\!\!\backslash\text{S})\circ\lambda x(\text{idk}\cdot(\text{what}\cdot x))\vdash\textsc{g}}/\!\!/L}{\textsc{amalgam}\circ\lambda x(\text{idk}\cdot(\text{what}\cdot x))\vdash\textsc{g}}\equiv}{\text{idk}\cdot(\text{what}\cdot\textsc{amalgam})\vdash\textsc{g}}\equiv$$

Here, 'idk' is short for 'I don't know', and has category S/Q; *what*, as usual, has category $\text{Q}/(\text{DP}\backslash\!\!\backslash\text{S})$. This proof shows that it makes sense for the expression *I don't know what* AMALGAM to function syntactically as if it were a (scope-taking) DP. The Curry-Howard denotation of this generalized quantifier is $\lambda P\exists x.Px \wedge$ I-don't-know (what P).

With this lemma in place, it is easy to see how the complete derivation of (277b) will go. Essentially, the synthetic quantifier phrase *I don't know what* AMALGAM takes scope over the rest of the sentence:

(279)
$$\dfrac{\dfrac{\dfrac{\lambda y(\text{idk}\cdot(\text{what}\cdot y))\vdash(\text{DP}\backslash\!\!\backslash\text{S})\backslash\!\!\backslash\text{S} \qquad \textsc{g}\circ\lambda x(\text{Sally}\cdot(\text{ate}\cdot x))\vdash\text{S}}{(\textsc{g}/\!\!/((\text{DP}\backslash\!\!\backslash\text{S})\backslash\!\!\backslash\text{S})\circ\lambda y(\text{idk}\cdot(\text{what}\cdot y)))\circ\lambda x(\text{Sally}\cdot(\text{ate}\cdot x))\vdash\text{S}}/\!\!/L}{(\text{idk}\cdot(\text{what}\cdot\textsc{amalgam}))\circ\lambda x(\text{Sally}\cdot(\text{ate}\cdot x))\vdash\text{S}}\equiv,\textsc{lex}}{\text{Sally}\cdot(\text{ate}\cdot(\text{idk}\cdot(\text{what}\cdot\textsc{amalgam})))\vdash\text{S}}\equiv$$

Reading from the bottom line upward: the first step is to allow the quantifier phrase [*I don't know what* AMALGAM] to take scope over *Sally ate* ___. As a result, on the second line from the bottom, we have a generalized quantifier taking scope over a DP remnant—this is the heart of the analysis. The derivation continues by allowing AMALGAM to take scope over the quantifier phrase (third line), and proceeding upwards in a manner similar to previous derivations.

Turning to the semantics, the fact that the symbol P occurs twice in the body of the semantic denotation ($\lambda F\lambda P\exists x.Px \wedge (FP)$) is what makes this construction a form of ellipsis: the content of the continuation P is used twice to build the semantic value of the complete sentence. In the Curry-Howard semantics of the derivation just sketched, F corresponds to the function from properties P to the proposition that the speaker doesn't know what has property P; and P corresponds to the property of being something that Sally will eat today. The net result is that (277b) is predicted to mean that there exists something that Sally is going to eat today, and the speaker doesn't know what Sally is going to eat today.

16.10 Semantic restrictions on sluicing: the Answer Ban

Not every inner antecedent gives rise to a successful sluice.

(280) a. Someone left, but I don't know who.
b. *John left, but I don't know who.

To a first approximation, setting aside sprouting examples, the wh-correlate (the inner antecedent) is usually indefinite. In fact, Jäger's (2001, 2005) analysis requires that the inner antecedent must always be indefinite. This is too restrictive:

(281) John left, but I don't know who else.

Although there is no prohibition against definite inner antecedents, we should and will say something about the conditions under which they are felicitous; see Barker (2013) for a more detailed discussion.

AnderBois (2011) argues that sluices are anaphoric to issues, in the sense of Inquisitive Semantics (e.g., Groenendijk and Roelofsen 2009, Mascarenhas 2009). More specifically, AnderBois (2011) argues that the antecedent must raise an issue, that is, have inquisitive content, and the sluiced interrogative must raise the same issue. In Inquisitive Semantics, questions, indefinites, disjunctions, and existential modals all give rise to inquisitive content. This correctly predicts that disjunctions can serve as inner antecedents, just like indefinites can:

(282) a. Someone left, but I don't know who.
b. John or Mary left, but I don't know which one.

One limitation of an inquisitive-semantics conception of sluicing is that licensing a sluice cannot be a purely semantic matter, in view of the case matching effects discussed above. But even on purely semantic grounds, the simple form of the anaphora-to-issues theory both overgenerates and undergenerates:

(283) a. John will leave or John won't leave, but I don't know which (one).
b. *John might leave, but I don't know which (one).

On the inquisitive-semantics account of Ciardelli et al. (2009), *might* in (283b) raises the same issue as the disjunctive antecedent in (283a). Yet the sentence with the modal does not license sluicing.

There is an additional difficulty related to undergeneration. Sprouting is a puzzle on a pure inquisitive-semantics approach, since it is far from clear how an antecedent such as *John left* raises the issue of when John left. That is what would be required to license a sprouting case such as *John left, but I don't know when*. And in fact, one and the same antecedent would have to give rise to an unbounded number of potential issues; for instance, in order to license the sluice *who else* in (281), *John left* would have to also give rise to the issue of who else besides John left.

Given these challenges to at least the simple version of the anaphora-to-issues theory, I will suggest that there is an independent semantic constraint at work in sluicing. It is inspired by AnderBois' approach, but different from it; see also a related proposal in Barros (2013). In particular, unlike AnderBois' hypothesis, it does not require that the antecedent raise an issue:

(284) **The Answer Ban**: the antecedent clause must not resolve, or even partially resolve, the issue raised by the sluiced interrogative.

Some examples will illustrate:

(285) #John left but I don't know who.

In (285), the interrogative raises the issue of who left. But the antecedent entails that John left, which settles (or at least partially settles) the issue. As we saw in (281), however, the fact that John left does not settle the issue of who *else* left, and the sluice is fine.

(286) a. #John or Mary left, but I don't know who.
b. John or Mary left, but I don't know which one.

In (286a), the issue is once again who left. The proposition that John or Mary left does not completely settle the issue, but it does partially resolve the issue, since it rules out possibilities in which neither John nor Mary left. But in (286b), the issue raised by the interrogative involves only a finite set of alternatives; as long as we take that set to contain exactly two alternatives involving John and Mary, then the proposition that John or Mary left does not resolve the issue raised by the interrogative, and the sluice is perfectly fine.

We should hasten to point out that there is a well-known class of cases in which a sluice antecedent seems to partially resolve the sluice, in apparent defiance of the Answer Ban.

(287) John met a woman, but I don't know who __.

If the issue raised by the sluiced clause were exactly the question denoted by the interrogative *who John met*, then the set of possible answers would involve both men and women. But (287) is interpreted as asserting the more specific claim that the speaker doesn't know which woman John met. Chung et al. (1995) call this 'Merger', and in their account, both the inner antecedent and wh-phrase impose semantic restrictions on one and the same variable in logical form. On the face of it, Merger examples appear to be inconsistent with the spirit of the Answer Ban, since the proposition that John met a woman is a partial answer to the question of who John met.

However, this conclusion only goes through if we assume that the issue raised by the sluice is identical with the denotation of the sluiced clause. This can't be right in general for any theory of questions: a use of the interrogative *who John met* typically does not ask for a complete specification of all the people John has ever met. Rather, it is limited in the familiar (if still mysterious) way that domain narrowing usually works. The net effect is that the question is interpreted as asking who John met out of some salient group of candidates that are relevant for some conversational purpose. If the speaker of (287) takes it for granted that the person John met was a woman, then the issue raised by the interrogative is the question of who John met from among the set of relevant women, an issue that is compatible with the Answer Ban.

Why would a grammar impose an Answer Ban? It is easy to understand the prohibition against re-raising a previously resolved issue in simple cases: it is incoherent to draw attention to the issue of who left if you already know who left. Addressing similar facts, Dayal and Schwarzschild (2010) point out that we shouldn't be surprised to discover that a sluice is infelicitous if the unsluiced discourse is infelicitous in the same way (*#John left, but I don't know who left*). But a coherence requirement fails to account for more complex situations:

(288) *Mary knows that John left, but Bill doesn't know who.

In (288), although Mary's knowledge settles the issue of who left, the issue can remain completely unresolved in Bill's mind; nevertheless, the sluice is degraded. The Answer Ban as stated in (284), however, depends only on the content of the antecedent clause *John left* and the sluice, and does not depend on anyone's epistemic state, so (288) is correctly predicted to be infelicitous. What we're suggesting is that the Answer Ban is a grammaticized constraint on epistemic coherence.

In sum, we have argued in this chapter for an anaphoric theory of sluicing. Like Jäger's proposal, it accounts for case matching and island insensitivity. Unlike Jäger's specific analysis, it also generalizes smoothly to sprouting and implicit argument sluices. Unlike any of its competitor accounts, it also easily handles Andrews Amalgams. The net result is a theory of sluicing on which sluicing amounts to anaphora to a scope remnant, i.e., anaphora to a continuation. To the extent that this account of sluicing is viable, it supports the main thesis of this book, which is that explicitly recognizing continuations is an essential element in a complete understanding of natural language composition.

17

Formal properties of NL_λ

NL_λ was introduced in chapter 13 as a completely ordinary multi-modal type-logical grammar, except for its one unusual structural postulate, repeated here:

(289) $\Sigma[\Delta] \equiv \Delta \circ \lambda\alpha\ \Sigma[\alpha]$

As discussed and illustrated in previous chapters, this is a form of lambda abstraction in the syntax, which we claim underpins the logic of scope-taking. In combination with the logical rules, this postulate says that in the continuation mode, an expression combines with its argument by surrounding it ('$\backslash\!\!\backslash$'), or by allowing the argument to do the surrounding ('$/\!\!/$').

The way that this is accomplished is by allowing a substructure Δ to take scope over a larger structure that contains it. As our notation emphasizes, the relationship between the focused structure Δ and the structure over which it takes scope is very much like the relationship between the argument and the abstract it combines with. As we have mentioned in the preface to Part II, the idea of allowing something like beta reduction in the syntax is in the spirit of Oehrle (1994), Muskens (2001), and de Groote (2002).

Admittedly, the postulate in (289) is not a typical structural postulate. For one thing, typical postulates adjust structures locally. For instance, here is a structural inference rule (not adopted here) that guarantees associativity for the merge mode:

(290) $p \cdot (q \cdot r) \equiv (p \cdot q) \cdot r$

This rule rearranges structures, but only across two levels of structural grouping. In contrast, the lambda postulate in (289) allows an in-situ scope-taker to take scope over a surrounding structure of unbounded size in one swoop.

For another thing, the postulate in (289) involves structures built out of lambdas and variables, which are by no means a typical part of structural inference rules.

So is the lambda-like structural postulate kosher? This chapter addresses this question by studying NL_{CL}, a type-logical grammar in which the work done by (289) is factored into a small set of perfectly well-behaved structural postulates. More specifically, the postulates of NL_{CL} conform to the general requirements placed on structural postulates studied by Restall (2000) in his chapter 11. As a result, we show in section 17.3 that Restall's proof of soundness and completeness holds for our logic as well. This means that NL_{CL} is sound and complete with respect to the same class of models as other more familiar substructural logics.

Furthermore, in section 17.4, we show that NL_{CL} does not disturb the structure of the underlying grammar NL. That is, NL_{CL} is conservative over the non-associative Lambek grammar: a sequent that contains only the merge mode is a theorem of NL iff it is is a theorem of NL_{CL}. This means that NL_{CL} can be used without worrying that the introduction of scope-taking might change the logic of the merge mode in any way.

Once we have established these formal properties of NL_{CL}, we will show that a suitably restricted version of NL_λ is equivalent to NL_{CL} in the following sense: given a sequent built up from formulas combined with $\cdot$ and $\circ$, if there is a derivation of that sequent in one of the logics, there is an equivalent derivation in the other. Two derivations are equivalent if they have the same assumptions and the same conclusion, reached via the same sequence of logical rules, with the same Curry-Howard semantic labeling.

The 'CL' in NL_{CL} stands for Combinatory Logic, though it could equally well stand for Continuation Logic. The rationale for this name, as we will explain below, is that the equivalence between NL_λ and NL_{CL} is directly analogous to the well-known equivalence between the lambda calculus and Combinatory Logic.

17.1 Scope-taking in type-logical grammars

There are a number of other type-logical analyses that address scope-taking in the literature. To start with, a limited form of scope taking results from adding associativity to the merge mode, that is, by adopting the structural postulate in (290). However, as pointed out by many (e.g., Moortgat 1997), this strategy only accounts for scope-takers that happen to be at the left or right edge of their scope domain, (e.g., *John saw everyone*), and does not account for scope-takers that are surrounded on both sides by their scope domain (*John saw everyone yesterday*).

Moortgat (1988, 1997) provides a more robust account of scope-taking by defining a type constructor q ('q' for quantification). The logic of q captures how an in-situ scope-taker interacts with its context: an expression in category $q(A, B, C)$ functions locally as an A, takes scope over a B, and functions in the larger context as an expression of category C. This is exactly what a scope-taking expression needs to do. However, the logical characterization of q is problematic. For instance, although it is easy to write a left rule (a rule of use) for q, a general right rule (a rule of proof) remains elusive. Furthermore, it is unsatisfactory that the many decompositions of q into structural postulates in the literature all require either more than two modes (e.g., Morrill 1994) or additional mechanisms to prevent commutativity from leaking into the merge mode (e.g., Barker and Shan 2006). It is thus worth noting that the rule of use for q is a theorem in our logic, where $q(A, B, C)$ is implemented as $C /\!\!/ (A \backslash\!\!\backslash B)$, as shown below in section 17.10.

In any case, empirically, as insightful as the q constructor is for characterizing normal in-situ scope-taking, it will not suffice for describing the kind of parasitic scope-taking argued for in Part II. The reason is that in order to recognize the nuclear scope of a host quantifier as a constituent (the essence of parasitic scope), we must be free to reason about continuations of the form $A \backslash\!\!\backslash B$ independently of the quantifiers that take them as arguments. But there is no way to isolate any category involving just A and B within the category $q(A, B, C)$.

Bernardi and Moortgat (2007), Moortgat (2009), Bernardi and Moortgat (2010) give a logic called Lambek-Grishin (LG) that provides connectives for quantification that make continuations explicit. However, the nuclear scope of a quantifier is still not a logical constituent in LG. As a result, it is likewise not clear how LG could account for the parasitic scope treatments of *same*, anaphora, verb phrase ellipsis, *average*, and sluicing. See section 18.2 for a more detailed discussion of LG.

17.2 $\mathbf{NL}_{CL}$: An equivalent logic with standard postulates

The postulate given above in (289) succinctly expresses the logic of scope-taking. However, as mentioned above, it is a somewhat unusual postulate. In this section we give a more cumbersome but equivalent logic that uses only standard postulates.

We define NL_{CL}, a non-associative Lambek grammar with the same two modes as NL_λ, namely, the merge mode and the continuation mode, as in chapter 13. However, whereas NL_λ builds augmented structures with λ and syntactic variables, NL_{CL} instead adds three atomic structures: I, B, and C. As we will explain, these atomic structures are analogous to the Combinatory Logic combinators **I**, **B**, and **C**, as named by Curry.

The logical inference rules of NL_{CL} are exactly as given above in (220) in chapter 13, repeated here (without change) for ease of reference:

(291)

$$\frac{}{A \vdash A}\ \text{Axiom}$$

$$\frac{\Gamma \vdash A \quad \Sigma[B] \vdash C}{\Sigma[\Gamma \cdot A \backslash B] \vdash C} \backslash L \qquad \frac{A \cdot \Gamma \vdash B}{\Gamma \vdash A \backslash B} \backslash R \qquad \frac{\Gamma \vdash A \quad \Sigma[B] \vdash C}{\Sigma[B/A \cdot \Gamma] \vdash C} /L \qquad \frac{\Gamma \cdot A \vdash B}{\Gamma \vdash B/A} /R$$

$$\frac{\Gamma \vdash A \quad \Sigma[B] \vdash C}{\Sigma[\Gamma \circ A \backslash\!\!\backslash B] \vdash C} \backslash\!\!\backslash L \qquad \frac{A \circ \Gamma \vdash B}{\Gamma \vdash A \backslash\!\!\backslash B} \backslash\!\!\backslash R \qquad \frac{\Gamma \vdash A \quad \Sigma[B] \vdash C}{\Sigma[B /\!\!/ A \circ \Gamma] \vdash C} /\!\!/ L \qquad \frac{\Gamma \circ A \vdash B}{\Gamma \vdash B /\!\!/ A} /\!\!/ R$$

These are the same logical rules that we have been using throughout Part II, and are standard in type-logical discussions, as in, e.g., Moortgat (1997:129).

In addition to the logical rules, NL_{CL} has three structural postulates:

(292) $$\frac{p}{p \circ \mathsf{I}}\,\mathsf{I} \qquad \frac{p \cdot (q \circ r)}{q \circ ((\mathsf{B} \cdot p) \cdot r)}\,\mathsf{B} \qquad \frac{(p \circ q) \cdot r}{p \circ ((\mathsf{C} \cdot q) \cdot r)}\,\mathsf{C}$$

These postulates are identical to the ones given in Barker (2007). Restall (2000:30) considers I (which he writes '0') as "a zero-place punctuation mark", where punctuation marks (p. 19) "stand to structures in the same way that connectives stand to formulae". Likewise, B and C are also zero-place punctuation marks. The double horizontal line indicates that these rules are bi-directional, i.e., inference in the top-to-bottom direction and in the bottom-to-top direction are both valid. Restall calls the top-to-bottom inference for the I postulate Push, and the other direction Pop.

In the form of an official inference rule, the I postulate (for instance) is written

(293) $$\frac{\Sigma[p] \vdash A}{\Sigma[p \circ \mathsf{I}] \vdash A},$$

and similarly for the other rules.

In the usual terminology for classifying structural postulates, I is a right identity with respect to $\circ$, B governs mixed commutativity involving $\cdot$ and $\circ$, and C governs mixed associativity involving $\cdot$ and $\circ$. However, we will suggest below other ways of understanding what these postulates are doing.

An example derivation will show how these postulates work together to achieve in-situ quantification for the sentence *John saw everyone*:

(294) $$\dfrac{\dfrac{\dfrac{\dfrac{\dfrac{\dfrac{\dfrac{\dfrac{\dfrac{\dfrac{\dfrac{\dfrac{\mathrm{DP} \vdash \mathrm{DP} \quad \dfrac{\mathrm{DP} \vdash \mathrm{DP} \quad \mathrm{S} \vdash \mathrm{S}}{\mathrm{DP} \cdot \mathrm{DP}\backslash \mathrm{S} \vdash \mathrm{S}}\backslash L}{\mathrm{DP} \cdot ((\mathrm{DP}\backslash \mathrm{S})/\mathrm{DP} \cdot \mathrm{DP}) \vdash \mathrm{S}}/L}{\text{john} \cdot (\text{saw} \cdot \mathrm{DP}) \vdash \mathrm{S}}\,\text{LEX}}{\text{john} \cdot (\text{saw} \cdot (\mathrm{DP} \circ \mathsf{I})) \vdash \mathrm{S}}\,\mathsf{I}}{\text{john} \cdot (\mathrm{DP} \circ ((\mathsf{B} \cdot \text{saw}) \cdot \mathsf{I})) \vdash \mathrm{S}}\,\mathsf{B}}{\mathrm{DP} \circ ((\mathsf{B} \cdot \text{john}) \cdot ((\mathsf{B} \cdot \text{saw}) \cdot \mathsf{I})) \vdash \mathrm{S}}\,\mathsf{B}}{(\mathsf{B} \cdot \text{john}) \cdot ((\mathsf{B} \cdot \text{saw}) \cdot \mathsf{I}) \vdash \mathrm{DP}\backslash\!\!\backslash \mathrm{S}}\backslash\!\!\backslash R \quad \mathrm{S} \vdash \mathrm{S}}{\mathrm{S}/\!\!/(\mathrm{DP}\backslash\!\!\backslash \mathrm{S}) \circ ((\mathsf{B} \cdot \text{john}) \cdot ((\mathsf{B} \cdot \text{saw}) \cdot \mathsf{I})) \vdash \mathrm{S}}/\!\!/L}{\text{everyone} \circ ((\mathsf{B} \cdot \text{john}) \cdot ((\mathsf{B} \cdot \text{saw}) \cdot \mathsf{I})) \vdash \mathrm{S}}\,\text{LEX}}{\text{john} \cdot (\text{everyone} \circ ((\mathsf{B} \cdot \text{saw}) \cdot \mathsf{I})) \vdash \mathrm{S}}\,\mathsf{B}}{\text{john} \cdot (\text{saw} \cdot (\text{everyone} \circ \mathsf{I})) \vdash \mathrm{S}}\,\mathsf{B}}{\text{john} \cdot (\text{saw} \cdot \text{everyone}) \vdash \mathrm{S}}\,\mathsf{I}$$

This derivation is equivalent to the NL_λ derivation given above in (224). That is, it differs only in the application of structural rules.

Since one of the distinctive advantages of NL_λ over some other approaches is the ability to handle higher-order continuations, which is what enables derivations of parasitic scope, we should demonstrate how NL_{CL} accounts for a parasitic scope example. Here is a derivation of *The same waiter served everyone*:

(295)

$$
\begin{array}{cl}
\vdots & \\
(\mathrm{the} \cdot (\mathrm{A} \cdot \mathrm{waiter})) \cdot (\mathrm{served} \cdot \mathrm{DP}) \vdash \mathrm{S} & \\
\hline
(\mathrm{the} \cdot (\mathrm{A} \cdot \mathrm{waiter})) \cdot (\mathrm{served} \cdot (\mathrm{DP} \circ \mathrm{I})) \vdash \mathrm{S} & \mathrm{I} \\
\hline
(\mathrm{the} \cdot (\mathrm{A} \cdot \mathrm{waiter})) \cdot (\mathrm{DP} \circ ((\mathrm{B} \cdot \mathrm{served}) \cdot \mathrm{I})) \vdash \mathrm{S} & \mathrm{B} \\
\hline
\mathrm{DP} \circ ((\mathrm{B} \cdot (\mathrm{the} \cdot (\mathrm{A} \cdot \mathrm{waiter}))) \cdot ((\mathrm{B} \cdot \mathrm{served}) \cdot \mathrm{I})) \vdash \mathrm{S} & \mathrm{B} \\
\hline
(\mathrm{B} \cdot (\mathrm{the} \cdot (\mathrm{A} \cdot \mathrm{waiter}))) \cdot ((\mathrm{B} \cdot \mathrm{served}) \cdot \mathrm{I}) \vdash \mathrm{DP}\backslash\!\!\backslash \mathrm{S} & \backslash\!\!\backslash R \\
\hline
(\mathrm{B} \cdot (\mathrm{the} \cdot ((\mathrm{A} \circ \mathrm{I}) \cdot \mathrm{waiter}))) \cdot ((\mathrm{B} \cdot \mathrm{served}) \cdot \mathrm{I}) \vdash \mathrm{DP}\backslash\!\!\backslash \mathrm{S} & \mathrm{I} \\
\hline
(\mathrm{B} \cdot (\mathrm{the} \cdot (\mathrm{A} \circ ((\mathrm{C} \cdot \mathrm{I}) \cdot \mathrm{waiter})))) \cdot ((\mathrm{B} \cdot \mathrm{served}) \cdot \mathrm{I}) \vdash \mathrm{DP}\backslash\!\!\backslash \mathrm{S} & \mathrm{C} \\
\hline
(\mathrm{B} \cdot (\mathrm{A} \circ ((\mathrm{B} \cdot \mathrm{the}) \cdot ((\mathrm{C} \cdot \mathrm{I}) \cdot \mathrm{waiter})))) \cdot ((\mathrm{B} \cdot \mathrm{served}) \cdot \mathrm{I}) \vdash \mathrm{DP}\backslash\!\!\backslash \mathrm{S} & \mathrm{B} \\
\hline
(\mathrm{A} \circ ((\mathrm{B} \cdot \mathrm{B}) \cdot ((\mathrm{B} \cdot \mathrm{the}) \cdot ((\mathrm{C} \cdot \mathrm{I}) \cdot \mathrm{waiter})))) \cdot ((\mathrm{B} \cdot \mathrm{served}) \cdot \mathrm{I}) \vdash \mathrm{DP}\backslash\!\!\backslash \mathrm{S} & \mathrm{B} \\
\hline
\mathrm{A} \circ ((\mathrm{C} \cdot ((\mathrm{B} \cdot \mathrm{B}) \cdot ((\mathrm{B} \cdot \mathrm{the}) \cdot ((\mathrm{C} \cdot \mathrm{I}) \cdot \mathrm{waiter})))) \cdot ((\mathrm{B} \cdot \mathrm{served}) \cdot \mathrm{I})) \vdash \mathrm{DP}\backslash\!\!\backslash \mathrm{S} & \mathrm{C} \\
\hline
((\mathrm{C} \cdot ((\mathrm{B} \cdot \mathrm{B}) \cdot ((\mathrm{B} \cdot \mathrm{the}) \cdot ((\mathrm{C} \cdot \mathrm{I}) \cdot \mathrm{waiter})))) \cdot ((\mathrm{B} \cdot \mathrm{served}) \cdot \mathrm{I})) \vdash (\mathrm{A})\backslash\!\!\backslash(\mathrm{DP}\backslash\!\!\backslash \mathrm{S}) \qquad \mathrm{DP}\backslash\!\!\backslash \mathrm{S} \vdash \mathrm{DP}\backslash\!\!\backslash \mathrm{S} & \backslash\!\!\backslash R \\
\hline
(\mathrm{DP}\backslash\!\!\backslash \mathrm{S})/\!\!/((\mathrm{A})\backslash\!\!\backslash(\mathrm{DP}\backslash\!\!\backslash \mathrm{S})) \circ ((\mathrm{C} \cdot ((\mathrm{B} \cdot \mathrm{B}) \cdot ((\mathrm{B} \cdot \mathrm{the}) \cdot ((\mathrm{C} \cdot \mathrm{I}) \cdot \mathrm{waiter})))) \cdot ((\mathrm{B} \cdot \mathrm{served}) \cdot \mathrm{I})) \vdash \mathrm{DP}\backslash\!\!\backslash \mathrm{S} & /\!\!/L \\
\hline
\mathrm{same} \circ ((\mathrm{C} \cdot ((\mathrm{B} \cdot \mathrm{B}) \cdot ((\mathrm{B} \cdot \mathrm{the}) \cdot ((\mathrm{C} \cdot \mathrm{I}) \cdot \mathrm{waiter})))) \cdot ((\mathrm{B} \cdot \mathrm{served}) \cdot \mathrm{I})) \vdash \mathrm{DP}\backslash\!\!\backslash \mathrm{S} & \mathrm{LEX} \\
\hline
(\mathrm{same} \circ ((\mathrm{B} \cdot \mathrm{B}) \cdot ((\mathrm{B} \cdot \mathrm{the}) \cdot ((\mathrm{C} \cdot \mathrm{I}) \cdot \mathrm{waiter})))) \cdot ((\mathrm{B} \cdot \mathrm{served}) \cdot \mathrm{I}) \vdash \mathrm{DP}\backslash\!\!\backslash \mathrm{S} & \mathrm{C} \\
\hline
(\mathrm{B} \cdot (\mathrm{same} \circ ((\mathrm{B} \cdot \mathrm{the}) \cdot ((\mathrm{C} \cdot \mathrm{I}) \cdot \mathrm{waiter})))) \cdot ((\mathrm{B} \cdot \mathrm{served}) \cdot \mathrm{I}) \vdash \mathrm{DP}\backslash\!\!\backslash \mathrm{S} & \mathrm{B} \\
\hline
(\mathrm{B} \cdot (\mathrm{the} \cdot (\mathrm{same} \circ ((\mathrm{C} \cdot \mathrm{I}) \cdot \mathrm{waiter})))) \cdot ((\mathrm{B} \cdot \mathrm{served}) \cdot \mathrm{I}) \vdash \mathrm{DP}\backslash\!\!\backslash \mathrm{S} & \mathrm{B} \\
\hline
(\mathrm{B} \cdot (\mathrm{the} \cdot ((\mathrm{same} \cdot \mathrm{I}) \cdot \mathrm{waiter}))) \cdot ((\mathrm{B} \cdot \mathrm{served}) \cdot \mathrm{I}) \vdash \mathrm{DP}\backslash\!\!\backslash \mathrm{S} & \mathrm{C} \\
\hline
(\mathrm{B} \cdot (\mathrm{the} \cdot (\mathrm{same} \cdot \mathrm{waiter}))) \cdot ((\mathrm{B} \cdot \mathrm{served}) \cdot \mathrm{I}) \vdash \mathrm{DP}\backslash\!\!\backslash \mathrm{S} \qquad \mathrm{S} \vdash \mathrm{S} & \mathrm{I} \\
\hline
\mathrm{S}/\!\!/(\mathrm{DP}\backslash\!\!\backslash \mathrm{S}) \circ ((\mathrm{B} \cdot (\mathrm{the} \cdot (\mathrm{same} \cdot \mathrm{waiter}))) \cdot ((\mathrm{B} \cdot \mathrm{served}) \cdot \mathrm{I})) \vdash \mathrm{S} & /\!\!/L \\
\hline
\mathrm{everyone} \circ ((\mathrm{B} \cdot (\mathrm{the} \cdot (\mathrm{same} \cdot \mathrm{waiter}))) \cdot ((\mathrm{B} \cdot \mathrm{served}) \cdot \mathrm{I})) \vdash \mathrm{S} & \mathrm{LEX} \\
\hline
(\mathrm{the} \cdot (\mathrm{same} \cdot \mathrm{waiter})) \cdot (\mathrm{everyone} \circ ((\mathrm{B} \cdot \mathrm{served}) \cdot \mathrm{I})) \vdash \mathrm{S} & \mathrm{B} \\
\hline
(\mathrm{the} \cdot (\mathrm{same} \cdot \mathrm{waiter})) \cdot (\mathrm{served} \cdot (\mathrm{everyone} \circ \mathrm{I})) \vdash \mathrm{S} & \mathrm{B} \\
\hline
(\mathrm{the} \cdot (\mathrm{same} \cdot \mathrm{waiter})) \cdot (\mathrm{served} \cdot \mathrm{everyone}) \vdash \mathrm{S} & \mathrm{I}
\end{array}
$$

Considerably more inferences are required when abstractions are accomplished step by step rather than in one long jump. However, since this derivation differs from the corresponding derivation given in chapter 14 only in the application of structural postulates, which do not affect the Curry-Howard labeling, the semantic value is exactly as for the equivalent derivation in NL_λ.

The derivations just shown establish that NL_λ and NL_{CL} can provide highly similar analyses of natural language phenomena. We will consider the exact nature of the equivalence between the logics in some detail, after first proving some results about NL_{CL}.

17.3 Soundness and completeness

NL_{CL} is sound and complete with respect to the usual class of relational models. We will give enough details to make it clear that soundness and completeness follows directly from the proofs given in Restall (2000), chapter 11.

A frame $\mathcal{F}$ for NL_{CL} consists of

- A (flat) set of points $\mathcal{P}$
- 3-place accessibility relations $R.$ and $R_\circ$
- 1-place predicates I, B, and C

A model $\mathfrak{M}$ for NL_{CL} is a frame along with an evaluation relation $\Vdash$ that satisfies the following:

$$x \Vdash Z/Y \text{ iff } \forall y, z.(R.xyz \wedge y \Vdash Y) \rightarrow z \Vdash Z$$
$$y \Vdash X\backslash Z \text{ iff } \forall x, z.(R.xyz \wedge x \Vdash X) \rightarrow z \Vdash Z$$

$$x \Vdash Z/\!\!/Y \text{ iff } \forall y, z.(R_\circ xyz \wedge y \Vdash Y) \rightarrow z \Vdash Z$$
$$y \Vdash X\backslash\!\!\backslash Z \text{ iff } \forall x, z.(R_\circ xyz \wedge x \Vdash X) \rightarrow z \Vdash Z$$

$$x \Vdash \mathsf{I} \text{ iff } x \in I$$
$$x \Vdash \mathsf{B} \text{ iff } x \in B$$
$$x \Vdash \mathsf{C} \text{ iff } x \in C$$
$$z \Vdash p \cdot q \text{ iff } \exists x, y.R.xyz \wedge x \Vdash p \wedge y \Vdash q$$
$$z \Vdash p \circ q \text{ iff } \exists x, y.R_\circ xyz \wedge x \Vdash p \wedge y \Vdash q$$

Restall (2000:249) provides an algorithm for constructing frame conditions corresponding to the structural postulates. Given our structural postulates, the algorithm produces the following frame conditions:

Structural postulate: Frame condition:

$$\frac{p}{p \circ \mathsf{I}} \qquad \forall pz.\,(p = z) \leftrightarrow (\exists i.\, R_{\circ}piz \wedge Ii)$$

$$\frac{p \cdot (q \circ r)}{q \circ ((\mathsf{B} \cdot p) \cdot r)} \qquad \forall pqrz.\,(\exists y.\, R.pyz \wedge R_{\circ}qry) \leftrightarrow (\exists bxy.\, R_{\circ}qyz \wedge R.xry \wedge R.bpx \wedge Bb)$$

$$\frac{(p \circ q) \cdot r}{p \circ ((\mathsf{C} \cdot q) \cdot r)} \qquad \forall pqrz.\,(\exists x.\, R.xrz \wedge R_{\circ}pqx) \leftrightarrow (\exists cxy.\, R_{\circ}pyz \wedge R.xry \wedge R.cqx \wedge Cc)$$

Theorem (Soundness and completeness): $X \vdash A$ is provable in NL_{CL} iff for every model $\mathfrak{M} = \langle \mathcal{F}, \models \rangle$ that satisfies the frame conditions above, $\forall x \in \mathcal{F}, x \models X \rightarrow x \models A$.

Proof: given in Restall (2000), theorems 11.20, 11.37.

17.4 NL_{CL} is conservative over NL

Because in-situ scope-taking requires establishing a long-distance dependency with medial embedded elements, it provides limited access to both associativity and commutativity. It is worth wondering whether commutativity could leak into the merge mode, in effect allowing illicit scrambling of argument positions. For instance, in Barker and Shan (2006), the simplest version of their structural postulates gives rise to commutativity in the presence of a right identity (see Barker and Shan 2006:footnote 2). Barker and Shan eventually adopt more specific postulates for independent reasons in a way that fortuitously blocks unwanted commutativity. In any case, we prove here that NL_{CL} does not have any commutativity problem even in its simplest, most general presentation.

Theorem (Conservativity): Let an NL sequent be a sequent built up only from the formulas and structures allowed in NL: $/, \backslash, \cdot$. An NL sequent is provable in NL_{CL} iff it is provable in NL.

Proof: The 'if' direction is easy, since every NL derivation is also an NL_{CL} derivation. In the 'only-if' direction, we need to show that if an NL sequent is not valid in NL, it is not valid in NL_{CL}.

The proof proceeds by extending a falsifying NL model to a falsifying NL_{CL} model. Suppose that an NL sequent ϕ is not valid in NL. Then there is a model $\mathcal{M}$ of NL, whose (flat) point-set is $\mathcal{P}$ and whose (only) ternary relation is R, such that there is some $x \in \mathcal{P}$ that falsifies ϕ.

We want to extend the model $\mathcal{M}$ of NL to a new model $\mathcal{M}_{CL}$ of NL_{CL} in which the same point x still falsifies ϕ. Without loss of generality, assume $\mathcal{P}$ contains no ordered pairs. Let a, i, b, and c be four distinct points not in $\mathcal{P}$ that are also not ordered pairs. Let the (flat) point-set $\mathcal{P}_{CL}$ of the new model be the smallest set such that

- $\mathcal{P}$ is a subset of $\mathcal{P}_{CL}$;
- a, i, b, c, are elements of $\mathcal{P}_{CL}$;
- the ordered pair $\langle x, y\rangle$ is in $\mathcal{P}_{CL}$ whenever both x and y are in $\mathcal{P}_{CL}$ and either x or y is not in $\mathcal{P} \cup \{a\}$.

As one might expect, we let i be the (only) point in the new model that satisfies the predicate I, and likewise for b and c and their respective predicates.

Let $R.$ and $R_\circ$, the three-place relations of $\mathcal{M}_{CL}$, be the smallest relations such that

- $R.xyz$ if $Rxyz$, for any $x, y, z \in \mathcal{P}$.
- $R.xy\langle x, y\rangle$ if either x or y is not in $\mathcal{P} \cup \{a\}$, for any $x, y \in \mathcal{P}_{CL}$.
- $R.aaa$.
- $R_\circ ziz$, for any $z \in \mathcal{P}_{CL}$.
- $R_\circ q\langle\langle b, p\rangle, r\rangle z$ if $R_\circ qry$ and $R.pyz$, for any $p, q, r, y, z \in \mathcal{P}_{CL}$.
- $R_\circ p\langle\langle c, q\rangle, r\rangle z$ if $R_\circ pqx$ and $R.xrz$, for any $p, q, r, x, z \in \mathcal{P}_{CL}$.

Note that $R.$ restricted to $\mathcal{P}$ coincides with R.

The recursive definition of $R_\circ$ is well-founded because the second argument to $R_\circ$ after "if" is always a proper subpart of the argument before "if". It is easy to check that $R.$ and $R_\circ$ satisfy the frame conditions. For instance, the frame condition for the right identity is precisely that $R_\circ piz$ iff $p = z$.

Let each atomic proposition's valuation in the new model be the union of $\{a\}$ and its valuation in the old model. In other words, if X is an atomic proposition in NL and $x \in \mathcal{P}_{CL}$, then let x satisfy X in the new model $\mathcal{M}_{CL}$ iff $x = a$ or x satisfies X in the old model $\mathcal{M}$. It now remains to extend this property from atomic propositions X to all structures and formulas X, by induction on X. The inductive steps are $\cdot$, $/$, and $\backslash$. Write $\Vdash$ for the satisfaction relation in the old model $\mathcal{M}$, and $\Vdash_{CL}$ for the satisfaction relation in the new model $\mathcal{M}_{CL}$.

If $X = X_1 \cdot X_2$, then we reason:

$$
\begin{array}{lll}
 & x \Vdash_{CL} X_1 \cdot X_2 & \\
\text{iff} & \exists y, z \in \mathcal{P}_{CL} : y \Vdash_{CL} X_1 \wedge z \Vdash_{CL} X_2 \wedge R.yzx & \text{(by the definition of } \Vdash_{CL}) \\
\text{iff} & R.aax \vee (\exists y \in \mathcal{P} : y \Vdash X_1 \wedge R.yax) & \text{(by induction hypothesis)} \\
 & \quad \vee (\exists z \in \mathcal{P} : z \Vdash X_2 \wedge R.azx) & \\
 & \quad \vee (\exists y, z \in \mathcal{P} : y \Vdash X_1 \wedge z \Vdash X_2 \wedge R.yzx) & \\
\text{iff} & x = a \vee \exists y, z \in \mathcal{P} : y \Vdash X_1 \wedge z \Vdash X_2 \wedge Ryzx & \text{(by definition of } R.) \\
\text{iff} & x = a \vee x \Vdash X_1 \cdot X_2 & \text{(by definition of } \Vdash)
\end{array}
$$

If $X = X_1/X_2$, then we reason:

$$
\begin{array}{lll}
 & x \Vdash_{CL} X_1/X_2 & \\
\text{iff} & \forall z \in \mathcal{P}_{CL} : (\exists y \in \mathcal{P}_{CL} : y \Vdash_{CL} X_2 \wedge R.xyz) & \text{(by definition of } \Vdash_{CL}) \\
 & \qquad \to z \Vdash_{CL} X_1 & \\
\text{iff} & \forall z \in \mathcal{P}_{CL} : (R.xaz \vee \exists y \in \mathcal{P} : y \Vdash X_2 \wedge R.xyz) & \text{(by induction hypothesis)} \\
 & \qquad \to (z = a \vee z \Vdash X_1) &
\end{array}
$$

Now, either $x \in \mathcal{P}$ or $x \notin \mathcal{P}$. If $x \in \mathcal{P}$, then the definition of R. reduces the last proposition above to $\forall z \in \mathcal{P} : (\exists y \in \mathcal{P} : y \Vdash X_2 \wedge Rxyz) \rightarrow z \Vdash X_1$, which is equivalent to $x \Vdash X_1/X_2$. If $x \notin \mathcal{P}$, then the definition of R. reduces the last proposition above to $x = a$. Hence $x \Vdash_{CL} X$ iff $x = a \vee x \Vdash X$, as desired. The \ case is like the / case.

Thus if x falsifies a sequent ϕ in NL, the same point x falsifies ϕ in NL_{CL}. Since NL_{CL} is sound, ϕ is not provable in NL_{CL}. QED.

17.5 The connection between NL_λ and NL_{CL}

The inspiration for NL_{CL} comes from the well-known equivalence between the lambda calculus and Combinatory Logic. More specifically, the postulates of NL_{CL} implement a version of Shönfinkel's embedding of λ-terms into Combinatory Logic. Adapting the presentation in Barendregt (1981:152), we define $\langle\cdot\rangle$, which maps an arbitrary λ-term into Combinatory Logic:

(296)
$$\begin{array}{rlrl} \langle x\rangle &\equiv x & \mathbb{A}(x,x) &\equiv \textsc{i} \\ \langle MN\rangle &\equiv \langle M\rangle\,\langle N\rangle & \mathbb{A}(x,M) &\equiv \textsc{k}M \quad (x \text{ not free in } M) \\ \langle \lambda x.M\rangle &\equiv \mathbb{A}(x,\langle M\rangle) & \mathbb{A}(x,MN) &\equiv \textsc{s}(\mathbb{A}(x,M))(\mathbb{A}(x,N)) \end{array}$$

where $\textsc{s}xyz \rightsquigarrow_{CL} xz(yz)$, $\textsc{k}xy \rightsquigarrow_{CL} x$, and $\textsc{i}x \rightsquigarrow_{CL} x$ as usual. As Barendregt shows, if $M \rightsquigarrow_\beta N$, then $\langle M\rangle \rightsquigarrow_{CL} \langle N\rangle$.

For example,

(297) $\langle \lambda x\lambda y.yx\rangle = \textsc{s}(\textsc{k}(\textsc{si}))(\textsc{s}(\textsc{kk})\textsc{i})$

We could use postulates that implement Shönkinkel's mapping exactly. However, the frame conditions and the conservativity proof for NL_{CL} given in the previous sections are simpler if we use instead a more efficient refinement of the mapping due to David Turner. We add the following clauses:

(298)
$$\begin{array}{rll} \mathbb{A}(x,MN) &\equiv \textsc{b}M(\mathbb{A}(x,N)) & (x \text{ not free in } M) \\ \mathbb{A}(x,MN) &\equiv \textsc{c}(\mathbb{A}(x,M))N & (x \text{ not free in } N) \end{array}$$

where $\textsc{b}xyz \rightsquigarrow_{CL} x(yz)$ and $\textsc{c}xyz \rightsquigarrow_{CL} xzy$. With these clauses added, we have

(299) $\langle \lambda x\lambda y.yx\rangle = \textsc{b}(\textsc{ci})\textsc{i}$

This is considerably simpler than the encoding given above in (297).

The two clauses in (298) match the B and C postulates of NL_{CL} closely. This correspondence is the heart of the equivalence between the two systems.

It would be reasonable to declare NL_{CL} to be the "real" logic of scope-taking, and define the lambda postulate to be a mere notational variant that succinctly summarizes a sequence of structural inferences in NL_{CL}. Instead, we will consider NL_λ to be an independently-defined logic, and establish conditions under which the two logics are equivalent.

17.6 Embedding $\mathbf{NL_\lambda}$ into $\mathbf{NL_{CL}}$

This section investigates the conditions under which a derivation in NL_λ has an equivalent derivation in NL_{CL}.

For instance, obviously, since NL_{CL} doesn't have any structures built from λ's and variables, a derivation in NL_λ will only have an equivalent derivation in NL_{CL} if the final sequent is λ-free.

In addition, the IBC variant of NL_{CL} does not allow abstraction out of arbitrary contexts. In order to characterize this restriction more precisely, we define the following class of structures:

(300) $\Gamma\lceil p\rceil ::= \quad p \;\mid\; p\circ q \;\mid\; q\cdot\Gamma\lceil p\rceil \;\mid\; \Gamma\lceil p\rceil\cdot q \;\mid\; \lambda y.\,\Gamma\lceil p\rceil$

Given a structure p, a $\lceil\,\rceil$-context will consist either of the empty context, or else the entire left element at the top level of a $\circ$ structure, or else a larger context built up from $\cdot$ and λ. We can impose these restrictions by replacing the original lambda postulate with one that mentions $\lceil\,\rceil$-contexts:

(301) $\Sigma\lceil\Delta\rceil \equiv \Delta\circ\lambda\alpha\;\Sigma\lceil\alpha\rceil$

To illustrate, the following (bidirectional) inferences are licensed by (301):

(302) $\dfrac{A}{A\circ\lambda xx} \quad \dfrac{A\circ B}{A\circ\lambda x(x\circ B)} \quad \dfrac{A\cdot B}{A\circ\lambda x(x\cdot B)} \quad \dfrac{\lambda x.(x\cdot B)}{B\circ\lambda y\lambda x(x\cdot y)}$

But not these:

(303) $\dfrac{(A\cdot B)\circ C}{A\circ\lambda x((x\cdot B)\circ C)} \quad \dfrac{A\circ B}{B\circ\lambda y(A\circ y)}$

The reason these last two inferences are not allowed is that abstraction across $\circ$ is forbidden unless the abstractee is the complete left element connected by $\circ$.

A note on the case in which $\Gamma\lceil p\rceil = p\circ q$: if this case is left out, there is still an equivalence between NL_λ and NL_{CL}, but only for theorems built entirely with $\cdot$. Some sequents built from $\circ$ will be theorems of NL_{CL} but not of NL_λ, for instance, $(S/\!\!/(DP\backslash\!\!\backslash S)\circ DP\backslash\!\!\backslash(S/DP))\cdot DP \vdash S$. See section 17.11 for a brief discussion of the symmetric case, i.e., $\Gamma\lceil p\rceil = q\circ p$, which is needed for sluicing.

In order to embed proofs in NL_λ into NL_{CL}, we can adapt the mapping given in the last section (which we continue to write $\langle\cdot\rangle$) in order to provide a mapping from structures in NL_λ (with the lambda postulate restricted to $\lceil\,\rceil$-contexts) into structures in NL_{CL}:

(304)
$$\begin{aligned}
\langle x\rangle &\equiv x\\
\langle p\cdot q\rangle &\equiv \langle p\rangle\cdot\langle q\rangle\\
\langle p\circ q\rangle &\equiv \langle p\rangle\circ\langle q\rangle\\
\langle \lambda x.p\rangle &\equiv \mathbb{A}(x,\langle p\rangle)
\end{aligned}$$

$$\begin{aligned}
\mathbb{A}(x,x) &\equiv \text{I}\\
\mathbb{A}(x,p\cdot q) &\equiv (\mathsf{B}\cdot p)\cdot\mathbb{A}(x,q) && (x \text{ not free in } p)\\
\mathbb{A}(x,p\cdot q) &\equiv (\mathsf{C}\cdot\mathbb{A}(x,p))\cdot q && (x \text{ not free in } q)\\
\mathbb{A}(x,x\circ q) &\equiv (\mathsf{C}\cdot\mathsf{I})\circ q && (x \text{ not free in } q)
\end{aligned}$$

The last clause handles abstraction of the left element of a $\circ$-structure, as discussed in the previous paragraph.

Before we can show how this mapping can help translate NL_λ derivations into NL_{CL} derivations, we must address the possibility of abstracting a variable past its lambda binder.

(305)
$$\dfrac{\dfrac{a\cdot(b\cdot c)}{b\circ\lambda x.a\cdot(x\cdot c)}}{b\circ((x\cdot c)\circ\lambda y\lambda x.a\cdot y)}$$

The occurrence of x in the final sequent is not in the scope of the lambda that binds it.

This sort of situation is reminiscent of scope extrusion in programming languages (e.g., Westbrook et al. 2010), which occurs when code containing a variable is executed outside the scope of the binder for that variable, usually causing a runtime error. In linguistics, it is reminiscent of unbound traces created by unrestricted Quantifier Raising, or by remnant movement (e.g., Heim and Kratzer 1998:222). In the current context, inference patterns like that in (305) interfere with translating from NL_λ to NL_{CL}, since $\langle\cdot\rangle$ maps the final sequent to a structure that contains a variable, and NL_{CL} structures do not contain variables.

We could consider further constraining the application of the lambda postulate in a way that prevented the undesired configuration from arising. However, this would spoil the correspondence between NL_λ and NL_{CL}. We can't easily constrain NL_{CL} in a parallel way, because the completeness proof relies on assuming that the parameters of the structural postulates (the *p*'s, *q*'s, and *r*'s) can be instantiated as any structure whatsoever.

Fortunately, it is not necessary to impose any special restrictions to avoid unbound variables. It is always possible to replace a derivation with unbound variables such as that in (305) with an equivalent derivation that does not involve any (even temporarily) unbound variables. This is because abstracting anything other than a formula is inefficient, in the sense that the abstracted structure must always eventually be moved back into its original position. This claim is made precise in the following theorem.

Theorem (Efficient Abstraction for NL$_\lambda$): given an arbitrary derivation in NL$_\lambda$ (with abstraction restricted to $\lceil\,\rceil$-contexts) there is an equivalent derivation in which no instance of the structural postulate has a premise of the form $q \circ \lambda x\Gamma\lceil x\rceil$ unless q is a (structure that consists entirely of a single) formula.

As a corollary, we can assume that any abstracted structure will always be a single formula. This means that the problematic derivations like the one in (305) can always be avoided.

Proof: Given an arbitrary derivation in NL$_\lambda$, consider all of the cases in which there is a structure $q \circ \lambda x\Gamma\lceil x\rceil$ that serves as the focussed part of the premise of an instance of the structural postulate in which q is not a formula. Choose the highest of these cases, if there is a unique highest instance; if not, choose an instance such that its depth in the proof is at least as small as that of any other. The strategy of the proof will be to push this inference upwards in the derivation until it is adjacent to an exactly canceling inference.

The proof proceeds by considering the adjacent inference immediately higher in the derivation. We illustrate with an instance of $\backslash R$:

(306)
$$\dfrac{\dfrac{A\cdot\Delta[q\circ\lambda x\Gamma[x]]\vdash B}{\Delta[q\circ\lambda x\Gamma[x]]\vdash A\backslash B}\,\backslash R}{\Delta[\Gamma[q]]\vdash A\backslash B}\,\lambda \quad\equiv\quad \dfrac{\dfrac{A\cdot\Delta[q\circ\lambda x\Gamma[x]]\vdash B}{A\cdot\Delta[\Gamma[q]]\vdash B}\,\lambda}{\Delta[\Gamma[q]]\vdash A\backslash B}\,\backslash R$$

Given the derivation fragment on the left, we can replace it with the equivalent fragment on the right. Although the initial premise and the final conclusion are identical, the order of the lambda instance and the $\backslash R$ instance have been swapped. Reversal of inference order is equally unproblematic for $/R$, $\bbslash R$, and $/\!\!/R$.

Similar arguments show that the lambda postulate can be pushed upwards past any L inference, although there are two configurations that deserve extra scrutiny. The first case involves a situation in which a complex structure targeted by the lambda postulate was only just introduced by an L rule:

(307)
$$\dfrac{\dfrac{A\vdash A \qquad B\circ\lambda x\Gamma[x]\vdash C}{(A\cdot A\backslash B)\circ\lambda x\Gamma[x]\vdash C}\,\backslash L}{\Gamma[A\cdot A\backslash B]\vdash C}\,\lambda \quad\equiv\quad \dfrac{A\vdash A \qquad \dfrac{B\circ\lambda x\Gamma[x]\vdash C}{\Gamma[B]\vdash C}\,\lambda}{\Gamma[A\cdot A\backslash B]\vdash C}\,\backslash L$$

Reading from top to bottom in the left-hand derivation, the $\backslash L$ rule creates the complex structure $A\cdot A\backslash B$, which is then targeted by the lambda postulate. But the equivalent derivation on the right demonstrates that there is no difficulty pushing the instance of the lambda postulate above the logical rule.

The second case that needs scrutiny involves $/\!\!/L$.

(308)
$$\dfrac{\dfrac{\lambda x\Gamma\lceil x\rceil\vdash A \qquad \Sigma[B]\vdash C}{\Sigma[B/\!\!/A\circ\lambda x\Gamma\lceil x\rceil]\vdash C}\,/\!\!/L}{\Sigma[\Gamma[B/\!\!/A]]\vdash C}\,\lambda$$

Once again, the worry is that if the occurrence of $\circ$ that is introduced by $/\!\!/L$ is the same $\circ$ mentioned in the lambda postulate, it will not be possible to swap the inferences. But the structure that undergoes beta reduction here is the formula $B/\!\!/A$, the principal formula of the $\backslash\!\!\backslash L$ inference, rather than a non-formula structure, contrary to assumption.

It remains only to consider the possibility that the adjacent inference is another instance of the structural postulate. If the two inferences target different structures for abstraction, then their order can be swapped without harm. For instance,

(309)
$$\cfrac{\cfrac{q \circ \lambda y \Gamma\lceil y \rceil}{q \circ \lambda y(y \circ \lambda x \Gamma\lceil x \rceil)}\,\lambda_2}{q \circ \lambda x \Gamma\lceil x \rceil}\,\lambda_1 \quad \equiv \quad \cfrac{\cfrac{q \circ \lambda y \Gamma\lceil y \rceil}{\Gamma\lceil q \rceil}\,\lambda_1}{q \circ \lambda x \Gamma\lceil x \rceil}\,\lambda_2$$

The inference λ_1 applies the postulate in the expansion direction (there is one more occurrence of $\circ$ in the premise than in the conclusion), and the inference λ_2 applies the postulate in the reduction direction (there is one fewer occurrence of $\circ$ in the premise). As the right hand derivation shows, their order can be safely reversed. (And in fact, in this configuration, the initial and final sequents are identical up to choice of variables, so the pair of inferences cancel each other out, and can both be removed without affecting the derivation.)

If two instances of the structural postulate do target the same structure, there are two ways this could happen. One possibility is that the upper inference is a beta expansion, in which case the targeted structure is re-abstracted to take scope over an even larger structure. But this violates the assumption that the original instance of the schema $q \circ \lambda x \Gamma\lceil x \rceil$ has a depth at least as small as any other. The other way that the adjacent inferences could target the same occurrence of $\circ$ is if the upper inference is a reduction, in which case the postulates exactly cancel each other out:

(310)
$$\cfrac{\cfrac{\Delta[\Gamma\lceil q \rceil] \vdash A}{\Delta[q \circ \lambda x \Gamma\lceil x \rceil] \vdash A}\,\lambda}{\Delta[\Gamma\lceil q \rceil] \vdash A}\,\lambda$$

Since the initial premise is identical to the final conclusion, both inferences can be removed without harming the derivation.

Since $\circ$ cannot occur in an axiom, and since the only way for the occurrence of $\circ$ in focus to be introduced into the proof is via an instance of the lambda postulate, it must always be possible to push the original instance of the lambda postulate upwards in the proof until it is adjacent to an exactly cancelling instance of the postulate, and can be removed. Since there are a finite number of cases to consider, they can all be eliminated one by one. QED.

We will call on the reasoning in this proof twice more in this chapter: there is an analogous theorem for NL$_{CL}$, and a similar argument will play an essential role in the decidability result below in section 17.9.

Theorem (Faithfulness of the $\langle\cdot\rangle$ mapping from λ-structures into CL-structures): For any structure p and context $\Gamma\lceil\ \rceil$,

(311) $$\frac{\langle p \circ \lambda x\Gamma\lceil x\rceil\rangle}{\langle\Gamma\lceil p\rceil\rangle}\ CL$$

This inference is written in the style of a structural inference; here, '*CL*' stands for some sequence of inferences consisting entirely of structural inferences in NL$_{CL}$. This theorem says that beta reduction (or, in the bottom-to-top inference direction, beta expansion) in NL$_\lambda$ can be faithfully simulated by the structural postulates of NL$_{CL}$.

Proof: The proof proceeds by induction on the complexity of the abstraction structure. The complexity of a variable or formula is 1; the complexity of the structure λxp is one more than the complexity of the structure p; and the complexity of the structure $p \cdot q$ is one more than the sum of the complexities of p and q.

Let $\lambda x\Gamma\lceil x|$ be a structure in NL$_\lambda$ with complexity c. The inductive assumption is that for any structure $\lambda x\Gamma'\lceil x\rceil$ whose complexity is less than c, $\langle p \circ \lambda x\Gamma'\lceil x\rceil\rangle \equiv_{CL} \langle\Gamma'\lceil p\rceil\rangle$, for all p.

The cases are laid out as in (300). If $\lambda x\Gamma\lceil x\rceil =$

λxx then $\langle p\circ\lambda x\Gamma\lceil x\rceil\rangle = \langle p\circ\lambda xx\rangle = \langle p\rangle\circ\langle\lambda xx\rangle = \langle p\rangle\circ \mathsf{I} \equiv_{CL} \langle p\rangle = \langle\Gamma\lceil p\rceil\rangle$, and the claim holds.

$\lambda x(x \circ q)$ then $\langle p\circ\lambda x\Gamma\lceil x\rceil\rangle = \langle p\circ\lambda x(x\circ q)\rangle = \langle p\rangle\circ\langle\lambda x(x\circ q)\rangle = \langle p\rangle\circ\mathbb{A}(x, \langle x\circ q\rangle) = \langle p\rangle\circ((\mathsf{C}\cdot\mathsf{I})\circ\langle q\rangle) \equiv_{CL} \langle p\rangle\circ\langle q\rangle = \langle p\circ q\rangle = \langle\Gamma\lceil p\rceil\rangle$, and the claim holds.

$\lambda x(q\cdot\Gamma'\lceil x\rceil)$ then $\langle p \circ \lambda x\Gamma\lceil x\rceil\rangle = \langle p\rangle\circ((\mathsf{B}\cdot\langle q\rangle)\cdot\langle\lambda x\Gamma'\lceil x\rceil\rangle) \equiv_{CL} \langle q\rangle\cdot(\langle p\rangle\circ\langle\lambda x\Gamma'\lceil x\rceil\rangle) = \langle q\rangle\cdot(\langle p\circ\lambda x\Gamma'\lceil x\rceil\rangle)$. By the inductive assumption, $\langle p\circ\lambda x\Gamma'\lceil x\rceil\rangle \equiv_{CL} \langle\Gamma'\lceil p\rceil\rangle$, and the claim holds.

$\lambda x(\Gamma'\lceil x\rceil\cdot q)$ (similar to the previous case).

The final case is when Γ is itself an abstraction, i.e., $\lambda x\Gamma\lceil x\rceil = \lambda x\lambda y\Gamma'\lceil y\rceil\lceil x\rceil$. We can assume that Γ' is structurally complex, and furthermore that the top connective is $\cdot$. Furthermore, there must be structures q and r such that $\Gamma' = q\cdot r$, since that is the only way to fit two distinct variables into a structure without abstracting illegally from the right side of $\circ$. Each of the unique occurrences of x and of y can be either in q or in r, so there are four subcases to consider. We begin by assuming that both x and y occur in q. Then we reason as follows:

$$
\begin{aligned}
(312)\quad \langle p \circ \lambda x \Gamma\lceil x \rceil\rangle &= \langle p \circ \lambda x \lambda y \Gamma'\lceil y \rceil\lceil x \rceil\rangle \\
&= \langle p \circ \lambda x \lambda y (q\lceil y \rceil\lceil x \rceil \cdot r)\rangle \\
&= \langle p\rangle \circ \langle \lambda x \lambda y (q\lceil y \rceil\lceil x \rceil \cdot r)\rangle \\
&= \langle p\rangle \circ \mathbb{A}(x, \langle \lambda y (q\lceil y \rceil\lceil x \rceil \cdot r)\rangle) \\
&= \langle p\rangle \circ \mathbb{A}(x, \mathbb{A}(y, \langle q\lceil y \rceil\lceil x \rceil \cdot r\rangle)) \\
&= \langle p\rangle \circ \mathbb{A}(x, \mathbb{A}(y, \langle q\lceil y \rceil\lceil x \rceil\rangle \cdot \langle r\rangle)) \\
&= \langle p\rangle \circ \mathbb{A}(x, (\mathsf{C} \cdot \mathbb{A}(y, \langle q\lceil y \rceil\lceil x \rceil\rangle)) \cdot \langle r\rangle) \\
&= \langle p\rangle \circ ((\mathsf{C} \cdot \mathbb{A}(x, \mathsf{C} \cdot \mathbb{A}(y, \langle q\lceil y \rceil\lceil x \rceil\rangle))) \cdot \langle r\rangle) \\
&= \langle p\rangle \circ ((\mathsf{C} \cdot ((\mathsf{B} \cdot \mathsf{C}) \cdot \mathbb{A}(x, \mathbb{A}(y, \langle q\lceil y \rceil\lceil x \rceil\rangle)))) \cdot \langle r\rangle) \\
&= \langle p\rangle \circ ((\mathsf{C} \cdot ((\mathsf{B} \cdot \mathsf{C}) \cdot \mathbb{A}(x, \langle \lambda y (q\lceil y \rceil\lceil x \rceil)\rangle))) \cdot \langle r\rangle) \\
&= \langle p\rangle \circ ((\mathsf{C} \cdot ((\mathsf{B} \cdot \mathsf{C}) \cdot \langle \lambda x \lambda y (q\lceil y \rceil\lceil x \rceil)\rangle)) \cdot \langle r\rangle) \\
&\equiv_{CL} ((\langle p\rangle \circ ((\mathsf{B} \cdot \mathsf{C}) \cdot \langle \lambda x \lambda y (q\lceil y \rceil\lceil x \rceil)\rangle)) \cdot \langle r\rangle \\
&\equiv_{CL} (\mathsf{C} \cdot (\langle p\rangle \circ \langle \lambda x \lambda y (q\lceil y \rceil\lceil x \rceil)\rangle)) \cdot \langle r\rangle \\
&= (\mathsf{C} \cdot \langle p \circ \lambda x \lambda y (q\lceil y \rceil\lceil x \rceil)\rangle) \cdot \langle r\rangle \\
&\equiv_{CL} (\mathsf{C} \cdot \langle \lambda y (q\lceil y \rceil\lceil p \rceil)\rangle) \cdot \langle r\rangle \quad \text{(by the inductive assumption)} \\
&= (\mathsf{C} \cdot \mathbb{A}(y, \langle q\lceil y \rceil\lceil p \rceil\rangle)) \cdot \langle r\rangle \\
&= \mathbb{A}(y, \langle q\lceil y \rceil\lceil p \rceil\rangle \cdot \langle r\rangle) \\
&= \mathbb{A}(y, \langle q\lceil y \rceil\lceil p \rceil \cdot r\rangle) \\
&= \langle \lambda y (q\lceil y \rceil\lceil p \rceil \cdot r)\rangle \\
&= \langle \Gamma\lceil p \rceil\rangle
\end{aligned}
$$

The other three subcases are similar. QED.

With Efficient Abstraction and Faithfulness in hand, we can provide an explicit mapping from NL_λ into NL_{CL}.

Theorem (Embedding of λ-free theorems of NL_λ in NL_{CL}): For any derivation in NL_λ (with abstraction restricted to $\lceil\ \rceil$-contexts) whose final sequent does not contain any λ-structures, there is an equivalent derivation in NL_{CL}.

Proof: The goal is to map a derivation in NL_λ onto a derivation in NL_{CL} in such a way that each sequent $\Gamma \vdash A$ in the NL_λ proof is mapped onto a corresponding sequent $\langle\Gamma\rangle \vdash A$ in the NL_{CL} derivation.

Starting with an arbitrary derivation in NL_λ in which abstraction is restricted to $\lceil\ \rceil$-contexts, and which has a lambda-free conclusion, we replace it with an equivalent derivation in which only formulas have been abstracted. We are guaranteed to be able to do this by the Efficient Abstraction proof given above. The derivation will consist entirely of inferences involving the axiom rule, the structural rule, and the logical rules. For axioms, $A \vdash A$ only if $\langle A\rangle \vdash A$, since for any formula A, $\langle A\rangle = A$. An inference involving the structural postulate in NL_λ will be replaced with an equivalent sequence of structural postulates from NL_{CL}, as guaranteed by the Faithfulness theorem proved immediately above. As for the logical rules, we begin with one of the R rules. Clearly, we have:

(313) $$\frac{A \cdot \Gamma \vdash B}{\Gamma \vdash A\backslash B}\backslash R \quad \text{iff} \quad \frac{\langle A \cdot \Gamma\rangle \vdash B}{\langle \Gamma\rangle \vdash A\backslash B}\backslash R$$

Each of the other R rules behaves similarly. It remains only to consider the L rules, for instance,

(314) $$\frac{\Gamma \vdash A \qquad \Sigma[B] \vdash C}{\Sigma[\Gamma \cdot A\backslash B] \vdash C}\backslash L \quad \text{iff} \quad \frac{\langle\Gamma\rangle \vdash A \qquad \langle\Sigma[B]\rangle \vdash C}{\langle\Sigma[\Gamma \cdot A\backslash B]\rangle \vdash C}\backslash L$$

The only possibility for concern would be if the B in $\Sigma[B]$ were embedded inside of a λ-structure. But Γ cannot contain any variables bound by λs within Σ. Therefore it is easy to see that $\langle\Sigma[\langle\Gamma\rangle \cdot A\backslash B]\rangle = \langle\Sigma[\Gamma \cdot A\backslash B]\rangle$. For instance, if $\Gamma = \lambda xx$, and $\Sigma[\,] = D{\cdot}([\,]{\circ}E)$, then $\langle\Sigma[\langle\Gamma\rangle{\cdot}A\backslash B]\rangle = \langle\Sigma[\mathsf{I}{\cdot}A\backslash B]\rangle = \langle D{\cdot}([\mathsf{I}{\cdot}A\backslash B]{\circ}E)\rangle = \langle\Sigma[\Gamma{\cdot}A\backslash B]\rangle \vdash C$, as desired. Similarly for the other L rules.

We have shown that for each inference in the NL_λ derivation, we can construct an equivalent sequence of inferences in NL_{CL}. If the final sequent in the NL_λ derivation is $\Gamma \vdash A$, the final sequent in the NL_{CL} derivation will be $\langle\Gamma\rangle \vdash A$. But since Γ is λ-free, $\Gamma = \langle\Gamma\rangle$. Finally, since the two proofs differ only in the application of structural rules, and since structural postulates do not affect the Curry-Howard semantic labeling, the semantic value of the proofs are equivalent. QED.

17.7 Embedding NL_{CL} into NL_λ

This section addresses the converse of the question investigated in the previous section, namely, the conditions under which a derivation in NL_{CL} has an equivalent derivation in NL_λ.

Once again, obviously, since NL_λ doesn't have the structures I, B, and C, the conclusion of the derivation in NL_{CL} must be IBC-free.

And once again, in addition, we must worry about abstracting non-formula structures.

(315) $$\frac{\dfrac{\dfrac{a \cdot b}{(a \circ \mathsf{I}) \cdot b}\,\mathsf{I}}{a \circ ((\mathsf{C} \cdot \mathsf{I}) \cdot b)}\,\mathsf{C}}{a \circ (((\mathsf{C} \circ \mathsf{I}) \cdot \mathsf{I}) \cdot b)}\,\mathsf{I}$$

Because there is no direct analog of the structures B or C in NL_λ, there is no straightforward way of simulating a derivation in which B or C, or structures containing them, serve as the target for abstraction.

However, just as for NL_λ, abstraction of a non-formula is always eliminable.

Theorem (Efficient Abstraction for NL_{CL}): Given an arbitrary derivation in NL_{CL}, there is an equivalent derivation in NL_{CL} in which no instance of the I postulate has a premise of the form $q \circ \mathsf{I}$ unless q is a formula; and in which no instance of the B postulate has a premise of the form $q \circ ((\mathsf{B} \cdot p) \cdot r)$ unless q is a formula; and in in which no instance of the C postulate has a premise of the form $q \circ ((\mathsf{C} \cdot p) \cdot r)$, unless q is a formula.

Proof sketch: The claims for I, B, and C must be considered simultaneously. The reason is that when adjacent instances of I, B, C can target the same occurrence of $\circ$, their order cannot be swapped. For instance,

(316)
$$\dfrac{\dfrac{\Sigma[p \circ ((\mathsf{C} \cdot \mathsf{I}) \cdot r)] \vdash A}{\Sigma[(p \circ \mathsf{I}) \cdot r] \vdash A}\,\mathsf{C}}{\Sigma[p \cdot r] \vdash A}\,\mathsf{I}$$

The order of the I and the C inferences cannot be reversed. Therefore, when eliminating abstraction of non-formulas, we must start with the highest inference in the chain, and then work our way down. The first step, then, is to find the set of all cases in which a non-formula has been abstracted, whether via I, B, and C, and begin by eliminating any instances with the smallest depth in the derivation. The proof then proceeds in a manner similar to the proof of Efficient Abstraction for NL_λ. QED.

Theorem (Embedding of IBC-free theorems of NL_{CL} in NL_λ): for any derivation in NL_{CL} whose conclusion does not contain the structures I, B, or C, there is an equivalent derivation in NL_λ.

Proof sketch: First, we replace the NL_{CL} derivation with an equivalent one in which abstraction is restricted to formulas, as guaranteed by the previous theorem. Then we replace each instance of I, B, and C with instances of the lambda postulate as follows:

(317)
$$\frac{p}{p \circ \mathsf{I}}\,\mathsf{I} \quad \sim \quad \frac{p}{p \circ \lambda xx}\,\lambda$$

$$\frac{p \cdot (q \circ r)}{q \circ ((\mathsf{B} \cdot p) \cdot r)}\,\mathsf{B} \quad \sim \quad \frac{p \cdot (q \circ r)}{q \circ \lambda x(p \cdot (x \circ r))}\,\lambda$$

$$\frac{(p \circ q) \cdot r}{p \circ ((\mathsf{C} \cdot q) \cdot r)}\,\mathsf{C} \quad \sim \quad \frac{(p \circ q) \cdot r}{p \circ \lambda x((x \circ q) \cdot r)}\,\lambda$$

Note that each of these applications of the lambda postulate obeys the restriction to $\ulcorner\urcorner$-contexts. Since the Efficient Abstraction theorem guarantees that structures such as B, $(\mathsf{B} \cdot p)$, etc. will not be the target of any structural postulate, it is straightforward to show that this mapping allows NL_λ to faithfully simulate the NL_{CL} derivation using the methods of the previous section. QED.

Thus NL_λ and NL_{CL} are equivalent: any sequent containing only structures built from $\cdot$ and $\circ$ will be a theorem of one just in case it is a theorem of the other. Furthermore, for each derivation in one system, there will be a matching derivation in the other that differs only in the application of structural rules, which means that the semantic values of the two derivations will be identical. Since NL_{CL} is conservative with respect to the non-associative Lambek grammar NL, NL_λ is too. As a result, NL_λ with restricted abstraction contexts can be used with full confidence that it is equivalent to an ordinary and well-behaved substructural grammar.

17.8 Cut elimination

It is common when studying substructural logics to worry about cut elimination. For instance, in Lambek (1958), cut elimination was crucial to proving decidability. We have not concentrated on issues of computational tractability in this book, with the exception of the discussion of computational tractability in section 12.2 for the grammar in Part I. Nevertheless, we will prove cut elimination here and, in the next section, decidability for NL_λ.

The cut rule, repeated here, characterizes transitivity of the logical system:

(318)
$$\frac{\Gamma \vdash A \qquad \Sigma[A] \vdash B}{\Sigma[\Gamma] \vdash B}\ \text{CUT}$$

The cut rule says that if Γ is a proof of A, and Σ is a proof of B that depends on proving A, then we can construct a new proof of B in which A has been replaced with the proof Γ. The formula A has been 'cut out' of the derivation.

A bit of standard vocabulary used below: we'll say that for each of the premises of a cut inference, the formula A targeted by the cut is the *cut formula* for that premise.

A cut elimination result says that any theorem that can be proved with the full system including the cut rule can be proved without using the cut rule. Lambek (1958) showed that NL enjoys cut elimination, and Moortgat (1997) reports that this is true as well for multi-modal versions of NL.

However, despite the close similarity of NL_λ and NL_{CL} to other systems that enjoy cut elimination, we should not take it for granted that cut elimination goes through for our logics too. As a case in point, the Lambek-Grishin calculus, a continuation-based type-logical grammar discussed in the next chapter, does not have cut admissibility either in its sequent presentation or in its natural deduction presentation, although there is a display presentation of Lambek-Grishin for which cut is admissible; see, e.g., Bastenhof (2013:67).

Therefore we will prove that NL_λ and NL_{CL} have cut elimination. Our proof strategy, just as it was above for completeness, will be to rely on Restall's general proof of cut elimination for Gentzen-style sequent systems. This strategy emphasizes the ordinariness and the standardness of our logics, and how they fit into a larger landscape of substructural logics.

In order for Restall's proof to apply, we need to demonstrate that our cut rule, our structural rule, and our logical rules conform to certain conditions.

First, there are a number of constraints on the form of the logical and structural rules (the 'parameter conditions', Restall 2000:114) that are clearly satisfied by all of our rules and postulates. In particular, there is no rule in which some element in the premise of a rule is duplicated in the conclusion.

In addition (Restall 2000:113), we must show that cuts are eliminable whenever one of the premises is an axiom. This is clearly the case for our grammars; see relevant details in, e.g., in chapter 1 of Jäger (2005).

We must also show what Restall (p. 115) 'calls eliminability of matching principal constituents' (reduction of principal cuts). Since this depends on only the logical rules, the discussion in Jäger once again provides full details.

The only remaining element in the preconditions for the proof is to demonstrate that every formula is either consequent regular or antecedent regular (or both). This precondition is in the service of showing that if one or the other cut formula is not principal, the cut can be pushed upwards in the proof. A *principal formula* is a new formula that is created by the inference rule; for instance, in the $\backslash R$ inference rule $\dfrac{A \circ \Gamma \vdash B}{\Gamma \vdash A\backslash B}$, $A\backslash B$ is the principal formula.

In fact, it turns out that every formula in our system is consequent regular. A formula A is *consequent regular* (in the context of our system) just in case the following two conditions hold: first, whenever a formula A is the goal of a sequent (i.e., the formula to the right of the turnstyle) but is not a principal formula, a cut on A against some sequent can be replaced by a cut on A in one of the premises. For instance,

(319)
$$\dfrac{\dfrac{\Gamma \vdash E \qquad \Delta[F] \vdash B/C}{\Delta[\Gamma \cdot E\backslash F] \vdash B/C}\backslash L \qquad \Sigma[B/C] \vdash D}{\Sigma[\Delta[\Gamma \cdot E\backslash F]] \vdash D}\text{CUT}$$

In this derivation, $A = B/C$ is the goal of the sequent $\Delta[\Gamma \cdot E\backslash F] \vdash B/C$, which we are cutting against $\Sigma[B/C] \vdash D$. Since the left premise of the cut is a instance of an $\backslash L$ inference, B/C is not a principal formula. This means that it must be identical to some formula in one of the premises (since sequent rules guarantee by construction that only principal formulas are new). The larger cut can be replaced with a smaller cut on the premise as follows:

(320)
$$\dfrac{\Gamma \vdash E \qquad \dfrac{\Delta[F] \vdash B/C \qquad \Sigma[B/C] \vdash D}{\Sigma[\Delta[F]] \vdash D}\text{CUT}}{\Sigma[\Delta[\Gamma \cdot E\backslash F]] \vdash D}\backslash L$$

We have pushed the cut upwards past the $\backslash L$ inference, that is, we have swapped the order of the two inferences.

The second condition for establishing consequent regularity is that whenever the cut formula A is the principal formula of the left premise of the cut, if it is not the principal formula of the right premise, once again the larger cut can be pushed upwards.

(321)
$$\dfrac{\Sigma \vdash F \qquad \dfrac{\Gamma[F] \vdash D \qquad \Delta[E] \vdash C}{\Delta[\Gamma[F] \cdot D\backslash E] \vdash C}\backslash L}{\Delta[\Gamma[\Sigma] \cdot D\backslash E] \vdash C}\text{CUT}$$

Assume the cut formula F is the principal formula of the left premise of the cut. Because the cut formula is not the principal formula of the $\backslash L$ inference, it must be inherited from one of the premises of the $\backslash L$ inference, in this case, its left premise. And once again, nothing prevents pushing the cut past the $\backslash L$ inference:

(322)
$$\dfrac{\dfrac{\Sigma \vdash F \qquad \Gamma[F] \vdash D}{\Gamma[\Sigma] \vdash D}\text{CUT} \qquad \Delta[E] \vdash C}{\Delta[\Gamma[\Sigma] \cdot D\backslash E] \vdash C}\text{CUT}$$

Establishing consequent regularity requires checking each inference in the system, but this is not difficult. Our logical rules are completely standard, so it is not surprising that they do not impede formulas being consequent regular.

In particular, inferences involving any of our structural rules in either NL_λ or in NL_{CL} do not interfere with establishing consequent regularity. The only potentially problematic case would be when the right premise of a cut is the conclusion of a structural inference. But since every formula in the conclusion of a structural inference also occurs in the premise of the inference, it follows that the cut formula occurs in the premise of the structural inference, so there is no obstacle to pushing the cut above the structural rule.

At this point, we can assert the following corollary of Restall's theorem 6.11:

Theorem (cut elimination): given that the parameter conditions, the eliminability of matching principal constituents, and the regularity condition hold, if $\Gamma \vdash A$ and $\Delta[A] \vdash B$ are provable, then $\Delta[\Gamma] \vdash B$ is also provable.

Proof: see Restall (2000):section 6.3. QED.

17.9 Decidability

Decidability is a property a logic has if it is always possible to figure out whether a sequent is a theorem (has a proof, has a derivation) in a bounded amount of time, where the bound is some concrete function of the complexity of the sequent to be proved.

Cut elimination is important for decidability. The reason is that if there are theorems that can only be completed using Cut, then during the course of trying to build a proof, we must constantly consider whether a cut might be needed.

(323)
$$\frac{\Gamma \vdash A \qquad \Sigma[A] \vdash B}{\Sigma[\Gamma] \vdash B}\text{CUT}$$

If the only way to prove the sequent $\Sigma[\Gamma] \vdash B$ is via a cut, the proof-search problem is to guess which A is going to work here. Since A does not correspond to any subpart of the conclusion sequent, it is unconstrained. We have to try A after A, and we may not know whether we've considered all of the relevant hypotheses. The cut elimination theorem from the previous section removes this worry, since it guarantees that we can ignore the cut rule while we search for a proof without worrying that we're missing out on finding derivations.

But cut elimination is not sufficient to guarantee decidability. After all, the distinctive feature of NL_λ is that we also have a kind of lambda expansion/reduction in the syntax. The structural postulate given in chapter 13 is a reversible inference, that is, it is bidirectional. In the discussion that follows, it will be helpful to keep track of the two directions separately:

(324)
$$\frac{\Sigma[\Delta\lceil A\rceil] \vdash B}{\Sigma[A \circ \lambda x\Delta\lceil x\rceil] \vdash B}\text{REDUCTION} \qquad \frac{\Sigma[A \circ \lambda x\Delta\lceil x\rceil] \vdash B}{\Sigma[\Delta\lceil A\rceil] \vdash B}\text{EXPANSION}$$

Since in proof search we are starting with the conclusion and trying to find appropriate premises, the names 'reduction' and 'expansion' are relative to the bottom-to-top direction of reading proofs. The problem for decidability is that there is no limit to the opportunities for expansion, since $B \equiv B \circ \lambda xx \equiv (B \circ \lambda xx) \circ \lambda xx \equiv ....$

Nevertheless, we have the following result:

Theorem (Decidability): NL_λ with abstraction restricted to $\lceil\ \rceil$-contexts is decidable.

Proof sketch: we will show that every derivation in NL_λ is equivalent to a derivation in which each inference has the subformula property. For our purposes, an inference has the subformula property just in case every formula in the premises corresponds to a unique (part of a) formula in the conclusion. It is easy to check that every logical rule in NL_λ has the subformula property.

In addition, for each logical rule, there is always exactly one logical connective in the conclusion that does not have a corresponding occurrence in the premises, namely, the logical connective introduced by the principal formula of the relevant inference. For instance, the $\backslash R$ rule has exactly one occurrence of the $\backslash$ connective in the conclusion that does not have a corresponding occurrence in the premise.

The subformula property, in conjunction with the observation that there is always one fewer logical connectives in the premises than in the conclusion, means that each application of a logical inference reduces the complexity of the material to be proven, where the relevant notion of complexity is the total number of logical connectives in the formulas in the premises.

At this point, we need only take into account the structural postulate. The postulate does have the subformula property—every formula in the premise also appears in the conclusion, and vice versa—but it does not eliminate any logical connective, so there is no guarantee that the premise is simpler than the conclusion.

Given an arbitrary proof in NL_λ, the strategy for proving decidability will be to replace each application of the structural postulate with an equivalent derived inference which does guarantee a strictly simpler set of premises.

The first step will be to push each expansion use of the postulate upwards in the proof until one of two things happens: either it encounters a matching reduction instance, in which case the two rules cancel each other out, and can be eliminated from the proof; or else the expansion is adjacent to a logical rule that introduces the occurrence of $\circ$. It turns out that the only candidate for such a logical rule is $/\!\!/L$. As we will explain, the combination of the expansion and the instance of $/\!\!/L$ can be viewed as a two-step rule that in aggregate has the desired simplification guarantee.

Therefore we will explore the conditions under which expansions can be pushed upwards.

Assume then that we have a structure of the form $q \circ \lambda x\Gamma\lceil x\rceil$ as the focused part of the premise of an instance of the structural postulate. By the Efficient Abstraction theorem, we can assume that q is a formula. By reasoning similar to the proof of the Efficient Abstraction theorem, we can push the structural inference higher in the proof until it reaches a logical inference that targets the $\circ$. The only logical rules that introduce $\circ$ into their conclusion are $\backslash\!\!\backslash L$ and $/\!\!/L$. But the premise of an expansion inference does not match the conclusion of $\backslash\!\!\backslash L$, since the expansion inference creates a structure of the form $\lambda x\Gamma\lceil x\rceil$ to the right of the occurrence of $\circ$, and the $\backslash\!\!\backslash L$ rule requires a formula in that position. Therefore the only logical rule that can introduce the $\circ$ in the premise of an expansion inference is $/\!\!/L$:

(325)
$$\dfrac{\dfrac{\lambda x\Gamma\lceil x\rceil \vdash A \qquad \Sigma\lceil B\rceil \vdash C}{\Sigma[B/\!\!/A \circ \lambda x\Gamma\lceil x\rceil] \vdash C}\,/\!\!/L}{\Sigma[\Gamma\lceil B/\!\!/A\rceil] \vdash C}\,\text{EXP} \quad \equiv \quad \dfrac{\lambda x\Gamma\lceil x\rceil \vdash A \qquad \Sigma[B] \vdash C}{\Sigma[\Gamma\lceil B/\!\!/A\rceil] \vdash C}\,/\!\!/L_\lambda$$

We can replace the adjacent pair of inferences on the left with the derived inference on the right, which we can call $/\!\!/L_\lambda$. By repeated application of this reasoning, every instance of expansion can either be eliminated, or replaced with an instance of $/\!\!/L_\lambda$.

Having eliminated all expansion inferences, we can eliminate reduction inferences in a similar fashion. Reasoning dually, beta *reduction* inferences can always be pushed *downwards* until the reduction encounters an instance of $\backslash\!\!\backslash R$ that targets the $\circ$ connective introduced by the reduction. And once again, we can replace the combination of the reduction and the instance of $\backslash\!\!\backslash R$ with a derived rule that captures their net effect:

(326)
$$\dfrac{\dfrac{\Gamma\lceil A\rceil \vdash B}{A \circ \lambda x\Gamma\lceil x\rceil \vdash B}\,\textsc{red}}{\lambda x\Gamma\lceil x\rceil \vdash A\backslash\!\!\backslash B}\,\backslash\!\!\backslash R \quad \equiv \quad \dfrac{\Gamma\lceil A\rceil \vdash B}{\lambda x\Gamma\lceil x\rceil \vdash A\backslash\!\!\backslash B}\,\backslash\!\!\backslash R_\lambda$$

We have two derived logical inferences: $\backslash\!\!\backslash R_\lambda$, and $/\!\!/ L_\lambda$. The $\backslash\!\!\backslash R_\lambda$ rule says that in-situ elements can take scope directly from embedded positions, without needing to first be abstracted leftwards. Dually, the $/\!\!/ L_\lambda$ rule says that a context can surround a scope-taker even when the scope-taker is embedded in a still larger surrounding context.

At this point, the logic contains the original logical rules, two derived logical rules, and no structural postulates. Each inference eliminates exactly one logical connective. As a result, no part of the proof can have a depth greater than the number of logical connectives in the final sequent. Since there is at most one way to apply each rule to a given occurrence of a logical connective, decidability follows immediately. QED.

If NL_λ (restricted to $\lceil\ \rceil$-contexts) is decidable, it follows that NL_{CL} is decidable (at least for IBC-free sequents), since an IBC-free sequent is derivable in NL_{CL} if and only if there is an equivalent derivation in NL_λ.

Adding the two derived logical rules to the standard logical rules leads to derivations of in-situ scope-taking:

(327)
$$\dfrac{\dfrac{\dfrac{\text{john} \cdot (\text{saw} \cdot \text{DP}) \vdash \text{S}}{\lambda x.\text{john} \cdot (\text{saw} \cdot x) \vdash \text{DP}\backslash\!\!\backslash\text{S}}\,\backslash\!\!\backslash R_\lambda \qquad \text{S} \vdash \text{S}}{\text{john} \cdot (\text{saw} \cdot \text{S}/\!\!/(\text{DP}\backslash\!\!\backslash\text{S})) \vdash \text{S}}\,/\!\!/ L_\lambda}{\text{john} \cdot (\text{saw} \cdot \text{everyone}) \vdash \text{S}}$$

In effect, we have compiled both parts of the structural rule into the logical rules. If we add these two derived logical rules to the grammar, we can eliminate the structural rules, and still derive all of the examples in Part II up to, but not including, sluicing (as discussed below in section 17.11).

Incidentally, if we carry this fusion strategy one step further, we derive the rule of use for Moortgat's q type constructor:

(328)
$$\dfrac{\dfrac{\Gamma\lceil A\rceil \vdash B}{\lambda x\Gamma\lceil x\rceil \vdash A\backslash\!\!\backslash B}\,\backslash\!\!\backslash R_\lambda \qquad \Sigma[C] \vdash D}{\Sigma[\Gamma\lceil C/\!\!/(B\backslash\!\!\backslash A)\rceil] \vdash D}\,/\!\!/ L_\lambda \quad \approx \quad \dfrac{\Gamma\lceil A\rceil \vdash B \qquad \Sigma[C] \vdash D}{\Sigma[\Gamma[q(A, B, C)]] \vdash D}\,q$$

We now have an explanation for why it was impossible to find a general right rule for the q type constructor: it is because the q inference represents the fusion of two logically distinct inferences, each with their own left and right rules.

In support of the usefulness of factoring the *q* into independent components, note that the decidable system here extends to parasitic scope, which requires the independent logical components to be interleaved in a way that cannot be duplicated by the *q* inference alone:

(329)
$$\dfrac{\dfrac{\dfrac{\dfrac{\dfrac{(\text{the}\cdot(\text{N/N}\cdot\text{waiter}))\cdot(\text{served}\cdot\text{DP})\vdash\text{S}}{\lambda x.(\text{the}\cdot(\text{N/N}\cdot\text{waiter}))\cdot(\text{served}\cdot x)\vdash\text{DP}\backslash\!\!\backslash\text{S}}\,\backslash\!\!\backslash R_\lambda}{\lambda y\lambda x.(\text{the}\cdot(y\cdot\text{waiter}))\cdot(\text{served}\cdot x)\vdash(\text{N/N})\backslash\!\!\backslash(\text{DP}\backslash\!\!\backslash\text{S})}\,\backslash\!\!\backslash R_\lambda \qquad \text{DP}\backslash\!\!\backslash\text{S}\vdash\text{DP}\backslash\!\!\backslash\text{S}}{\lambda x.(\text{the}\cdot((\text{DP}\backslash\!\!\backslash\text{S})/\!\!/((\text{N/N})\backslash\!\!\backslash(\text{DP}\backslash\!\!\backslash\text{S}))\cdot\text{waiter}))\cdot(\text{served}\cdot x)\vdash\text{DP}\backslash\!\!\backslash\text{S}}\,/\!\!/L_\lambda}{\lambda x.(\text{the}\cdot(\text{same}\cdot\text{waiter}))\cdot(\text{served}\cdot x)\vdash\text{DP}\backslash\!\!\backslash\text{S}}\,\text{LEX} \qquad \text{S}\vdash\text{S}}{\dfrac{(\text{the}\cdot(\text{same}\cdot\text{waiter}))\cdot(\text{served}\cdot\text{S}/\!\!/(\text{DP}\backslash\!\!\backslash\text{S}))\vdash\text{S}}{(\text{the}\cdot(\text{same}\cdot\text{waiter}))\cdot(\text{served}\cdot\text{everyone})\vdash\text{S}}\,\text{LEX}}\,/\!\!/L_\lambda$$

Although the innermost pair of $/\!\!/L_\lambda$ and $\backslash\!\!\backslash R_\lambda$ could be fused into a single instance of the *q* inference, the outermost pair could not.

17.10 Proof search with gaps

From the point of view of decidability, gaps are a challenge, since they allow us to posit new structure during the course of a proof search, in which case we lose the subformula property. An extension of the technique developed in the previous section allows derivations with gaps without giving up decidability.

(330)
$$\dfrac{\Gamma[B\cdot A]\vdash C}{\Gamma[A]\vdash B\backslash\!\!\backslash C}\,\backslash\!\!\backslash R_{lgap} \qquad \dfrac{\Gamma[A\cdot B]\vdash C}{\Gamma[A]\vdash B\backslash\!\!\backslash C}\,\backslash\!\!\backslash R_{rgap}$$

Since each of these inferences has the subformula property, and moreover, eliminates a logical connective, adding them to the logic will not compromise decidability.

To illustrate these logical rules in action, here is a derivation of the wh-question *Who did John see* (with *did* suppressed for simplicity):

(331)
$$\dfrac{\dfrac{\dfrac{\text{john}\cdot(\text{see}\cdot\text{DP})\vdash\text{S}}{\text{john}\cdot\text{see}\vdash\text{DP}\backslash\!\!\backslash\text{S}}\,\backslash\!\!\backslash R_{gap} \qquad \text{Q}\vdash\text{Q}}{\text{Q}/(\text{DP}\backslash\!\!\backslash\text{S})\cdot(\text{john}\cdot\text{see})\vdash\text{Q}}\,/L}{\text{who}\cdot(\text{john}\cdot\text{see})\vdash\text{Q}}\,\text{LEX}$$

Incidentally, the inference rules $\backslash\!\!\backslash R_{lgap}$ and $\backslash\!\!\backslash R_{rgap}$ given in (330) allow embedded sprouting of the sort illustrated above in (269) as simple parasitic scope:

(332)

$$\dfrac{\dfrac{\dfrac{\lambda y\lambda x(x\cdot(\text{bidk}\cdot(\text{when}\cdot y)))\;\vdash\;(\text{ADV}\backslash\!\!\backslash \text{S})\backslash\!\!\backslash((\text{ADV}\backslash\!\!\backslash \text{S})\backslash\!\!\backslash \text{S}) \qquad \dfrac{\dfrac{\dfrac{(\text{john}\cdot(\text{left}\cdot\text{ADV}))\vdash \text{S}}{(\text{john}\cdot\text{left})\vdash \text{ADV}\backslash\!\!\backslash \text{S}}\backslash\!\!\backslash R_{rgap}\quad \text{S}\vdash\text{S}}{(\text{john}\cdot\text{left})\circ(\text{ADV}\backslash\!\!\backslash \text{S})\backslash\!\!\backslash \text{S}\vdash \text{S}}\backslash\!\!\backslash L}{}}{(\text{john}\cdot\text{left})\circ(\text{WHENSLGAP}\circ\lambda y\lambda x(x\cdot(\text{bidk}\cdot(\text{when}\cdot y))))\vdash \text{S}}\backslash\!\!\backslash L}{(\text{john}\cdot\text{left})\circ\lambda x(x\cdot(\text{bidk}\cdot(\text{when}\cdot\text{WHENSLGAP})))\vdash\text{S}}}{(\text{john}\cdot\text{left})\cdot(\text{bidk}\cdot(\text{when}\cdot\text{WHENSLGAP}))\vdash\text{S}}\equiv$$

As before, WHENSLGAP has category $(\text{ADV}\backslash\!\!\backslash \text{S})^{(\text{ADV}\backslash\!\!\backslash \text{S})}$, where $\text{ADV} = (\text{DP}\backslash\text{S})\backslash(\text{DP}\backslash\text{S})$. The logical inference rules, with the behavior of gaps compiled in, infer the possible location of the silent adverbial automatically.

17.11 Sluicing and unrestricted abstraction

NL_λ restricted to $\lceil\,\rceil$ contexts and NL_{CL} are not able to derive the full range of sluicing derivations given above in chapter 16. The reason is that sluicing requires abstraction of a scope-remnant, which requires abstracting a structure across a $\circ$. For instance, the derivation given above in (255) begins as follows:

(333)

$$\dfrac{\dfrac{\lambda x(x\cdot\text{left})\circ\lambda y((\text{someone}\circ y)\cdot(\text{bidk}\cdot(\text{who}\cdot\text{SG})))\vdash\text{S}}{(\text{someone}\circ\lambda x(x\cdot\text{left}))\cdot(\text{bidk}\cdot(\text{who}\cdot\text{SG}))\vdash\text{S}}\equiv}{(\text{someone}\cdot\text{left})\cdot(\text{bidk}\cdot(\text{who}\cdot\text{SG}))\vdash\text{S}}\equiv$$

As the top line shows, the derivation depends crucially on abstracting the non-formula structure $\lambda x(x\cdot\text{left})$.

One way to extend the expressive power to handle sluicing is to add $q\circ p$ to the set of contexts in (300) that the structural postulate of NL_λ is allowed to abstract over. Equivalently, we could add a postulate like the following to NL_{CL}:

(334)

$$\dfrac{p\circ q}{q\circ(\text{I}'\cdot p)}\;\text{I}'$$

On the one hand, the completeness proof and the conservativity proof could easily be adjusted to accommodate this extra postulate.

On the other hand, the Efficient Abstraction theorems would not hold of either extended logic, since it would no longer be true that the order of adjacent instances of the structural postulates could be swapped without affecting the result of the proof. One way to see why this is so is to carefully examine the derivation of basic sluicing in section 16.2, tracking where each occurrence of $\circ$ enters and exits the derivation.

In the absence of an Efficient Abstraction result, new techniques would be needed to establish any equivalence result between NL_λ with restricted abstraction and $\text{NL}_{\text{IBCI}'}$. Decidability would also need to be re-evaluated.

Another approach worth considering would be to remove all restrictions on abstraction. In the case of NL$_\lambda$, this would mean allowing the lambda postulate to abstract across any structure without restriction. In the case of NL$_{CL}$, this would mean adding the following two postulates to I, B, and C:

(335) $$\frac{p \circ (q \circ r)}{q \circ ((\mathsf{B}' \cdot p) \circ r)}\ \mathsf{B}' \qquad \frac{(p \circ q) \circ r}{p \circ ((\mathsf{C}' \cdot q) \circ r)}\ \mathsf{C}'$$

Once again, these new postulates would be compatible with the completeness proof and with the conservativity proof. And once again, new techniques would be needed to establish any equivalence or decidability results.

18

Scope needs *delimited* continuations

In this chapter, we will discuss some other continuation-based systems that provide analyses of some of the phenomena addressed in this book, concentrating on scope-taking and dynamic anaphora. We will suggest in each case that the other analyses are incomplete in a way that our analyses are not. We want to emphasize at the outset, however, that the points of agreement between our project and these other approaches are much deeper and stronger than any points of disagreement.

There are two kinds of continuations: delimited, and undelimited. To appreciate the difference, consider an expression embedded in a larger context. For the sake of concreteness, let's assume that the larger context is a single utterance, and that the utterance consists of a single complex sentence. As always, a continuation of the expression is a portion of the surrounding context. In general, any specific expression will have many continuations, depending on how much of the surrounding context the continuation captures. One continuation might be the context up to the closest enclosing nominal, as we proposed for certain uses of *same* in section 14.1; another might be the context up to the closest enclosing clause, as we proposed for most uses of distributive quantifiers in natural language. These are *delimited* continuations: continuations that correspond to a proper part of the surrounding context.

An undelimited continuation is a continuation that contains the entire rest of the context, no matter how large it is. In computational terms, a delimited continuation of category $A\backslash\!\!\backslash B$ denotes a function from objects of type A to objects of type B. An undelimited continuation of category $A \rightarrow \bot$, for comparison, denotes a function on objects of type A that never returns.

In geometry, the difference between delimited and undelimited is analogous to the difference between a line segment and a ray: a line segment has a definite endpoint, but a ray has only a starting point and an direction, and continues indefinitely.

Formal systems (grammars, logics) that deal in undelimited continuations are quite different from those that deal in delimited ones. The reason is that a delimited continuation is, by definition, embedded within a larger context. That means that the continuation must produce a value that the larger context needs. In the formal systems we have been considering, that entails that the continuation must have a result type, in order to fit into the larger composition. For this reason, Wadler (1994) calls delimited continuations 'composable': the inner continuation returns a value of the type expected by the outer continuation.

Undelimited continuations are, by definition, unembedded. That means that the formal system does not need to track what kind of result the continuation returns. In fact, it is not even necessary to know what the type of that result will be.

We will discuss two examples of formal systems that adapt undelimited continuations to model scope, one based on the $\lambda\mu$-calculus (de Groote 2001), and one based on the Lambek-Grishin calculus (Moortgat 2009, Bernardi and Moortgat 2007, Bernardi and Moortgat 2010, Bastenhof 2012, Bastenhof 2013). We will also discuss the continuation-based account of discourse anaphora of (de Groote 2006). Although that analysis does not make explicit use of undelimited continuations, it does limit the result type of a continuation in a similar way.

In contrast with these, the grammars we have considered so far in this book have all involved delimited continuations. In fact, we believe that only delimited continuations are a good fit for modeling scope in natural language. The reason is simple: the scope-takers we have considered so far in natural language are always able to take scope over a region that is smaller than the entire utterance. That is, the scope takers we've studied are all composable. In particular, the combination of a scope-taker with its nuclear scope can always form a proper subpart of a larger structure. These are the hallmarks of delimited continuations.

The need for delimited continuations becomes even more clear when we consider cases in which the scope-taking element changes the result type of the expression it takes scope over. This means that no single result type, whether the result type is conceived of as $\bot$ or as $\texttt{t}$, will suffice. To see what is at issue, consider the following phrase:

(336) a book [the author of which] I know

In this example, the wh-word *which* takes scope over the bracketed determiner phrase. That is, the context *the author of* [ ] has type DP\\DP: it is the kind of context that takes a determiner phrase plug and returns a determiner phrase. For instance, if we plug in the determiner phrase *Waverly*, we get the determiner phrase *the author of Waverly*. However, in this case, the bracketed phrase does not function as a determiner phrase (for instance, if we replace the bracketed phrase with a simple determiner phrase, the result is ungrammatical: **a book Waverly I know*). Rather, the bracketed phrase must function as a relative pronoun, similar to *that*, as in *a book that I know*. Thus if REL is the category of a relative pronoun, the category of *which* in (336) must be REL//(DP\\DP): the sort of expression that plugs into a hole of type DP, takes scope over an DP, and changes it into a REL.

In other words, the use of *which* in (336) changes the expression it takes scope over from a determiner phrase into a relative pronoun. If $\bot$ or $\texttt{t}$ is our only result type, we are faced with a problem, since we appear to need two distinct result types (namely, DP and REL).

In sum, the fact that scope-taking expressions in natural language are always able to take scope over a proper subpart of the sentences in which they occur, and the fact that scope-taking expressions are able to explicitly change the result type of the expressions they take scope over, strongly suggests that the scope-taking mechanism for natural language must deliver delimited continuations.

There may be other phenomena in natural language that also require delimited continuations, such as the compositional semantics of focus (see, e.g., Barker 2004, and Bekki and Asai 2009).

Even if we are right—that scope requires delimited continuations—that does not mean that undelimited continuations have no applications in natural language. Modifying the continuation-based approach proposed in Kubota and Uegaki (2009), Barker et al. (2010) argue that undelimited continuations are exactly the right tool for modeling expressives such as *damn*, which arguably always make their semantic contribution only over the entire utterance at once. In the terminology of Potts (2003), Harris and Potts (2009), they are speaker-oriented.

(337) John pretended that he walked the damn dog

In this example, the negative content contributed by *damn* remains a commitment of the speaker, and cannot be a report of an opinion held by John but not the speaker. Barker et al. (2010) suggest that this top-level-only behavior is a good match for undelimited continuations.

18.1 The $\lambda\mu$-calculus applied to scope

Building on ideas of Griffin (1990), Parigot (1992) develops an extension of the lambda calculus in order to model the computational content of classical proofs. That is, the Curry-Howard isomorphism shows that intuitionistic proofs correspond to terms in the lambda calculus (glossing over some complications). But there are classical theorems that cannot be proved intuitionistically, famously, e.g., $p \vee \neg p$, the law of the excluded middle. If classical proofs do not correspond to the lambda calculus, what sort of computational system do they correspond to? One answer, it turns out, is the $\lambda\mu$-calculus, which depends on continuations.

de Groote (2001) uses the $\lambda\mu$-calculus to model quantifier scope and at least some scope ambiguity. In addition to ordinary variables (‘x’), λ-abstracts (‘$\lambda x M$’), and applications (‘MN’), the $\lambda\mu$-calculus has μ-variables (‘α’), μ-abstracts (‘$\mu\alpha M$’), and naming constructions (‘αM’). In addition to the usual β-reduction of the λ-calculus:

(338) β-reduction: $(\lambda x M)\, N \leadsto M\{x \mapsto N\}$

there are two new reduction rules:

(339) μ-reduction: $(\mu\alpha M)\, N \leadsto \mu\alpha.M\{\alpha m \mapsto \alpha(m\, N)\}$

where '$M\{\alpha m \mapsto \alpha(m\,N)\}$' is the term M with each occurrence of 'αm' replaced by '$\alpha(m\,N)$', and

(340) μ'-reduction: $M\,(\mu\alpha N) \rightsquigarrow \mu\alpha.N\{\alpha n \mapsto \alpha(M\,n)\}$

where '$N\{\alpha n \mapsto \alpha(M\,n)\}$' is the term N with each occurrence of 'αn' replaced by '$\alpha(M\,n)$'. Although Parigot mentions μ'-reduction, his official calculus does not have μ'-reduction, since it renders the calculus non-confluent. But non-confluence is a virtue in this application, since it will give rise to the two scope readings.

As we'll see momentarily, the μ- and μ'- reduction rules allow a scope-taking expression to take scope incrementally by repeatedly taking scope over each adjacent functor. This is the essence of continuations, of course: something in argument position consuming a superordinate functor.

de Groote adds to the $\lambda\mu$-calculus a rule that he calls 'simplification':

(341) Simplification: $\mu\alpha M \rightsquigarrow M\{\alpha N \mapsto N\}$

Simplification extinguishes the functor-climbing potential of a μ-term. Thus it plays a role roughly analogous to our LOWER type-shifter in Part I.

We can now assign *someone* the term $\mu\alpha.\exists x.\alpha x$; *loves* the constant **loves**; and *everyone* the term $\mu\beta.\forall y.\beta y$. Then we have two distinct reduction paths for *Someone loves everyone*.

First, linear scope:

(342) $(\mu\alpha.\exists x.\alpha x)(\mathbf{loves}\ (\mu\beta.\forall y.\beta y))$
$$\rightsquigarrow \mu\alpha.\exists x.\alpha(\mathbf{loves}\ (\mu\beta.\forall y.\beta y)\ x)$$
$$\rightsquigarrow \mu\alpha.\exists x.\alpha((\mu\beta.\forall y.\beta(\mathbf{loves}\ y))\ x)$$
$$\rightsquigarrow \mu\alpha.\exists x.\alpha(\mu\beta.\forall y.\beta(\mathbf{loves}\ y\ x)$$
$$\rightsquigarrow \exists x.\forall y.\mathbf{loves}\ y\ x$$

The last step involves two applications of Simplification.

Second, inverse scope:

(343) $(\mu\alpha.\exists x.\alpha x)(\mathbf{loves}\ (\mu\beta.\forall y.\beta y))$
$$\rightsquigarrow (\mu\alpha.\exists x.\alpha x)(\mu\beta.\forall y.\beta(\mathbf{loves}\ y))$$
$$\rightsquigarrow \mu\beta.\forall y.\beta((\mu\alpha.\exists x.\alpha x)(\mathbf{loves}\ y))$$
$$\rightsquigarrow \mu\beta.\forall y.\beta(\mu\alpha.\exists x.\alpha(\mathbf{loves}\ y\ x))$$
$$\rightsquigarrow \forall y.\exists x.\mathbf{loves}\ y\ x$$

The addition of the simplification rule is crucial for the application to scope-taking. In the original $\lambda\mu$-calculus, reduction continues until every scope-taking expression takes scope over the entire sentence (or else gets trapped underneath a λ; we're ignoring Parigot's 'renaming' reduction rule). That's what it means to be an undelimited continuation: to take scope over an undelimited region of the context.

In most instances, then, the only way for a scope-taker to take anything less than scope over the entire utterance is for the simplification rule to apply.

The syntactic category of an undelimited continuation is simpler than that of a delimited one. If every scope-taker takes scope over the entire utterance, there is no need to specify either the category over which the expression takes scope—there is no choice in the matter—nor is there any need to specify the category of the expression that results from the scope-taker combining with its nuclear scope; again, there is no choice in the matter.

As for taking scope over expressions that are not clauses, note that if the simplification rule fires at the wrong moment, the result is incoherent:

(344) $(\mu\alpha.\exists x.\alpha x)(\mu\beta.\forall y.\beta(\mathbf{loves}\, y)) \rightsquigarrow (\exists x.x)(\forall y.\mathbf{loves}\, y)$

For this reason, de Groote requires the simplification rule to only apply to expressions of type `t`, i.e., only when the scope-taking operator has taken scope exactly over a clause.

Thus in order for the simplification rule to work, it is necessary to make assumptions about the syntactic category of the complete expression. In many cases, this is harmless: in many discussions of scope, the scope-taker is embedded inside a declarative sentence (type `t`), and likewise the syntactic category of the sentence as a whole is also `t`. But assuming that the type of the delimited continuation will match the type of the final result is highly limiting, and empirically inadequate. In terms of the delimited continuations we've been using throughout the book, it means that the only possible category for a scope-taking expression is $\mathrm{S}/\!\!/(A\backslash\!\!\backslash \mathrm{S})$, for any choice of A: the category over which the scope-taker takes scope is fixed in advance for all scope-takers, and the result category must always be the same as the scope target.

When other expression types besides plain clauses are involved, the situation becomes more complex. For instance, if the category of the sentence as a whole differs from the category over which a scope-taker takes scope, there is a conflict:

(345) a. Someone knows [who everyone spoke to]
b. Someone knows [who bought what]

In (345a), a universal quantifier takes scope over an embedded question, and in (345b), a wh-word takes scope over an embedded question. At the same time, a different quantifier takes scope over the matrix clause, which remains category `t`. These circumstances create incompatible requirements for the types of the scope-taking expressions, as well as for the restriction on the simplification rule.

For this reason, choosing a result type in advance is not only contrary to the spirit of undelimited continuations, it creates empirical problems for the application to natural language scope.

In addition, requiring the result category to be the same as the scope target also creates difficulties. Many of the analyses given through this book rely on a scope-taker being able to change the category of the expression over which it takes scope. Our analysis of binding in Part I, for instance, depends on a pronoun changing the category of an expression from A to DP $\rhd A$. Likewise, we analyzed in-situ wh-expressions as changing the category of the expression they take scope over from A to $B?A$, for a variety of choices of B (where usually $B =$ DP).

In addition, many of the analyses we have proposed rely on assuming a wide variety of scope targets. This is true for the treatment of gaps, reflexives and idioms in reconstruction cases, negative polarity licensing, the scope-taking of *same* in nominals, parasitic scope in general, and sluicing. In other words, the many analyses throughout this book taken together support the claim that for a fully general treatment of scope-taking, it must be possible for all three of the categories involved in characterizing scope-taking to differ from one another: the local syntactic category of the scope-taker, the scope of the expression over which the scope-taker takes scope, and the category of the expression that results from combining the scope-taker with its nuclear scope. That is, if a scope-taker has category $C /\!\!/ (A \backslash\!\!\backslash B)$, it must be possible to choose A, B and C independently.

So the $\lambda\mu$-calculus has limitations as a model of natural language scope. However, we endorse the basic insight that scope-taking in natural language involves continuations, and that scope ambiguity is a matter of the order in which reduction occurs (i.e., evaluation order).

18.2 The Lambek-Grishin calculus and scope

Moortgat (2009), Bernardi and Moortgat (2007), Bernardi and Moortgat (2010), Bastenhof (2012), Bastenhof (2013) and others have studied an extension of Lambek grammar (Lambek 1958) due to Grishin (1983). Despite the fact that the Lambek-Grishin calculus, unlike the $\lambda\mu$-calculus, is able to maintain a distinction between local category, scope-target, and result category of a scope-taker, there are complications on the semantic side that arise once again, though in a different way, from the fact that the continuations involved are undelimited.

The project of applying the Lambek-Grishin calculus to natural language scope seeks to explain scope-taking as a consequence of completing a symmetry of the ordinary Lambek grammar with respect to negation. Dual to the merge mode used throughout this book, i.e., $/$, $\times$, and $\backslash$, in addition, we now have $\obslash$ ("left coimplication"), $\otimes$ ("cotensor"), and $\oslash$ ("right coimplication"). In the terminology of Linear Logic (Girard 1987), the ordinary merge connectives are a multiplicative conjunction, and its Lambek-Grishin dual is a multiplicative disjunction.

The symmetry is beautiful. Cotensor is the mirror image of tensor, with the mirror placed at the turnstyle. In particular, the counterpart of the Right rules for Slash and Backslash are the Left rules for Coimplication Left and Coimplication Right. For instance,

(346) $$\frac{\Gamma \vdash A \qquad \Delta[B] \vdash C}{\Delta[(B/A) \cdot \Gamma] \vdash C}\ /L \qquad \frac{C \vdash \Delta[B] \qquad A \vdash \Gamma}{C \vdash \Delta[\Gamma \circ (A \oslash B)]}\ \oslash R$$

On the left, we have our usual rule $/L$ introducing a function/argument articulation on the left side of the turnstyle. On the right, we have the mirror-image rule, introducing a cofunction/coargument articulation on the right side of the turnsytle. As Bernardi and Moortgat (2007) put it, the tensor mode composes values, and the cotensor mode composes contexts.

In addition to the logical rules, which in some sense merely complete a symmetry latent in the original Lambek grammar, Grishin (1983) proposes a set of structural postulates, including the following:

(347)
$(P1)\quad (A \oslash B) \times C \vdash A \oslash (B \times C)$
$(P2)\quad C \times (A \oslash B) \vdash A \oslash (C \times B)$
$(P3)\quad C \times (B \oslash A) \vdash (C \times B) \oslash A$
$(P4)\quad (B \oslash A) \times C \vdash (B \times C) \oslash A$

An example derivation shows how these postulates allow a coimplication introduced at the sentential level (top of the derivation) to end up embedded in-situ in a DP position (bottom of the derivation):

(348)
$$\dfrac{\dfrac{\dfrac{\dfrac{\dfrac{\dfrac{\text{alice} \times (\text{thinks} \times (\text{DP} \times \text{left})) \vdash \text{S} \qquad \text{S} \vdash \text{S}}{\text{alice} \times (\text{thinks} \times (\text{DP} \times \text{left})) \vdash (\text{S} \oslash \text{S}) \oplus \text{S}}\ \oslash R}{(\text{S} \oslash \text{S}) \oslash (\text{alice} \times (\text{thinks} \times (\text{DP} \times \text{left}))) \vdash \text{S}}\ \oslash L}{\text{alice} \times ((\text{S} \oslash \text{S}) \oslash (\text{thinks} \times (\text{DP} \times \text{left}))) \vdash \text{S}}\ \text{P2}}{\text{alice} \times (\text{thinks} \times ((\text{S} \oslash \text{S}) \oslash (\text{DP} \times \text{left}))) \vdash \text{S}}\ \text{P2}}{\text{alice} \times (\text{thinks} \times (((\text{S} \oslash \text{S}) \oslash \text{DP}) \times \text{left})) \vdash \text{S}}\ \text{P1}}{\text{alice} \times (\text{thinks} \times (\text{someone} \times \text{left})) \vdash \text{S}}\ \text{LEX}$$

The proposed category for the scope-taking quantifier *someone* is $(\text{S} \oslash \text{S}) \oslash \text{DP}$. As Moortgat (2012) puts it, "In general, an expression of type $(B \oslash C) \oslash A$ behaves locally as an A within a context of type B; it then acts as a function transforming B into C." This is exactly what is needed for natural language scope-taking. Thus LG elegantly models the syntactic behavior of scope-taking.

In order to understand the nature of the syntactic explanation offered by the Grishin postulates, note that P1 and P2 are highly similar in form to the structural postulates for NL_{CL} derived in section 17.2.

(349) $\dfrac{(A \oslash B) \times C}{A \oslash (B \times C)} P1 \quad \approx \quad \dfrac{(p \circ q) \cdot r}{p \circ ((\mathsf{C} \cdot q) \cdot r)} \mathsf{C}$

$\dfrac{C \times (A \oslash B)}{A \oslash (C \times B)} P2 \quad \approx \quad \dfrac{p \cdot (q \circ r)}{q \circ ((\mathsf{B} \cdot p) \cdot r)} \mathsf{B}$

One difference stems from the fact that the NL_{CL} postulates are bidirectional inferences, so the structural constants *B* and *C* are needed to leave a trail of breadcrumbs. This enables a quantifier expression to move off to take scope in a way that (the element that conceptually serves the role of) its trace variable can find its way back down to the original position of the scope-taker when the direction of the postulates are reversed. (This remark about breadcrumbs will make more sense when looking at an NL_{CL} derivation such as (294) or (295).) Another difference is that the connectives in the postulates from NL_{CL} are structural connectives, '·' and '∘', rather than syntactic category connectives as in the Grishin postulates. Nevertheless, despite these differences, these two pairs of rules accomplish the same result in a highly similar manner, namely, allowing a scope-taker to interact with distant syntactic elements.

On the semantic side, the fit is less natural. The standard semantics for cotensor and coimplication involves undelimited continuations, as spelled out by, e.g, Curien and Herbelin (2000) or Wadler (2003). The specific formal language Bernardi and Moortgat use for their semantic labeling based on this general reasoning is a minor variant of Curien and Herbelin's (2000) $\lambda\mu\tilde{\mu}$-calculus. This semantic labeling does not deliver the meanings needed for natural language scope-taking without extension.

One way to see this is to consider the syntactic category assigned to a scope-taking DP, namely, $(S \oslash S) \oslash DP$. Figuring out the semantic type of a value of category $(S \oslash S) \oslash DP$ requires some careful reasoning. Starting as simply as possible, a value of category *A* is the kind of object that can combine with a continuation of category *A* to form a complete computation. Likewise, the value of category $A \backslash B$ is a function from values of category *A* to values of category *B*. A continuation of category $A \backslash B$, then, is an ordered pair $\langle v, \kappa \rangle$ in which *v* is a value of category *A*, and κ is a continuation of category *B*. The computation is completed by applying the function to *v*, and then cutting the result of the function/argument application with the continuation κ. Here, 'cutting' means feeding the value (matter) to the continuation (antimatter).

(350) $A \times (A \backslash B) \vdash B \qquad\qquad B \vdash (B \oslash C) \oplus C$

By mirrored reasoning, a continuation of category $B \oslash C$ is a cofunction from continuations of category *C* to continuations of category *B*. A *value* of category $B \oslash C$ is an object that can combine with a continuation of category $B \oslash C$ to form a complete computation. In (350), what the continuation $B \oslash C$ needs in order to complete the computation expressed by the sequent is a value of type *B*, and a continuation of category *C*. Thus the natural semantic value for $B \oslash C$ is an ordered pair $\langle v, \kappa \rangle$, where v is a value of category *B*, and κ is a continuation of category *C*.

Taking this reasoning one step further, a value in category (S $\oslash$ S) $\obslash$ DP—our target category, the category proposed for a scope-taking DP—will be an ordered pair $\langle\kappa, v\rangle$ in which κ is a continuation of category S $\oslash$ S, and v is a value of category DP.

The problem, then, is that the natural semantics for category (S $\oslash$ S) $\obslash$ DP does not correspond in any direct way to a generalized quantifier meaning. Instead, it is an ordered pair in which the DP is separate from the function that applies at the clausal level. As a result, there is no direct way for a quantifier in the first component to bind (or affect in any way) the value of the DP component.

Some additional mechanism is required. Rather than computing with terms in this formal system directly, Bernardi and Moortgat (2007) and Bernardi and Moortgat (2010) map $\lambda\mu\tilde{\mu}$-terms into typed (intuitionistic) lambda terms via a Continuation Passing Style transform similar to the ones discussed in chapter 12. The extra expressive power provided by the CPS transform allows lexical items to denote functions that do not correspond to any expression in the $\lambda\mu\tilde{\mu}$ language. This in turn allows the lexical items to extend the expressive power of the Lambek-Grishin grammars to simulate the behavior of delimited continuations.

There is some motivation for continuizing the semantics that is independent of the application to scope-taking, namely, if the semantic labeling is not itself continuized, it is not confluent. The choice of a CPS evaluation regime restores confluence.

Note that, e.g., Barker (2002) shows that a CPS transform itself introduces enough continuation-passing to cover a significant amount of the semantics of scope-taking. The net result in the complete LG system is that the semantics part of the syntax and semantics of scope-taking do not follow from the Lambek-Grishin system alone. The question, then, is how much of the scope-taking is due to the Grishin postulates, and how much of the explanation of scope-taking is due to the extra power provided by the CPS transform.

To drive this point home, Bastenhof (2013) shows that if we provide the Lambek-Grishin system with a particular formal language for representing the meanings of expressions and derivations, it is possible to derive the full power of Hendriks' (1993) Flexible Montague Grammar, giving a robust account of scope that does not use the Grishin postulates given in (347) at all.

It appears, then, that the Grishin interaction postulates are neither sufficient nor necessary for modeling scope.

Furthermore, as we saw above in the previous section in the discussion of the $\lambda\mu$-calculus, in order for the natural language quantifiers to take scope over embedded expressions at all, it is necessary to choose in advance the result type of the complete computation. Bernardi and Moortgat choose `t` as the result type, just as in de Groote (2001); but as discussed in the previous section, there is no single choice for a result type that is adequate in general.

18.3 A continuation-based grammar for dynamic semantics

de Groote (2006) develops a continuation-based grammar that reconstructs the main results of Dynamic Predicate Logic (Groenendijk and Stokhof 1991). The starting point is to conceive of a discourse as a function from an initial set of discourse referents to a truth value. This means that an individual sentence needs two things in order to produce a complete discourse: an initial list of discourse referents, and the rest of the discourse—that is, the sentence's continuation. If `[e]` is the semantic type of a list of discourse referents, then a continuized sentence denotation has type

(351) $\texttt{[e]} \rightarrow (\texttt{[e]} \rightarrow \texttt{t}) \rightarrow \texttt{t}$

This is a function from a list of discourse referents to a function from continuations to truth values, where a continuation (the rest of the discourse) is itself a function from a list of discourse referents to a truth value.

This gives us the following analysis of a standard example of dynamic discourse anaphora:

(352) (John entered) (and (he$_0$ sat))	$\lambda i\kappa.\textbf{entered}\, j \wedge \textbf{sat}\, i_0 \wedge \kappa(j{:}i)$
John entered	$\lambda i\kappa.\textbf{entered}\, j \wedge \kappa(j{:}i)$
John	$\lambda Pik.Pj(j{:}i)\kappa$
entered	$\lambda xi\kappa.\textbf{entered}\, x \wedge \kappa i$
and (he$_0$ sat)	$\lambda pi\kappa.pi(\lambda j.\textbf{sat}\, i_0 \wedge \kappa j)$
and	$\lambda qpi\kappa.pi(\lambda j.qj\kappa)$
he$_0$ sat	$\lambda i\kappa.\textbf{sat}\, i_0 \wedge \kappa i$
he$_0$	$\lambda Pi\kappa.Pi_n i\kappa$
sat	$\lambda xi\kappa.\textbf{sat}\, x \wedge \kappa i$

Here, 'i_n' is the nth member of the list i. Some details to note: the generalized quantifier *John* evaluates its continuation κ with respect to a list $j : i$ of individuals, where '$j : i$' is the list of individual i with j prefixed to it. The dynamic conjunction *and* evaluates its first argument (the right conjunct) with respect to a list of discourse referents j which the left conjunct may have updated with additional discourse referents. So the left conjunct *John entered* adds John to the set of discourse referents, and the right conjunct *he$_0$ sat* targets the position in the list that contains the individual dynamically added by the left conjunct.

Thus, as explained above in chapter 3, continuizing the category S leads naturally to the dynamic-semantics conception of sentence meaning as an update on context.

If we have the following expression meanings

(353) a donkey $= \lambda Qik.\exists y.\textbf{donkey}\, y \wedge Qy(y{:}i)\kappa$

(354) every $= \lambda PQi\kappa.\forall x.Pxi(\lambda i.\text{True}) \rightarrow Pxi(\lambda j.Qx(x{:}j)(\lambda i.\text{True})$

then we have an analysis of donkey anaphora as in *Every farmer with a donkey beats it* (see de Groote 2006 for full details). In slightly more detail, in the value for *a donkey*, the existential quantifier selects an entity, and places it on the updated list of discourse referents. In the value for *every*, whenever a choice of x satisfies the restriction P, then a list of discourse referents with x added to it will also satisfy the nuclear scope Q. Here, $\lambda i.$True is a trivial continuation that ignores the current set of discourse referents and simply returns True.

Once again, the grammar makes assumptions about the result type of the complete discourse. The assumption is that the result type is `t`, the type of a declarative sentence. To see why this choice is forced, note that many of the conjuncts in the logical representations in the derivation given just above have the form κi, which must therefore evaluate to a truth value. Moreover, it is assumed by the inner workings of the lexical entry for *every* that discourses must evaluate to truth values, since the denotation for *every* relies on the assumption that both its restriction P and its nuclear scope Q produce a truth value after being fed an appropriate pair of arguments.

As a result of building in this reliance on truth value result types, it is unclear even how to extend the account to simple yes/no questions such as

(355) Does every farmer who owns a donkey beat it?

The problem is that the internal semantics of the determiner *every* requires continuations to have type $\texttt{[e]} \rightarrow \texttt{t}$, but yes/no questions do not denote truth values.

It will be necessary to add a more flexible category system that can track the result types of various operators, allowing different scope-takers to deliver different result categories, perhaps along the lines of the system in Part I.

18.4 Monads

Another strategy for scaling up the approach in de Groote (2006) would start by replacing the system with a functionally equivalent State monad. As Wadler (1995, 1994) explains, monads are a technique for adding a layer to a computation for managing a particular side effect. The state monad adds the ability to examine and modify a store of information, here, a list of discourse referents.

There are many useful monads. Besides the State monad, monads that are especially useful for natural language include the Reader monad, the List monad, and the Continuation monad. Individual monads can be characterized by specifying a unit function, and a bind function. The bind function is sometimes written '$\star$'; as for the name, it is not exactly what linguists think of as binding, though there is a connection that we will not elaborate on here.

Giorgolo and Asudeh (2011) show how to use a State monad to account for dynamic binding, including donkey anaphora.

For the State monad, the unit function maps any ordinary denotation into a monadic value that maintains state information. In the dynamic anaphora application under consideration here, the state will be a simple list of discourse referents. So the unit will take an ordinary denotation of type a and return a monadic object of type $[e] \to (a, [e])$, where '$(a, [e])$' is the type of an ordered pair consisting of a denotation of type a and a list of individuals.

(356) $unit = \lambda x.\lambda i.\langle x, i\rangle$

(357) $p \star f = \lambda i.\text{let } \langle x, j\rangle \text{ be } pi \text{ in } fxj$

The unit lifts a denotation into the monad type by turning it into something that expects to receive an input state (here, i). It does not make any use of the input state, but it does include the state in its output, the ordered pair $\langle x, i\rangle$.

The bind function takes an ordinary denotation of type a and a function f mapping monadic objects of type a onto a monadic object of type b, i.e., $a \to \texttt{[e]} \to \texttt{[e]} \to (a, \texttt{[e]})$. In words, bind applies the left monadic object u to the initial state i, producing an ordered pair $\langle x, j\rangle$ consisting of a denotation x and an updated state j. Then bind returns the ordered pair delivered by applying f first to the newly-computed object x and then to the updated state j.

Monads must also obey certain constraints which guarantee that their components are well-behaved in certain ways. For instance, in a genuine monad, $p \star \texttt{unit} = p$ for all monadic objects p. The constraints are called 'laws', and we will not pause to present them here; see, e.g., Wadler (1995) for details.

The easiest place to see the correspondence between the dynamic grammar from de Groote (2006) and the State monad is to consider the function denoted by dynamic conjunction given in (352):

(358) $p \text{ and } q = \lambda ik.pi(\lambda j.qjk)$

Just as in the definition of bind immediately above in (357), the left conjunct p is applied to the input state i, and then the right conjunct q is applied to the updated state j.

The conception of programming with monads is that it is possible to construct a program without any thought of side effects, then add side effects after the fact simply by lifting the original computation into a monad.

Shan (2001a) introduced monads for analyzing natural language. In particular, he pointed out (p. 289) that a Reader monad is well-suited for modeling the relationship between an extensional (non-monadic) grammar and an intensional (monadic) grammar. Ben-Avi and Winter (2007) develop a closely similar technique in considerably more detail. The monadic type constructor M that is relevant for intensionalization maps an extensional meaning of type a to a monadic object of type $s \to a$. That is, the monadic version of an expression in category a is a function from worlds (type s) to objects of type a.

There is a monad called the Continuation monad. The Continuation monad is at least as expressive as any other monad, in the sense that all other monads (the Reader monad, the State monad, the List monad, etc.) can be simulated using a continuation monad. Although the dynamic grammar of de Groote (2006) discussed in the previous section is not exactly in the form of a continuation monad, it still gives a sense of how continuations can be used to reproduce the functionality of a State monad.

Monads, like continuations, are able to regulate order of evaluation. Indeed, it is the order-sensitive nature of monads that de Groote (2006) exploits in order to derive the linear order asymmetries that characterize dynamic semantics. This is because the bind operation guarantees that the left argument of bind will always be evaluated before the right argument of bind. See Wadler (1994:43) for a discussion of how a continuation monad can guarantee a call-by-value evaluation discipline even when the monad is implemented within a language that is evaluated in a call-by-name discipline.

We should add that the framework of de Groote (2006) is both elegant and flexible. For example, Bumford and Barker (2013) show how to adapt the basic technique to implement Brasoveanu's (2011) compositional account of *different*. Kobele (2012) adapts the technique to provide a non-movement analysis of quantifier scope within a Minimalist syntax. For a third example, de Groote and Lebedeva (2010), Lebedeva (2012) extend this system to give a compositional account of presupposition accommodation.

Nevertheless, the continuation-passing in de Groote (2006), as well as the official Continuation monad, is less flexible than the full power of (delimited) continuations. The reason is that the monad technique depends upon the monadic operations returning a result whose type is once again a member of the same monadic type. In our terms, monads in general are limited to having the input type and the result type both be members of the same monadic type. This is roughly equivalent in our systems of restricting every scope-taker to a category of the form $C /\!\!/ (A \backslash\!\!\backslash B)$ where $C = B$. As Wadler (1994:47) remarks, "there is no reason why the type p of a composable continuation need be the same as the type o returned by the entire computation". He sketches how to allow for arbitrary layers of composable (delimited) continuations, in the spirit of Danvy and Filinski (1989).

In sum, we conclude that any fully general empirically adequate account of scope-taking requires delimited, composable continuations. Undelimited continuations are not adequate in the general case, though they may have applications in natural language semantics other than scope-taking. In particular, we conclude that it is necessary for a continuation-based system to allow the result type delivered by a scope-taking element to differ from the type of the expression over which the scope-taker takes scope.

Afterword: the logic of evaluation order

The formal systems in Part I and Part II are quite different, not only formally, but in substance: although the grammar in Part I seeks to explain crossover, the grammar in Part II generates crossover examples as easily as it generates non-crossover examples; likewise, in the other direction, the parasitic scope of Part II is not easily translatable to the tower system.

On the one hand, this a good thing: we have presented two very different projects, both of which show how a continuation-based approach can provide new insights. The differences between the analyses emphasize that using continuations is a perspective, method, a tool—not a theory. We shouldn't expect two different continuation-based analyses to necessarily be compatible any more than we should expect two different Quantifier Raising analyses to necessarily be compatible, or two possible-worlds analyses, or two analyses involving mereological fusion.

On the other hand, both projects involve scope-taking and binding, and it is worthwhile asking whether they could be unified. Is there something about the type-logical framework that is fundamentally at odds with imposing a left-to-right evaluation regime? Certainly not: Barker and Shan (2006) present a type-logical analysis that gives an evaluation-order account of crossover.

But it remains possible that there is something about parasitic scope that is incompatible with explicit control over evaluation order. We will show that this is not the case by sketching a way to add control over evaluation order to NL_{CL}.

Working within NL_{CL}, we begin by replacing (only) the postulate B with the following variant:

(359) $$\frac{p \cdot (q \circ r)}{q \circ ((\mathsf{B} \cdot p) \cdot r)}\,\mathsf{B} \qquad \frac{p \cdot (q \circ r)}{q \circ ((\mathsf{B}'' \circ p) \cdot r)}\,\mathsf{B}''$$

The idea is that abstracting something (q) across a structure to its left (p) turns the abstracted-over structure into an island. In the variant rule given here, this is accomplished by hiding p behind a newly-introduced occurrence of $\circ$. Since abstraction from the right element of a $\circ$ structure is not allowed, no part of p can be abstracted out of it, and crossover is blocked.

(360) a. Everyone loves his mother
b. everyone $\circ$ ((C $\cdot$ I) $\cdot$ (his $\circ$ ((B$''$ $\circ$ loves) $\cdot$ ((C $\cdot$ I) $\cdot$ mother)))) $\vdash$ S

(361) a. ?His mother loves everyone
b. everyone $\circ$ ((B$''$ $\circ$ (his $\circ$ ((C $\cdot$ I) $\cdot$ mother))) $\cdot$ ((B$''$ $\circ$ loves) $\cdot$ I)) $\vdash$ S

For the grammatical sentence in (360), we have given the sequent just before an application of the B$''$ postulate allows *his* to take parasitic scope over the nuclear scope of *everyone*. For the crossover violation in (361), we have given the sequent just before *his* would be about to take parasitic scope. But the B$''$ postulate does not apply, thanks to the presence of the blocking occurrence of $\circ$. It is not possible to complete the derivation, and (361) is correctly predicted to be ungrammatical.

As for extending this strategy to reconstruction examples, it is not difficult to adapt the fronting analysis of chapter 5. If we have a new atomic structure F (for 'fronting'), then the fronting rule is once again purely a matter of a syntactic adjustment: $p \circ q \Rightarrow (\mathsf{F} \cdot p) \cdot q$. This structural rule says that an F-marked constituent p that is linearly adjacent to some q can be treated as equivalent to having abstracted p from some gap position within q. If we assign *which* the structure $\mathsf{F} \cdot \mathrm{Q} /\!\!/ ((\mathrm{DP}/\mathrm{N}) \backslash\!\!\backslash \mathrm{S})$, and provide also associativity specific to fronting (i.e., $\mathsf{F} \cdot (p \cdot q) \Rightarrow (\mathsf{F} \cdot p) \cdot q$), then with a gap of category $(\mathrm{DP}^{\mathrm{DP}} \backslash\!\!\backslash \mathrm{S}) /\!\!/ (\mathrm{DP}^{\mathrm{DP}} \backslash\!\!\backslash \mathrm{S})$, the reconstruction example *Which of his$_i$ relatives does everyone$_i$ love* __ can be derived with reconstructed binding, but ?*Which of his$_i$ relatives* __ *loves everyone$_i$* is correctly predicted to be a crossover violation.

In other words, it is feasible to translate the evaluation-order explanation of crossover developed in Part I into the specific type-logical approach developed in Part II.

Notes on exercises

1. $\dfrac{\mathrm{S} \mid \mathrm{S}}{\mathrm{DP}\backslash\mathrm{S}} \equiv \mathrm{S}/\!\!/((\mathrm{DP}\backslash\mathrm{S})\backslash\!\!\backslash\mathrm{S})$ and $\dfrac{\forall x.[\,]}{\textbf{left}\ x} \equiv \lambda\kappa.\forall x.\kappa(\textbf{left}\ x)$.

2. $h[\,] = \textbf{thinks}[\,]$

3. $$\left(\begin{array}{cc} \dfrac{C \mid D}{A} & \dfrac{D \mid E}{A\backslash B} \\ \textit{left.exp} & \textit{right.exp} \\ \dfrac{g[\,]}{x} & \dfrac{h[\,]}{f} \end{array}\right) = \begin{array}{c} \dfrac{C \mid E}{B} \\ \textit{left.exp right.exp} \\ \dfrac{g[h[\,]]}{f(x)} \end{array}$$

4. $$\left(\begin{array}{cc} \dfrac{\mathrm{S} \mid \mathrm{S}}{(\mathrm{DP}\backslash\mathrm{S})/\mathrm{DP}} & \dfrac{\mathrm{S} \mid \mathrm{S}}{\mathrm{DP}} \\ \textit{loves} & \textit{everyone} \\ \dfrac{[\,]}{\textbf{loves}} & \dfrac{\forall y.[\,]}{y} \end{array}\right) = \begin{array}{c} \dfrac{\mathrm{S} \mid \mathrm{S}}{(\mathrm{DP}\backslash\mathrm{S})} \\ \textit{loves everyone} \\ \dfrac{\forall y.[\,]}{\textbf{loves}\ y} \end{array}$$

Note that there is only one set of brackets in the result semantics instead of two, i.e., the semantic value is not $\dfrac{[\forall y.[\,]]}{\textbf{loves}\ y}$. One way to determine which brackets can be removed and when is to convert to flat notation, which has no brackets at all, and back again:

$$\frac{[\forall y.[\,]]}{\textbf{loves}\ y} \equiv \lambda\kappa\forall y.\kappa(\textbf{loves}\ y) \equiv \frac{\forall y.[\,]}{\textbf{loves}\ y}$$

5. $$\left(\begin{array}{cc} \dfrac{\mathrm{DP} \rhd \mathrm{S} \mid \mathrm{S}}{\mathrm{DP}} & \dfrac{\mathrm{S} \mid \mathrm{S}}{\mathrm{DP}\backslash\mathrm{DP}} \\ \textit{his} & \textit{mother} \\ \dfrac{\lambda y.[\,]}{y} & \dfrac{[\,]}{\textbf{mom}} \end{array}\right) = \begin{array}{c} \dfrac{\mathrm{DP} \rhd \mathrm{S} \mid \mathrm{S}}{\mathrm{DP}} \\ \textit{his mother} \\ \dfrac{\lambda y.[\,]}{\textbf{mom}\ y} \end{array}$$

$$\left(\begin{array}{cc} \dfrac{\mathrm{DP} \rhd \mathrm{S} \mid \mathrm{DP} \rhd \mathrm{S}}{(\mathrm{DP}\backslash\mathrm{S})/\mathrm{DP}} & \dfrac{\mathrm{DP} \rhd \mathrm{S} \mid \mathrm{S}}{\mathrm{DP}} \\ \textit{loves} & \textit{his mother} \\ \dfrac{[\,]}{\textbf{loves}} & \dfrac{\lambda y.[\,]}{\textbf{mom}\ y} \end{array}\right) = \begin{array}{c} \dfrac{\mathrm{DP} \rhd \mathrm{S} \mid \mathrm{S}}{\mathrm{DP}\backslash\mathrm{S}} \\ \textit{loves his mother} \\ \dfrac{\lambda y.[\,]}{\textbf{loves}(\textbf{mom}\ y)} \end{array}$$

6. $\dfrac{\lambda y \forall x.[\,]x}{\textbf{loves}\ y\ (\textbf{mom}\ x)}$

7.

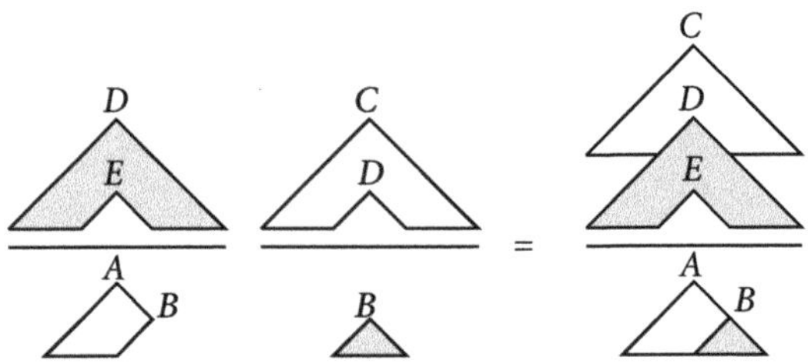

8.
$$\begin{array}{c} \mathrm{S}\,|\,\mathrm{DP} \rhd \mathrm{S} \\ \hline \mathrm{DP} \\ \textit{everyone} \\ \forall x.[\;]x \\ \hline x \end{array} \left(\begin{array}{c} \mathrm{S}\;|\;\mathrm{S} \\ \hline (\mathrm{DP}\backslash\mathrm{S})/\mathrm{DP} \\ \textit{loves} \\ [\;] \\ \hline \textbf{loves} \end{array} \left(\begin{array}{c} \mathrm{DP} \rhd \mathrm{S}\,|\,\mathrm{S} \\ \hline \mathrm{DP} \\ \textit{his} \\ \lambda y.[\;] \\ \hline y \end{array} \begin{array}{c} \mathrm{DP} \rhd \mathrm{S}\,|\,\mathrm{DP} \rhd \mathrm{S} \\ \hline \mathrm{DP}\backslash\mathrm{DP} \\ \textit{mother} \\ [\;] \\ \hline \textbf{mom} \end{array} \right)\right)$$

$$= \begin{array}{c} \mathrm{DP} \rhd \mathrm{S}\,|\,\mathrm{DP} \rhd \mathrm{S} \\ \hline \mathrm{S} \\ \textit{Everyone loves his mother} \\ \lambda y \forall x.[\;]x \\ \hline \textbf{loves (mom } y\textbf{)}\ x \end{array}$$

Because the right-to-left variant of the combination schema forces *outside* corners to match, the pattern of lifting must be different from the derivation in (31). It is not possible to LOWER, so the derivation can't be completed. Note that the semantic value is highly similar to the crossover derivation computed for exercise 4.

9. The tower convention for syntactic categories says that any category of the form $Z /\!\!/ (X \backslash\!\!\backslash Y)$ can be completely equivalently written as $\dfrac{\mathrm{Z}|\mathrm{Y}}{\mathrm{X}}$, no matter whether X, Y, or Z are atomic category symbols or complex. This means that the element underneath the horizontal line is always a constituent, whether or not it is itself complex. Therefore we have the following equivalences:

$$\begin{array}{c} \mathrm{E}\,|\,\mathrm{F} \\ \hline \mathrm{C}\,|\,\mathrm{D} \\ \hline \mathrm{A} \end{array} \equiv \begin{array}{c} \mathrm{E}\;|\;\mathrm{F} \\ \hline \left(\begin{array}{c} \mathrm{C}\,|\,\mathrm{D} \\ \hline \mathrm{A} \end{array} \right) \end{array} \equiv \frac{\mathrm{E}\;|\;\mathrm{F}}{C /\!\!/ (A \backslash\!\!\backslash D)} \equiv E /\!\!/ \left((C /\!\!/ (A \backslash\!\!\backslash D)) \backslash\!\!\backslash F \right)$$

10. The tower convention for semantic values says that any semantic value of the form $\lambda\kappa.g[\kappa x]$ can be completely equivalently written as $\dfrac{g[\;]}{x}$. So we have the following equivalences:

$$\begin{array}{c} h[\;] \\ \hline g[\;] \\ \hline x \end{array} \equiv \begin{array}{c} h[\;] \\ \hline \left(\begin{array}{c} g[\;] \\ \hline x \end{array} \right) \end{array} \equiv \frac{h[\;]}{\lambda\kappa.g[\kappa x]} \equiv \lambda\gamma.h[\gamma(\lambda\kappa.g[\kappa x])]$$

11. $\big(\lambda F\gamma.F(\lambda x.\gamma(\lambda\kappa.\kappa x))\big)\big(\lambda\kappa\forall x.\kappa x\big) = \lambda\gamma\forall x.\gamma(\lambda\kappa.\kappa x)$

12.

```
                                          E
            E       A       AE      M E       A
1. MAE   2. MA   3. M E   4. M    5.  A    6. M
```

13. Pronouns can bind other pronouns. Apply BIND to the leftmost pronoun:

$$
\begin{array}{c} \mathrm{S}\,|\,\mathrm{DP}\rhd\mathrm{S} \\ \hline \mathrm{DP} \\ \textit{someone} \\ \exists x.\,([\,]\,x) \\ \hline x \end{array}
\left(\left(\begin{array}{c} \mathrm{DP}\rhd\mathrm{S}\,|\,\mathrm{DP}\rhd\mathrm{S} \\ \hline ((\mathrm{DP}\backslash\mathrm{S})/\mathrm{DP}/\mathrm{S}) \\ \textit{told} \\ [\,] \\ \hline \textbf{told} \end{array}
\begin{array}{c} \mathrm{DP}\rhd\mathrm{S}\,|\,\mathrm{DP}\rhd\mathrm{S} \\ \hline \mathrm{DP} \\ \textit{everyone} \\ \forall y.\,[\,] \\ \hline y \end{array}\right)\right.
$$

$$
\left.\left.\left(\begin{array}{c} \mathrm{DP}\rhd\mathrm{S}\,|\,\mathrm{DP}\rhd\mathrm{S} \\ \hline \mathrm{DP} \\ \textit{he} \\ \lambda x.[\,]\,x \\ \hline x \end{array}
\left(\begin{array}{c} \mathrm{DP}\rhd\mathrm{S}\,|\,\mathrm{DP}\rhd\mathrm{S} \\ \hline (\mathrm{DP}\backslash\mathrm{S})/\mathrm{DP} \\ \textit{saw} \\ [\,] \\ \hline \textbf{saw} \end{array}
\begin{array}{c} \mathrm{DP}\rhd\mathrm{S}\,|\,\mathrm{S} \\ \hline \mathrm{DP} \\ \textit{him} \\ \lambda y.[\,] \\ \hline y \end{array}\right)\right)\right)\right)
$$

14. The derivation of the embedded clause is the crucial part:

$$
\begin{array}{c|c} \mathrm{DP}\rhd\mathrm{S} & \mathrm{DP}\rhd\mathrm{S} \\ \hline \mathrm{S} & \mathrm{S} \\ \hline \multicolumn{2}{c}{\mathrm{DP}} \\ \multicolumn{2}{c}{\textit{everyone}} \\ \multicolumn{2}{c}{[\,]} \\ \hline \multicolumn{2}{c}{\forall x.[\,]} \\ \hline \multicolumn{2}{c}{x} \end{array}
\left(\begin{array}{c|c} \mathrm{DP}\rhd\mathrm{S} & \mathrm{DP}\rhd\mathrm{S} \\ \hline \mathrm{S} & \mathrm{S} \\ \hline \multicolumn{2}{c}{(\mathrm{DP}\backslash\mathrm{S})/\mathrm{DP}} \\ \multicolumn{2}{c}{\textit{saw}} \\ \multicolumn{2}{c}{[\,]} \\ \hline \multicolumn{2}{c}{[\,]} \\ \hline \multicolumn{2}{c}{\textbf{saw}} \end{array}
\begin{array}{c|c} \mathrm{DP}\rhd\mathrm{S} & \mathrm{S} \\ \hline \mathrm{S} & \mathrm{S} \\ \hline \multicolumn{2}{c}{\mathrm{DP}} \\ \multicolumn{2}{c}{\textit{her}} \\ \multicolumn{2}{c}{\lambda y.[\,]} \\ \hline \multicolumn{2}{c}{[\,]} \\ \hline \multicolumn{2}{c}{y} \end{array}\right)
$$

$$
\begin{array}{c|c} \mathrm{DP}\rhd\mathrm{S} & \mathrm{S} \\ \hline \mathrm{S} & \mathrm{S} \\ \hline \multicolumn{2}{c}{\mathrm{S}} \\ \multicolumn{2}{c}{\textit{everyone saw her}} \\ \multicolumn{2}{c}{\lambda y.[\,]} \\ \hline \multicolumn{2}{c}{\forall x.[\,]} \\ \hline \multicolumn{2}{c}{\textbf{saw}\ y\ x} \end{array}
\quad \overset{\textsc{lower}}{\Rightarrow} \quad
\begin{array}{c|c} \mathrm{DP}\rhd\mathrm{S} & \mathrm{S} \\ \hline \multicolumn{2}{c}{\mathrm{S}} \\ \multicolumn{2}{c}{\textit{everyone saw her}} \\ \multicolumn{2}{c}{\lambda y.[\,]} \\ \hline \multicolumn{2}{c}{\forall x.\textbf{saw}\ y\ x} \end{array}
$$

An internal application of LOWER enforces embedded scope. Crucially, the semantic effect of the pronoun is on a higher layer than the quantificational effect of *everyone*.

15.

$$
\begin{array}{c} \mathrm{DP}\bbslash\mathrm{S}\,|\,\mathrm{DP}\bbslash\mathrm{S} \\ \hline \mathrm{DP} \\ \textit{Mary} \\ [\,] \\ \hline \textbf{m} \end{array}
\left(\begin{array}{c} \mathrm{DP}\bbslash\mathrm{S}\,|\,\mathrm{DP}\bbslash\mathrm{S} \\ \hline (\mathrm{DP}\backslash\mathrm{S})/\mathrm{S} \\ \textit{thinks} \\ [\,] \\ \hline \textbf{thinks} \end{array}
\left(\begin{array}{c} \mathrm{DP}\bbslash\mathrm{S}\,|\,\mathrm{DP}\bbslash\mathrm{S} \\ \hline \mathrm{DP} \\ \textit{John} \\ [\,] \\ \hline \textbf{j} \end{array}
\left(\begin{array}{c} \mathrm{DP}\bbslash\mathrm{S}\,|\,\mathrm{DP}\bbslash\mathrm{S} \\ \hline (\mathrm{DP}\backslash\mathrm{S})/\mathrm{DP} \\ \textit{likes} \\ [\,] \\ \hline \textbf{likes} \end{array}
\begin{array}{c} \mathrm{DP}\bbslash\mathrm{S}\,|\,\mathrm{S} \\ \hline \mathrm{DP} \\ \_\_ \\ \lambda y.[\,] \\ \hline y \end{array}\right)\right)\right)
$$

$$
= \begin{array}{c} \mathrm{DP}\bbslash\mathrm{S}\,|\,\mathrm{S} \\ \hline \mathrm{S} \\ \textit{Mary thinks John likes}\ \_\_ \\ \lambda y.[\,] \\ \hline \textbf{thinks}(\textbf{likes}\ y\ \textbf{j})\textbf{m} \end{array}
\quad \overset{\textsc{lower}}{\Rightarrow} \quad
\begin{array}{c} \mathrm{DP}\bbslash\mathrm{S} \\ \textit{Mary thinks John likes}\ \_\_ \\ \lambda y.\textbf{thinks}(\textbf{likes}\ y\ \textbf{j})\textbf{m} \end{array}
$$

16. Prohibit gaps of the form $A /\!\!/ A$ when $A = ((B/C) \backslash\!\!\backslash D)$. If the subcategory beneath the lowest horizontal line has the form B/C, then the gap must be on a right branch. (This solution is incomplete, but can be generalized.)

17. Making the right-to-left variant of the combination schema available allows derivation of the ungrammatical superiority violation **What did who eat* __. Here is a derivation of the question body *did who eat* __, omitting *did* for clarity:

$$\begin{array}{c}\text{DP?S}|\text{S}\\ \hline \text{DP}\\ \textit{who}\\ \textbf{who}(\lambda x.[\,])\\ \hline x\end{array}\left(\begin{array}{c}\text{DP?S}|\text{DP?S}\\ \hline (\text{DP}\backslash\text{S})/\text{DP}\\ \textit{eat}\\ [\,]\\ \hline \textbf{eat}\end{array}\quad\begin{array}{c}\text{DP}\backslash\!\!\backslash(\text{DP?S})|\text{DP?S}\\ \hline \text{DP}\\ \_\_\\ \lambda y.[\,]\\ \hline y\end{array}\right)$$

$$=\begin{array}{c}\text{DP?S}|\text{S}\\ \hline \text{DP}\\ \textit{who}\\ \textbf{who}(\lambda x.[\,])\\ \hline x\end{array}\quad\begin{array}{c}\text{DP}\backslash\!\!\backslash(\text{DP?S})|\text{DP?S}\\ \hline \text{DP}\backslash\text{S}\\ \textit{eat}\,\_\_\\ \lambda y.[\,]\\ \hline \textbf{eat}\;y\end{array}=\begin{array}{c}\text{DP}\backslash\!\!\backslash(\text{DP?S})|\text{S}\\ \hline \text{S}\\ \textit{(did) who eat}\,\_\_\\ \lambda y.\textbf{who}(\lambda x.[\,])\\ \hline \textbf{eat}\;y\;x\end{array}\quad\begin{array}{c}\text{LOWER}\\ \Rightarrow\end{array}\quad\begin{array}{c}\text{DP}\backslash\!\!\backslash(\text{DP?S})\\ \textit{(did) who eat}\,\_\_\\ \lambda y.\textbf{who}(\lambda x.\textbf{eat}\;y\;x)\end{array}$$

Remember that the variant combination schema matches *outside* corners. This question body is ready to combine with the fronted instantiation of *what* given by $\lambda\kappa.\textbf{what}(\lambda x.\kappa x)$:$(\text{DP?(DP?S)})/(\text{DP}\backslash\!\!\backslash(\text{DP?S}))$.

18. This is primarily an exercise in using linear semantic values rather than semantic towers. It is necessary to LIFT the expressions *John*, *left*, and *slept* before beginning combination. For the sake of simple expressions, beta reduction has been performed at the earliest possible moment. For the schema for *and*, we instantiate $A = \text{DP}\backslash\text{S}$, and $B = \text{S}$.

$$\begin{array}{c}\text{S}|\text{S}\\ \hline \text{DP}\\ \textit{John}\\ \lambda\kappa.\kappa\textbf{j}\end{array}\left(\begin{array}{c}\text{S}|\text{S}\\ \hline \text{DP}\backslash\text{S}\\ \textit{left}\\ \lambda\kappa.\kappa\;\textbf{left}\end{array}\left(\begin{array}{c}\left(\left(\dfrac{\text{S}|\text{S}}{\text{DP}\backslash\text{S}}\Big\backslash\dfrac{\text{S}|\text{S}}{\text{DP}\backslash\text{S}}\right)\Big/\dfrac{\text{S}|\text{S}}{\text{DP}\backslash\text{S}}\right)\\ \textit{and}\\ \lambda rl\kappa.(l\kappa)\wedge(r\kappa)\end{array}\quad\begin{array}{c}\text{S}|\text{S}\\ \hline \text{DP}\backslash\text{S}\\ \textit{slept}\\ \lambda\kappa.\kappa\;\textbf{slept}\end{array}\right)\right)$$

$$=\begin{array}{c}\text{S}|\text{S}\\ \hline \text{DP}\\ \textit{John}\\ (\lambda\kappa.\kappa\textbf{j})\end{array}\quad\begin{array}{c}\text{S}|\text{S}\\ \hline \text{DP}\backslash\text{S}\\ \textit{left and slept}\\ (\lambda\kappa.(\kappa\;\textbf{left})\wedge(\kappa\;\textbf{slept}))\end{array}=\begin{array}{c}\text{S}|\text{S}\\ \hline \text{S}\\ \textit{John left and slept}\\ (\lambda\kappa.\kappa\;((\textbf{left}\;\textbf{j})\wedge(\textbf{slept}\;\textbf{j})))\end{array}$$

$$\begin{array}{c}\text{LOWER}\\ \Rightarrow\end{array}\quad\begin{array}{c}\text{S}\\ \textit{John left and slept}\\ (\textbf{left}\;\textbf{j})\wedge(\textbf{slept}\;\textbf{j})\end{array}$$

19. The point of this exercise is to make sure that coordinating a DP that lives at the individual level (type `t`) with a generalized quantifier goes smoothly.

$$\left(\begin{array}{c}\text{S}|\text{S}\\ \hline \text{DP}\\ \textit{John}\\ \lambda\kappa.\kappa\textbf{j}\end{array}\begin{array}{c}\left(\left(\dfrac{\text{S}|\text{S}}{\text{DP}}\Big\backslash\dfrac{\text{S}|\text{S}}{\text{DP}}\right)\Big/\dfrac{\text{S}|\text{S}}{\text{DP}}\right)\\ \textit{and}\\ \lambda rl\kappa.(l\kappa)\wedge(r\kappa)\end{array}\begin{array}{c}\text{S}|\text{S}\\ \hline \text{DP}\\ \textit{everyone}\\ \lambda\kappa.\forall x.\kappa x\end{array}\right)\begin{array}{c}\text{S}|\text{S}\\ \hline \text{DP}\backslash\text{S}\\ \textit{left}\\ \lambda\kappa.\kappa\;\textbf{left}\end{array}$$

$$= \begin{array}{c}\frac{\mathrm{S}|\mathrm{S}}{\mathrm{DP}} \\ \textit{John and everyone} \\ \lambda\kappa.(\kappa\mathbf{j}) \wedge (\forall x.\kappa x)\end{array} \quad \begin{array}{c}\frac{\mathrm{S}\,|\,\mathrm{S}}{\mathrm{DP\backslash S}} \\ \textit{left} \\ \lambda\kappa.\kappa\ \mathbf{left}\end{array} = \begin{array}{c}\frac{\mathrm{S}|\mathrm{S}}{\mathrm{DP}} \\ \textit{John and everyone left} \\ \lambda\kappa.\kappa\ \big((\mathbf{left\ j}) \wedge (\forall x.\mathbf{left}\ x)\big)\end{array} \quad \overset{\text{LOWER}}{\Rightarrow} \quad \begin{array}{c}\mathrm{S} \\ \textit{John and everyone left} \\ (\mathbf{left\ j}) \wedge (\forall x.\mathbf{left}\ x)\end{array}$$

The right conjunct entails the left conjunct. The interpretation is paraphrased by 'Not only John, but indeed, everyone, left'.

20. Argument Raising produces a shifted functor that takes the same number of arguments as the original; Value Raising produces a shifted functor that takes one more argument than the original. If we tried to modify Argument Raising to also add an extra argument, the shifted derivations would never resolve: as mentioned in the text, for every application of Value Raising that adds an argument place, there must be a corresponding application of Argument Raising higher in the structure to return the argument-place count to normal.

21. The type-shifter solution simply changes a trailing S^- to S: for all choices of A and B, shift $B /\!\!/ (A \backslash\!\!\backslash \mathrm{S}^-)$ to $B /\!\!/ (A \backslash\!\!\backslash \mathrm{S})$. This rule says in effect that an S^- is a kind of S, i.e., that the category S^- is contained within the category S. See Bernardi (2002), Bernardi and Szabolcsi (2008) for a more sophisticated approach to category inferences applied to negative polarity. As for the lexical ambiguity approach, we simply provide multiple lexical entries. The two approaches are compatible: we can imagine that the variant lexical entries are created by the type-shifter. The issue is a familiar one: can the type-shifter be limited in its domain to the lexicon, or must it be part of the active grammar? For instance, the FRONT type-shifter must be part of the active grammar, since the analysis of pied piping requires FRONT to apply to an expression that has been built up by merge operations. Are there parallel arguments for the issue here? There is yet a third solution, in which the LOWER type-shifter is adjusted to match either S in the top right corner or S^-. The next two exercises show that this third solution would be incomplete.

22.
$$\begin{array}{c}\frac{\mathrm{S}|\mathrm{S}^-}{\mathrm{DP}} \\ \textit{no one} \\ \frac{\neg\exists x.[\ ]}{x}\end{array} \left(\left(\begin{array}{c}\frac{\mathrm{S}^-\ |\ \mathrm{S}^-}{((\mathrm{DP\backslash S})/\mathrm{DP})/\mathrm{DP}} \\ \textit{gave} \\ \frac{[\ ]}{\mathbf{gave}}\end{array} \quad \begin{array}{c}\frac{\mathrm{S}^-|\mathrm{S}^-}{\mathrm{DP}} \\ \textit{anyone} \\ \frac{\exists y.[\ ]}{y}\end{array} \right) \begin{array}{c}\frac{\mathrm{S}^-|\mathrm{S}}{\mathrm{DP}} \\ \textit{anything} \\ \frac{\exists z.[\ ]}{z}\end{array} \right)$$

Conceptually what is going on is that *anyone* transmits the fact that it has been licensed to other negative polarity items downstream. Note that the trailing S^- of *anything* has been replaced by S by one of the mechanisms discussed in the answer to the previous exercise.

23.
$$\begin{array}{c}\frac{\mathrm{S}|\mathrm{S}}{\mathrm{DP}} \\ \textit{no one} \\ \frac{\neg\exists x.[\ ]}{x}\end{array} \left(\begin{array}{c}\frac{\mathrm{S}\ |\ \mathrm{S}^-}{(\mathrm{DP\backslash S})/\mathrm{S}} \\ \textit{doubts} \\ \frac{[\ ]}{\mathbf{doubts}}\end{array} \left(\begin{array}{c}\frac{\mathrm{S}^-|\mathrm{S}}{\mathrm{DP}} \\ \textit{anyone} \\ \frac{\exists y.[\ ]}{y}\end{array} \quad \begin{array}{c}\frac{\mathrm{S}\ |\ \mathrm{S}}{\mathrm{DP\backslash S}} \\ \textit{left} \\ \frac{[\ ]}{\mathbf{left}}\end{array} \right) \right)$$

This derivation is neutral across the two solutions proposed in the answer to exercise 15. Either there is a type-shifter that shifts the category of *no one* to $\mathrm{S} /\!\!/ (\mathrm{DP} \backslash\!\!\backslash \mathrm{S})$ and *anyone* to $\mathrm{S}^- /\!\!/ (\mathrm{DP} \backslash\!\!\backslash \mathrm{S})$, or else these two words have these categories as variant lexical items.

24.
$$
\begin{array}{c}\dfrac{\mathrm{S}|\mathrm{S}}{\mathrm{DP}}\\ \textit{a donkey}\\ \lambda\kappa.\exists x.\mathbf{donk}\,x \wedge \kappa x\end{array}
\left(\left(\left(\dfrac{\mathrm{S}|\mathrm{S}}{\mathrm{DP}}\Big\backslash\dfrac{\mathrm{S}|\mathrm{S}}{\mathrm{DP}}\right)\Big/\dfrac{\mathrm{S}|\mathrm{S}}{\mathrm{DP}}\right)
\begin{array}{c}\\ \textit{or}\\ \lambda rl\kappa.(l\kappa)\vee(r\kappa)\end{array}
\begin{array}{c}\dfrac{\mathrm{S}|\mathrm{S}}{\mathrm{DP}}\\ \textit{a goat}\\ \lambda\kappa.\exists y.\mathbf{goat}\,x \wedge \kappa x\end{array}\right)
$$

$$
= \begin{array}{c}\dfrac{\mathrm{S}|\mathrm{S}}{\mathrm{DP}}\\ \textit{a donkey or a goat}\\ \lambda\kappa.(\exists x.\mathbf{donk}\,x \wedge \kappa x)\vee(\exists y.\mathbf{goat}\,y\wedge\kappa y)\end{array}
$$

$$
\overset{\text{BIND}}{\Rightarrow}\quad \begin{array}{c}\dfrac{\mathrm{S}|\mathrm{DP}\rhd\mathrm{S}}{\mathrm{DP}}\\ \textit{a donkey or a goat}\\ \lambda\kappa.(\exists x.\mathbf{donk}\,x \wedge (\kappa xx))\vee(\exists y.\mathbf{goat}\,y\wedge(\kappa yy))\end{array}
$$

Combining this derivation with the simple case of donkey anaphora in (150):

$$
\begin{array}{c}\dfrac{\mathrm{S}\ |\ \mathrm{S}}{(\mathrm{S/S})/\mathrm{S}}\\ \textit{if}\\ \dfrac{\neg[\;]}{\lambda pq.p\wedge\neg q}\end{array}
\left(\begin{array}{c}\dfrac{\mathrm{S}|\mathrm{DP}\rhd\mathrm{S}}{\mathrm{DP}}\\ \textit{a donkey or a goat}\\ \dfrac{\left(\lambda R.\left(\begin{array}{c}(\exists x.\mathbf{donk}\,x\vee(Rxx))\vee\\(\exists y.\mathbf{goat}\,y\vee(Ryy))\end{array}\right)\right)(\lambda z.[\;])}{z}\end{array}
\begin{array}{c}\dfrac{\mathrm{DP}\rhd\mathrm{S}|\mathrm{DP}\rhd\mathrm{S}}{\mathrm{DP\backslash S}}\\ \textit{entered}\\ \dfrac{[\;]}{\mathbf{entered}}\end{array}\right)
\left(\begin{array}{c}\dfrac{\mathrm{DP}\rhd\mathrm{S}|\mathrm{S}}{\mathrm{S}}\\ \textit{it left}\\ \dfrac{\lambda x.[\;]}{\mathbf{left}\ x}\end{array}\right)
$$

$$
= \begin{array}{c}\dfrac{\mathrm{S}|\mathrm{S}}{\mathrm{S}}\\ \textit{If a donkey or a goat entered, it left}\\ \dfrac{\neg\left(\left(\lambda R.\left(\begin{array}{c}(\exists x.\mathbf{donk}\,x\wedge(Rxx))\vee\\(\exists y.\mathbf{goat}\,y\wedge(Ryy))\end{array}\right)\right)(\lambda zx.[\;])\right)}{(\mathbf{entered}\ z)\wedge\neg(\mathbf{left}x)}\end{array}
\overset{\text{LOWER}}{\Rightarrow}
\begin{array}{c}\mathrm{S}\\ \textit{If a donkey or a goat entered, it left}\\ \neg\left(\begin{array}{c}(\exists x.\mathbf{donk}\,x\wedge((\mathbf{entered}\ x)\wedge\neg(\mathbf{left}\ x)))\\ \vee(\exists y.\mathbf{goat}\,y\wedge((\mathbf{entered}\ y)\wedge\neg(\mathbf{left}\ y)))\end{array}\right)\end{array}
$$

We have adjusted the form of the semantic value of *a donkey or a goat* in order to be able to display it as a semantic tower. Crucially, the outer negation of the *if* takes scope over the disjunction. The net truth conditions on this construal says that there is no donkey who entered without leaving, and there is no goat who entered without leaving.

25. $((\mathrm{S\backslash S})\backslash\!\!\backslash\mathrm{S})/\!\!/((\mathrm{S\backslash S})\backslash\!\!\backslash\mathrm{S})$

26.
$$
\begin{array}{c}\dfrac{\mathrm{DP}\backslash\!\!\backslash\mathrm{S}|\mathrm{S}}{\mathrm{DP}}\\ \text{—}\\ \dfrac{\lambda y.[\;]}{y}\end{array}
\left(\begin{array}{c}\dfrac{\mathrm{S}\ |\ \mathrm{S}}{(\mathrm{DP\backslash S})/\mathrm{DP}}\\ \textit{owns}\\ \dfrac{[\;]}{\mathbf{owns}}\end{array}
\left(\lambda P.\begin{array}{c}\dfrac{\mathrm{S}|\mathrm{S}}{\mathrm{DP}}\Big/\mathrm{N}\\ \textit{a}\\ \dfrac{\exists x.\,Px\wedge[\;]}{x}\end{array}
\begin{array}{c}\mathrm{N}\\ \textit{donkey}\\ \mathbf{donkey}\\ \\ \end{array}\right)\right)
$$

$$
\overset{\text{BIND}}{\Rightarrow}\quad
\begin{array}{c}\dfrac{\mathrm{DP}\backslash\!\!\backslash\mathrm{S}|\mathrm{S}}{\mathrm{DP}}\\ \text{—}\\ \dfrac{\lambda y.[\;]}{y}\end{array}
\left(\begin{array}{c}\dfrac{\mathrm{S}\ |\ \mathrm{S}}{(\mathrm{DP\backslash S})/\mathrm{DP}}\\ \textit{owns}\\ \dfrac{[\;]}{\mathbf{owns}}\end{array}
\begin{array}{c}\dfrac{\mathrm{S}|\mathrm{DP}\rhd\mathrm{S}}{\mathrm{DP}}\\ \textit{a donkey}\\ \dfrac{\exists x.\,\mathbf{donk}\,x\wedge([\;]\,x)}{x}\end{array}\right)
=
\begin{array}{c}\dfrac{\mathrm{DP}\backslash\!\!\backslash\mathrm{S}|\mathrm{S}}{\mathrm{DP}}\\ \text{—}\\ \dfrac{\lambda y.[\;]}{y}\end{array}
\begin{array}{c}\dfrac{\mathrm{S}|\mathrm{DP}\rhd\mathrm{S}}{\mathrm{DP\backslash S}}\\ \textit{owns a donkey}\\ \dfrac{\exists x.\,\mathbf{donk}\,x\wedge([\;]\,x)}{\mathbf{owns}\ x}\end{array}
$$

$$\overset{\textsc{lift,lift}}{\Rightarrow}\quad \begin{array}{c} \text{S}\ |\ \text{S} \\ \hline \text{DP}\mathbin{\backslash\!\!\backslash}\text{S}\ |\ \text{S} \\ \hline \text{DP} \\ \_\_ \\ [\ ] \\ \hline \lambda y.[\ ] \\ \hline y \end{array} \qquad \begin{array}{c} \text{S}\ |\ \text{DP} \rhd \text{S} \\ \hline \text{S}\ |\ \text{S} \\ \hline \text{DP}\backslash\text{S} \\ \textit{owns a donkey} \\ \exists x.\,\textbf{donk}\,x \wedge ([\ ]\,x) \\ \hline [\ ] \\ \hline \textbf{owns}\ x \end{array} \quad \overset{\textsc{lower}}{\Rightarrow} \quad \begin{array}{c} \text{S}\ |\ \text{DP} \rhd \text{S} \\ \hline \text{DP}\mathbin{\backslash\!\!\backslash}\text{S} \\ \_\_\ \textit{owns a donkey} \\ \exists x.\,\textbf{donk}\,x \wedge ([\ ]\,x) \\ \hline \lambda y.\textbf{owns}\ x\ y \end{array}$$

Note that we apply LIFT to the entire gap expression, but only to the lower part of the binder *a donkey*. This is what enables the indefinite to take scope wider than the relative clause. We complete the derivation of *farmer who __ owns a donkey* by using the same lexical entries for *farmer* and for the relative pronoun who_{rel} given in (183), except that they must each undergo LIFT (choosing $B = \text{S}$) in order to combine with the version of __ *owns a donkey* derived here.

27. The easiest way is just to add another layer:

$$\begin{array}{c} \begin{array}{c} \text{S}\ |\ \text{DP} \rhd \text{S} \\ \hline \text{S}\ |\ \text{DP} \rhd \text{S} \\ \hline \text{DP} \end{array} \Big/ \begin{array}{c} \text{S}\ |\ \text{DP} \rhd \text{S} \\ \hline \text{S}\ |\ \text{DP} \rhd \text{S} \\ \hline \text{N} \end{array} \\ \textit{every} \\ \begin{array}{c} \neg\exists x.g[\lambda y.Px \wedge \neg([\ ]y)] \\ \hline i[\ ] \\ \hline x \end{array} \Big/ \begin{array}{c} g[\ ] \\ \hline i[\ ] \\ \hline P \end{array} \end{array}$$

The middle layer can be repeated for as many layers as desired. Another strategy would be to give pronouns the schematic category $(\text{DP} \rhd A)/\!\!/(\text{DP}\backslash\!\!\backslash A)$, which would allow stacking any number of binders on a single layer (other changes would be needed to make this work).

28. We're aiming for a bound reading of *Someone*$_i$ *called every boy who met her*$_i$.

$$\begin{array}{c} \text{S}\ |\ \text{DP} \rhd \text{S} \\ \hline \text{S}\ |\ \text{S} \\ \hline \text{DP} \\ \textit{Someone} \\ \forall z.([\ ]\,z) \\ \hline [\ ] \\ \hline z \end{array} \left(\begin{array}{c} \text{DP} \rhd \text{S}\ |\ \text{DP} \rhd \text{S} \\ \hline \text{S}\ |\ \text{S} \\ \hline (\text{DP}\backslash\text{S})/\text{DP} \\ \textit{called} \\ [\ ] \\ \hline [\ ] \\ \hline \textbf{called} \end{array} \left(\begin{array}{c} \text{DP} \rhd \text{S}\ |\ \text{DP} \rhd \text{S} \\ \hline \dfrac{\text{S}\ |\ \text{S}}{\text{DP}} \Big/ \text{N} \\ \textit{every} \\ [\ ] \\ \hline \lambda P.\ \dfrac{\forall x.\ Px \rightarrow [\ ]}{x} \end{array} \quad \begin{array}{c} \text{DP} \rhd \text{S}\ |\ \text{S} \\ \hline \text{N} \\ \textit{boy who \_\_ met her} \\ \lambda y.\,[\ ] \\ \hline \lambda x.\textbf{boy}\,x \wedge (\textbf{met}\,y\,x) \end{array} \right)\right)$$

The quantifier *someone* first undergoes the BIND typshifter, then *LIFT* applies to its lower level. The truth conditions give *someone* wide scope: there is a person z such that z called every boy who met z.

29. • The geach rule (e.g., Jacobson 1999:120) says that if a functor combines with an argument containing a pronominal dependency, then the resulting expression will contain a pronominal dependency. Translated into our notation:

$$\begin{array}{ccc} A/B & \mathbf{g} & \dfrac{D \rhd C \mid D \rhd C}{A/B} \\ exp & \Rightarrow & exp \\ f & & \dfrac{[\,]}{f} \end{array}$$

That is, if A/B is the category of an expression that is about to combine with an argument that does not contain any pronouns, then $\dfrac{D \rhd C \mid D \rhd C}{A/B}$ is the category the expression would need to have in order to be able to combine with an argument containing one pronominal dependency in a way that transmits the dependency to the larger expression. But this, of course, is just a special case of our LIFT. • As for Right Node Raising, we'll discuss a simpler derivation that contains all of the essential moves, namely, *Betty loves, but Mary hates, her mother.* Jacobson's analysis of Right Node Raising depends on the free availability of function composition (which Jacobson sometimes calls 'compose', e.g., Jacobson (1999:120)). Unlike most combinatory categorial grammars (and, looking ahead to Part II, unlike most type-logical grammars), the grammars in this book do not make use of function composition. This is not because we think function composition is not a necessary tool—indeed, it is necessary for a number of coordination constructions, including Right Node Raising (see Kubota and Levine 2012, Kubota 2013 for a recent discussion). Rather, it is because we want to emphasize that nothing in our system depends on function composition. But for the purposes of this exercise, we need function composition. And, just like Jacobson, and Steedman (2000, 2012), in order for function composition to work, we need the following two type-shifters:

$$\begin{array}{ccc} \mathrm{A} & \textbf{lift} & \mathrm{B}/(\mathrm{A}\backslash\mathrm{B}) \\ exp & \Rightarrow & exp \\ x & & \lambda f.fx \end{array} \qquad \begin{array}{ccc} A/B & \textbf{compose} & (\mathrm{A}/\mathrm{C})/(\mathrm{B}/\mathrm{C}) \\ exp & \Rightarrow & exp \\ f & & \lambda gx.f(gx) \end{array}$$

Of course, *lift* is just our LIFT generalized to the merge modality.

$$\begin{array}{ccccccccc} \mathrm{DP} & \text{LIFT} & \dfrac{\mathrm{S} \mid \mathrm{S}}{\mathrm{DP}} & \text{BIND} & \dfrac{\mathrm{S} \mid \mathrm{DP} \rhd \mathrm{S}}{\mathrm{DP}} & \textbf{lift} & \dfrac{\mathrm{S} \mid \mathrm{DP} \rhd \mathrm{S}}{\mathrm{S}/(\mathrm{DP}\backslash\mathrm{S})} & \textbf{compose} & \dfrac{\mathrm{S} \mid \mathrm{DP} \rhd \mathrm{S}}{(\mathrm{S}/\mathrm{DP})/((\mathrm{DP}\backslash\mathrm{S})/\mathrm{DP})} \\ Mary & \Rightarrow & Mary & \Rightarrow & Mary & \Rightarrow & Mary & \Rightarrow & Mary \\ \mathbf{m} & & \dfrac{[\,]}{\mathbf{m}} & & \dfrac{[\,]\,\mathbf{m}}{\mathbf{m}} & & \dfrac{[\,]\,\mathbf{m}}{\lambda f.f\mathbf{m}} & & \dfrac{[\,]\,\mathbf{m}}{\lambda gx.gx\mathbf{m}} \end{array}$$

With this derived expression, we can continue:

$$\left(\left(\dfrac{\mathrm{S} \mid \mathrm{DP} \rhd \mathrm{S}}{\mathrm{S}/\mathrm{DP}} \Bigg\backslash \dfrac{\mathrm{S} \mid \mathrm{DP} \rhd \mathrm{S}}{\mathrm{S}/\mathrm{DP}}\right) \Bigg/ \dfrac{\mathrm{S} \mid \mathrm{DP} \rhd \mathrm{S}}{\mathrm{S}/\mathrm{DP}}\right) \left(\begin{array}{cc} \dfrac{\mathrm{S} \mid \mathrm{DP} \rhd \mathrm{S}}{(\mathrm{S}/\mathrm{DP})/((\mathrm{DP}\backslash\mathrm{S})/\mathrm{DP})} & \dfrac{\mathrm{DP} \rhd \mathrm{S} \mid \mathrm{DP} \rhd \mathrm{S}}{(\mathrm{DP}\backslash\mathrm{S})/\mathrm{DP}} \\ Mary & hates \\ \dfrac{[\,]\,\mathbf{m}}{\lambda gx.gx\mathbf{m}} & \dfrac{[\,]}{\mathbf{hates}} \end{array}\right)$$

$$\begin{array}{c} but \\ \lambda rl\kappa.(l\kappa) \wedge (r\kappa) \end{array}$$

The rest of the derivation is routine. The net truth conditions require that Betty loves Betty's mother, but Mary hates Mary's mother. The point is more compelling with quantificational binders, and the derivation is only mildly more complex. In any case, there is no difficulty distributing a pronoun-containing argument across coordinated binders. • In order to arrive at an account of paycheck pronouns, all we need to do is instantiate the pronoun schema $(A \rhd B) /\!\!/ (A \backslash\!\!\backslash B)$ with a choice for A that allows an upstream DP to bind into it. Here, the choice will be $A = \text{pn} = \dfrac{\text{DP} \rhd \text{S} \mid \text{S}}{\text{DP}}$, with $B = \text{S}$. We're aiming at a paycheck interpretation for *Mary spent it* on which it can mean 'Mary spent her paycheck':

$$\begin{array}{c} \begin{array}{c|c} \text{pn} \rhd \text{S} & \text{pn} \rhd \text{S} \\ \hline \text{S} & \text{DP} \rhd \text{S} \end{array} \\ \hline \text{DP} \\ \textit{Mary} \\ \underline{[\ ]} \\ \underline{[\ ]\,\mathbf{m}} \\ \mathbf{m} \end{array} \left(\begin{array}{c} \begin{array}{c|c} \text{pn} \rhd \text{S} & \text{pn} \rhd \text{S} \\ \hline \text{DP} \rhd \text{S} & \text{DP} \rhd \text{S} \end{array} \\ \hline (\text{DP}\backslash\text{S})/\text{DP} \\ \textit{spent} \\ \underline{[\ ]} \\ \underline{[\ ]} \\ \mathbf{spent} \end{array} \quad \begin{array}{c} \begin{array}{c|c} \text{pn} \rhd \text{S} & \text{S} \\ \hline \text{DP} \rhd \text{S} & \text{S} \end{array} \\ \hline \text{DP} \\ \textit{it} \\ \underline{\lambda f.[\ ]} \\ \underline{\lambda x.[\ ]} \\ fx \end{array} \right) \begin{array}{c} \text{LOWER,LOWER} \\ \Rightarrow \end{array} \quad \begin{array}{c} \text{pn} \rhd \text{S} \\ \textit{Mary spent it} \\ \lambda f.\mathbf{spent}(f\mathbf{m})\ \mathbf{m} \end{array}$$

Just like an unbound ordinary pronoun, a sentence with this final category is a request from the pragmatic context to supply a value for the pn dependency, which semantically will be a function of type $\mathsf{e} \to \mathsf{e}$. Like Jacobson, in order to get the desired interpretation, we need only assume that the paycheck function was made salient from previous discourse.

30. We proceed exactly as for the call-by-name case, except that we use the call-by-value translation.

$$\begin{aligned} ([(\lambda x\mathrm{I})\Omega]\mathrm{I}) &= (\underline{(\lambda\kappa.[\lambda x\mathrm{I}](\lambda m.[\Omega](\lambda n.mn\kappa)))\mathrm{I}}) \\ &= ([\lambda x\mathrm{I}](\lambda m.[\Omega](\lambda n.mn\mathrm{I}))) \\ &= (\underline{(\lambda\kappa.\kappa(\lambda x[\mathrm{I}]))(\lambda m.[\Omega](\lambda n.mn\mathrm{I}))}) \\ &= (\underline{(\lambda m.[\Omega](\lambda n.mn\mathrm{I}))(\lambda x[\mathrm{I}])}) \\ &= ([\Omega](\lambda n.(\lambda x[\mathrm{I}])n\mathrm{I})) \end{aligned}$$

We still have a way to go here, but it's clear that it is always the leftmost redex that is simulated next. Since we now have the infinite loop Ω in leftmost position, the reduction is doomed.

31. Let L and R be the categories of two expressions that we are trying to combine. The Slash, Backslash, and Front rules will contribute at most one way each of producing a combined expression. If neither L nor R have more than one level, we are done (base case). If L has more than one layer, choose D, E, and A such that $L = \dfrac{D \mid E}{A}$. Assume that there are only a finite number of ways of combining A and R (recursive assumption). Then the LiftRight clause will contribute at most one new way of combining L and R for each way of combining A and R. Symmetrically for R and LiftLeft. If both L and R have more than one layer, then the Combination rule will contribute at most one new way of combining L and R for each way of combining proper subparts of parts of L and R. In each case, the recursive assumption involved two categories that had a strictly smaller number of layers than the original L and R. Eventually, the recursion will arrive at the case where L and R each have only one level, and we've reached the base case. At this point in our reasoning, we need only consider the Lower rule. In order to

execute the Lower rule, we can wait until all of the other ways of combining L and R have been found. Then the Lower rule will contribute at most one new way of combining L and R for each old way of combining them. The new way may itself trigger the side condition for the Lower rule; but since the new way involves a category that has a strictly smaller number of layers than the original way of combining L and R, the total number of new ways of combining L and R via the Lower rule must be finite.

32. Binding and NPI licensing require that a syntactic part of the dependent element match a syntactic part of the element that is doing the binding or the licensing. The only combination rules that require matching of any kind between parts of the two towers being combined are Slash, Backslash, Lower, and the Combination rule. Clearly, Slash and Backslash operate only on the bottom layer, and so are not relevant for binding and NPI licensing, which always take place on higher layers. The Lower rule does require matching, but only on different layers, and so is also irrelevant. But if the Lower rule is adjusted so that it is triggered by any matching categories, i.e.:

$$\begin{array}{c} \dfrac{A|B}{B} \\ \textit{phrase} \\ \dfrac{f[\ ]}{x} \end{array} \quad \overset{\text{LOWER}'}{\Rightarrow} \quad \begin{array}{c} A \\ \textit{phrase} \\ f[x] \end{array}$$

where B is allowed to be any category, then binding and NPI licensing become possible again. Unfortunately, so does crossover:

$$\begin{array}{c} \dfrac{S \,|\, S}{DP \rhd S \,|\, S} \\ DP \\ \textit{he} \\ \dfrac{[\ ]}{\lambda x.[\ ]} \\ x \end{array} \left(\begin{array}{c} \dfrac{S \,|\, S}{S \,|\, S} \\ (DP\backslash S)/DP \\ \textit{loves} \\ \dfrac{[\ ]}{[\ ]} \\ \textbf{loves} \end{array} \quad \begin{array}{c} \dfrac{S \,|\, DP \rhd S}{S \,|\, S} \\ DP \\ \textit{everyone} \\ \dfrac{\forall y.[\ ]\,y}{[\ ]} \\ y \end{array} \right) = \begin{array}{c} \dfrac{S \,|\, DP \rhd S}{DP \rhd S \,|\, S} \\ S \\ \textit{He loves everyone} \\ \dfrac{\forall y.[\ ]\,y}{\lambda x.[\ ]} \\ \textbf{loves}\ y\ x \end{array}$$

$$\overset{\text{LOWER}}{\Rightarrow} \begin{array}{c} \dfrac{S \,|\, DP \rhd S}{DP \rhd S} \\ \textit{He loves everyone} \\ \dfrac{\forall y.[\ ]\,y}{\lambda x.\textbf{loves}\ y\ x} \end{array} \quad \overset{\text{LOWER}'}{\Rightarrow} \quad \begin{array}{c} S \\ \textit{He loves everyone} \\ \forall y.\textbf{loves}\ y\ y \end{array}$$

As for re-introducing an evaluation order asymmetry, there are endless possibilities. For instance, note that a legitimate binding/licensing configuration can be localized to the combination of two adjacent expressions, such that the binder/licensor category is on the right-hand edge of the rightmost category, and the bindee/licensee category is one level lower on the on the left-hand edge of the leftmost expression.

Here are derivations of the six readings of *Someone gave everyone nothing* that do not make use of the Combination rule. Note that all of the derivations require three continuation layers, i.e., they all finish with three applications of Lower.

```
exists > forall > nothing:
someone gave everyone nothing S Lower LiftR Lower LiftL Lower LiftL
   Backlash someone (S//(DP\\S))
   gave everyone nothing (S//((S//((DP\S)\\S))\\S)) LiftRight LiftLeft
     Slash gave everyone (S//(((DP\S)/DP)\\S)) LiftLeft Slash
       gave (((DP\S)/DP)/DP)
       everyone (S//(DP\\S))
     nothing (S//(DP\\S))
forall > exists > nothing:
someone gave everyone nothing S Lower LiftL Lower LiftR Lower LiftL
   Backlash someone (S//(DP\\S))
   gave everyone nothing (S//((S//((DP\S)\\S))\\S)) LiftRight LiftLeft
     Slash gave everyone (S//(((DP\S)/DP)\\S))
       gave (((DP\S)/DP)/DP)
       everyone (S//(DP\\S))
     nothing (S//(DP\\S))
forall > nothing > exists:
someone gave everyone nothing S Lower LiftL Lower LiftL Lower LiftR
   Backlash someone (S//(DP\\S))  exists
   gave everyone nothing (S//((S//((DP\S)\\S))\\S)) LiftRight LiftLeft
     Slash gave everyone (S//(((DP\S)/DP)\\S)) LiftLeft Slash
       gave (((DP\S)/DP)/DP)
       everyone (S//(DP\\S))
     nothing (S//(DP\\S))
exists > nothing > forall:
someone gave everyone nothing S Lower LiftR Lower LiftL Lower LiftL
   Backlash someone (S//(DP\\S))
   gave everyone nothing (S//((S//((DP\S)\\S))\\S)) LiftLeft LiftRight
     Slash gave everyone (S//(((DP\S)/DP)\\S)) LiftLeft Slash
       gave (((DP\S)/DP)/DP)
       everyone (S//(DP\\S))
     nothing (S//(DP\\S))
nothing > exists > forall:
someone gave everyone nothing S Lower LiftL Lower LiftR Lower LiftL
   Backlash someone (S//(DP\\S))
   gave everyone nothing (S//((S//((DP\S)\\S))\\S)) LiftLeft LiftRight
     Slash gave everyone (S//(((DP\S)/DP)\\S)) LiftLeft Slash
       gave (((DP\S)/DP)/DP)
       everyone (S//(DP\\S))
     nothing (S//(DP\\S))
```

```
nothing > forall > exists:
someone gave everyone nothing S Lower LiftL Lower LiftL Lower LiftR
   Backlash someone (S//(DP\\S))
   gave everyone nothing (S//((S//((DP\S)\\S))\\S)) LiftLeft LiftRight
     Slash gave everyone (S//(((DP\S)/DP)\\S)) LiftLeft Slash
       gave (((DP\S)/DP)/DP)
       everyone (S//(DP\\S))
     nothing (S//(DP\\S))
```

Bibliography

AnderBois, Scott. 2011. Sluicing as anaphora to issues. In *Proceedings of SALT*, 20, 451–470.

Baker, Carl Leroy. 1968. Indirect questions in English. Ph.D. thesis, University of Illinois.

Bar-Hillel, Yehoshua. 1953. A quasi-arithmetical notation for syntactic description. *Language* 29(1):47–58.

Barendregt, Henk P. 1981. *The lambda calculus: Its syntax and semantics*. Amsterdam: Elsevier.

Bargmann, Sascha, Christopher Götze, Thomas Weskott, Anke Holler, and Gert Webelhuth. 2013. An empirical investigation into binding-theoretic reconsruction effects in restrictive relative clauses of German. University of Frankfurt and Göttingen manuscript.

Barker, Chris. 2001. Continuations: In-situ quantification without storage or type-shifting. In Hastings et al. (2001).

Barker, Chris. 2002. Continuations and the nature of quantification. *Natural Language Semantics* 10(3):211–242.

Barker, Chris. 2004. Continuations in natural language. In *CW'04: Proceedings of the 4th ACM SIGPLAN continuations workshop*, ed. Hayo Thielecke, 1–11. Tech. Rep. CSR-04-1, School of Computer Science, University of Birmingham.

Barker, Chris. 2005. Remark on Jacobson 1999: Crossover as a local constraint. *Linguistics and Philosophy* 28(4):447–472.

Barker, Chris. 2007. Parasitic scope. *Linguistics and Philosophy* 30(4):407–444.

Barker, Chris. 2009. Reconstruction as delayed evaluation. In *Theory and evidence in semantics*, eds. Erhard W. Hinrichs and John A. Nerbonne, 1–28. Center for the Study of Language and Information, Stanford University.

Barker, Chris. 2012. Quantificational binding does not require c-command. *Linguistic Inquiry* 43(4):614–633.

Barker, Chris. 2013. Scopability and sluicing. *Linguistics and Philosophy* 36(3):187–223.

Barker, Chris. 2014a. Evaluation order, crossover, and reconstruction. New York University manuscript.

Barker, Chris. 2014b. Scope. In *Handbook of contemporary semantic theory, 2nd edition*, eds. Shalom Lappin and Chris Fox. Oxford: Blackwell.

Barker, Chris, Raffaella Bernardi, and Chung-chieh Shan. 2010. Principles of interdimensional meaning interaction. In *Proceedings from Semantics and Linguistic Theory XX*, eds. Nan Li and David Lutz, 109–127. Ithaca: Cornell University Press.

Barker, Chris, and Pauline Jacobson. 2007. Introduction: Direct compositionality. In *Direct compositionality*, eds. Chris Barker and Pauline Jacobson, 1–19. New York: Oxford University Press.

Barker, Chris, and Chung-chieh Shan. 2006. Types as graphs: Continuations in type-logical grammar. *Journal of Logic, Language and Information* 15(4):331–370.

Barker, Chris, and Chung-chieh Shan. 2008. Donkey anaphora is in-scope binding. *Semantics and Pragmatics* 1(1):1–46.

Barros, Matthew. 2013. Harmonic sluicing: Which remnant/correlate pairs work, and why. In *Proceedings of SALT* 23, 295–315.

Barwise, Jon, and Robin Cooper. 1981. Generalized quantifiers and natural language. *Linguistics and Philosophy* 4:159–219.

Bastenhof, Arno. 2012. Polarities in logic and semantics. In *Logic, language and meaning*, 230–239. Berlin: Springer.

Bastenhof, Arno. 2013. Categorial symmetry. Ph.D. thesis, Utrecht University.

Bäuerle, Rainer, Christoph Schwarze, and Arnim von Stechow, eds. 1983. *Meaning, use and interpretation of language*. Berlin: Walter de Gruyter.

Beck, Sigrid. 2000. The semantics of different: Comparison operator and relational adjective. *Linguistics and Philosophy* 23(2):101–139.

Bekki, Daisuke, and Kenichi Asai. 2009. Representing covert movements by delimited continuations. In *Proceedings of the 6th international workshop on logic and engineering of natural language semantics*. Japanese Society of Artificial Intelligence.

Ben-Avi, Gilad, and Yoad Winter. 2007. A modular approach to intensionality. In *Proceedings of Sinn und Bedeutung 11 (2006)*, ed. Estela Puig-Waldmüller. Barcelona, Spain: Universitat Pompeu Fabra.

Berman, Stephen. 1987. Situation-based semantics for adverbs of quantification. *University of Massachusetts Occasional Papers* 12:45–68.

Bernardi, Raffaella. 2002. Reasoning with polarity in categorial type logic. Ph.D. thesis, Utrecht Institute of Linguistics (OTS), Utrecht University.

Bernardi, Raffaella, and Michael Moortgat. 2007. Continuation semantics for symmetric categorial grammar. In *Proceedings of WoLLIC'2007: 14th workshop on logic, language, information and computation*, 53–71. Lecture Notes in Computer Science 4576, Berlin: Springer.

Bernardi, Raffaella, and Michael Moortgat. 2010. Continuation semantics for the Lambek-Grishin calculus. *Information and Computation* 208(5):397–416.

Bernardi, Raffaella, and Richard Moot. 2001. Generalized quantifiers in declarative and interrogative sentences. *Journal of Language and Computation* 1(3):1–19.

Bernardi, Raffaella, and Anna Szabolcsi. 2008. Optionality, scope, and licensing: An application of partially ordered categories. *Journal of Logic, Language and Information* 17(3).

Brasoveanu, Adrian. 2007. Structured nominal and modal reference. Ph.D. thesis, Rutgers, The State University of New Jersey.

Brasoveanu, Adrian. 2011. Sentence-internal *different* as quantifier-internal anaphora. *Linguistics and Philosophy* 34(2):93–168.

Brasoveanu, Adrian, and Donka F Farkas. 2011. How indefinites choose their scope. *Linguistics and Philosophy* 34(1):1–55.

Bresnan, Joan. 1994. Linear order vs. syntactic rank: Evidence from weak crossover. In *CLS 30-1: The main session*. Chicago Linguistic Society.

Bresnan, Joan. 1998. Morphology competes with syntax: Explaining typological variation in weak crossover effects. In *Is the best good enough? Optimality and competition in syntax*, eds. Pilar Barbosa, Danny Fox, Paul Hagstrom, Martha McGinnis, and David Pesetsky, 59–92. Cambridge: MIT Press.

Brody, Michael, and Anna Szabolcsi. 2003. Overt scope in Hungarian. *Syntax* 6(1):19–51.

Bumford, Dylan. 2013. Incremental quantification. New York University unpublished manuscript.

Bumford, Dylan, and Chris Barker. 2013. Association with distributivity and the problem of multiple antecedents for singular *different*. *Linguistics and Philosophy* 36(5): 355–369.

Büring, Daniel. 2001. A situation semantics for binding out of DP. In Hastings et al. (2001), 56–75.

Büring, Daniel. 2004. Crossover situations. *Natural Language Semantics* 12(1):23–62.

Büring, Daniel. 2005. *Binding theory*. Cambridge University Press.

Carlson, Greg N. 1987. Same and different: Some consequences for syntax and semantics. *Linguistics and Philosophy* 10(4):531–565.

Charlow, Simon. 2009. Inverse linking, superiority, and QR. Submitted to the ESSLLI student session.

Charlow, Simon. 2010. Two kinds of binding out of DP. Talk handout, NYU Linguistics.

Charlow, Simon. 2014. On the semantics of exceptional scope. Ph.D. thesis, New York University.

Chierchia, Gennaro. 1991. Functional WH and weak crossover. In *Proceedings of the 10th West Coast Conference on Formal Linguistics*, ed. Dawn Bates, 75–90. Stanford, CA: Center for the Study of Language and Information.

Chierchia, Gennaro. 1993. Questions with quantifiers. *Natural Language Semantics* 1(2):181–234.

Chierchia, Gennaro. 1995. *The dynamics of meaning: Anaphora, presupposition, and the theory of grammar*. Chicago: University of Chicago Press.

Chierchia, Gennaro. 2013. *Logic in grammar: Polarity, free choice, and intervention*. Oxford University Press.

Chomsky, Noam. 1973. Conditions on transformations. In *A festschrift for Morris Halle*, eds. Stephen R. Anderson and Paul Kiparsky, 232–286. New York: Holt, Rinehart and Winston.

Chung, Sandra. 2013. Syntactic identity in sluicing: How much and why. *Linguistic Inquiry* 44(1): 1–44.

Chung, Sandra, William A Ladusaw, and James McCloskey. 1995. Sluicing and logical form. *Natural Language Semantics* 3(3):239–282.

Ciardelli, Ivano, Jeroen Groenendijk, and Floris Roelofsen. 2009. Attention! *might* in inquisitive semantics. In *Proceedings of SALT*, vol. 19, 91–108.

Collins, Chris, and Paul M. Postal. 2014. *Classical neg raising*. Cambridge: MIT Press.

Comorovski, Ileana. 1996. *Interrogative phrases and the syntax-semantics interface*. Dordrecht: Kluwer.

Cresti, Diana. 1995. Extraction and reconstruction. *Natural Language Semantics* 3:79–122.

Curien, Pierre-Louis, and Hugo Herbelin. 2000. The duality of computation. In *ICFP '00: Proceedings of the ACM international conference on functional programming*, vol. 35(9) of *ACM SIGPLAN Notices*, 233–243. New York: ACM Press.

Danvy, Olivier, and Andrzej Filinski. 1989. A functional abstraction of typed contexts. Tech. Rep. 89/12, DIKU, University of Copenhagen, Denmark. <http://www.daimi.au.dk/~danvy/Papers/fatc.ps.gz> (Accessed: May 17, 2014).

Danvy, Olivier, and Andrzej Filinski. 1990. Abstracting control. In *Proceedings of the 1990 ACM conference on Lisp and functional programming*, 151–160. New York: ACM Press.

Dayal, Veneeta. 1995. Licensing any in non-negative/non-modal contexts. In *Proceedings of SALT 5*, 72–93.

Dayal, Veneeta. 1996. *Locality in wh quantification: Questions and relative clauses in Hindi*. Dordrecht: Kluwer.

Dayal, Veneeta. 1998. *Any* as inherently modal. *Linguistics and Philosophy* 21(5):433–476.

Dayal, Veneeta, and Roger Schwarzschild. 2010. Definite inner antecedents and wh-correlates in sluices. *Rutgers Working Papers in Linguistics* 3:92–114.

Dekker, Paul J.E. 2012. *Dynamic semantics*, vol. 91. Berlin: Springer.

Dowty, David R. 1985. A unified indexical analysis of *same* and *different*: A response to Stump and Carlson. Paper presented at *University of Texas workshop on syntax and semantics, Austin, Texas* March 22–24.

Dowty, David R. 1994. The role of negative polarity and concord marking in natural language reasoning. In *Proceedings from Semantics and Linguistic Theory IV*, eds. Mandy Harvey and Lynn Santelmann. Ithaca: Cornell University Press.

Dowty, David R. 2007. Compositionality as an empirical problem. In *Direct compositionality*, eds. Chris Barker and Pauline Jacobson, 23–101. Oxford University Press.

van Eijck, Jan, and Christina Unger. 2010. *Computational semantics with functional programming*. Cambridge: Cambridge University Press.

Elbourne, Paul. 2006. *Situations and individuals*. Cambridge: MIT Press.

Elbourne, Paul. 2009. Bishop sentences and donkey cataphora: A response to Barker and Shan. *Semantics and Pragmatics* 2(1):1–7.

Evans, Gareth. 1977. Pronouns, quantifiers, and relative clauses (i). *Canadian Journal of Philosophy* 7(3):467–536.

Evans, Gareth. 1980. Pronouns. *Linguistic Inquiry* 11(2):337–362.

Farkas, Donka. 2003. Quantifier scope and syntactic islands. In *Semantics*, vol. 2. *Generalized quantifiers and scope*, ed. Javier Gutiérrez-Rexach. New York: Routledge.

Felleisen, Matthias. 1987. The calculi of λ_v-CS conversion: A syntactic theory of control and state in imperative higher-order programming languages. Ph.D. thesis, Computer Science Department, Indiana University. Also as Tech. Rep. 226.

Fry, John. 1997. Negative polarity licensing at the syntax-semantics interface. In *Proceedings of the 35th annual meeting of the Association for Computational Linguistics and 8th conference of the European chapter of the Association for Computational Linguistics*, eds. Philip R. Cohen and Wolfgang Wahlster, 144–150. San Francisco, CA: Morgan Kaufmann.

Fry, John. 1999. Proof nets and negative polarity licensing. In *Semantics and syntax in Lexical Functional Grammar: The resource logic approach*, ed. Mary Dalrymple, chap. 3, 91–116. Cambridge: MIT Press.

Gazdar, Gerald. 1980. A cross-categorial semantics for coordination. *Linguistics and Philosophy* 3(3):407–409.

Geurts, Bart. 1996. On *no*. *Journal of Semantics* 13(1):67–86.

Giannakidou, Anastasia. 2011. Positive polarity items and negative polarity items: Variation, licensing, and compositionality. In *Semantics: An international handbook of natural language and meaning*, eds. Claudia Maienborn, Klaus Von Heusinger, and Paul Portner, vol. 33, 1660–1712. Walter de Gruyter.

Giorgolo, Gianluca, and Ash Asudeh. 2011. $\langle m, \eta, \star \rangle$. In *Proceedings of Sinn und Bedeutung 16*.

Girard, Jean-Yves. 1987. Linear logic. *Theoretical Computer Science* 50:1–101.

Griffin, Timothy G. 1990. A formulae-as-types notion of control. In *POPL '90: Conference record of the annual ACM symposium on principles of programming languages*, 47–58. New York: ACM Press.

Grishin, V.N. 1983. On a generalization of the Ajdukiewicz-Lambek system. In *Studies in nonclassical logics and formal systems*, ed. A.I. Mikhailov 315–334. Moscow: Navka.

Groenendijk, Jeroen, and Floris Roelofsen. 2009. Inquisitive semantics and pragmatics. In *Proceedings of SPR-09, ILCLI international workshop on semantics, pragmatics, and rhetoric.*

Groenendijk, Jeroen, and Martin Stokhof. 1990. Dynamic Montague grammar. In *Papers from the 2nd symposium on logic and language*, eds. László Kálmán and László Pólos, 3–48. Budapest: Akadémiai Kiadó.

Groenendijk, Jeroen, and Martin Stokhof. 1991. Dynamic predicate logic. *Linguistics and Philosophy* 14(1):39–100.

de Groote, Philippe. 2001. Type raising, continuations, and classical logic. In van Rooy and Stokhof (2001), 97–101.

de Groote, Philippe. 2002. Towards abstract categorial grammars. In *Proceedings of the 40th annual meeting of the Association for Computational Linguistics*, 148–155. San Francisco, CA: Morgan Kaufmann.

de Groote, Philippe. 2006. Towards a Montagovian account of dynamics. In *Proceedings from Semantics and Linguistic Theory 16*. Ithaca: Cornell University Press.

de Groote, Philippe, and Ekaterina Lebedeva. 2010. Presupposition accommodation as exception handling. In *Proceedings of the 11th annual meeting of the special interest group on discourse and dialogue*, 71–74. Association for Computational Linguistics.

Grosu, Alexander, and Manfred Krifka. 2007. The gifted mathematician that you claim to be: Equational intensional 'reconstruction' relatives. *Linguistics and Philosophy* 30(4): 445–485.

Harris, Jesse A, and Christopher Potts. 2009. Perspective-shifting with appositives and expressives. *Linguistics and Philosophy* 32(6):523–552.

Hastings, Rachel, Brendan Jackson, and Zsofia Zvolensky, eds. 2001. *Proceedings from Semantics and Linguistic Theory* 11. Ithaca: Cornell University Press.

Heim, Irene. 1982. The semantics of definite and indefinite noun phrases. Ph.D. thesis, Department of Linguistics, University of Massachusetts.

Heim, Irene. 1983. File change semantics and the familiarity theory of definiteness. In Bäuerle et al. (1983), 164–189.

Heim, Irene. 1990. E-type pronouns and donkey anaphora. *Linguistics and Philosophy* 13(2): 137–177.

Heim, Irene, and Angelika Kratzer. 1998. *Semantics in generative grammar*. Oxford: Blackwell.

Hendriks, Herman. 1988. Type change in semantics: The scope of quantification and coordination. In *Categories, polymorphism and unification*, eds. Ewan Klein and Johan F. A. K. van Benthem, 96–119. Centre for Cognitive Science, University of Edinburgh.

Hendriks, Herman. 1990. *Flexible Montague Grammar*. Institute for Language, Logic and Information, Universiteit van Amsterdam.

Hendriks, Herman. 1993. Studied flexibility: Categories and types in syntax and semantics. Ph.D. thesis, Institute for Logic, Language and Computation, Universiteit van Amsterdam.

Heycock, Caroline. 1995. Asymmetries in reconstruction. *Linguistic Inquiry* 547–570.

Hornstein, Norbert. 1995. *Logical form: From GB to Minimalism*. Oxford: Blackwell.

Jacobs, Joachim. 1980. Lexical decomposition in Montague Grammar. *Theoretical Linguistics* 7:121–136.

Jacobson, Pauline. 1999. Towards a variable-free semantics. *Linguistics and Philosophy* 22(2): 117–184.

Jacobson, Pauline. 2002. The (dis)organization of the grammar: 25 years. *Linguistics and Philosophy* 25(5–6):601–626.

Jäger, Gerhard. 2001. Indefinites and sluicing. A type-logical approach. In van Rooy and Stokhof (2001), 114–119.

Jäger, Gerhard. 2005. *Anaphora and type-logical grammar*. Trends in Logic 24, Berlin: Springer.

Johnson, Kyle. 2012. Recoverability of deletion. Manuscript, University of Massachusetts at Amherst.

Kamp, Hans. 1981. A theory of truth and semantic representation. In *Formal methods in the study of language: Proceedings of the 3rd Amsterdam Colloquium*, eds. Jeroen Groenendijk, Theo Janssen, and Martin Stokhof, 277–322. Amsterdam: Mathematisch Centrum.

Kayne, Richard S. 1998. Overt vs. covert movements. *Syntax* 1(2):128–191.

Keenan, Edward L. 1987. Semantic case theory. In *Proceedings of the sixth Amsterdam Colloquium*, 109–132. ITLI University of Amsterdam.

Keenan, Edward L. 1992. Beyond the Frege boundary. *Linguistics and Philosophy* 15(2):199–221.

Keenan, Edward L., and Leonard M Faltz. 1985. *Boolean semantics for natural language*. Reidel: Dordrecht.

Kennedy, Christopher, and Jason Stanley. 2009. On 'average'. *Mind* 118(471): 583–646.

Kluck, Marina Elisabeth. 2011. Sentence amalgamation. Ph.D. thesis, University of Groningen.

Kobele, Gregory M. 2012. Importing Montagovian dynamics into minimalism. In *Logical aspects of computational linguistics*, 103–118. Springer.

Kratzer, Angelika. 1989. An investigation of the lumps of thought. *Linguistics and Philosophy* 12: 607–653.

Krifka, Manfred. 1995. The semantics and pragmatics of polarity items. *Linguistic Analysis* 25: 209–257.

Kroch, Anthony S. 1974. The semantics of scope in English. Ph.D. thesis, Massachusetts Institute of Technology. Reprinted by New York: Garland, 1979.

Kubota, Yusuke. 2013. Japanese non-constituent coordination. *Linguistic Inquiry*. To appear.

Kubota, Yusuke, and Robert Levine. 2012. Against ellipsis: Arguments for the direct licensing of non-canonical coordinations. Ohio State University manuscript.

Kubota, Yusuke, and Wataru Uegaki. 2009. Continuation-based semantics for conventional implicatures: The case of Japanese benefactives. In *Proceedings from Semantics and Linguistic Theory 19*, eds. Satoshi Ito and Ed Cormany, 306–323. Ithaca: Cornell University Press.

Kuno, Susumu, and Jane J. Robinson. 1972. Multiple wh questions. *Linguistic Inquiry* 3:463–487.

Ladusaw, William A. 1979. Polarity sensitivity as inherent scope relations. Ph.D. thesis, Department of Linguistics, University of Massachusetts. Reprinted by New York: Garland, 1980.

Lakoff, George. 1974. Syntactic amalgams. In *Papers from the tenth regional meeting: Chicago Linguistic Society*.

Lambek, Joachim. 1958. The mathematics of sentence structure. *The American Mathematical Monthly* 65(3):154–170.

Lebedeva, Ekaterina. 2012. Expression de la dynamique du discours à l'aide de continuations. Ph.D. thesis, Université de Lorraine.

Lev, Thomas. 2005. Donkey pronouns: Void descriptions? In *Proceedings of NELS 35*, vol. 2, 379–390. University of Massachusetts, Amherst: GLSA.

Linebarger, Marcia Christine. 1980. The grammar of negative polarity. Ph.D. thesis, Massachusetts Institute of Technology.

Mascarenhas, Salvador. 2009. Inquisitive semantics and logic. Master's thesis, ILLC, University of Amsterdam.

Mascarenhas, Salvador. 2011. Licensing by modification: The case of positive polarity pronouns. In *Proceedings of Sinn und Bedeutung*, vol. 16.

May, Robert C. 1977. The grammar of quantification. Ph.D. thesis, Department of Linguistics and Philosophy, Massachusetts Institute of Technology. Reprinted by New York: Garland, 1991.

Merchant, Jason. 2001. *The syntax of silence: Sluicing, islands, and the theory of ellipsis*. Oxford University Press.

Moltmann, Friederike. 1992. Reciprocals and *same/different*: Towards a semantic analysis. *Linguistics and Philosophy* 15(4):411–462.

Montague, Richard. 1974. The proper treatment of quantification in ordinary English. In *Formal philosophy: Selected papers of Richard Montague*, ed. Richmond H. Thomason, 247–270. New Haven: Yale University Press.

Moortgat, Michael. 1988. *Categorial investigations: Logical and linguistic aspects of the Lambek calculus*. Dordrecht: Foris.

Moortgat, Michael. 1997. Categorial type logics. In *Handbook of logic and language*, eds. Johan F. A. K. van Benthem and Alice G. B. ter Meulen, chap. 2. Amsterdam: Elsevier Science.

Moortgat, Michael. 2009. Symmetric categorial grammar. *Journal of Philosophical Logic* 38: 681–710.

Moortgat, Michael. 2012. Typelogical grammar. *The Stanford encyclopedia of philosophy*. Available at <http://plato.stanford.edu/entries/typelogical-grammar> (Accessed: May 17, 2014).

Morrill, Glyn. 1994. *Type-logical grammar: Categorial logic of signs*. Dordrecht: Kluwer.

Morrill, Glyn, Oriol Valentín, and Mario Fadda. 2011. The displacement calculus. *Journal of Logic, Language and Information* 20(1):1–48.

Munn, Alan. 1994. A minimalist account of reconstruction asymmetries. In *Proceedings of NELS*, vol. 24, 397–410. Citeseer.

Muskens, Reinhard. 2001. λ-grammars and the syntax-semantics interface. In van Rooy and Stokhof (2001), 150–155.

Oehrle, Richard T. 1994. Term-labeled categorial type systems. *Linguistics and Philosophy* 17(6): 633–678.

Parigot, Michel. 1992. λμ-calculus: An algorithmic interpretation of classical natural deduction. In *Proceedings of LPAR '92: International conference on logic programming and automated reasoning*, ed. Andrei Voronkov, 190–201. Lecture Notes in Artificial Intelligence 624, Berlin: Springer.

Partee, Barbara Hall. 1987. Noun phrase interpretation and type-shifting principles. In *Studies in discourse representation theory and the theory of generalized quantifiers*, eds. Jeroen Groenendijk, Dick de Jongh, and Martin Stokhof, 115–143. Groningen-Amsterdam Studies in Semantics 8, Dordrecht: Foris.

Partee, Barbara Hall, and Mats Rooth. 1983. Generalized conjunction and type ambiguity. In Bäuerle et al. (1983), 361–383.

Penka, Doris. 2012. Split scope of negative indefinites. *Language and Linguistics Compass* 6(8): 517–532.

Penka, Doris, and Hedde Zeijlstra. 2005. Negative indefinites in Dutch and German. Paper presented at *the 20th Comparative Germanic Syntax Workshop, Tilburg.*

Plotkin, Gordon D. 1975. Call-by-name, call-by-value and the λ-calculus. *Theoretical Computer Science* 1(2):125–159.

Postal, Paul Martin. 1971. *Cross-over phenomena.* New York: Holt, Rinehart and Winston.

Potts, Christopher. 2003. The logic of conventional implicatures. Ph.D. thesis, University of California, Santa Cruz.

Reinhart, Tanya. 1983. *Anaphora and semantic interpretation.* London: Croom Helm.

Restall, Greg. 2000. *An introduction to substructural logics.* London: Routledge.

Reynolds, John C. 1993. The discoveries of continuations. *Lisp and Symbolic Computation* 6(3–4):233–247.

Romero, Maribel. 1998. Focus and reconstruction effects in wh-phrases. Ph.D. thesis, University of Massachusetts Amherst.

van Rooy, Robert, and Martin Stokhof, eds. 2001. *Proceedings of the 13th Amsterdam Colloquium.* Institute for Logic, Language and Computation, Universiteit van Amsterdam.

Ross, John Robert. 1969. Guess who? In *Papers from the fifth regional meeting of the Chicago Linguistic Society*, eds. R. I. Binnick, A. Davison, G. M. Green, and J. L. Morgan, 252–286.

Rullmann, Hotze. 1995. Maximality in the semantics of wh-constructions. Ph.D. thesis, University of Massachusetts, Amherst.

Safir, Ken. 1999. Vehicle change and reconstruction in Ā-Chains. *Linguistic Inquiry* 30(4): 587–620.

Safir, Ken. 2004a. *The syntax of anaphora.* New York: Oxford University Press.

Safir, Ken. 2004b. *The syntax of (in)dependence.* Cambridge: MIT Press.

Sauerland, Uli. 2005. DP is not a scope island. *Linguistic Inquiry* 36(2):303–314.

Schlenker, Philippe. 2007. Anti-dynamics: Presupposition projection without dynamic semantics. *Journal of Logic, Language and Information* 16(3):325–356.

Shan, Chung-chieh. 2001a. Monads for natural language semantics. In *Proceedings of the ESSLLI-2001 student session*, ed. Kristina Striegnitz, 285–298. Helsinki: 13th European Summer School in Logic, Language and Information.

Shan, Chung-chieh. 2001b. A variable-free dynamic semantics. In van Rooy and Stokhof (2001), 204–209.

Shan, Chung-chieh. 2002a. A continuation semantics of interrogatives that accounts for Baker's ambiguity. In *Proceedings from Semantics and Linguistic Theory* 12, ed. Brendan Jackson, 246–265. Ithaca: Cornell University Press.

Shan, Chung-chieh. 2002b. Temporal versus non-temporal "when". *Snippets* 6:14–15. <http://www.ledonline.it/snippets/allegati/snippets6005.pdf> (Accessed: May 17, 2014).

Shan, Chung-chieh. 2003a. Linguistic side effects. Talk slides, NEPLS 8; <http://www.cs.rutgers.edu/~ccshan/nepls8/talk.pdf> (Accessed: May 17, 2014).

Shan, Chung-chieh. 2003b. Quantifier strengths predict scopal possibilities of Mandarin Chinese *wh*-indefinites. Draft manuscript, Harvard University; http://www.cs.rutgers.edu/~ccshan/mandarin/paper.pdf> (Accessed: May 17, 2014).

Shan, Chung-chieh. 2004. Polarity sensitivity and evaluation order in type-logical grammar. In *Proceedings of the 2004 human language technology conference of the North American chapter of the Association for Computational Linguistics*, eds. Susan Dumais, Daniel Marcu, and Salim Roukos, vol. 2, 129–132. Somerset, NJ: Association for Computational Linguistics.

Shan, Chung-chieh. 2005. Linguistic side effects. Ph.D. thesis, Harvard University.

Shan, Chung-chieh, and Chris Barker. 2006. Explaining crossover and superiority as left-to-right evaluation. *Linguistics and Philosophy* 29(1):91–134.

Shan, Chung-chieh, and Balder David ten Cate. 2002. The partition semantics of questions, syntactically. In *Proceedings of the ESSLLI-2002 student session*, ed. Malvina Nissim, 255–269. Trento, Italy: 14th European Summer School in Logic, Language and Information.

Solomon, Michael. 2011. True distributivity and the functional interpretation of indefinites. New York University unpublished manuscript.

Sportiche, Dominique. 2006. Reconstruction, binding, and scope. *The Blackwell companion to syntax*, vol. 4:35–93.

Steedman, Mark. 2000. *The syntactic process*. Cambridge: MIT Press.

Steedman, Mark. 2012. *Taking scope: The natural semantics of quantifiers*. Cambridge: MIT Press.

Sternefeld, Wolfgang. 1997. The semantics of reconstruction and connectivity. Arbeitspapiere des SFB 340 97, Universität Stuttgart and Tübingen.

Sternefeld, Wolfgang. 2001. Semantic vs. syntactic reconstruction. In *Linguistic form and its computation*, eds. Hans Kamp, Antje Rossdeutscher, and Christian Rohrer, 145–182. Stanford, CA: CSLI Publications.

Stone, Matthew. 1992. *Or* and anaphora. In *Proceedings from Semantics and Linguistic Theory* 2, eds. Chris Barker and David Dowty, 367–385. Columbus: Ohio State University.

Stump, Gregory. 1982. A GPSG fragment for dependent nominals. Ohio State University Manuscript.

de Swart, Henriëtte. 1998. Licensing of negative polarity items under inverse scope. *Lingua* 105: 175–200.

de Swart, Henriëtte. 2000. Scope ambiguities with negative quantifiers. In *Reference and anaphoric relations*, eds. Klaus von Heusinger and Urs Egli, 118–142. Dordrecht: Kluwer.

Szabolcsi, Anna. 1989. Bound variables in syntax (are there any?). In *Semantics and contextual expression*, eds. Renate Bartsch, Johan F. A. K. van Benthem, and Peter van Emde Boas, 295–318. Dordrecht: Foris.

Szabolcsi, Anna. 1992. Combinatory grammar and projection from the lexicon. In *Lexical matters*, eds. Ivan A. Sag and Anna Szabolcsi, 241–269. CSLI Lecture Notes 24, Stanford, CA: Center for the Study of Language and Information.

Szabolcsi, Anna. 2004. Positive polarity—negative polarity. *Natural Language and Linguistic Theory* 22(2):409–452.

Szabolcsi, Anna. 2010. *Quantification*. Cambridge University Press.

Tancredi, Christopher Damian. 1992. Deletion, deaccenting, and presupposition. Ph.D. thesis, Massachusetts Institute of Technology.

Valentín, Oriol. 2012. Theory of discontinuous lambek calculus. Ph.D. thesis, Universitat Autonòma de Barcelona.

Wadler, Philip L. 1994. Monads and composable continuations. *Lisp and Symbolic Computation* 7(1):39–56.

Wadler, Philip L. 1995. Monads for functional programming. In *Advanced functional programming: 1st international spring school on advanced functional programming techniques*, eds. Johan Jeuring and Erik Meijer, 24–52. Lecture Notes in Computer Science 925, Berlin: Springer.

Wadler, Philip L. 2003. Call-by-value is dual to call-by-name. In *ICFP '03: Proceedings of the ACM international conference on functional programming*, vol. 38(9) of *ACM SIGPLAN Notices*. New York: ACM Press.

Westbrook, Edwin, Mathias Ricken, Jun Inoue, Yilong Yao, Tamer Abdelatif, and Walid Taha. 2010. Mint: Java multi-stage programming using weak separability. In *PLDI '10: Proceedings of the ACM conference on programming language design and implementation*. New York: ACM Press.

Zweig, Eytan. 2008. Dependent plurals and plural meaning. Ph.D. thesis, New York University.

Index

OXFORD STUDIES IN THEORETICAL LINGUISTICS

Published

1 The Syntax of Silence
Sluicing, Islands, and the Theory of Ellipsis
by Jason Merchant

2 Questions and Answers in Embedded Contexts
by Utpal Lahiri

3 Phonetics, Phonology, and Cognition
edited by Jacques Durand and Bernard Laks

4 At the Syntax-Pragmatics Interface
Concept Formation and Verbal Underspecification in Dynamic Syntax
by Lutz Marten

5 The Unaccusativity Puzzle
Explorations of the Syntax-Lexicon Interface
edited by Artemis Alexiadou, Elena Anagnostopoulou, and Martin Everaert

6 Beyond Morphology
Interface Conditions on Word Formation
by Peter Ackema and Ad Neeleman

7 The Logic of Conventional Implicatures
by Christopher Potts

8 Paradigms of Phonological Theory
edited by Laura Downing, T. Alan Hall, and Renate Raffelsiefen

9 The Verbal Complex in Romance
by Paola Monachesi

10 The Syntax of Aspect
Deriving Thematic and Aspectual Interpretation
Edited by Nomi Erteschik-Shir and Tova Rapoport

11 Aspects of the Theory of Clitics
by Stephen Anderson

12 Canonical Forms in Prosodic Morphology
by Laura J. Downing

13 Aspect and Reference Time
by Olga Borik

14 Direct Compositionality
edited by Chris Barker and Pauline Jacobson

15 A Natural History of Infixation
by Alan C. L. Yu

16 Phi-Theory
Phi-Features Across Interfaces and Modules
edited by Daniel Harbour, David Adger, and Susana Béjar

17 French Dislocation
Interpretation, Syntax, Acquisition
by Cécile De Cat

18 Inflectional Identity
edited by Asaf Bachrach and Andrew Nevins

19 Lexical Plurals
by Paolo Acquaviva

20 Adjectives and Adverbs
Syntax, Semantics, and Discourse
Edited by Louise McNally and Christopher Kennedy

21 InterPhases
Phase-Theoretic Investigations of Linguistic Interfaces
edited by Kleanthes Grohmann

22 Negation in Gapping
by Sophie Repp

23 A Derivational Syntax for Information Structure
by Luis López

24 Quantification, Definiteness, and Nominalization
edited by Anastasia Giannakidou and Monika Rathert

25 The Syntax of Sentential Stress
by Arsalan Kahnemuyipour

26 Tense, Aspect, and Indexicality
by James Higginbotham

27 Lexical Semantics, Syntax, and Event Structure
edited by Malka Rappaport Hovav, Edit Doron, and Ivy Sichel

28 About the Speaker
Towards a Syntax of Indexicality
by Alessandra Giorgi

29 The Sound Patterns of Syntax
edited by Nomi Erteschik-Shir and Lisa Rochman

30 The Complementizer Phase
edited by Phoevos Panagiotidis

31 Interfaces in Linguistics
New Research Perspectives
edited by Raffaella Folli and Christiane Ulbrich

32 Negative Indefinites
by Doris Penka

33 Events, Phrases, and Questions
by Robert Truswell

34 Dissolving Binding Theory
by Johan Rooryck and Guido Vanden Wyngaerd

35 The Logic of Pronominal Resumption
by Ash Asudeh

36 Modals and Conditionals
by Angelika Kratzer

37 The Theta System
Argument Structure at the Interface
edited by Martin Everaert, Marijana Marelj, and Tal Siloni

38 Sluicing
Cross-Linguistic Perspectives
edited by Jason Merchant and Andrew Simpson

39 Telicity, Change, and State
A Cross-Categorial View of Event Structure
edited by Violeta Demonte and Louise McNally

40 Ways of Structure Building
edited by Myriam Uribe-Etxebarria and Vidal Valmala

41 The Morphology and Phonology of Exponence
edited by Jochen Trommer

42 Count and Mass Across Languages
edited by Diane Massam

43 Genericity
edited by Alda Mari, Claire Beyssade, and Fabio Del Prete

44 Strategies of Quantification
edited by Kook-Hee Gil, Steve Harlow, and George Tsoulas

45 Nonverbal Predication
Copular Sentences at the Syntax-Semantics Interface
by Isabelle Roy

46 Diagnosing Syntax
edited by Lisa Lai-Shen Cheng and Norbert Corver

47 Pseudogapping and Ellipsis
by Kirsten Gengel

48 Syntax and its Limits
edited by Raffaella Folli, Christina Sevdali, and Robert Truswell

49 Phrase Structure and Argument Structure
A Case Study of the Syntax-Semantics Interface
by Terje Lohndal

50 Edges in Syntax
Scrambling and Cyclic Linearization
by Heejeong Ko

51 The Syntax of Roots and the Roots of Syntax
edited by Artemis Alexiadou, Hagit Borer, and Florian Schäfer

52 Causation in Grammatical Structures
edited by Bridget Copley and Fabienne Martin

53 Continuations and Natural Language
Chris Barker and Chung-chieh Shan

Published in association with the series
The Oxford Handbook of Linguistic Interfaces
edited by Gillian Ramchand and Charles Reiss

In preparation

External Arguments in Transitivity Alternations
by Artemis Alexiadou, Elena Anagnostopoulou, and Florian Schäfer

Modality Across Syntactic Categories
edited by Ana Arregui, Mari Luisa Rivero, and Andrés Pablo Salanova

Phi Syntax
A Theory of Agreement
by Susana Béjar

Stratal Optimality Theory
by Ricardo Bermúdez Otero

Phonology in Phonetics
by Abigail Cohn

Generality and Exception
by Ivan Garcia-Alvarez

The Morphosyntax of Gender
by Ruth Kramer

The Semantics of Evaluativity
by Jessica Rett

Computing Optimality
by Jason Riggle

Pragmatic Aspects of Scalar Modifiers
by Osamu Sawada

Gradience in Split Intransitivity
by Antonella Sorace

The manufacturer's authorised representative in the EU for product safety is Oxford University Press España S.A. of el Parque Empresarial San Fernando de Henares, Avenida de Castilla, 2 – 28830 Madrid (www.oup.es/en or product.safety@oup.com). OUP España S.A. also acts as importer into Spain of products made by the manufacturer.

www.ingramcontent.com/pod-product-compliance
Ingram Content Group UK Ltd.
Pitfield, Milton Keynes, MK11 3LW, UK
UKHW020923170926
475595UK00031B/45
9780199575015